BICENTENNIAL
1807
⊛WILEY
2007
BICENTENNIAL

THE WILEY BICENTENNIAL—KNOWLEDGE FOR GENERATIONS

*E*ach generation has its unique needs and aspirations. When Charles Wiley first opened his small printing shop in lower Manhattan in 1807, it was a generation of boundless potential searching for an identity. And we were there, helping to define a new American literary tradition. Over half a century later, in the midst of the Second Industrial Revolution, it was a generation focused on building the future. Once again, we were there, supplying the critical scientific, technical, and engineering knowledge that helped frame the world. Throughout the 20th Century, and into the new millennium, nations began to reach out beyond their own borders and a new international community was born. Wiley was there, expanding its operations around the world to enable a global exchange of ideas, opinions, and know-how.

For 200 years, Wiley has been an integral part of each generation's journey, enabling the flow of information and understanding necessary to meet their needs and fulfill their aspirations. Today, bold new technologies are changing the way we live and learn. Wiley will be there, providing you the must-have knowledge you need to imagine new worlds, new possibilities, and new opportunities.

Generations come and go, but you can always count on Wiley to provide you the knowledge you need, when and where you need it!

WILLIAM J. PESCE
PRESIDENT AND CHIEF EXECUTIVE OFFICER

PETER BOOTH WILEY
CHAIRMAN OF THE BOARD

Introduction to Programming Using Visual Basic

Evangelos Petroutsos, Patrick G. McKeown,
Rod Stephens, Jim Keogh, Thearon Willis,
Bryan Newsome, and Bill Sempf

with Rachelle Reese

BICENTENNIAL
BICENTENNIAL
1807
WILEY
2007
BICENTENNIAL
BICENTENNIAL
BICENTENNIAL

Credits

PUBLISHER
Anne Smith

ACQUISITIONS EDITOR
Lois Ann Freier

MARKETING MANAGER
Jennifer Slomack

SENIOR EDITORIAL ASSISTANT
Tiara Kelly

PRODUCTION MANAGER
Kelly Tavares

PRODUCTION ASSISTANT
Courtney Leshko

CREATIVE DIRECTOR
Harry Nolan

COVER DESIGNER
Hope Miller

COVER PHOTO
Gary Cornhouse/Digital Vision/Getty Images

Wiley 200th Anniversary Logo designed by: Richard J. Pacifico

This book was set in Times New Roman by Techbooks, printed and bound by R.R. Donnelley.

The cover was printed by R.R. Donnelley.

Microsoft product screen shot(s) reprinted with permission from Microsoft Corporation.

This book is printed on acid free paper. ∞

To order books or for customer service please, call 1-800-CALL WILEY (225-5945).

ISBN-13 978-0-470-10188-9

Printed in the United States of America

10 9 8 7 6 5 4 3 2 1

College classrooms bring together learners from many backgrounds, with a variety of aspirations. Although the students are in the same course, they are not necessarily on the same path. This diversity, coupled with the reality that these learners often have jobs, families, and other commitments, requires a flexibility that our nation's higher education system is addressing. Distance learning, shorter course terms, new disciplines, evening courses, and certification programs are some of the approaches that colleges employ to reach as many students as possible and help them clarify and achieve their goals.

Wiley Pathways books, a new line of texts from John Wiley & Sons, Inc., are designed to help you address this diversity and the need for flexibility. These books focus on the fundamentals, identify core competencies and skills, and promote independent learning. Their focus on the fundamentals helps students grasp the subject, bringing them all to the same basic understanding. These books use clear, everyday language and are presented in an uncluttered format, making the reading experience more pleasurable. The core competencies and skills help students succeed in the classroom and beyond, whether in another course or in a professional setting. A variety of built-in learning resources promote independent learning and help instructors and students gauge students' understanding of the content. These resources enable students to think critically about their new knowledge and apply their skills in any situation.

Our goal with *Wiley Pathways* books—with their brief, inviting format, clear language, and core competencies and skills focus—is to celebrate the many students in your courses, respect their needs, and help you guide them on their way.

CASE Learning System

To meet the needs of working college students, *Introduction to Programming Using Visual Basic* uses a four-part process called the CASE Learning System:

- ▲ C: Content
- ▲ A: Analysis
- ▲ S: Synthesis
- ▲ E: Evaluation

Based on Bloom's taxonomy of learning, CASE presents key topics in programming using Visual Basic in easy-to-follow chapters. The text then prompts analysis, synthesis, and evaluation with a variety of learning aids and assessment tools. Students move efficiently from reviewing what they have learned, to acquiring new information and skills, to applying their new knowledge and skills to real-life scenarios.

Using the CASE Learning System, students not only achieve academic mastery of introductory programming *topics,* but they master real-world *skills* related to that content. The CASE Learning System also helps students become independent learners, giving them a distinct advantage in the field, whether they are just starting out or seeking to advance in their careers.

Organization, Depth, and Breadth of the Text

▲ **Modular Format.** Research on college students shows that they access information from textbooks in a non-linear way. Instructors also often wish to reorder textbook content to suit the needs of a particular class. Therefore, although *Introduction to Programming Using Visual Basic* proceeds logically from the basics to increasingly more challenging material, chapters are further organized into sections that are self-contained for maximum teaching and learning flexibility.

▲ **Numeric System of Headings.** *Introduction to Programming Using Visual Basic* uses a numeric system for headings (e.g., 2.3.4 identifies the fourth subsection of Section 3 of Chapter 2). With this system, students and teachers can quickly and easily pinpoint topics in the table of contents and the text, keeping class time and study sessions focused.

▲ **Core Content.** The topics in *Introduction to Programming Using Visual Basic* are organized into twelve chapters.

Chapter 1, An Introduction to Programming and Visual Basic, introduces students to the fundamentals of programming using Microsoft Visual Studio 2005 and Microsoft Visual Basic 2005. The chapter begins with some basic programming concepts, such as a discussion of the six basic operations that all computers perform, what an algorithm is, and the three basic control structures that are used in programming. It then provides a brief description of programming languages, including the concepts of event-driven and object-oriented programs, and describes the role that Visual Studio and Visual Basic play in program development. Next, the chapter covers the role of solutions and projects in creating a program with Visual Basic. Windows Forms, which are used to create the user interface for a Windows application, are also introduced, along with the basic steps for adding user interface elements, known as controls, to a Windows Form. The chapter concludes with a look at event-driven programming and provides opportunity for students to write their first code.

Chapter 2, Using Variables, Constants, and Operators, examines how to store and perform operations on data within a program. The chapter teaches students how to create and use variables to store values that change, how to convert data from one type to another, how to use constants and enumerations to store data values that do not change, and how to perform operations on a program's data.

Chapter 3, Managing Program Flow, outlines how to break down what a program should do into steps and write code that describes those steps to the compiler. The chapter begins by exploring the role that pseudocode (algorithms) and flowcharts play in designing program flow. The chapter then teaches students how to write code that makes decisions, and how to write code that performs repetitive tasks. The chapter concludes with an examination of Visual Studio debugging tools, and describes how to use these tools to find and fix problems in code.

Chapter 4, Saving Time with Reusable Code, teaches students how to write code that is reusable and that can handle unexpected events that generate exceptions. The chapter begins with a discussion of how to create functions and procedures that can be called from different places in a program. Next, it provides a more in-depth look at object-oriented programming and introduces students to important .NET Framework objects. It then teaches students how to use classes instantiated as objects and shared classes to perform procedures common to multiple applications. The chapter concludes with a section on how to use the Exception object to implement exception handling in an application.

Chapter 5, Using Arrays and Collections, covers the processing of data using arrays and collections. The chapter begins with a look at how arrays are used to store and process list data in memory, and teaches students how to declare, populate, and retrieve data from a single-dimensional array. The chapter then examines the procedures used to process list data, and discusses how to find the minimum value, find the maximum value, add the values in an array, and sort arrays. The chapter also covers how to process tables of data, using two-dimensional arrays. The chapter concludes with an exploration of how to use two powerful classes for working with lists: the ArrayList class and the Hashtable class.

Chapter 6, Handling User Input and Formatting Output, focuses on how to design a user interface that is effective and easy-to-use. The first section covers how to select the most appropriate control to meet an input or output requirement and how to allow users to navigate through a form using the keyboard. It also introduces the Anchor and Dock properties and shows students how to add controls to a form dynamically. The chapter also covers string manipulation and formatting concerns, and concludes with a look at formatting numeric and date variables.

Chapter 7, Building Menus and Toolbars, teaches students how to design a user interface that includes menus, toolbars, and status information. It begins with a discussion of menu design considerations, and then examines how to use the MenuStrip control to add a menu to a form. It also addresses how to add dynamic menus, including adding menu items at runtime, and how to use the ContextStrip to add context-sensitive menus. The final section examines how to use the ToolStrip control, the StatusStrip control, and the ToolStripContainer control to add toolbars and status bars that can be customized by the user.

Chapter 8, Creating Your Own Classes, teaches students how to build their own classes and use them in their projects. Topics covered include creating classes to promote code reusability, declaring a class and creating properties and methods, and a number of more advanced techniques, such as read-only properties, custom enumerations, shared properties and methods, and overloading. The chapter also examines how to use inheritance, including calling methods on the base class and the derived class, and constructors.

Chapter 9, Accessing Data, provides an overview of key concepts and procedures with respect to relational databases, a key concern given that many applications create and store data in relational databases. The chapter begins with a look at relational database concepts, including fields, records, relationships, and normalization. Next, the chapter looks at Structured Query Language (SQL), and teaches students how to perform selection queries using a SELECT statement, and action queries using INSERT, UPDATE, and DELETE. The chapter concludes with an examination of how to access data using ADO.NET and how to bind relational data to controls.

Chapter 10, Programming Input and Output, examines the concepts behind file input and output. It teaches students how to save data to a file and read data from a file using Visual Basic, how to use the Graphics object to draw to the screen, and how to generate a document to be printed and send it to the printer a user selects.

Chapter 11, Deploying Your Application, addresses the considerations involved in preparing an application to run outside Visual Studio. It looks first at concepts related to planning a deployment and installation, including identifying dependencies and choosing a type of deployment. Next it discusses how to prepare an application for deployment, and compares three types of installations supported for applications you build using the.NET Framework 2.0. It concludes by teaching students how to create a Windows Installer Setup program.

Chapter 12, Building Web Applications, helps students leverage their knowledge of Visual Basic by applying it to the Web. To do so, it provides a basic introduction to Hypertext Markup Language (HTML), the language used to build Web documents. The chapter explains how a Web application works, discusses HTML fundamentals, including how to create lists, tables and forms with HTML, and concludes with a look at how to build a simple Web application using ASP.NET.

Pre-reading Learning Aids

Each chapter of *Introduction to Programming Using Visual Basic* features the following learning and study aids to activate students' prior knowledge of the topics and orient them to the material.

▲ **Pre-test.** This pre-reading assessment tool in multiple-choice format not only introduces chapter material, but it also helps students anticipate the chapter's learning outcomes. By focusing students' attention on what they do not know, the self-test provides students with a benchmark against which they can measure their own progress. The pre-test is available online at www.wiley.com/college/petroutsos.

▲ **What You'll Learn in This Chapter.** This bulleted list focuses on subject matter that will be taught. It tells students what they will be learning in this chapter and why it is significant for their careers. It will also help students understand why the chapter is important and how it relates to other chapters in the text.

▲ **After Studying This Chapter, You'll Be Able To.** This list emphasizes capabilities and skills students will learn as a result of reading the chapter. It sets students up to synthesize and evaluate the chapter material, and relate it to the real world.

Within-text Learning Aids

The following learning aids are designed to encourage analysis and synthesis of the material, support the learning process, and ensure success during the evaluation phase:

▲ **Introduction.** This section orients the student by introducing the chapter and explaining its practical value and relevance to the book as a whole. Short summaries of chapter sections preview the topics to follow.

▲ **"For Example" Boxes.** Found within each section, these boxes tie section content to real-world examples, scenarios, and applications.

▲ **Figures and Tables.** Line art and photos have been carefully chosen to be truly instructional rather than filler. Tables distill and present information in a way that is easy to identify, access, and understand, enhancing the focus of the text on essential ideas.

▲ **Self-Check.** Related to the "What You'll Learn" bullets and found at the end of each section, this battery of short answer questions emphasizes student understanding of concepts and mastery of section content. Though the questions may either be discussed in class or studied by students outside of class, students should not go on before they can answer all questions correctly.

▲ **Key Terms and Glossary.** To help students develop a professional vocabulary, key terms are bolded in the introduction, summary, and when they first appear in the chapter. A complete list of key terms appears at the end of each chapter and again in a glossary at the end of the book with brief definitions. Knowledge of key terms is assessed by all assessment tools (see below).

▲ **Summary.** Each chapter concludes with a summary paragraph that reviews the major concepts in the chapter and links back to the "What You'll Learn" list.

Evaluation and Assessment Tools

The evaluation phase of the CASE Learning System consists of a variety of within-chapter and end-of-chapter assessment tools that test how well students have learned the material. These tools also encourage students to extend their learning into different scenarios and higher levels of understanding and thinking. The following assessment tools appear in every chapter of *Introduction to Programming Using Visual Basic:*

▲ **Summary Questions** help students summarize the chapter's main points by asking a series of multiple choice and true/false questions that emphasize student understanding of concepts and mastery of chapter content. Students should be able to answer all of the Summary Questions correctly before moving on.

▲ **Applying This Chapter** questions drive home key ideas by asking students to synthesize and apply chapter concepts to new, real-life situations and scenarios.

▲ **You Try It** questions are designed to extend students' thinking, and so are ideal for discussion or writing assignments. Using an open-ended format and sometimes based on Web sources, they encourage students to draw conclusions using chapter material applied to real-world situations, which fosters both mastery and independent learning.

▲ **Post-test** should be taken after students have completed the chapter. It includes all of the questions in the pre-test, so that students can see how their learning has progressed and improved. The post-test is available online at www.wiley.com/college/petroutsos.

Instructor Package

Introduction to Programming Using Visual Basic is available with the following teaching and learning supplements. All supplements are available online at the text's Book Companion Web site, located at www.wiley.com/college/petroutsos.

▲ **Instructor's Resource Guide.** Provides the following aids and supplements for teaching an introduction to databases course:

• *Sample syllabus.* A convenient template that instructors may use for creating their own course syllabi.

• *Teaching suggestions.* For each chapter, these include a chapter summary, learning objectives, definitions of key terms, lecture notes, answers to select text question sets, and at least 3 suggestions for classroom activities, such as ideas for speakers to invite, videos to show, and other projects.

▲ **PowerPoint Slides.** Key information is summarized in 10 to 15 PowerPoint slides per chapter. Instructors may use these in class or choose to share them with students for class presentations or to provide additional study support.

▲ **Test Bank.** One test per chapter, as well as a mid-term, and two finals: one cumulative, one non-cumulative. Each includes true/false, multiple choice, and open-ended questions. Answers and page references are provided for the true/false and multiple choice questions, and page references for the open-ended questions. Questions are available in Microsoft Word and computerized test bank formats.

Student Project Manual

The inexpensive *Introduction to Programming Using Visual Basic Project Manual* contains activities (an average of five projects per textbook chapter) designed to help students apply textbook concepts in a practical way. Easier exercises at the beginning graduate to more challenging projects that build critical-thinking skills.

Taken together, the content, pedagogy, and assessment elements of *Introduction to Programming Using Visual Basic* offer the career-oriented student the most important aspects of programming as well as ways to develop the skills and capabilities that current and future employers seek in the individuals they hire and promote. Instructors will appreciate its practical focus, conciseness, and real-world emphasis.

We would like to thank the following reviewers for their feedback and suggestions during the text's development. Their advice on how to shape *Introduction to Programming Using Visual Basic* into a solid learning tool that meets both their needs and those of their busy students is deeply appreciated.

Jimmy Chen, Salt Lake Community College
Larry Hardy, Georgia Perimeter College
Kris Stengel, North Harris College
Neal Stenlund, Northern Virginia Community College
Don Stroup, Ivy Tech Community College

We would also like to thank Carol Traver for all her hard work in formatting and preparing the manuscript for production.

BRIEF CONTENTS

CONTENTS

1

AN INTRODUCTION TO PROGRAMMING AND VISUAL BASIC

Starting Point

Go to www.wiley.com/college/petroutsos to assess your knowledge of the basics of programming and Visual Basic.
Determine where you need to concentrate your effort.

What You'll Learn in This Chapter

▲ Operations all computers perform
▲ Basic control structures
▲ Programming languages and the need for just-in-time compilation
▲ Programming in Windows
▲ Object-oriented programming
▲ The programming process
▲ The purpose and key features of the Visual Basic programming environment
▲ The relationship between a solution and a project
▲ How to create Windows application projects
▲ Forms and form properties
▲ Controls
▲ The role of events in Windows programming and how to build a simple program that responds to events
▲ How to test code

After Studying This Chapter, You'll Be Able To

▲ Identify the types of operations a computer carries out in order to prepare to write a program
▲ Identify the steps required to prepare to write a program
▲ Install and get help in Visual Studio
▲ Write pseudocode as preparation for creating a program
▲ Create an IPO table as preparation for creating a program
▲ Create a Windows application project
▲ Use the Solution Explorer window to manage the files in a project
▲ Customize the Visual Studio environment to make it easier to work in
▲ Add a form to a project
▲ Set form properties by using the Properties window
▲ Add TextBox, Label, and Button controls to a form
▲ Set control properties by using the Properties window
▲ Add code to a form event
▲ Add code to a control event
▲ Test code by debugging

INTRODUCTION

This chapter introduces the fundamentals of programming using Microsoft Visual Studio 2005 and Microsoft Visual Basic 2005. The first section introduces you to some basic programming concepts and the role that Visual Studio and Visual Basic play in program development. In the second section, you will learn about solutions and projects and become familiar with the Visual Studio development environment. In the third section, you will learn about Windows Forms. A Windows form allows you to create the user interface for a Windows application. In the fourth section, you will look at the basic steps for adding user interface elements, known as controls, to a Windows form. In the final section, you will learn about event-driven programming and write your first code.

1.1 Getting Familiar with Programming

No doubt, you have used many applications. But have you thought about what goes on behind the scenes or the tools used to create that application? In this section, you'll discover the difference between source code and a compiled program. Next, you'll learn some basics about the development environment you will be using: Visual Studio. After that, you'll learn the fundamental steps for preparing to install and installing Visual Studio. Finally, you'll learn about the documentation and help features available for learning about Visual Studio and Visual Basic.

1.1.1 An Introduction to Programming

Before you begin to think about creating a computer program, it's useful to understand the six operations that all computers can carry out. Understanding these operations will help you when you start writing programs. These are the six operations a computer can perform:

1. Input data
2. Store data in internal memory
3. Perform arithmetic on data
4. Compare two values and select one of two alternative actions
5. Repeat a group of actions any number of times
6. Output the results of processing

These six operations are depicted in Figure 1-1, where each operation is numbered. Let's discuss each of these operations in a little more detail:

1. **Input data:** For a computer to be able to process data, it must first be able to accept input of data. Data is typically input from a keyboard or

Figure 1-1

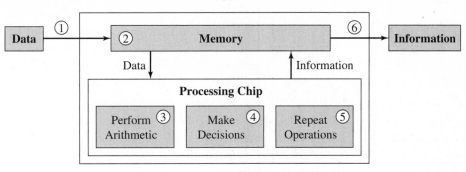

The six computer operations.

mouse, but it can also come from other sources, such as a bar-code reader like those used at checkout terminals. Input can also come from some type of sensor or from a data file on a computer disk. For example, with a word processor, the letters of the alphabet, numbers, and punctuation symbols form the data that is processed by the computer. New documents are created by entering data from the keyboard, and existing documents are loaded from a hard drive or flash memory.

2. **Store data in memory:** After data has been input, it is stored in internal memory. Each memory location that holds data is assigned a name, which the instructions use to perform the processing. Because the values in a memory location can change as the process occurs, the memory locations are called **variables.** For example, the current balance in your checking account would typically be stored in a single memory location and be identified by a variable name. The instructions for processing this data are also stored in memory.

3. **Perform arithmetic on data:** Once data and instructions have been input and stored, arithmetic operations can be performed on the variables that represent the data. This includes addition, subtraction, multiplication, division, and raising to a power. The processing chip of the computer carries out these operations by retrieving the data from memory and then performing the processing based on instructions from the programmer. How does a word processor or computer game work if all the computer can do is perform arithmetic? The answer is that everything in a computer—numbers, letters, graphics, and so on—is represented by numbers, and all processing is handled through some type of arithmetic operation.

4. **Compare two values and select one of two alternative actions:** To do anything other than the simplest processing, a computer must be able to choose between two sets of instructions to execute. It does this by

comparing the contents of two memory locations and, based on the result of that comparison, executing one of two groups of instructions. For example, when you carry out the spell-checking operation, the computer checks each word to determine whether it matches a word in the computer's dictionary. Based on the result of this comparison, the word is accepted or flagged for you to consider changing.

5. **Repeat a group of actions any number of times:** Although you could carry out all the preceding operations with a typewriter or handheld calculator, repeating actions is something the computer does better than any person or any other type of machine. Because a computer never tires or becomes bored, it can be instructed to repeat some action as many times as needed, without fear of an error occurring due to the constant repetition. The capability of a computer to repeat an operation is what most clearly sets it apart from all other machines. The spell-checking operation mentioned earlier is an example of a repeated action: The program repeatedly checks words until it comes to the end of the document.

6. **Output the results of processing:** After the processing has been completed and the required information generated, to be of any use, the information must be output. Output of processed information can take many forms: It can be displayed on a monitor, printed on paper, stored as files on a disk, and so on. Output is accomplished by retrieving information from a memory location and sending it to the output device. For example, when you complete your work with a word processor, the resulting information is displayed on your monitor and saved to a file, and you may also print it for distribution to others.

1.1.2 Programs and Programming

To carry out any of the six operations just discussed, you must be able to provide instructions to the computer, in the form of a program. The most important thing about programming is that it is a form of problem solving, and the objective is to develop the step-by-step process—the logic—that will solve the problem. Step-by-step logic of this type is referred to as an **algorithm.** You have worked with algorithms before; a set of directions to a party is an algorithm, as is a recipe to make spaghetti sauce or to bake a cake. For a computer program, you must develop a set of instructions for solving a problem, using only the six operations of a computer. This is the most difficult part of programming.

Many times, a program fails to work because the programmer attempts to write the program before developing the correct algorithm for solving the problem. Only after you have developed the logic of the solution can you consider actually writing the instructions for the computer.

Control Structures

All computer programs are created using just three types of logic, or, as they are known in programming, **control structures:** the sequence, decision, and repetition control structures.

The **sequence control structure** includes the input, storage, arithmetic, and output computer operations discussed earlier. It is so called because all four of these operations can be performed without any need to make a decision or repeat an operation. At its simplest, *sequence* means one program instruction follows another, in order. The programmer must determine the proper sequence for the instructions.

The **decision control structure** is the same as the decision-making computer operation discussed earlier. It enables the programmer to control the flow of operations by having the user or data determine which operation is to be performed next.

Finally, the **repetition control structure** is used to repeat one or more operations. The number of repetitions depends on the user or the data, but the programmer must include a way to terminate the repetition process.

All algorithms are created by performing the six operations of a computer, using combinations of these three control structures. When you learn how to create the logic for these three control structures, you will find that writing meaningful and useful programs is a matter of combining the structures to create more complex logic.

Programming Languages

When you have developed the logic for solving a problem, you can think about writing the actual instructions that the computer will use in implementing the logic. Computer programs must be written in one of various **programming languages,** such as **Visual Basic.** Each of these languages uses a restricted vocabulary and a very structured syntax (similar to grammar) that the computer can understand. Although a great deal of research is ongoing to create computers that can accept instructions using conversational English, currently no computers can do so.

Within a computer, the data and instructions are represented in the **binary number system** as a series of 0s and 1s. This form of representation is used because the computer has only two electrical states, on and off, corresponding to 1 and 0. Using a string of transistors that act as switches, the computer can represent a number, a character, or an instruction as a series of on/off states. All processing is carried out in the binary number system. For example, a computer carries out all arithmetic in binary instead of in the decimal number system that humans use. The binary form of the instructions is called **machine language** because this is the language that computers use to carry out their operations. An example of the machine language statements necessary to sum the digits 1 to 100 for a computer using an Intel CPU chip is shown in Figure 1-2.

Figure 1-2

Machine Language Command	Explanation
10111000 00000000 00000000	Set Total Value to 0
10111001 00000000 01100100	Set Current Value to 100
00000001 11001000	Add Current Value to Total Value
01001001	Subtract 1 from Current Value
01110101 11111011	If Current Value is not 0, repeat

A machine language program.

Programming the very first computers, which had to be done in binary, was very difficult and time-consuming. Now, we have English-like programming languages, such as Visual Basic, that are referred to as **high-level languages** because they are closer to the level of the human programmer than to the level of the machine. Before the statements in a high-level program can be used to direct the actions of a computer, they must be translated into machine language. Files on a Windows-based computer with an .exe file extension are machine language programs that have been translated from some high-level language. They can be executed with no translation because they are already in a binary form. Until recently, this was a direct translation from high-level language to machine language by a software program known as a **compiler** or an interpreter, depending on whether the code was translated as a unit or line by line; Figure 1-3 shows how the direct translation process works.

The problem with the direct translation approach is that different types of computers have different machine languages, so a program would have to be translated differently for an Apple computer than for a Windows computer. To make it possible for the same program to run on all types of computers, the concept of

Figure 1-3

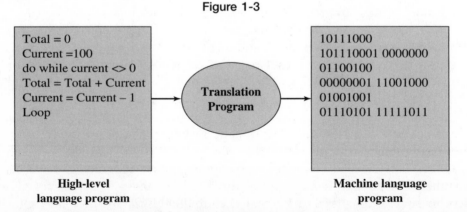

High-level   Machine language
language program   program

The direct translation process.

Figure 1-4

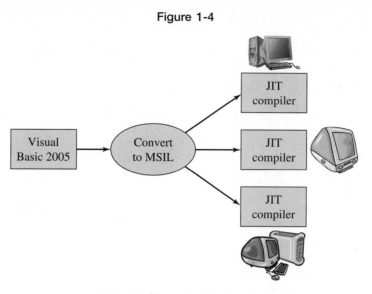

Use of MSIL and JIT compilers.

the **just-in-time (JIT) compiler** was developed. With this approach, a high-level program is translated or compiled into an intermediate form that is machine independent. The two approaches to this use of a JIT compiler are Java from Sun Microsystems and the **.NET Framework** from Microsoft, of which Visual Basic 2005 is a part. In the case of Java, the intermediate form is called **byte-code,** and for the .NET Framework, it is called **Microsoft Intermediate Language (MSIL).** Once converted, a Visual Basic 2005 program is compiled into MSIL; the JIT compiler on any computer can convert it into machine language for that particular machine. This process for MSIL is shown in Figure 1-4.

Whereas the Java approach works only for programs written in Java, the .NET Framework approach works for all languages that have been revised to work under that framework. At this time, these include Visual Basic, C# (pronounced "c-sharp"), and C++ (pronounced "c plus plus") .NET. This means that if you are using one of these languages, it can be compiled in MSIL and combined with other programs in MSIL and then sent to the JIT compiler, which for the .NET Framework is called the **Common Language Runtime (CLR).**

1.1.3 Programming in Windows

As you are probably aware, most personal computers today run some form of the Microsoft Windows operating system, such as Windows 2000, Windows XP, or Windows Server 2003. With Windows being the primary operating system for personal computers, learning to program in the Windows environment has become a critical skill for anybody who is interested in working in information systems. To program in Windows, you first need to understand a little about how Windows works.

Figure 1-5

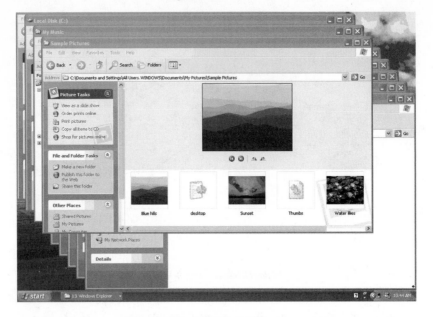

Windows in Windows XP.

To understand the workings of Windows, you need to understand three key concepts: windows, events, and messages. A **window** is any rectangular region on the screen that has its own boundaries. All visible components run in their own windows. For example, when you use a word processor, a document window displays the text you are entering and editing. When you retrieve a file, you do this from a **dialog box** that is a window that displays on top of other windows. Similarly, when an error message is displayed, it is done in a window. Figure 1-5 shows a Windows XP screen with several types of windows displayed.

As a part of its operations, the Windows operating system constantly monitors all the windows on the screen for signs of activity, termed **events.** An event can be a mouse click or a double-click, a keypress, or a change in a window caused by an entry of text in it.

When an event occurs, the corresponding window sends a message to the operating system, which processes the message and then broadcasts it to other windows. When they receive a message, the other windows take actions based on their own sets of instructions. Programming in Windows requires that you learn how to work with windows, events, and messages. For this reason, programming in Windows is usually termed **event-driven programming** because all actions are driven by events. Although this may sound complicated, languages such as Visual Basic make it easy to create Windows-based applications by providing you with the necessary tools.

Event-driven programming is quite different from traditional approaches to programming, where the program itself controls the actions that take place and the order in which those actions occur. With traditional programs, execution of the program starts with the first instruction and continues through the remaining instructions, making decisions as to which instructions will be executed, depending on the data that are input. The main program may use smaller subprograms to handle parts of the processing. This type of programming is referred to as **procedural programming,** and it works very well for such activities as processing a large number of grades at the end of a term or printing payroll checks at the end of a pay period. However, with the move toward widespread use of graphical user interfaces (GUIs), the trend is toward using event-driven programming.

Visual Basic is an event-driven language that does not follow a predefined sequence of instructions; it responds to events to execute different sets of instructions, depending on which event occurs. The order in which events—such as mouse clicks, keystrokes, or even other sets of instructions—occur controls the order of events in Visual Basic and other event-driven languages. For that reason, an event-driven program can execute differently each time it is run, depending on what events occur.

1.1.4 Introduction to Object-Oriented Programming

In addition to being event driven, Visual Basic is an **object-oriented (OO) language.** An OO language is one that encapsulates functionality into classes. The beauty of Visual Basic is that, unlike with many other OO languages, you do not have to know how to create objects to use them. Visual Basic automatically creates for you, the programmer, new instances of many objects from a wide variety of built-in templates.

What distinguishes OO programming from earlier languages is that objects combine programming instructions, or **code,** with data. Previous attempts to structure programs in such a way that large problems could be broken down into smaller problems separated the code from the data. The problem with this approach is that if the data changes, the code might not work with the new data. With OO programming, the combination of code and data avoids this problem. For example, instead of writing code to deal with customers and then using that code with different customer data for each customer, the code and data are combined into an **object** for each customer. The objects for multiple customers are very similar, with the exception of the data component, so you can use them in similar ways.

To understand OO programming, you need to understand a number of concepts and terminology. First, in order to create an object, you must first create a **class**—that is, a template with data and procedures from which objects are created. One way of looking at this is to think of a class as a cookie cutter and

Figure 1-6

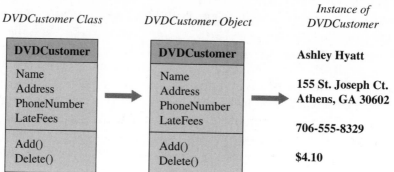

A class, an object, and an instance.

the actual object as the resulting cookie.[1] All the actual work in creating an object is accomplished in creating the class; an **object** is created by defining it to be an **instance** of a class.

Objects have two key elements: properties and methods. Some objects also have events. **Properties** of objects are simply the attributes associated with the object, such as the object's name, color, and so on. **Methods** are a set of predefined activities that an object can carry out. For example, consider the customer objects mentioned earlier; they could be instances of a class called DVDCustomer, which has have the properties and methods shown in Figure 1-6. Note that the DVDCustomer class has Name, Address, PhoneNumber, and LateFees properties. The class also has the Add and Delete methods to add and delete customers. Note that there is also an object named DVDCustomer for a DVD rental store, and there is an instance of this object for Ashley Hyatt that contains properties particular to her.

Three key characteristics of OO programming are encapsulation, inheritance, and polymorphism. **Encapsulation** refers to the requirement that it should never be possible to work with variables in an object directly; the variables must be addressed through the object's properties and methods. This implies a black-box view of an object, in which the programmer does not need to know what is going on inside the object but only needs to know how to work with the object's methods and properties. For example, you would not be able to change the values of the DVDCustomer object without going through the properties of the object; you cannot get into the object except through the properties.

Inheritance refers to the capability to create child classes that descend from a parent class. This capability makes it easier to build new child classes by having them inherit properties and methods from a parent class. For example, the class DVDCustomer inherits the properties and methods from a more general

Customer class, which itself inherits properties and methods from an even more general Person class.

Finally, **polymorphism** is related to inheritance in that a child class can inherit all the characteristics and capabilities of the parent class but then add or modify some of them so the child class is different from the parent class. For example, the DVDCustomer class inherits the Name, Address, and PhoneNumber properties from the Customer class and then adds the LateFees property that is particular to DVDCustomer.

As another example of objects, consider a soccer ball. The SoccerBall class inherits properties and methods from the more general Ball class. These properties include diameter, weight, color, and so on. Methods for the soccer ball include rolling and bouncing. If you apply the Kick event to the soccer ball, then, depending on the ball's diameter and weight, it will roll and bounce a certain distance. It is important to note that the instructions for a method are already a part of Visual Basic, but the programmer must write the instructions to tell the object how to respond to an event. You combine objects with properties or methods by using a period, or dot, and you combine objects with events by using an underscore character. Continuing the soccer ball example, you might have a property definition through the following statement to define the color of the ball:

```
Ball.Color = White
```

Similarly, the Roll method of the soccer ball is referenced by the dot property as shown here:

```
Ball.Roll
```

Finally, the Kick event is applied to the soccer ball as follows, causing the ball to roll:

```
Ball.Kick
```

Working with Visual Basic involves combining objects with the instructions on how each object should respond to a given event. For example, you might have a button for which the instructions are to display a message; instructions for another button might be to exit the program. These instructions are referred to as the *code* for the program

1.1.5 The Programming Process

Creating an application using an OO programming language such as Visual Basic is much easier than working with a traditional programming language. Instead of having to develop the logic for the entire program as you would with a procedural language, you can divide the program logic into small, easily handled parts by working with objects and events. For each object, you determine the events that you want the object to respond to and then develop code to have the object provide the desired response. All the necessary messages between objects in Windows are handled by Visual Basic, thereby significantly reducing the work you must do to create an application.

The manner in which you create a Visual Basic project is also different from traditional programming. Instead of having to create an entire program before testing any part of it, with Visual Basic, you can use **interactive development** to create an object, write the code for it, and test it before going on to other objects. For example, assume that a store named Vintage DVDs that rents only "old" movies on DVD has asked you to create a Visual Basic project that calculates taxes on a DVD rental and sums the taxes and price to compute the amount due. With Visual Basic, you can create the objects and code to calculate the taxes and amount due and test them to ensure their correctness before going on to the rest of the project.

Although creating an application in Visual Basic is easier than working with a procedural language, you still need to follow a series of steps to ensure correctness and completeness of the finished product:

1. Define the problem.
2. Create an interface.
3. Develop logic for action objects.
4. Write and test code for action objects.
5. Test the overall project.
6. Document the project in writing.

Note that it may be necessary to repeat or iterate through these steps to arrive at an acceptable final solution to the original problem. The following sections discuss each of these steps and apply them to a part of the situation just mentioned—that is, creating an application to calculate the taxes and amount due on a DVD rental.

Step 1: Define the Problem

Before you can develop any computer application, it is absolutely necessary to clearly define your objective—that is, the problem to be solved. Only then can you begin to develop the correct logic to solve the problem and incorporate that logic into a computer application. Ensuring that the correct problem is being solved requires careful study of why a problem exists. Maybe an organization is currently handling some repetitive process manually and wants to use a computer to automate it. Or perhaps management has a complicated mathematical or financial problem that cannot be solved by hand. Or maybe a situation has occurred or will occur that cannot be handled by an existing program.

The problem identification step should include identification of the data to be input to the program and the desired results to be output from the program. Often,

Figure 1-7

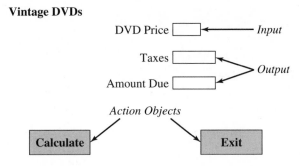

A sketch of the interface for Vintage DVDs.

these two items are specified by a person or an agency other than the programmer. Much grief can be avoided if these input and output requirements are incorporated into the programmer's thinking at this early stage of program development. Unclear thinking at this stage may cause the programmer to write a program that does not correctly solve the problem at hand, a program that correctly solves the wrong problem, or a combination of both. Therefore, the programmer must spend as much time as necessary to truly identify and understand the problem.

Because Visual Basic is a visual language, a good way to understand what is required to solve the problem is to sketch the interface, showing the various objects that will be part of the project. Not only does this help you understand the problem, it is also a good way for you to communicate your understanding to other people. As a part of this sketch, you should denote the input and output objects and the objects for which code is needed to respond to events, the so-called **action objects.** A sketch of the proposed solution for the DVD rental problem is shown in Figure 1-7. In looking at the solution, you see one input—the price of the DVD—and two outputs—the taxes and the amount due. There are also two action objects—a calculation button and an exit button. If there are multiple forms, they should all be sketched, with input, output, and action objects.

Step 2: Create an Interface

After you have defined the problem and, using a sketch of the interface, decided on the objects that are necessary for your project, you are ready to create the interface. Creating the interface with Visual Basic is quite easy: You select objects from those available and place them on the form. This process should follow the sketch done earlier. Although you have not yet been introduced to the wide variety of objects available for creating Visual Basic projects, you can work on the logic for the Vintage DVDs problem with just four types of objects: the form, buttons for action, text boxes for input and output, and labels for descriptors. The interface is shown in Figure 1-8.

Figure 1-8

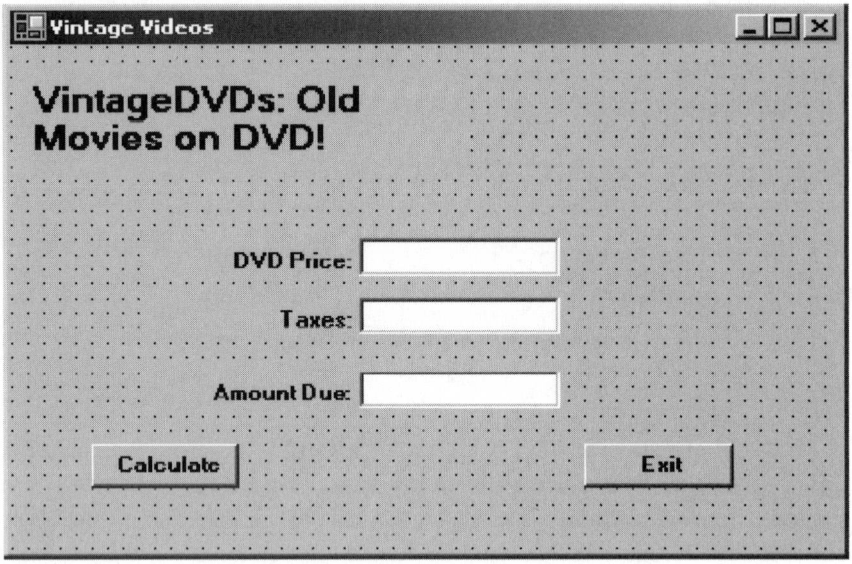

The interface for Vintage DVDs.

Step 3: Develop Logic for Action Objects

After you have clearly identified the problem and created the interface, the next step is to develop the logic for the action objects in the interface. This is the step in the development process during which you have to think about what each action object must do in response to an event. No matter how good your interface, if you don't develop the appropriate logic for the action objects, you will have great difficulty creating a project that solves the problem defined earlier.

To help with this logical development for the action objects, there are two useful tools for designing programming applications: IPO tables and pseudocode. **IPO (input/processing/output) tables** show the inputs to an object, the required outputs for that object, and the processing that is necessary to convert the inputs into the desired outputs. When you have an IPO table for an object, you can write a pseudocode procedure to complete the logic development step.

Writing **pseudocode** involves writing the code for the object in structured English rather than in a computer language. After you have developed an IPO table and the pseudocode for each object, it is easy to write a **procedure** in Visual Basic to carry out the necessary processing.

Let's begin by developing the logic for the Calculate button, using an IPO table. The IPO table for the Calculate button has as input the price of a DVD. The processing involves the calculation necessary to compute the desired

Figure 1-9

Input	Processing	Output
Video price	Taxes = 0.07 × Price	Taxes
	Amount due = Price + Taxes	Amount due

An IPO table for the Calculate button.

output: the amount of the sale. As mentioned earlier, in many cases, the program designer has no control over the input and output, which are specified by somebody else—either the person for whom the application is being developed or, if you are a member of a team and are working on one part of an overall application, the overall design. After you are given the specified input and output, your job is to determine the processing necessary to convert the inputs into desired outputs. Figure 1-9 shows the IPO table for the Calculate button. IPO tables are needed for all objects that involve input, output, and processing. (We won't create an IPO table for the Exit button because it simply terminates the project.)

After you have developed the IPO table for each action object, you should then develop a pseudocode procedure for each one. Pseudocode is useful for two reasons. First, you can write the procedure for the object in English, without worrying about the special syntax and grammar of a computer language. Second, pseudocode provides a relatively direct link between the IPO table and the computer code for the object because you use English to write instructions that can then be converted into program instructions. Often, this conversion from pseudocode statement to computer language instruction is virtually line for line.

There are no set rules for writing pseudocode; you can personalize the method you use for going from the IPO table to the computer program. The pseudocode should be a set of clearly defined steps that enables a reader to see the next step to be taken under any possible circumstance. Also, the language and syntax should be consistent so that the programmer will be able to understand his or her own pseudocode at a later time.

Let's write a pseudocode procedure for the Vintage DVDs Calculate object. Note that this pseudocode program follows the information in the IPO table shown in Figure 1-9:

```
Begin procedure
    Input DVD Price
    Taxes = 0.07 × DVD Price
    Amount Due = DVD Price + Taxes
    Output Taxes and Amount Due
End procedure
```

This small example has only one object for which an IPO table and pseudocode are needed. However, in most situations, there are numerous objects for which you need to develop the logic using these tools.

Step 4: Write and Test Code for Action Objects

After you have created the Visual Basic interface and developed the logic for the action objects, using IPO tables and pseudocode, you must write procedures in Visual Basic for each action object. This code should provide instructions to the computer to carry out one or more of the six operations listed earlier. Although creating the interface is important, writing the code is the essence of developing an application.

After you have written the code for an action object, the second part of this step is to test that object and correct any errors; you should not wait until the entire project is complete. You should use the interactive capabilities of Visual Studio to test the code of each and every object as it is written. This process is referred to as **debugging,** and it involves trying to remove all of the errors, or **bugs.**

Step 5: Test the Overall Project

After you have tested the code for each action object individually, the next step is to test the overall project and correct any errors that may still exist or that may be the result of incorrect communication between objects. At this stage, it is necessary to determine whether the results obtained from the project meet the objectives outlined in the problem definition step. If the project does not meet the final user's needs, then the developer must analyze the results and the objectives to find out where they diverge. After the analysis, the developer should trace through the program development procedure and correct the algorithm, IPO tables, pseudocode, and final code for one or more objects to find the cause of the difference between the objectives and the final project.

Step 6: Document the Project in Writing

An important part of writing any computer software is the documentation of the software. Documentation helps users by providing instructions and suggestions on using the software. Documentation helps other programmers who may need to make changes or correct the programs.

Internal documentation usually includes comments within the program that are intermingled with the program statements to explain the purpose and logic of the program elements. This type of documentation is essential to the maintenance of software, especially by someone other than the original programmer. By being able to read the original programmer's purpose for a part of a program or a program statement, a different programmer can make any needed corrections or revisions. Without internal documentation, it can be extremely difficult for anyone to understand the purpose of parts of the program. And if a programmer is unclear about what's going on in the program, making needed changes is very difficult

Written documentation includes books, manuals, and pamphlets that give instructions on using the software and also discuss the objectives and logic of the software. The documentation should include a user's guide and programmer documentation. The user's guide provides complete instructions on accessing the software, entering data, interpreting output, and understanding error messages. The programmer documentation should include various descriptive documents that allow for maintenance of the software. These may include pseudocode of sections of the program, a listing of the program, and a description of required input values and the resulting output.

FOR EXAMPLE

Creating an Area Calculator

Say that you work for a construction company. You need to build a program that can accept the length and width of a room, in feet and inches, and calculate its area in both inches and feet and inches. The program will be a Windows application.

You analyze the program requirements. You determine that the application needs two actions: a Calculate action and an Exit action.

The Calculate action needs to accept four input values: WidthFeet, WidthInches, LengthFeet, and LengthInches. These values will be entered by a user. You also determine that the program must output two values: TotalAreaInches and TotalAreaFeet. TotalAreaFeet is a decimal value that is the area calculated in square feet. TotalAreaInches is a whole number that is the area calculated in square inches.

You sketch the IPO table shown in Figure 1-10.

Figure 1-10

Input	Processing	Output
LengthFeet	TotalLengthInches = LengthFeet $\times$ 12 + LengthInches	AreaFeet
LengthInches	TotalWidthInches = WidthFeet $\times$ 12 + WidthInches	AreaInches
WidthFeet	TotalAreaInches = TotalLengthInches $\times$ TotalWidthInches	
WidthInches	AreaFeet = TotalAreaInches/12	
	AreaInches = Remainder of TotalAreaInches/12	

An IPO table for the area calculator.

(Continued)

You write the following pseudocode for the procedure:

```
Begin Procedure
Input LengthFeet, LengthInches, WidthFeet, WidthInches
TotalLengthInches = LengthFeet * 12 + LengthInches
TotalWidthInches = WidthFeet * 12 + WidthInches
TotalAreaInches = TotalLengthInches * TotalWidthInches
TotalAreaFeet = TotalAreaInches / 144
End Procedure
```

You sketch the interface and identify four fields used for input, two fields use for output, and two buttons.

You implement the interface by using a Visual Basic Windows form. You add TextBox controls for the Input fields and Label controls for the output fields. You also add Label controls to identify each input field. Next, you write and test the code for both buttons. After testing all functionality, you create the documentation.

SELF-CHECK

- Describe how an application written in Visual Basic 2005 is converted to machine language.
- Compare a class, an object, and an instance.
- Define encapsulation.
- Identify the six steps in creating a Windows application.

1.2 Working with Visual Studio

Visual Studio is the integrated development environment (IDE) used to create programs with Visual Basic. An IDE is an application that provides tools for creating, debugging, and modifying application code. In the next sections, you will learn how to install Visual Studio and how to use the online help system.

1.2.1 Installing Visual Studio

You can avoid frustrations when installing Visual Studio by first making sure your system can run Visual Studio. You don't want to begin the installation only to have the Setup Wizard display the dreadful message that it cannot install the application because your computer is not capable of supporting it. Visual Studio has the following hardware requirements:

▲ 600MHz or faster CPU
▲ 192MB or more of RAM
▲ 2GB of disk space

Your computer probably meets or surpasses these requirements if you purchased it within the past few years.

Typically, software—not hardware—is at the center of installation troubles. Not everyone keeps up-to-date with Microsoft's latest service packs. A **service pack** is a group of enhancements to Windows that usually patch security gaps in the original Windows release. Visual Studio requires you to have certain service packs installed on your computer before running the Setup Wizard. You can download service packs free of charge from www.microsoft.com. To install Visual Studio, you must be running one of the following:

▲ Windows 2000 with Service Pack 4 (SP4)
▲ Windows XP with SP2
▲ Windows Server 2003 with SP1

The installation of Visual Studio is straightforward and should take an hour to an hour and a half. You begin the installation by closing down any applications that are open on your computer. Next, you place Installation Disc 1 into your CD drive, and Windows automatically starts the Setup Wizard, which walks you through the installation. You also use the Setup Wizard to uninstall Visual Studio and to add or remove components to the installation that have not yet been installed. During the installation process, you have the opportunity to install all the components, select the components you want to install, or accept the default components that Microsoft suggests you install. You probably want to install the components that are selected by default. If you need a feature that you do not install now, sometime in the future, you can use the Setup Wizard again to install any component that was not originally installed. You will probably not need to add a new component later, however, because nearly all the components that you need are part of the default installation.

1.2.2 Getting Help with Visual Studio and Visual Basic

As you learn to program in Visual Basic, you may often need to look up how to do something in the documentation. This is normal. Even experienced programmers rely heavily on the documentation to find the best way to accomplish

Figure 1-11

The Document Explorer toolbar.

a task. The .NET Framework is a rich library with a huge number of objects. No one can be expected to remember how to use them all. Fortunately, Visual Studio and Visual Basic provide powerful tools for gaining access to the information you need.

The most straightforward use of the documentation requires little more than clicking on or in the object that you have a question about and pressing the F1 key to launch context-sensitive help. For instance, in any project, you can click somewhere on an object and press F1. The Microsoft Document Explorer launches documentation about that object loaded. The **Document Explorer** offers a sophisticated set of tools, mostly represented in the Document Explorer toolbar, shown in Figure 1-11. The tools you find there give you various ways to access the documentation, as follows. The toolbar's first section has navigation buttons, a refresh button, and font size maintenance. It also has the following buttons:

▲ **How Do I:** The How Do I button has preset questions that relate to the selected topic and may help with general queries about certain types of development. If you are stuck, give it a try.

▲ **Search:** Clicking the Search button allows for phrase searching.

▲ **Index and Contents:** The Index button and Contents button allow browsing through the index or table of contents of the documentation.

▲ **Help Favorites:** You can save favorites in the Help Favorites just as you can in Internet Explorer. The double arrow is handy: It synchronizes the Contents panel with the page you are currently viewing.

▲ **Ask a Question:** The Ask a Question button takes you directly to the NNTP Newsgroups (using a web-based viewer) hosted by Microsoft, where you can ask questions and have them answered by Microsoft MVPs, authors, and other experts.

These options are only one part of the documentation in Visual Studio. IntelliSense shows information from the user documentation when you rest the mouse cursor over a piece of code. The Properties window shows the documentation for a property when it is selected. And don't overlook the online tools that Microsoft provides. You can open the Help menu and select Technical Support to access a wealth of information available on the Web, right from inside Visual Studio.

FOR EXAMPLE

Getting Help

Say you are creating an application and want to use a control you have never used before. You drag the control onto your form and select it, and then you press F1. Visual Studio automatically goes out to the Internet to locate the documentation for that control. Later, you decide you want to know how other developers have used the control, so you click Ask a Question to go out to the NNTP Newsgroups.

SELF-CHECK

- What must you do before you install Visual Studio?
- How can you easily obtain information about how to use an object?
- Why would you use the Index button to locate product documentation?

1.3 Creating Solutions and Projects

When you create an application, you create multiple files. Some of these files contain **source code** (the human-readable instructions the program will execute) and are compiled as part of your application. You might also create graphics files, documentation files, and data files. Visual Studio allows you to organize all the files associated with an application into a **project.**

A single project is suitable for a simple application, but a more complex application might include multiple projects. A **solution** allows you to organize the files for one or more projects.

1.3.1 Creating a Windows Application Project

All applications are created as a project. It is fairly easy to create a new project, as you'll learn shortly. You use the New Project dialog box (shown in Figure 1-12), in which you select a project type and template. Visual Studio enables you to create projects in Visual Basic and other programming languages, as well. Here, you select Visual Basic as the project type.

In the New Project dialog box, several templates are displayed in the Templates window. A template contains the basic ingredients needed to create

Figure 1-12

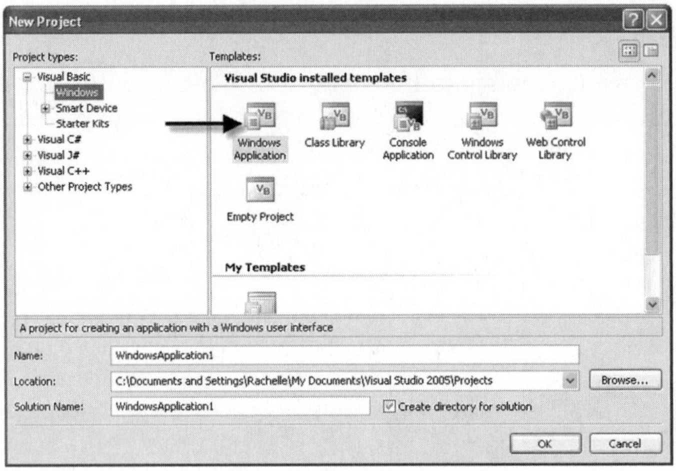

The New Project dialog box.

a specific kind of Visual Basic program. You see the templates Windows Application, Class Library, Windows Control Library, ASP.NET Web Application, ASP.NET Web Service, and others. You'll start learning to program by using the **Windows Application** template. A Windows application creates an .exe when it is compiled.

After you select Windows Application as the template for your project, a new Windows application project opens, showing a blank form and the Properties window. The **blank form** is where you create the screens that allow a user to interact with your application. You use the Properties window to define characteristics of the blank form. The default settings are sufficient for most applications you build. However, you probably want to change the text that appears at the top of the form to something that better describes the purpose of the form.

1.3.2 Using the Solution Explorer Window

Solutions and projects hold forms and other project files in folders. In fact, solutions and projects are represented by folders in the Visual Studio Projects directory of your My Documents folder. The **Solution Explorer** is Visual Studio's tool that allows you to manage the files in a project.

If you envision your projects like folders, you can imagine that you would group similar folders together in a folder. That's what solutions do: They are both physically and logically folders full of projects.

Figure 1-13

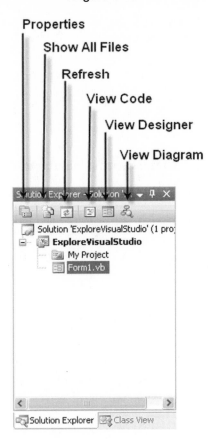

The Solution Explorer.

Figure 1-13 shows the important files in a project, along with a whole bunch of buttons above to help to manage them.

To open a file, you double-click the file's icon or name. To rename, copy, or delete a file, you right-click the file and choose the desired action from the context-sensitive menu that appears. In the Solution Explorer, you can also make a new folder and move files into it. And you can right-click a project to add a new form or support file.

The buttons above the files themselves are the most significant part of the Solution Explorer. They are, from left to right:

▲ **Properties:** Opens the Properties window.

▲ **Show All Files:** Shows hidden files.

▲ **Refresh:** Checks the solution folder for new files that may have been added by another tool.

▲ **View Code:** Opens the selected file in Code view. You use **Code view** to write source code.

▲ **View Designer:** Opens the selected file in Design view. You use **Design view** to design what your application looks like.

▲ **View Class Diagram:** Opens the Class Designer for the project. The **Class Designer** allows you to view how the classes in the project are related. You'll learn about classes later in the book. For now, just think of them as being definitions for objects in a project.

1.3.3 Customizing the Visual Studio Environment

You can customize the Visual Studio environment to make it easier to work in. All the tools, windows, and views are part of an Integrated Development Environment (IDE) that each user can customize. This makes organization of your personal development space a lot easier.

Most often, you will want to move around a tool window to put it in a more convenient spot. You can display a tool window in the following ways:

▲ **Floating:** A floating window is very mobile. You can drag it around by its handles to place it anywhere you want.

▲ **Dockable:** When you drag a dockable window, Visual Studio gives you the option to dock the window. When you **dock** a window, you anchor it to an edge so that it always stays in that location. There are several options for docking a window. If you drag the window over the top, bottom, left, or right arrow, it docks to that side. When a window is docked, it has a thumbtack that you can pin or unpin. When **pinned**, it stays on the side, moving the Design view over. When unpinned, it slides out of the way, toward the side it is pinned to.

▲ **Tabbed:** You can drag a window to the center and have it become a tab at the top of the view window, like the Form1.vb and Form2.vb files in Figure 1-14. If you drag the window to the center of the four-pointed star, it makes the window a tab in the other central windows.

FOR EXAMPLE

Configuring Your Environment

Say you are creating an application and want to cause the Properties window to float above other windows so you can move it to a convenient place. You click its title bar and drag it away from its docked position. Later, you decide that you want it above the Solution Explorer window, so you move it over the Solution Explorer window and highlight the arrow that points up.

Figure 1-14

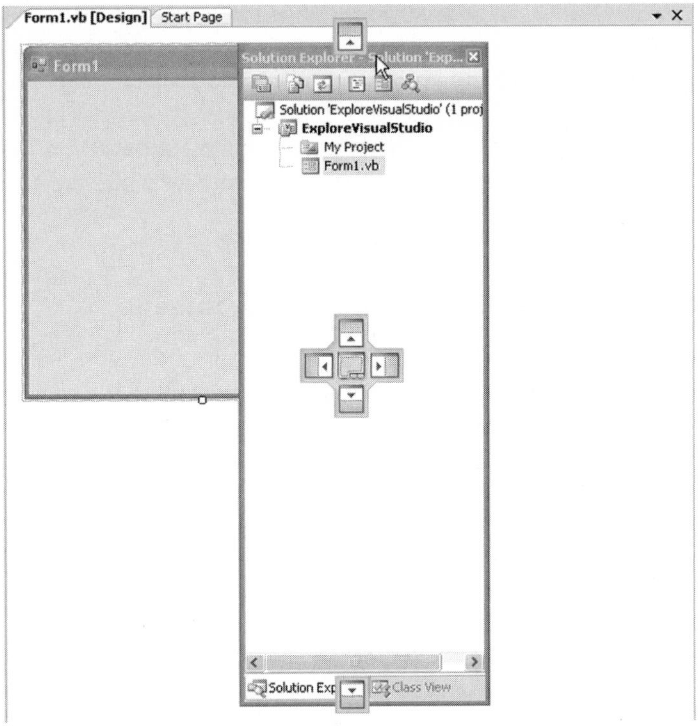

Moving windows.

SELF-CHECK

- Describe how a solution and a project are related.
- Describe a case in which you would create a folder inside a project.
- Compare and contrast the three ways to display windows in Visual Studio.

1.4 Understanding Forms

When you create a Windows application project, Visual Studio adds a default form to the project. You use a form to create the program's user interface. Each form in an application acts as a window or a dialog box.

In the following sections, you'll learn how to set properties on the default form. You'll also learn how to create additional forms in a project.

1.4.1 Defining a Form

A **form** is a member of the System.Windows.Forms.Form class. System. Windows.Forms is a namespace. The .Net Framework uses **namespaces** to organize and group classes that are related. A form has all the properties, methods, and events defined by the Form class. For instance, the Form class has a Show method that allows you to display the form. Each object based on the Form class in a project has a name. You use that name when accessing the form in code.

1.4.2 Working with Forms in Design View

When you open a Windows application project, you see the Design view. The Design view is where the GUI work takes place. Generally speaking, anytime you are working with what the form looks like, not code, you are working with the Design view. The term **designer window** refers to the actual place you do the work. The term *Design view* refers to the state of the file.

In general, Design view is the core part of Visual Studio. Many of the other tools in Visual Studio depend on the Design view, in fact, and are disabled when you use another view, such as Code view, to work on a project.

The designer tabs have the word [Design] in the tab name, as shown in Figure 1-15, to indicate that you are using the Design view. Tabs are used in

Figure 1-15

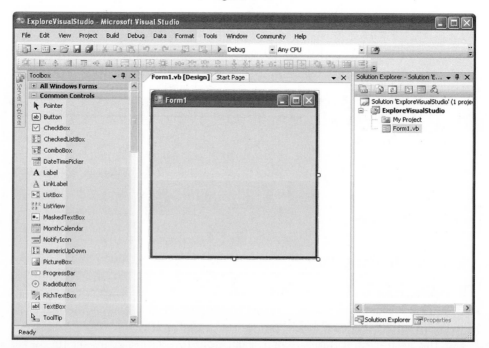

A form in Design view.

Figure 1-16

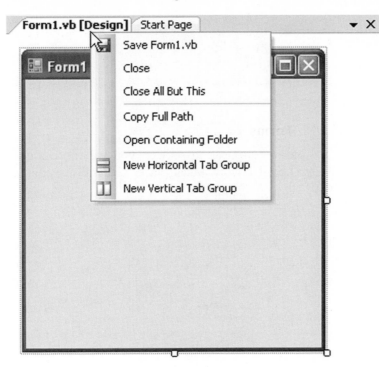

Managing tab groups.

the Design and Code views. A light gray tab represents views of files that are open but not active. An asterisk (*) next to the filename means that you've made changes but not yet saved the file.

The white tab is active and contains the editable form. When you have more than one form open, you can edit only the active form. You can drag the tabs to the left and right to change their order. Right-clicking a tab opens a menu from which you can choose several screen-management options, as shown in Figure 1-16. You can save and close files from this menu, or get information, such as the current path or the containing folder. You can display files as horizontal or vertical tab groups. **Tab groups** make it easier to copy information from one form into another. For example, you can have one set of pages on the top half of the screen and another on the bottom half, and you can copy from one and paste into the other without changing screens.

1.4.3 Setting Form Properties

A form has multiple properties that determine how it looks and acts. As you have already learned, a property is a value that describes an object. You can set

Figure 1-17

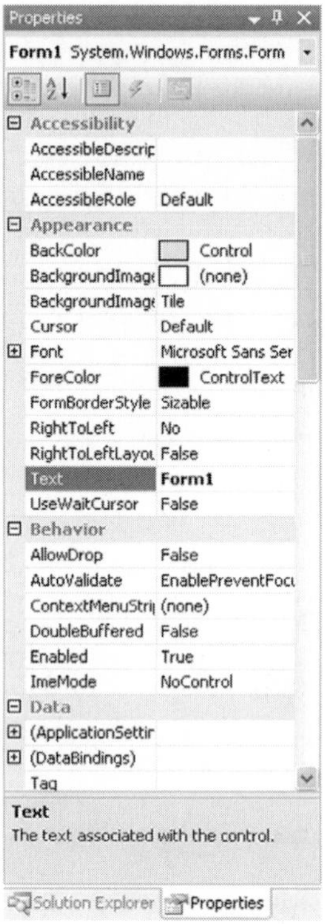

The Properties window.

properties at design time or at runtime. Setting a property at design time means setting it when you are creating the application. Setting a property at runtime (**runtime** refers to the state an application is in when it is executing) means setting it by writing code.

You set a property at design time by using the Properties window. The Properties window, shown in Figure 1-17, is usually on the right side of the screen. It contains all the editable values associated with a form. If the Properties window isn't on the right side of the screen, you can find it by opening the View menu and choosing Properties, or you can press F4.

At the top of the Properties window, you see the form element whose properties are listed. The Properties window has a toolbar. For now, just notice that the leftmost button causes the properties to be listed by type. The second button causes the properties to be listed in alphabetical order. A description of the selected property is shown beneath the list of properties.

You set a property at runtime by using code like this:

```
form_name.propertyname = propertyvalue
```

For example, to set the Text property of Form1 to "My First Program," you use the following code:

```
Form1.Text = "My First Program"
```

The Text property sets the text that displays in the form's title bar. Notice that "My First Program" is enclosed in quotation marks. That's because it is a string literal value. **String** is a programming term for textual data. A **literal** is a value that you type directly into code.

A form has a large number of properties. You'll have a chance to use many of them as you work your way through this book. For now, let's just look at a few of the important ones:

▲ **(Name):** Specifies the name you will use to reference an object in code. The (Name) property is really not a property at all. You can change (Name) in the Properties window, but you cannot change it in code.

▲ **BackColor:** Sets the background color of the form.

▲ **ControlBox:** Is set to True or False to determine whether the icon to the left of the form's title should be displayed. ControlBox shows a Windows-controlled menu when it is clicked.

▲ **FormBorderStyle:** Determines whether the form is resizable, a dialog, or a toolbox window.

▲ **HelpButton:** Determines whether a Help button appears on the title bar.

▲ **MaximizeBox:** Determines whether the Maximize button appears on the title bar.

▲ **MaximumSize:** Determines the maximum size for the window.

▲ **MinimizeBox:** Determines whether the Minimize button appears on the title bar.

▲ **MiminumSize:** Determines the minimum size for the window.

▲ **ShowInTaskbar:** Determines whether the window should be listed in the Windows taskbar.

▲ **Size:** Determines the starting size of the window. Sets the height and width.

▲ **StartPosition:** Determines where the form is displayed when it is first shown.

1.4.4 Adding a Form to a Project

Most Windows applications you build require multiple forms. For example, you might have an application that has a main form but that allows users to configure the application by using a Properties dialog. The Properties dialog would be a separate form.

To add a form to a project, you right-click the project name in Solution Explorer, open the Add menu, and choose Windows Form. Visual Studio has a number of **templates** for standard forms, as shown in Figure 1-18. You can choose one of them or you can choose Windows Form to add a blank form. You give the form a name and click Add.

Figure 1-18

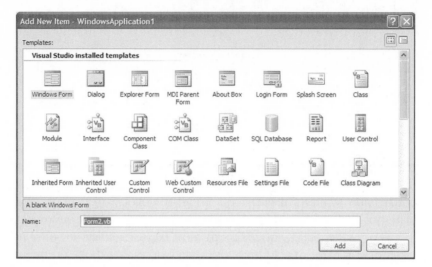

The Add New Item dialog box.

If your project has multiple forms, you need to designate one as the startup form. The **startup form** is the one that displays when the application first launches. To designate a startup form, you right-click the project in Solution Explorer and choose Properties. On the Application tab, you select the appropriate form from the Startup Form drop-down list, as shown in Figure 1-19.

Figure 1-19

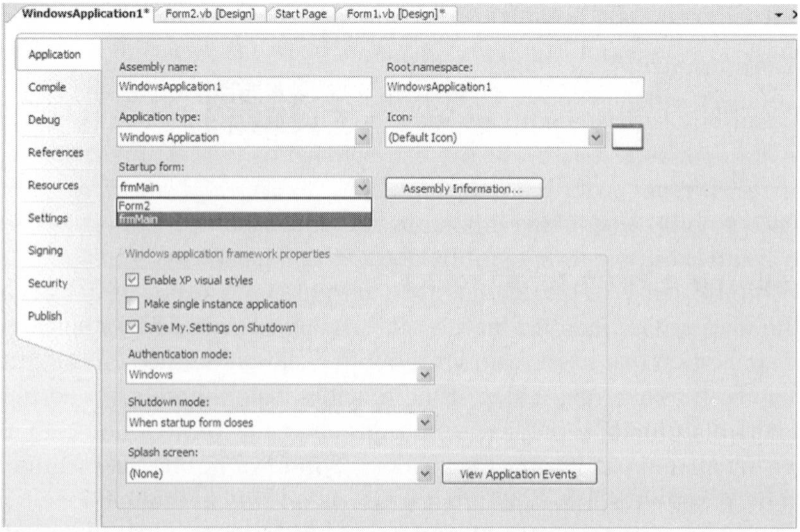

Setting the startup form.

FOR EXAMPLE

Using Multiple Forms

Say that you are writing an application that allows a user to perform various types of measurement conversion. The main form has four buttons: Distance, Temperature, Volume, and Weight. Each button displays a form that performs the relevant conversions. You configure the main form as the startup form.

You set the Text property and the (Name) property for each form as shown in Table 1-1.

Table 1-1: Form Property Settings

Form	Text	(Name)
Main form	Measurement Converter	frmMain
Distance calculations form	Distance Calculator	frmDistance
Temperature calculations form	Temperature Calculator	frmTemp
Volume calculations form	Volume Calculator	frmVolume
Weight calculations form	Weight Calculator	frmWeight

The forms do not require minimize or maximize buttons. Therefore, you set the MinimizeBox and MaximizeBox properties to False.

To show the Distance Calculator form, you use the following code:

```
frmDistance.Show
```

SELF-CHECK

- List some reasons you might need multiple forms in a project.
- To enable users to minimize, maximize, and resize a window, what properties should you set?
- Describe a situation in which you would set the Text property of a form at runtime instead of at design time.

1.5 Using Controls

Controls are special objects that allow you to add functionality to a form. Like forms (and pretty much everything else in Visual Basic), they are defined by classes. This means they have properties, methods, and events.

In the following sections, you'll learn how to add controls to a form. Although a large number of controls are available, the following sections focus on three simple but commonly used controls: the Label, Textbox, and Button controls.

1.5.1 Using the Toolbox to Add Controls

On the left side of the project window is a tab called the **toolbox** that expands into a list of tools when you hover the mouse over it. You use these tools to transform a blank form into an interactive screen for an application. The tools are organized into groups. You select the name of the group to see a list of tools in that group. You are likely to use the Common Controls tool group (see Figure 1-20) more than the other groups because it contains buttons, check boxes, and other controls that are frequently used in applications.

You can keep the toolbox open by first opening it with the mouse and then clicking the pushpin icon at the top of the toolbox. You can then drag and drop tools onto your form without having to open and close the toolbox each time. You click the pushpin icon again to return the toolbox to its tab position.

When you want to use a control on a form, you drag that control from the toolbox and drop it onto the form. You can adjust the control on the form by first selecting the control. Sizing handles appear around the control. You can then do any of the following:

Figure 1-20

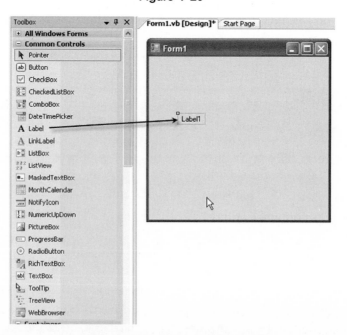

The Common Controls tool group.

Figure 1-21

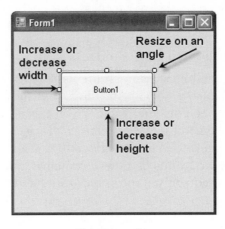

Sizing handles.

▲ Change the size of the control by dragging the sizing handles.
▲ Reposition the control on the blank form by dragging the center of the control to the new location.
▲ Remove a control by selecting it and pressing Delete.

You can adjust the size of a control on a form to fit your design by using the sizing handles that appear when you select the control. Visual Basic changes the Height and Width properties of the control to reflect the new size as you resize the control.

There are typically eight sizing handles around a control (see Figure 1-21). One sizing handle is in each corner of a control, and another is on each side of the control.

The right- and left-side sizing handles move the corresponding size out and in to make the control wider or narrower. The top- and bottom-side sizing handles move the corresponding side up and down, making the control taller or shorter. The corner sizing handles resize the control in any direction. As a corner sizing handle is dragged on an angle, the sides of the control attached to that handle move up and out or down and in, depending on the direction that the sizing handle is dragged.

Professional developers usually keep the size of a type of control the same throughout an application. For example, all Button controls are adjusted to the size of the Button control that has the longest button text (i.e., the text that appears on the button).

1.5.2 Setting Control Properties

Each control has a set of properties that define a characteristic or behavior of the control. The kinds of properties that are available depend on the type of control. For example, the FontColor property of the Label control sets the color of the label. The list of properties appears in the Properties window when you select the control. You can select a control from the drop-down list in the Properties window, or you can select a control by clicking it on the form.

Like a form, each control you add to a form also has a name. You can set the (Name) property for the control at design time through the Properties window, but you cannot set it at runtime.

You can also set a control's location on the form and the control's size through its properties. The control's location on the form is set through the X and Y properties. To access them in the Properties window, you expand Location. X and Y refer to the coordinates of the control's top-left corner in relation to the form's top-left corner. You can adjust the size of a control by setting the Width and Height properties, which are located in the Properties window under Size. You can also set them in code. However, to do so you use the Top property and the Left property:

```
lblName.Top = 40
lblName.Left = 10
```

This code sets the leftmost pixel of the control to 40 pixels from the edge of the form and the topmost pixel of the control to 10 pixels from the top of the form.

1.5.3 Adding a TextBox Control to a Form

A **TextBox control** enables a user to enter text into a field. Text can include letters, numbers, and other characters. You use a TextBox control anytime a user needs to be able to type a value.

You should rename the TextBox control, using a name that reflects the content of the text box. For example, you might name a TextBox control txtCustomerFirstName if the text box will contain the first name of a customer. Naming your TextBox controls in this way makes them more meaningful when you refer to them in your code. Using a prefix that identifies the control as a TextBox control (e.g., txt) is also useful for helping you understand the code you have written. You can change the name of a TextBox control by selecting the control, right-clicking, and clicking Properties from the pop-up menu. Then you type the new name in the (Name) property.

By default, the TextBox control accepts one line of text from the user and has only the two horizontal sizing handles. However, you can have the user enter multiple lines into a TextBox control by selecting the right arrow located near the upper-right corner of the text box. The Tasks pop-up menu appears (see Figure 1-22). You select the MultiLine check box to convert from a single-line text box to a multiline text box. After you make this selection, the eight sizing handles appear around the TextBox control. You can use them to resize the TextBox control to display multiple lines of text.

You access the text entered in a TextBox control by using the TextBox control's Text property. For example, to set the value of txtCustomerFirstName in code, you use this:

```
txtCustomerFirstName.Text = "John"
```

Figure 1-22

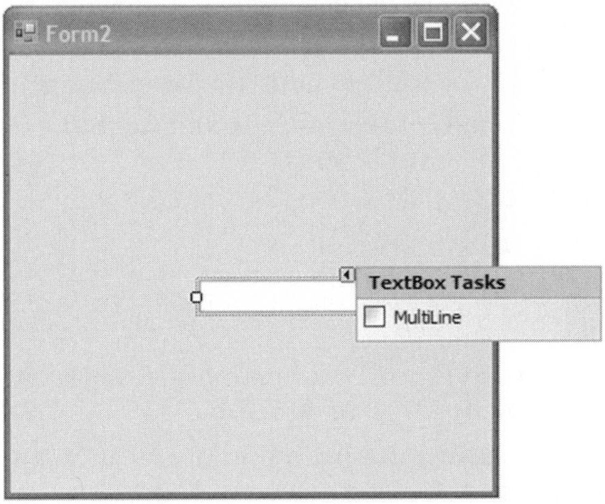

The MultiLine check box.

You can also retrieve the text a user types into a TextBox control and use it to set another property. For example, to set the Text property of txtHomeState to the value stored in txtWorkState, you use this:

```
txtHomeState.Text = txtWorkState.Text
```

By default, a user can edit the contents of a TextBox control. However, sometimes you place information into a TextBox control that you do not want the user to change, such as a customer account number. You can prevent the user from changing the contents of a TextBox control by setting the ReadOnly property of the TextBox control to True. The ReadOnly property tells Visual Basic whether to permit changes to the contents of the TextBox control. You set the ReadOnly property by using the following code:

```
txtAccountNumber.ReadOnly = True
```

Notice that you do not enclose True in quotes. True is a literal value, but it is not a string. It is a Boolean. A **Boolean** is a special type of property that can only be set to True or False.

The default values of the TextBox control's properties may or may not be appropriate for your application. You can change the default values by using the Properties list. You highlight the property and then enter the new value for the property. The following are some properties that are commonly changed:

▲ **MaxLength:** Sets the maximum number of characters a user can enter into the text box.

▲ **Multiline:** Determines whether one or multiple lines can be entered into the text box. You set the Multiline property to False for a single line or

True for multiple lines. If you are allowing multiple lines, you might also want to enable either horizontal or vertical scrollbars.

▲ **ScrollBars:** Determines whether horizontal scrollbars, vertical scrollbars, both, or neither are added to the text box.

▲ **Font:** Designates a font for text entered into the text box; you can choose from a list of available fonts.

▲ **ForeColor and BackColor:** Sets the foreground and background colors for the text box, respectively; you can choose a color from a palette of available colors.

▲ **TextAlign:** Aligns text within the text box; options are Left, Center, and Right.

1.5.4 Adding a Label Control to a Form

A **Label control** is used to display text on a form that identifies controls, provides instructions for using the application, and generally communicates to the user. For example, a label is typically used to identify a TextBox control; for example, the text "Customer First Name:" could be a Label control placed to the left or at the top of a TextBox control on a form.

You can modify the appearance of a Label control by changing its properties in the Properties window. You can use the Text property to change the text of a Label control and the ForeColor and BackColor properties to change the foreground and background colors of a Label control, respectively. You use the Font property to change the font of the Label control's text.

By default, a Label control's AutoSize property is set to True. This means that the control is automatically resized horizontally as you enter text. You can move the control, but you cannot change its size. When the AutoSize property is set to True, all text is displayed on a single line. If you want to wrap text or manage the size of the Label control yourself, you set the AutoSize property to False.

1.5.5 Adding a Button Control to a Form

A **Button control** simulates a push button on a form and is used to start, confirm, or cancel an operation. For example, you can use an OK button on a dialog box. The user confirms an action by clicking OK.

You should rename the Button control to reflect the action of the button (e.g., btnOK, btnCancel). You rename a Button control by setting its (Name) property.

You can modify the appearance of the label on a Button control by changing other Button control properties. You change the text of the label on a Button control by using the Button control's Text property. You change the font of the label by choosing a new value for the Font property. You click the Font property to display a list of other available fonts. You can reposition a label on a Button control by using the TextAlign property. You can click the TextAlign

FOR EXAMPLE

Designing a Temperature Conversion Form

Say that you are writing an application that allows a user to perform various types of measurement conversion. The main form has four buttons: Distance, Temperature, Volume, and Weight. Each button displays a form that performs the relevant conversions. You are designing the temperature conversion form. One way to design it would be to add one TextBox control named txtTemp, one Label control named lblConvertedTemp, and two Button controls: btnConvertToCelsius and btnConvertToFahrenheit.

property to see a diagram that illustrates where you can position the text. The choices are top, middle, or bottom and left, center, or right. You specify values by using the ContentAlignment enumeration. An **enumeration** is a set of descriptive words mapped to numeric values. For example, to have the text aligned bottom center, you use this code:

```
btnSetLabel.TextAlign = ContentAlignment.BottomCenter
```

You can prevent a Button control from being accidentally pushed by setting the Enabled property of the Button control to False. There are two ways to set the Enabled property: You can either open the Properties window and change the Enabled property to False or, from you can use the following code:

```
btnOK.Enabled = False
```

In this case, btnOK is the Button control name, and Enabled is the name of the property. You enable the Button control by changing the Enabled property to True or by adding the following code:

```
btnOK.Enabled = True
```

SELF-CHECK

- Identify the properties you would use to reposition a control in code.
- Compare and contrast the Label control and the TextBox control. Give examples of when you would use each.
- List some uses of the Button control.
- Describe the steps you would take to change the text of a Label control in code.

1.6 Writing an Event-Driven Program

A Visual Basic application is an event-driven application. As you have learned, an event is something that happens when an application runs, such as the clicking of a button. You can write code to respond to an event that is important to an application and ignore other events because Visual Basic has a default response for every event.

For example, you can write code that executes when the user clicks a button because that event is important to the application. You do not have to write code that executes when a form is loaded unless you want something special to happen when that event occurs.

1.6.1 Understanding Form Events

A **form event** is an event that occurs when something happens to a form. The default form event is the Load event, which occurs when a form is loaded into memory. An event is associated with a special type of subprocedure known as an **event procedure** or **event handler.** The **syntax** (i.e., the general grammar for using a subprocedure, function, or method) for a form's Load event procedure looks like this:

```
Private Sub frmMain_Load _
    (ByVal sender As System.Object, ByVal e As _
        System.EventArgs) Handles MyBase.Load
'Enter your code here
End Sub
```

In this case, the event belongs to a form named frmMain. Notice that the event is named with the name of the form, an underscore, and then the name of the event. A space and then an underscore character are used to wrap the text to the next line. Visual Basic sees each line as a separate line of code unless an underscore is used. In this case, we have to wrap to the next line so that the code can fit on the page of the book. In the development environment, there is no wrap.

Next, you see two arguments in parentheses. You shouldn't worry too much about them for now. An **argument** is used to pass data to a procedure. In this case, the operating system is passing data to the frmMain_Load event procedure. You'll learn more about arguments later in the book.

You know that this is an event procedure because of the Handles keyword. The **Handles keyword** identifies the event the procedure will handle. In this case, it will handle the Form class's Load event. **MyBase** is a special word that refers to an object's **base class** (i.e., the class on which the object is based). The base class for frmMain is System.Windows.Forms.Form.

The following line of code has been added:

```
'Enter your code here
```

Figure 1-23

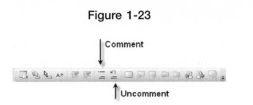

The Comment and Uncomment buttons.

This line is not really code; it is a comment. A **comment** is a line of code that is not compiled and executed. Instead, you use it to document your code. In Visual Basic, you add a comment to your code by preceding the line with an apostrophe. A quick way to comment lines of code is to select them and click the Comment Out button on the toolbar (see Figure 1-23). The Uncomment button removes the comment apostrophes.

The event procedure terminates with End Sub. This tells the compiler that the subprocedure is over.

The following are some other form events you might use:

▲ **Activated:** Occurs when a form becomes the active form (i.e., is brought into the foreground).
▲ **Shown:** Occurs when a form displays.
▲ **Deactivated:** Occurs when a different window becomes active.
▲ **FormClosing:** Occurs before a form closes.
▲ **Move:** Occurs when a user moves the window.

You add code to a form event if you want to do something in response to the event. For example, you might want to display a dialog, asking a user to confirm whether a form should close. To do so, you add code to the FormClosing event.

1.6.2 Using the Code Window

You place code that you want to execute in response to an event in the event procedure. When you double-click the form or a control, the event procedure for the default event displays. If you have not added code to the default event, a new event procedure is created. You can avoid creating a new event procedure by clicking View Code. Visual Studio displays the code page without creating a new event procedure. The code window is shown in Figure 1-24.

If you add an event procedure for a control or a form and then change that control's name, the name of the event procedure does not change automatically. You need to change the name in the event procedure manually.

The left drop-down box at the top of the window contains a list of objects on the form and the name of the form. If the object in the left box is a control or a form's events, the right drop-down box contains a list of events associated

Figure 1-24

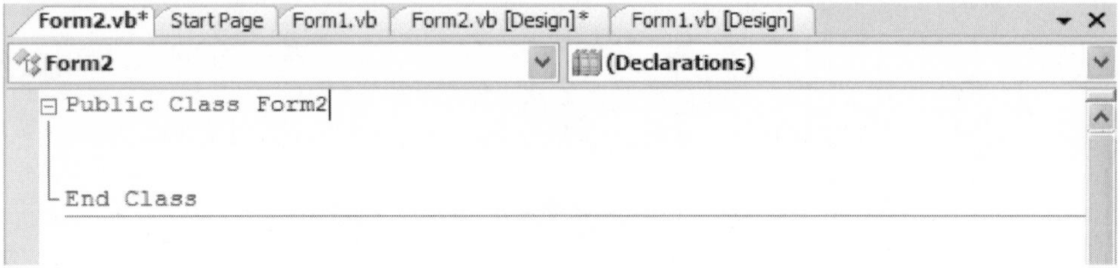

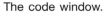

```
Form2.vb*   Start Page   Form1.vb   Form2.vb [Design]*   Form1.vb [Design]          ▾ ×
⁕⁑ Form2                                    ▾   📄 (Declarations)                     ▾
  ⊟ Public Class Form2
  │
  │
  └ End Class
```

The code window.

with the events in the left box. You can select an event from the list, and Visual Basic .NET displays the corresponding event procedure.

The problem with using Code view is that you need to know what to type. To help get started, you can use some very productive code-based tools, such as **IntelliSense.** When you type an object name and then a period, a special context-sensitive menu (the IntelliSense menu) appears, as shown in Figure 1-25. This menu shows the properties and methods the object supports.

1.6.3 Understanding Control Events

Most controls support events. One of those events is the default event, which is the event procedure that is created when you double-click a control in Design view. The following are the default events for the controls we have discussed so far:

Figure 1-25

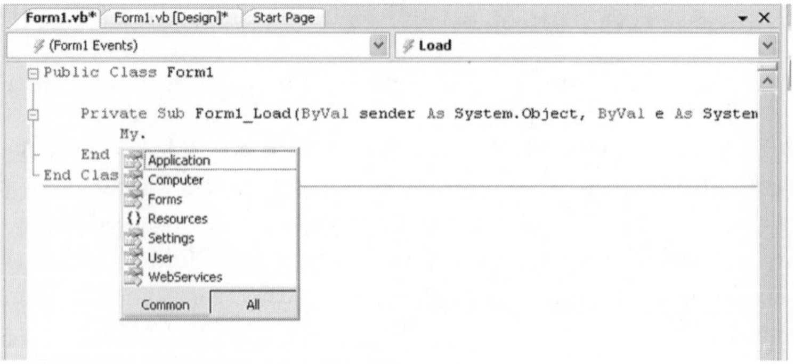

```
Form1.vb*   Form1.vb [Design]*   Start Page                                         ▾ ×
⚡ (Form1 Events)                          ▾   ⚡ Load                                 ▾
  ⊟ Public Class Form1
  │
  ⊟     Private Sub Form1_Load(ByVal sender As System.Object, ByVal e As Systen
            My.
      End   ┌─────────────────────┐
  └ End Clas │ 🔧 Application      │
            │ 🔧 Computer         │
            │ 🔧 Forms            │
            │ {} Resources        │
            │ 🔧 Settings         │
            │ 🔧 User             │
            │ 🔧 WebServices      │
            ├──────────┬──────────┤
            │ Common   │   All    │
            └──────────┴──────────┘
```

Using IntelliSense.

▲ **Button:** The Click event occurs when the user clicks the left mouse button on the button.

▲ **TextBox:** The TextChanged event occurs each time the Text property changes.

▲ **Label:** The Click event occurs when the user clicks the left mouse button on the label.

You add code to control events to cause something to happen when an event occurs. For example, to cause the Text property of the Label control to be set to the same value as the Text property in the Label control when a user clicks the btnSetLabel Button control, you add the following code:

```
Private Sub btnSetLabel_Click _
    (ByVal sender As System.Object, ByVal e As _
    System.EventArgs) Handles btnSetLabel.Click
        lblName.Text = txtName.Text
End Sub
```

Controls support other types of events as well. For example, the TextBox control supports a LostFocus event that occurs when the user moves focus away from the control by pressing Tab or clicking somewhere else on the screen. You might want to use the LostFocus event to process the text entered instead of using the TextChanged event. The TextChanged event occurs each time a character in the control is changed. It is important to understand the circumstances under which an event fires to make sure it is the best event to execute a specific piece of code.

1.6.4 Testing Your Code

You can run an application inside the IDE to test it. This is known as debugging. To start the application, you either open the Debug menu and choose Start Debugging, click the Start Debugging icon on the toolbar (refer to Figure 1-16), or press F5. Your application starts, and you can test each feature where you have added code to make sure it works the way it should.

When you have finished testing, you can return to the design environment by doing one of the following:

▲ Close the application.

▲ Open the Debug menu and choose Stop Debugging.

▲ Press Ctrl+Alt+Break.

▲ Click the Stop Debugging button on the toolbar.

FOR EXAMPLE

Coding the Temperature Conversion Form

Say you are writing an application that allows a user to perform various types of measurement conversion. The main form has four buttons: Distance, Temperature, Volume, and Weight. Each button displays a form that performs the relevant conversions. On the Temperature Conversion form, you add one TextBox control named txtTemp, one Label control named lblConvertedTemp, and two Button controls: btnConvertToCelsius and btnConvertToFahrenheit. You add code to the Click event of each button to retrieve data from TextBox. Text, perform the necessary calculation, and set the Text property of lblConvertedTemp to the converted value.

SELF-CHECK

- List the steps you would take to view the code for the Click event for btnStart.
- List the steps you would take to add code to an event procedure that is not a control's default event procedure.
- Describe how IntelliSense can help you program faster and more accurately.
- Identify each part of the event procedure syntax.
- List the steps you would take to test the txtAddress_TextChanged event procedure.

SUMMARY

In this chapter, you have learned the fundamental concepts and procedures necessary to begin programming in Visual Basic. You have learned about fundamental programming concepts, including event-driven programming and object-oriented programming. You have also learned the steps you must take to create a program. You have learned that Visual Studio is an IDE that provides you with the tools you need to write code and compile a Visual Basic application. You have also learned that Visual Studio uses projects to organize the files needed for an application and solutions to group multiple related projects. You have also learned that forms are used to provide the user interface for a Windows application and that a form is actually an object of the System.Windows.Forms.Form class. You have learned how to add TextBox, Label, and Button controls to a form and set control properties to create a user interface. You have also learned that Windows programs are based on events, and you have learned how to write a simple event procedure.

KEY TERMS

Action object

Algorithm

Argument

Base class

Binary number system

Blank form

Boolean

Bug

Button control

Bytecode

Class

Class Designer

Code

Code view

Common Language Runtime (CLR)

Comment

Compiler

Control

Control structure

Debugging

Decision control structure

Design view

Designer window

Dialog box

Document Explorer

Dock

Encapsulation

Enumeration

Event

Event-driven programming

Event handler

Event procedure

Form

Form event

Handles keyword

High-level language

Inheritance

Input/Processing/Output (IPO) Table

Instance

Integrated Development Environment (IDE)

IntelliSense

Interactive development

IPO table

JIT compiler

Label control

Literal

Machine language

Method

Microsoft Intermediate Language

MSIL

MyBase

Namespace

.NET Framework

Object

Object-oriented language

Pinned

Polymorphism

Procedural programming

Procedure

Programming language

Project

Property

Pseudocode

Repetition control structure

Runtime

Sequence control structure

Service pack

Solution

Solution Explorer

Source code

Startup form

String

Syntax

Tab group

Template

TextBox control

Toolbox

Variable

Visual Basic

Visual Studio

Window

Windows Application

ASSESS YOUR UNDERSTANDING

Go to www.wiley.com/college/petroutsos to evaluate your knowledge of the basics of programming and Visual Basic.

Measure your learning by comparing pre-test and post-test results.

Summary Questions

1. Source code must be compiled before it can execute. True or False?
2. A computer performs all processing through arithmetic. True or False?
3. Which of the following is not a control structure?
    (a) decision control structure
    (b) input control structure
    (c) repetition control structure
    (d) sequence control structure
4. Each bit of data in a computer is represented by a number in the base-10 system. True or False?
5. Procedural programming is used for Windows applications that have a GUI. True or False?
6. A/an _____ is an object loaded in memory.
    (a) class
    (b) procedure
    (c) instance
    (d) variable
7. When programming with Visual Basic, you must wait to test your application until every object has been coded. True or False?
8. Which of the following do you identify during the problem identification step?
    (a) action objects
    (b) controls you will add to the form
    (c) calculations you will perform
9. Creating an interface is the first step in the programming process. True or False?
10. When discussing program design, what does the acronym IPO stand for?
    (a) Internet public objects
    (b) input/processing/output
    (c) international programming organization
    (d) initial process organization

11. If you have designed a good-looking interface, testing the code is not important. True or False?

12. At which stage of a project do you determine whether the results obtained meet the objectives outlined in the problem definition step?

    (a) documentation

    (b) coding

    (c) testing the overall project

    (d) designing the interface

13. If a program has enough comments, they are the only documentation required. True or False?

14. Which of the following provides a program written in Visual Studio 2005 with access to operating system features and libraries for performing various functions?

    (a) IntelliSense

    (b) the CLR

    (c) the .NET Framework

15. Which of the following operating system configurations will run Visual Studio 2005?

    (a) Windows XP with SP1

    (b) Windows Server 2003 with no service pack

    (c) Windows 2000 Professional with SP4

16. You have added a control to a form. How can you easily get help on how to use the control?

    (a) Select the control and press F1.

    (b) Right-click the control and choose Help.

    (c) Right-click the control and choose View Code.

    (d) Select the control and press F2.

17. A Windows application project creates a dynamic link library (DLL) when compiled. True or False?

18. The Solution Explorer window lists all the files in a project. True or False?

19. A docked window in Visual Studio can be pinned or unpinned. True or False?

20. Which namespace contains the Form object used in a Windows application?

    (a) System.Windows.Forms

    (b) System.Forms

    (c) Windows.Application.Forms

    (d) Application.Forms

21. An asterisk (*) next to a filename in a tab means that you have not made changes since you changed the file. True or False?

22. Which form property cannot be changed in code?

    (a) Height

    (b) BackColor

    (c) (Name)

    (d) ShowInTaskbar

23. A project can have only a single startup form. True or False?

24. Which sizing handle would you use to make a control both taller and wider?

    (a) a corner handle

    (b) the right handle

    (c) the left handle

    (d) the bottom handle

25. Which pair of properties do you use to set a control's location on a form?

    (a) Top, Left

    (b) Bottom, Right

    (c) X, Y

    (d) PositionX, PositionY

26. By default, a TextBox control allows a user to enter multiple lines of text. True or False?

27. A Label control can wrap text only if the AutoSize property is set to True. True or False?

28. Which Button control property setting prevents a button from accidentally being pushed?

    (a) Activated = False

    (b) Enabled = False

    (c) Deactivated = True

    (d) Disabled = True

29. Which event is the default event for a form?

    (a) FormClosing

    (b) Activated

    (c) Load

    (d) Move

30. In Code view, you must select an object in the left-hand drop-down list before you can select an event. True or False?

31. What is the default event of the Label control?
    (a) Click
    (b) LostFocus
    (c) TextChanged
    (d) Change
32. Which key do you press to cause an application to start up?
    (a) F1
    (b) F3
    (c) F5
    (d) F7

Applying This Chapter

1. You are planning to install Visual Studio. Your computer has the following configuration: 800MHz processor, 512MB RAM, 20GB hard disk with 1GB free disk space, and Windows 2000 Professional with SP3. Can you install Visual Studio? If not, what changes must you make?

2. You are building an application that will include several image files. You want to make the image files easy to find. What should you do?

3. What is wrong with the following code?

```
frmConfiguration.Text = Configuration Settings
```

4. You add a TextBox control to a form. You cannot increase its height. Why not?

5. You add the following code to a form:

```
Private Sub txtName_TextChanged _
    (ByVal sender As System.Object, ByVal e As _
    System.EventArgs) Handles txtName.TextChanged
    txtName.ReadOnly = True
End Sub
```

You press F5 to run the application and type in the txtName field. You can enter only a single character. Why?

Installing Visual Studio

You plan to install Visual Studio to support application development using Visual Basic 2005. You do not plan to develop any applications using Visual C# or Visual C++. You have not yet decided whether you are going to build Windows applications or web applications.

1. Discuss the benefits and drawbacks of installing the Visual C# language component.
2. Discuss the benefits and drawbacks of installing web development components.
3. What can you do if you do not install the web development components and later decide to build a web-based application?

Configuring a Project

You are creating an order entry application for a customer. The customer has provided you with a requirements document and the Excel spreadsheet that is currently used to enter orders.

1. Discuss the benefits of adding these files to your project.
2. How would you ensure that these files were easy to identify?

Creating Forms

You are creating an order entry application for a customer. The application must allow users to view customer details and inventory details as well as enter orders. The application must also allow users to enter configuration settings. It should also display an About dialog box.

1. Identify the forms you need to add to the project.
2. Which form should you designate as the startup form?

Designing a Form

You are creating a form that will be used in a customer service application. The form will be used to enter details about a service call. The form will retrieve information from a database that stores customer information, based on a customer's name. The customer's name must not be modified after the data is retrieved. However, any other information can. The form must show the customer's name, phone number, and address. It must allow a user to enter a description of the problem and the resolution. The user must be able to submit the data to a database and print the data.

1. Sketch the form. Identify which types of controls you should use for each element.
2. Will any of the controls be multiline?
3. Will any of the controls be ReadOnly at design time?

Programming Events

You are creating a form that will be used in a customer service application. The form will be used to enter details about a service call. The form will retrieve information from a database that stores customer information, based on a customer's name. The customer's name must not be modified after the data is retrieved. However, any other information can. The form must show the customer's name, phone number, and address. It must allow a user to enter a description of the problem and the resolution. The phone number field can contain only numeric characters. The user must be able to submit the data to a database and print the data. The user must be prompted when to save data when the form is closed.

1. Identify the events procedures you need to create to provide the needed functionality.

2
USING VARIABLES, CONSTANTS, AND OPERATORS

Starting Point

Go to www.wiley.com/college/petroutsos to assess your knowledge of variables, constants, and operators.
Determine where you need to concentrate your effort.

What You'll Learn in This Chapter

▲ Variables and how to declare them
▲ Conversion between data types
▲ Constants and how to declare them
▲ Operations on variables

After Studying This Chapter, You'll Be Able To

▲ Declare and use variables
▲ Convert values from one data type to another
▲ Declare and use constants
▲ Use operators to perform calculations and other operations

INTRODUCTION

One of the primary things a program does is manipulate data. Therefore, you must understand how to store and perform operations on data within a program. In the first section, you will learn how to create and use variables to store values that change. In the second section, you will learn how to convert data from one type to another. In the third section, you will learn how to use constants to store data values that do not change. In the final section, you will learn how to perform operations on a program's data.

2.1 Declaring and Using Variables

Before you can write a program, you need to understand how data is represented in a program and how a variable uses memory. First, you'll learn about how data is stored in the memory of a computer. Next, you'll learn about the data types available with Visual Basic 2005. Following that, you'll learn how to declare a variable and you'll learn about variable scope. Finally, you'll learn how to assign values to and retrieve values from a variable.

2.1.1 Understanding Variables

Variables are among the most fundamental building blocks of a program. A **variable** is a program object that stores a value. The value can be a number, a letter, a string, a date, a structure that contains other values, or an object that represents both data and related actions.

When a variable contains a value, a program can manipulate it. A program can perform arithmetic operations on numbers, string operations on strings (such as **concatenation,** which involves appending one string onto the end of another, using substrings, and finding a target within a string), date operations (such as finding the difference between two dates and adding a time period to a date), and so forth.

Four factors determine a variable's exact behavior:

▲ **Data type** determines the kind of the data (integer, character, string, and so forth).

▲ **Scope** defines what code within the current module can access the variable.

▲ **Accessibility** determines what code in other modules can access the variable.

▲ **Lifetime** determines how long the variable's value is valid.

This chapter examines data types in detail.

2.1.2 Understanding How a Variable Uses Memory

The most limited resource on a computer is typically its **memory,** which is the area of the computer where operating system code and program code are stored when the computer is on. It is important that you try to get the most out of the available memory. Whenever you create a variable, you are using a piece of memory, so you should strive to use as few variables as possible and use the variables that you do have in the most efficient manner.

Today, absolute optimization of variables is not something you need to go into a deep level of detail about, for two reasons. First, computers have far more memory these days than they used to; the days when programmers tried to cram payroll systems into 32KB of memory are long gone. Second, compilers have a great deal of intelligence built in these days, to help generate the most optimized code possible.

Computers use the **binary** numbering system to represent all data as a pattern that includes only 1s and 0s. Take a simple integer, 27. In binary code (**base 2**), the number 27 is represented as 11011, each digit referring to a power of 2. The diagram in Figure 2-1 shows how you represent 27 in the more familiar **base 10,** or decimal, format, in which each digit of a number represents a power of 10, and then in base 2.

Although this may appear to be a bit obscure, look what's happening. In base 10, the decimal system that you're familiar with, each digit fits into a "slot." This slot represents a power of 10—the rightmost slot represents 10 to the power 0, the second represents 10 to the power 1, and so on. If you want to know what number the pattern represents, you take each slot in turn, multiply it by the value it represents, and add the results.

The same applies to binary; it just seems more complicated than decimal because you're not familiar with dealing with base 2. To convert a number from

Figure 2-1

10^7	10^6	10^5	10^4	10^3	10^2	10^1	10^0
10,000,000	1,000,000	100,000	10,000	1,000	100	10	1
0	0	0	0	0	0	2	7

In base-10, each digit represents a power of ten. To find what number the "pattern of base-10 digits" represents, you multiply the relevant number by the power of ten that the digit represents and add the results.

$$2 \times 10 + 7 \times 1 = 27$$

2^7	2^6	2^5	2^4	2^3	2^2	2^1	2^0
128	64	32	16	8	4	2	1
0	0	0	1	1	0	1	1

In base-2, or binary, each digit represents a power of two. To find what number the "pattern of binary digits" represents, you multiply the relevant number by the power of two that the digit represents and add the results.

$$1 \times 16 + 1 \times 8 + 1 \times 2 + 1 \times 1 = 27$$

Representing the number 27 in base 10 and base 2.

Table 2-1: Units of Measurement

Unit	Abbreviation	Number of Bytes
Kilobyte	KB	1,024 (i.e., 2^{10})
Megabyte	MB	1,048,576 (i.e., 2^{20})
Gigabyte	GB	1,073,741,842 (i.e., 2^{30})
Terabyte	TB	2^{40}
Petabyte	PB	2^{50}

base 2 to base 10, you take the digit in each slot in turn and multiply that power of 2 by the number that the slot represents (0 or 1). Then you add all the results together to get the number.

In computer terms, a binary slot is called a **bit** (also referred to as a binary digit). It is the smallest possible unit of information, the answer to a single yes/no question, represented by a part of the computer's circuitry that either has electricity flowing in it or not. The reason there are eight slots/bits on the diagram in Figure 2-1 is that there are 8 bits in a byte. A **byte** is the unit of measurement that you use when talking about computer memory.

A **kilobyte (KB)** is 1,024 bytes. You use 1,024 rather than 1,000 because 1,024 is the 10th power of 2, so as far as the computer is concerned, it's a "round number." Computers don't tend to think of things in terms of 10s like you do, so 1,024 is more natural to a computer than 1,000.

Likewise, a **megabyte (MB)** is 1,024 kilobytes, or 1,048,576 bytes. Again, that is another round number because it is the 20th power of 2. A **gigabyte (GB)** is 1,024 megabytes, or 1,073,741,824 bytes. (Again, think 2 to the power of 30, and you're on the right lines.) Finally, a **terabyte (TB)** is 2 to the 40th power, and a **petabyte (PB)** is 2 to the 50th power. These units are summarized in Table 2-1.

So what's the point of all this? Well, it's worth having an understanding of how computers store variables so that you can design your programs better. Suppose your computer has 256MB of memory. That's 262,144KB, or 268,435,456 bytes, or (multiply by 8) 2,147,483,648 bits. As you write your software, you have to make the best possible use of this available memory.

2.1.3 Understanding Data Types

When you define a variable, you must tell Visual Basic the type of data that should be stored in it. This is known as the *data type,* and all programming languages have a vast array of different data types to choose from. The data type of a variable has a great impact on how the computer runs the code. Table 2-2 summarizes Visual Basic's elementary data types.

Table 2-2: Visual Basic Data Types

Data Type	Size	Values
Boolean	2 bytes	True or False
Byte	1 byte	0 to 255 (unsigned byte)
SByte	1 byte	−128 to 127 (signed byte)
Char	2 bytes	0 to 65,535 (unsigned character)
Short	2 bytes	−32,768 to 32,767
UShort	2 bytes	0 through 65,535 (unsigned short)
Integer	4 bytes	−2,147,483,648 to 2,147,483,647
UInteger	4 bytes	0 through 4,294,967,295 (unsigned integer)
Long	8 bytes	−9,223,372,036,854,775,808 to 9,223,372,036,854,775,807
ULong	8 bytes	0 through 18,446,744,073,709,551,615 (unsigned long)
Decimal	16 bytes	0 to +/−79,228,162,514,264,337,593,543,950,335 with no decimal point; 0 to +/− 7.9228162514264337593543950335 with 28 places
Single	4 bytes	−3.4028235E+38 to −1.401298E−45 for negative values; 1.401298E−45 to 3.4028235E+38 for positive values
Double	8 bytes	−1.79769313486231570E+308 to −4.94065645841246544E−324 for negative values; 4.94065645841246544E−324 to 1.79769313486231570E+308 for positive values
String	Depends on length of string	Depending on the platform, a string can hold approximately 0 to 2 billion **Unicode** characters (Unicode is a character encoding scheme that supports international character sets.)
Date	8 bytes	January 1, 0001 0:0:00 to December 31, 9999 11:59:59 pm
Object	4 bytes	**Reference** to an object instance (a pointer to the memory location where an object is loaded)

The System namespace also provides integer data types that specify the number of bits explicitly: Int16, Int32, Int64, UInt16, UInt32, and UInt64. For example, Int32 represents a 32-bit integer. Using this type instead of Integer emphasizes the fact that the variable uses 32 bits. That can sometimes make code clearer. For example, suppose that you need to call an application programming interface (API) function that takes a 32-bit integer as a parameter.

Let's take a closer look at a few of the data types:

▲ **Boolean:** This data type holds the word True or False and is used to test the condition of a statement. The number 0 is used to represent the word False, and the number 1 is used to represent the word True. Boolean variables are used as flags to indicate whether part of the code should execute.

▲ **Char:** This data type holds a character. A character can be any character on the keyboard, including numbers, punctuation, and characters you do not see, such as a space or tab. A number represents each character from 0 to 65,535. The number that represents a character is stored in a Char variable. For example, the letter A is represented as the number 65. When you type the letter A, the number 65 is stored as the letter A inside your computer. The U.S. character set requires 1 byte; however, 2 bytes are necessary to accommodate the international character set. Char values are enclosed in double quotation marks (").

▲ **Byte:** This data type holds a positive number from 0 to 255. Byte variables are commonly used to store small whole number and binary streams.

▲ **Date:** This data type holds date and time information. Date variables are commonly used to perform date calculations, such as subtracting a birth date from today's date to calculate a person's age. Values assigned to a Date variable must appear in the format of a date and be enclosed inside a pair of # characters. For example, to set the DueDate variable to March 4, 2007, you use the following code:

```
DueDate = #3/4/2007#
```

You can also set a variable to a time or a date/time value. You can specify time in hours, minutes, and seconds, using either a 12-hour or 24-hour clock. For example, to set the ClosingTime variable to 5:00 p.m., you could use either of these:

```
ClosingTime = #5:00:00 PM#
ClosingTime = #17:00:00#
```

To set a variable to store both the date and the time parts, you use a literal that includes both. For example, to set the MeetingTime variable to December 12, 2008, at 2:30 p.m., you use the following code:

```
MeetingTime = #12/12/2008 2:30:00 PM#
```

▲ **Decimal:** This data type holds a value that has a decimal. The value can be a decimal value, a whole number, or a mixed number. It is good programming style, however, to use an Integer variable instead of a Decimal variable if the value is a whole number because an Integer uses less memory than a Decimal value. It is recommended that you use Decimal to store monetary values because money data is typically stored with only two digits of precision (i.e., two digits to the right of the decimal point). Decimal is a fixed decimal point value, not a floating-point value. Therefore, it is less subject to precision errors due to rounding than the Single or Double data types.

▲ **Double:** This data type holds a very large or very small value. A very small number is a decimal value that requires more than 28 decimal places. Double variables are typically used in scientific and engineering calculations.

▲ **Integer:** This data type holds a whole number. The whole number can be from −2,147,483,648 to 2,147,483,647 and is used for arithmetic and as a counter for a loop. An Integer variable is not used to store a value that contains a decimal.

▲ **Object:** This data type references any kind of value. Object data may reserve more memory than is required to store a value. It is good programming style to use a data type that is appropriate for the variable rather than an Object data type.

▲ **Long:** This data type holds a whole number from −9,223,372,036,854,775,808 to 9,223,372,036,854,775,807.

▲ **Short:** This data type holds a whole number from −32,768 to 32,767

▲ **String:** This data type holds more than one character and is commonly used to store textual data. For example, "Bob" is a value that can be stored in a String variable. String values are enclosed in double quotation marks ("). A String variable can hold a space (e.g., " ").

Selecting the best type of variable for an application is tricky because you may be unsure which variable type is the most efficient to use. Choosing a variable type that is too small to store your data causes subtle errors in a program, known as bugs. When in doubt, you should use the variable type that will hold the most data. For example, if you prompt the user of a program to enter a whole number, which you will store in a variable, do you use a Byte, Short, Integer, or Long variable type? An error occurs if you choose a Byte and the user enters the number 256 because Byte can store numbers only from 0 to 255.

Therefore, it is best to use a variable type that can store a larger number, such as an Integer.

When selecting the best data type, you should consider not only memory consumption but also performance. Because of the way current processors operate, the following guidelines will provide the best performance for applications that perform a lot of computations:

▲ Use Integer for signed whole numbers.

▲ Use UInteger for unsigned whole numbers.

▲ Use Double for numbers that include decimal points.

2.1.4 Declaring Variables

A **reserved word** is a keyword or function name used by Visual Basic. You cannot use a reserved word for any other purpose. **Dim** is the reserved word that tells Visual Basic that you are declaring a variable. **As** is a reserved word that tells Visual Basic that you are declaring the variable as a particular data type. To declare a variable, you specify the Dim reserved word, the variable name, the As reserved word, and the data type of the variable. The general syntax is shown here:

```
{Dim | Private | Static} name AS datatype [=value]
```

Here's an example:

```
Dim decProductPrice As Decimal
```

In this example, Visual Basic knows how much memory to reserve for the variable because you specified the data type of the variable. It's important to use the appropriate data type for a variable so that you do not reserve more memory than is required to hold the value that you assign to the variable.

You can declare multiple variables on the same line of code, as long as each variable is the same data type. You must use a comma to separate variable names. Here's an example:

```
Dim decProductPrice, decSalesTaxRate As Decimal
```

Declaring multiple variables on the same line saves space in your code and is a convenient way to organize variable names.

You need to be sure to use good programming style when deciding on a name for a variable. A variable name should begin with an abbreviation of the variable's data type. The abbreviation is in lowercase. The rest of the variable's name should reflect the kind of data stored in the variable. The variable name can be a combination of words, such as FirstName. The first letter of each word should be uppercase.

Another way to declare a variable is to use a **data type character** in the declaration. The following are the data type characters:

Character	Data Type
%	Integer
&	Long
@	Decimal
!	Single
#	Double
$	String

You can specify a variable's data type by adding a data type character after a variable's name when you declare it. When you use the variable later, you can omit the data type character if you like. For example, the following code declares the variable num_desserts as a Long and the variable satisfaction_quotient as a Double:

```
Dim num_desserts&
Dim satisfaction_quotient#
```

A **compiler option** is a setting in Visual Basic that determines what things are checked during compilation and what types of operations can be compiled without error. When the Option Explicit compiler option is set to On, you must declare all variables before you use them. If the Option Explicit compiler option is set to Off, Visual Basic automatically creates a new variable whenever it sees a variable that it has not yet encountered. For example, the following code doesn't explicitly declare any variables:

```
Option Explicit Off
Public Class Form1
...
Public Sub CountManagers()
    num_managers = 20
    Label.Text = num_managrs
End Sub
...
End Class
```

As it executes the code, Visual Basic sees the first statement, num_managers = 0. It doesn't recognize the variable num_managers, so it creates it.

Keeping Option Explicit turned off can lead to two very bad problems. First, it silently hides typographical errors. If you look closely at the previous code, you'll see that the misspelled variable num_managrs is displayed in Label.Text instead of the correctly spelled variable num_managers. Because Option Explicit is off, Visual Basic assumes that you want to use a new variable, so it creates num_managrs.

The second problem that occurs when Option Explicit is turned off is that Visual Basic doesn't really know what you will want to do with the variables it creates for you. It doesn't know whether you will use a variable as an Integer, a Double, a String, or a PictureBox. Even after you assign a value to the variable (say, Integer), Visual Basic doesn't know whether you will always use the variable as an Integer or whether you might later want to save a String in it.

To keep its options open, Visual Basic creates **undeclared variables** as generic objects. It can then fill an undeclared variable with just about anything. Unfortunately, this can make the code much less efficient than it needs to be. For example, programs are much better at manipulating integers than they are at manipulating objects. If you are going to use a variable as an integer, creating it as an object makes the program run much more slowly.

2.1.5 Naming Rules and Conventions

When declaring variables and when naming controls and objects, you need to be aware of a few rules. These are:

▲ A variable name must begin with a letter or an underscore.
▲ Other characters can consist of letters, numbers, and underscores.
▲ You cannot include spaces in a variable name.
▲ A variable name can be up to 255 characters.

It is standard practice to use an abbreviation of the data type as a prefix. For example, you might use either "int" or "i" to prefix a variable of type Integer.

2.1.6 Assigning and Retrieving Values

The **assignment operator** (=) is used to assign a value to a variable. The assignment operator is placed on the right side of the variable name. To the right of the = can be a value, a variable, or an expression. This right side must match the variable type; for example, a Date variable must be assigned a value in the format of a date.

You do not use quotations marks (" ") around numbers that are assigned to a variable that is a Boolean, Decimal, Double, or Integer data type. You do place quotation marks around numbers and characters that are assigned to a String variable or a Char variable.

If you assign a character or String data to an Integer variable without using quotation marks, an error message is displayed, saying that the name is not declared. Visual Basic assumes that the data is a name of a variable that you forgot to declare.

If you assign a number to a Char or String variable without using quotation marks, you receive an error message, saying that an integer value cannot be converted to a character variable.

You use the name of a variable in your code whenever you want to use the value stored in the variable. When your program runs, the variable name is replaced by the value of the variable. You do not see the value replace the variable name because normally you cannot see your code when your program is running. A variable name can be used in any expression that can use a value.

Suppose that you want to calculate a 5% sales tax rate on a $100 purchase. The expression you need to write is 100 * 0.05. Instead of using actual values in your program, you can use variables to represent the purchase price and the sales tax rate by assigning 100 to the decProductPrice variable and 0.05 to the decSalesTaxRate variable. The variable names rather than the values are then used, in the expression decSalesTaxRate * decProductPrice.

Make sure to spell a variable name exactly the way the variable name was spelled when you declared the variable; otherwise, you receive an error message when you try to run your program. For example, decSalesTaxRate and SalesTaxRate are two different variable names; although both contain SalesTaxRate, they may be different sales tax rates.

You should never place a variable name within quotation marks. If you do, the variable name is treated as a string value rather than the name of a variable. Let's say that you write "strCustomerFirstName" in a program when you want to refer to the contents stored in the variable strCustomerFirstName. Visual Basic treats "strCustomerFirstName" as a literal value because the name is enclosed in quotation marks, and does not replace "strCustomerFirstName" with the value stored in the variable strCustomerFirstName.

You can include the current value of a variable in the updated value by using the variable name. Let's say that you want to increase the current value of decProduct-Price by 10% and then save the new price to the decProductPrice variable. The new price is 110% of the current price, which is stored in the decProductPrice:

```
Dim decProductPrice As Decimal = 100
decProductPrice = decProductPrice * 1.10
```

Visual Basic multiplies the value stored in decProductPrice by 1.10, which is the current price plus 10%, and assigns the product of the calculation to decProductPrice.

A common error is to use a variable that has not been assigned the correct value. You can avoid this type of error by assigning an initial value to a variable, either when the variable is declared or shortly after the variable is declared. The process of assigning an initial value to a variable is called **initializing** a variable.

Any value can be the initial value assigned to a variable. Programmers typically use a value that cannot be confused with a typical value that is assigned to the variable. Zero is a good initial value for a variable that is used to store a number (e.g., decProductPrice) because the actual value—the price of a product—is usually greater than zero.

You can initialize a variable when you declare the variable by using an assignment operator (i.e., the = sign) after the declaration. Here's an example:

```
Dim decProductPrice As Decimal = 0
```

Alternatively, you can assign the initial value to the variable immediately after the variable is declared, as in the following example:

```
Dim decProductPrice As Decimal
decProductPrice = 0
```

The initial value that you assign to a variable remains until another value is assigned to the variable by a different line of code in the application.

You can initialize more than one variable when you declare multiple variables at the same time by separating the declarations with commas. To declare two decimal variables and initialize both to zero, you use this:

```
Dim decProdPrice As Decimal = 0, decSalesTaxRate As _
    Decimal = 0
```

Variables that are declared and initialized in the same Dim statement can be different data types. For example, VB .NET allows this:

```
Dim decProdNumber As Integer = 0, decSalesTaxRate _
    As Decimal = 0
```

If you do not specify an initial value when you declare a variable, the variable will automatically be initialized to a default value. Numeric-type variables will be initialized to 0, String variables will be initialized to Nothing, Boolean variables will be initialized to False, and a Date variable will be initialized to 1/1/0001 at 12:00 AM.

FOR EXAMPLE

Declaring Variables

Say that you are creating a payroll application. The application will allow a payroll administrator to enter a person's name, Social Security number, address, whether the person is paid a salary or hourly, whether the person is exempt (i.e., does not receive overtime pay), the monthly salary, the hourly wage, the date the person was hired, the date the person last received a wage increase, and the number of dependents claimed for withholding. The Social Security number will be used as a unique identifier for the employee and should not be entered with spaces or hyphens.

You need to store the data the user enters in variables. You want to use variables that will be the most memory efficient. You also want to name the variables so that you know the data type they store and their purpose. Therefore, you declare the variables as follows:

```
Dim strName, strAddress As String
Dim bytNumDependents As Byte
```

(Continued)

```
Dim intSSN As Integer
Dim bIsHourly, bIsExempt As Boolean
Dim sngHourlyPay, sngMonthlyPay As Single
Dim dtHireDate, dtRaiseDate As Date
```

Another programmer notes that the program's performance might be improved if you change sngHourlyPay, sngMonthlyPay, and bytNumDependents as follows:

```
Dim dblHourlyPay, dblMonthlyPay As Double
Dim intNumDependents As Integer
```

You analyze the impact on memory use and decide to make the change.

Yet another programmer then notes that some calculations on a Double value might cause imprecision due to rounding errors. That programmer recommends that you change dblHourlyPay and dblMonthlyPay as follows:

```
Dim decHourlyPay, decMonthlyPay As Decimal
```

You do some research and realize that the programmer is right. You make the change to the code.

SELF-CHECK

- Identify a situation in which you would use a variable.
- Illustrate how the number 426 is stored in memory. How many bytes does it require?
- You need to create a variable that will store the current temperature as a whole number in degrees Fahrenheit. Compare the use of SByte, Short, and Integer and list the advantages and potential disadvantages of each.
- Identify the dangers of setting the Option Explicit compiler option to Off.
- Write a variable declaration for a variable that stores a person's middle initial.

2.2 Converting Between Data Types

Sometimes it is necessary to assign the value in one variable to a variable of a different data type. In such a case, the value must be converted to the data type of the destination variable. In this section you will learn about the issues that

arise when converting between data types and the functions available to allow
you to safely convert data to a different data type.

2.2.1 Understanding Data Type Conversion

Normally, you assign a value to a variable that has the same data type as the
value. For example, you assign a string value to a string variable, you assign an
integer value to an integer variable, and so forth. Whether you can assign a value
of one type to a variable of another type depends on whether the conversion is
a narrowing or widening conversion.

A **narrowing conversion** is one in which data is converted from one type
to another type that cannot hold all the possible values allowed by the original
data type. For example, the following code copies the value from a Long variable into an Integer variable:

```
Dim intNumber As Integer
Dim lngNumber As Long
intNumber = lngNumber
```

A Long value can hold values that are too big to fit in an Integer, so this is a
narrowing conversion. The value contained in the Long variable may or may not
fit in the Integer

The following code shows a less obvious example:

```
Dim intNumber As Integer
Dim strText As String
intNumber = strText
```

Here, the code assigns the value in a String variable to an Integer variable. If the
string happens to contain a number (e.g., "10" or "1.23"), the assignment works.
If the string contains a nonnumeric value (e.g., "Hello"), however, the assignment fails with an error.

If you have the Option Strict compiler option turned on (it is off by default),
Visual Basic does not allow implicit narrowing conversions. If Option Strict is
off, Visual Basic attempts an implicit narrowing conversion and throws an error
if the conversion fails (e.g., if you try to copy the Integer value 900 into a Byte
variable). It is a good idea to turn Option Strict on. You can do so either through
project properties or by adding the following code before the class declaration
of your form:

```
Option Strict On
Public Class Form1

Private Sub Form1_Load(ByVal sender As _
    System.Object,ByVal e As System.EventArgs) _
    Handles MyBase.Load

End Sub
End Class
```

Figure 2-2

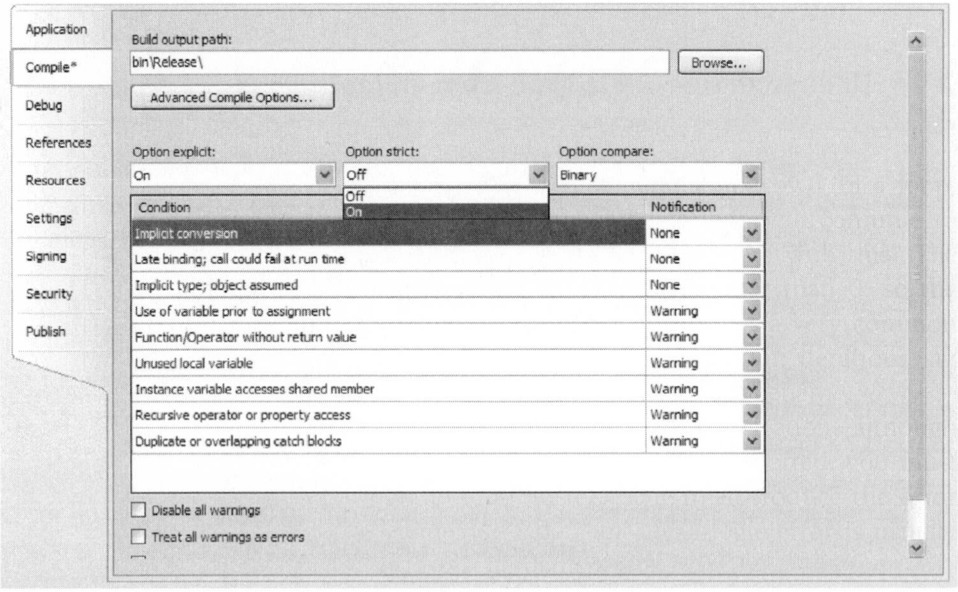

Setting Option Strict on.

To enable Option Strict for the entire project, in Solution Explorer, you right-click the name of the project, choose Properties, and then click the Compile tab. In the Option Strict drop-down list, you select On (see Figure 2-2).

In contrast to a narrowing conversion, a **widening conversion** is one where the new data type is always big enough to hold the old data type's values. For example, a Long is big enough to hold any Integer value, so copying an Integer value into a Long variable is a widening conversion. Visual Basic allows widening conversions. Note that some widening conversions can still result in data loss. For example, a Decimal variable can store more significant digits than a Single variable can. A Single can hold any value that a Decimal can but not with the same precision. If you assign a Decimal value to a Single variable, you may lose some **precision** (i.e., some of the digits to the right of the decimal point).

2.2.2 Using Data Type Conversion Functions

To make a narrowing conversion with Option Strict turned on, you must explicitly use a data type **conversion function,** which is a function that can be used to convert one data type to another. Visual Basic attempts the conversion and throws an error if it fails. The CByte function converts a numeric value into a

Byte value, so you could use the following code to copy an Integer value into a Byte variable:

```
Dim intNumber As Integer
Dim bytValue As Byte
bytValue = CByte(intNumber)
```

If the Integer variable contains a value less than 0 or greater than 255, the value does not fit in a Byte variable, so CByte throws an error.

Table 2-3 lists Visual Basic's data type conversion functions.

The CInt and CLng functions round fractional values to the nearest whole number. If the fractional part of a number is exactly .5, the functions round to the nearest even whole number. For example, 0.5 rounds to 0, 0.6 rounds to 1, and 1.5 rounds to 2.

In contrast, the Fix and Int functions truncate fractional values. Fix truncates toward zero, so Fix(−0.9) is 0, and Fix(0.9) is 0. Int truncates downward, so Int(−0.9) is −1, and Int(0.9) is 0. Fix and Int also differ from CInt and CLng because they return the same data type they are passed.

Table 2-3: Data Type Conversion Functions

Function	Converts To
CBool	Boolean
CByte	Byte
CChar	Char
CDate	Date
CDbl	Double
CDec	Decimal
CInt	Integer
CLng	Long
CObj	Object
CSByte	Sbyte
CShort	Short
CSng	Single
CStr	String
CUInt	UInteger
CULng	ULong
CUShort	UShort

The Val function begins at the beginning of a string and returns the numbers it encounters until it reaches a character. It ignores spaces and treats a . like a decimal point. For example, the following would set dblMyValue to 111.0:

```
Dim dblMyValue As Double
Dim strAddress As String = "111 West Main Street"
dblMyValue = Val(strAddress)
```

The CType function takes as parameters a value and a data type, and it converts the value into that type, if possible. For example, the following code uses CType to perform a narrowing conversion from a Long to an Integer:

```
Dim intNumber As Integer
Dim lngNumber As Long = 100
intNumber = CType(lngNumber, Integer)
```

Because the value of a_long can fit within an integer, the conversion succeeds.

2.2.3 Validating Data: Fundamental Concepts

As you have seen, converting data from one type to another succeeds only if the data types are compatible. Therefore, you must add code to a program to **validate** (i.e., ensure that the data can be converted to the necessary data type and is within an expected range) any data entered by the user before assigning it to a variable that requires a data type other than String or Object. The IsDate function allows you to test a value to determine whether it is a valid date. It returns a Boolean. To determine whether the text a user enters can be converted to a Date data type, you use the following code:

```
Dim bIsValidDate As Boolean
Dim datOrderDate As Date
bIsValidDate = IsDate(txtDate.Text)
If bIsValidDate Then
    datOrderDate = CDate(txtDate.Text)
Else
    MsgBox("Invalid Date")
End If
```

This code example requires some explanation. First, it sets the value of bIsValidDate by calling the IsDate function and passing the value the user entered in the control named txtDate. Next, this code example uses an If...Then statement to test the value of bIsValidDate. The **If...Then statement** is a decision control structure that accepts an expression that evaluates to either True or False. If the expression evaluates to True, the code that follows the If statement executes. If the expression evaluates to False, the code that follows the Else statement executes. The code uses another function we have not yet discussed: The MsgBox function displays a dialog box with a message. You pass the message you want to display as a String.

The IsNumeric function is used to verify that a value contains a valid number. It does not distinguish between whole numbers and decimal numbers. Like IsDate, it returns a Boolean value and can be used in a similar test, as follows:

```
Dim bIsNumber As Boolean
Dim intAge As Integer
bIsNumber = IsNumeric(txtAge.Text)
If bIsNumber Then
    intAge = CInt(txtAge.Text)
Else
    MsgBox("Enter a number")
End If
```

FOR EXAMPLE

Validating Data

Say that you are creating a payroll application. You declare the variables as follows:

```
Dim strName, strAddress As String
Dim intNumDependents As Integer
Dim intSSN As Integer
Dim decHourlyPay As Double
Dim dtHireDate, dtRaiseDate As Date
```

You are creating the form that users will use to enter the data. You have added a TextBox control to the form for each value and a Button control to process the values entered. You need to add code to the Button control to fill the variable with data from the TextBox controls. Option Strict is On, so you must perform explicit data type conversions. You add the following code to the btnSubmit Click event:

```
strName = txtName.Text
strAddress = txtAddress.Text
intNumDependents = CInt(txtNumDependents.Text)
intSSN = CInt(txtSSN.Text)
decHourlyPay = CDec(txtPay.Text)
dtHireDate = CDate(txtHireDate.Text)
dtRaiseDate = CDate(txtRaiseDate.Text)
```

You test the application and determine that it works when a user enters a valid value in each field but that an error occurs when some values are entered in the txtNumDependents, txtSSN, txtPay, txtHireDate, and txtRaise-Date fields. You realize that you need to add additional code to ensure that

(Continued)

users enter valid values. You change the code to validate the data entered in the txtSSN, txtNumDependents, txtPay, txtHireDate, and txtRaiseDate TextBox controls, as follows:

```
strName = txtName.Text
strAddress = txtAddress.Text
If IsNumeric(txtNumDependents.Text) Then
    intNumDependents = CInt(txtNumDependents.Text)
Else
    MsgBox("Enter a number in the Dependents field.")
End If
If IsNumeric(txtSSN.Text) Then
    intSSN = CInt(txtSSN.Text)
Else
    MsgBox("Enter a number in the SSN field.")
End If
If IsNumeric(txtPay.Text) Then
    decHourlyPay = CDec(txtPay.Text)
Else
    MsgBox("Enter a number in the Hourly Pay field.")
End If
If IsDate(txtHireDate.Text) Then
    dtHireDate = CDate(txtHireDate.Text)
Else
    MsgBox("Enter a date in the Hire Date field.")
End If

If IsDate(txtRaiseDate.Text) Then
    dtRaiseDate = CDate(txtRaiseDate.Text)
Else
    MsgBox("Enter a date in the Raise Date field.")
End If
```

SELF-CHECK

- Compare and contrast a narrowing conversion and a widening conversion. Give an example of each.
- Write code to convert from a Double to a Single data type. Change the code to use the CType function.
- Write code to convert from a Long to an Integer data type. Change the code to use the CType function.
- Compare and contrast data validation and data conversion.

2.3 Using Literals, Constants, and Enumerations

Sometimes you need to use values that remain constant throughout the execution of a program. For example, you might define DiscountRate as a constant if it is not likely to change. This section begins by looking at literal values and how you can make them type safe. Next, this section looks at the reasons and procedure for declaring constants. This section wraps up with a look at how to declare an enumeration.

2.3.1 Making Literals Type Safe

A *literal* is a value that is typed directly into an expression. For example, you can use the literal value "Enter Your Name" in a Label control:

```
lblName.Text = "Enter Your Name"
```

In some cases, you might need to ensure that Visual Basic treats a literal value as a specific data type. In such a case, you use the literal type characters shown in Table 2-4 in the expression.

For example, suppose that the following code is the first use of the variables i and ch (with Option Explicit turned off). Normally, Visual Basic would make i an Integer because the value 123L fits in an Integer. Because the literal value 123 ends with the L character, however, the value is a Long, so the variable i is

Table 2-4: Literal Type Characters

Data Type	Type Character
Short	S
UShort	US
Integer	I
UInteger	UI
Long	L
ULong	IL
Decimal	D
Single	F (for floating point; a term that describes a moving decimal point)
Double	R (for real; some programming languages use the term Real instead of Double)
Char	c (lowercase)

also a Long. Similarly, Visual Basic would normally make variable ch a String because the value "X" looks like a string. The "c" following the value tells Visual Basic to make this a Char variable instead, as shown here:

```
i = 123L
ch = "X"c
```

Visual Basic also lets you precede a literal integer value with &H to indicate that it is hexadecimal (i.e., base 16) or &O to indicate that it is octal (i.e., base 8). For example, the following three statements set the variable flags to the same value:

```
flags = 100     'Decimal 100.
flags = &H64
'Hexadecimal &H64 = 6 * 16 + 4 = 96 + 4 = 100.
flags = &O144 'Octal &O144 =
     '1 * 8 * 8 + 4 * 8 + 4 = 64 + 32 + 4 = 100.
```

The first statement uses the decimal value 100, the second uses the hexadecimal value &H64, and the third uses the octal value &O144.

Sometimes you must use literal type characters to make a value match a variable's data type. Consider the following example:

```
Dim ch As Char
ch = "X" ' Error because "X" is a String.
ch = "X"c ' Okay because "X"c is a Char.
Dim amount As Decimal
amount = 12.34 ' Error because 12.34 is a Double.
amount = 12.34D ' Okay because 12.34D is a Decimal.
```

The first assignment in this code tries to assign the value "X" to a Char variable. This throws an error because "X" is a String value. While it is obvious to a programmer that this code is trying to assign the character X to the variable, Visual Basic thinks the types don't match. The second assignment statement works because it assigns the Char value "X"c to the variable. The next assignment fails when it tries to assign the Double value 12.34 to a Decimal variable. The final assignment works because the value 12.34D is a Decimal literal.

The following code shows another way to accomplish these assignments. This version uses the data type conversion functions CChar and CDec to convert the values into the proper data types:

```
ch = CChar("X")
amount = CDec(12.34)
```

Using data type characters, literal type characters, and Visual Basic's default data type assignments can lead to very confusing code. You cannot expect every programmer to notice that a particular variable is a Single because it is followed by ! in its first use but not in others. You can make your code less confusing by using variable declarations that include explicit data types.

2.3.2 Declaring Constants

If you need to use a literal in more than one place in your code, it is a good idea to define it as a constant. A **constant** is an object that stores a literal value and that value cannot change during program execution. Using a constant ensures that you use a consistent value each time the literal is used and saves you work.

Imagine that you have these two methods, each of which does something with a given file on the computer's disk:

```
Public Sub DoSomething()
    'What's the filename?
    Dim strFileName As String = "c:\Temp\Demo.txt"
    'Open the file
    . . .
End Sub
Public Sub DoSomethingElse()
    'What's the filename?
    Dim strFileName As String = "c:\Temp\Demo.txt"
    'Do something with the file
    . . .
End Sub
```

(Obviously, this example omits the code that actually manipulates the file.) The code that defines the string literal gives the name of a file twice. This is poor programming practice because if both methods are supposed to access the same file, if that filename changes, this change has to be made in two separate places.

In this instance, both methods are next to each other and the program itself is small, but imagine having a massive program in which a separate string literal pointing to the file is defined in 10, 50, or even 1,000 places. If you need to change the filename, you have to change it many times. This is exactly the kind of thing that leads to serious problems when maintaining software code.

Rather than using a string literal, you need to define a filename globally and then use that global symbol for the filename in the code. This is what a constant is. It is, in effect, a special kind of variable that cannot actually be varied when the program is running

The syntax for declaring a constant is as follows:

```
Const name [As type] = initialization_expression
```

If you have Option Strict turned on, you must include the constant's data type. A constant can only be an intrinsic type (i.e., Boolean, Byte, Short, Integer,

Long, Decimal, Single, Double, Char, String, Date, or Object) or the name of an enumerated type. *initialization_expression* assigns the constant its never-changing value. You cannot use variables in the *initialization_expression*, but you can use conversion functions, such as Cint. You can also use the values of previously defined constants and enumeration values. The expression can include type characters such as # or &H, and if the declaration doesn't include a type statement (and Option Explicit is off), the type of the value determines the type of the constant.

The following code demonstrates these capabilities:

```
Const MAX_VALUES As Integer = CInt(123.45)
Const MASK_READ As Long = &H1000&
Const MASK_WRITE As Long = &H2000&
```

The first statement uses the CInt function to convert the value 123.45 into an integer constant. The second and third statements set the values of two Long constants to hexadecimal values. The names of the constants are shown here in all uppercase. This is not a requirement, but makes them easier to identify in your code.

2.3.3 Declaring and Using Enumerations

So far, the variables you've seen have had virtually no limitations on the kinds of data you can store in them. Technical limits notwithstanding, if you have a variable defined As Integer, you can put any number you like in it, provided that it is within the limits of an Integer (−2,147,483,648 to 2,147,483,647). The same holds true for String and Double. You have seen another variable type, however, that has only two possible values: Boolean variables can be either True or False and nothing else.

Often, when writing code, you want to limit the possible values that can be stored in a variable. For example, if you have a variable that stores the number of doors a car has, do you really want to be able to store the value 163,234?

Enumerations allow you to build a new type of variable, based on one of the data types Integer, Long, Short, or Byte. This variable can be set to one value of a set of possible values that you define, and it can ideally prevent someone from supplying invalid values. It is used to provide clarity in the code because it can describe a particular value.

For example, suppose that you are building a large application where users can have one of three access levels: clerk, supervisor, and administrator. You could define an enumerated type named AccessLevel to allow the values Clerk, Supervisor, and Administrator. In this case, if you declare a variable to be of type AccessLevel, Visual Basic allows the variable to take only those values.

The following code shows a simple example. It defines the AccessLevel type and declares the variable m_AccessLevel, using the type. Next, an expression sets the variable m_AccessLevel to AccessLevel.Supervisor. Notice that the value is prefixed with the enumerated type's name:

```
Enum AccessLevel
    Clerk
    Supervisor
    Administrator
End Enum
' The user's access level.
Private m_AccessLevel As AccessLevel
' Set supervisor access level.
m_AccessLevel = AccessLevel.Supervisor
```

The basic syntax for declaring an enumerated type is as follows:

```
Enum name [As type]
    value_name [= initialization_expression]
    value_name [= initialization_expression]
...
End Enum
```

The type value must be an integral type and can be Byte, Short, Integer, or Long. If you omit this value, Visual Basic stores the enumerated type values as integers. The *value_name* pieces are the names you want to allow the enumerated type to have. You can include an *initialization_expression* for each value if you like. This value must be compatible with the underlying data type (i.e., Byte, Short, Integer, or Long). If you omit a value's initialization expression, the value is set to 1 greater than the previous value. The first value is 0 by default. For example, in the previous example, Clerk = 0, Supervisor = 1, and Administrator = 2.

The following code changes the default assignments so Clerk = 10, Supervisor = 11, and Administrator = −1:

```
Public Enum AccessLevel
    Clerk = 10
    Supervisor
    Administrator = -1
End Enum
```

Usually, all that's important about an enumerated type is that its values are unique, so you don't need to explicitly initialize the values.

If you have a value that can take only a fixed number of values, you should probably make it an enumerated type. Also, if you discover that you have defined a series of constants to represent related values, you should consider converting them into an enumerated type. Then you can gain the benefits of Visual Basic's improved type checking and IntelliSense.

FOR EXAMPLE

Declaring Constants

Say that you are creating a payroll application. You need to ensure that an employee is paid 1.5 times his or her normal wage for hours over 8 hours in a day or 40 hours in a week. Any hours over 10 hours in a day must be paid at twice the employee's hourly wage.

Because the values will be used several times in the program, you decide to create constants, and you declare the following constants:

```
Const OTPAY = 1.5D
Const DTPAY = 2.0D
Const OTPAYDAYTHRESHOLD = 8I
Const OTPAYWEEKTHRESHOLD = 40I
Const DTPAYDAYTHRESHOLD = 10I
```

The program must also support three categories of employees: contract, hourly, and salary. You decide to create an enumeration to support this requirement. You declare the enumeration as follows:

```
Enum EmployeeType
     Contract = 1
     Hourly = 2
     Salary = 3
End Enum
```

You declare a variable to hold the employee type, as follows:

```
Dim etType As EmployeeType
```

When you enter the code, IntelliSense automatically displays a list of valid settings.

SELF-CHECK

- Discuss the advantages and disadvantages of using literals with a type character.
- Identify situations in which it is better to define a constant than to use a literal.
- Give an example of a situation in which you would create an enumeration. Discuss how doing so would make it easier to write and understand your code.

2.4 Working with Operators

Now that you have a general understanding of how to store data and move it between variables, it is time to discuss how to manipulate data using arithmetic and comparison operators. This section looks first at simple expressions that perform a single computation. Next, it looks at more complex expressions and examines how to control the **order of precedence**.

2.4.1 Performing Mathematical Operations

An expression uses an **operator** to tell Visual Basic to perform an operation using values on either side of the operator. These values are called **operands.** For example, 7 + 5 is an expression. The + is the symbol for the addition operator. The numerals 7 and 5 are operands.

There are basically four types of operators that you use in programs. These are arithmetic operators, comparison operators, logical operators (also known as bitwise operators), and bit shift operators. **Arithmetic operators** tell Visual Basic to perform arithmetic. **Comparison operators** tell Visual Basic to compare the operand on the left side of the operator with the operand on the right side of the operator. If they compare, the operator returns a True; otherwise, the operator returns a False. **Bitwise operators (logical operators) and bit shift** operators perform operations on the bits of an operand. We'll look at arithmetic operators here.

The arithmetic operators are as follows: **exponentiation** (^), which is used for scientific notation; negation (−), used for a value less than zero; multiplication (*); division (/); addition (+); subtraction (−); **modulo** (Mod), which is used for obtaining the remainder of a division operation; and string concatenation (&), which is used for combining two strings.

Let's look at a simple example:

```
Dim intYears As Integer = 0, intDays As Integer = 0
intYears = CInt(txtYears.Text)
intDays = intYears * 356
lblDays.Text = "It has been " & CStr(intDays) _
    & "days"
```

First, you declare a variable named intYears, obtain the value entered into the txtYears TextBox control, and multiply it by 356 to determine the number of days. You then use the concatenation operator to format the results and display them in lblDays. Notice that this example uses the CInt and CStr conversion functions to convert the data between String (the data type for the Text property of the Label and TextBox controls) and Integer.

Be careful using the Integer data type with the division (/) operator. If Option Strict is set to On, an error occurs when you try to compile the following code:

```
Dim intSalesByYear As Integer = 0
Dim intAvSalesPerDay As Integer = 0
intAvSalesPerDay = intSalesByYear / 356
```

If Option Strict is set to Off, the result is rounded to the nearest whole number, resulting in loss of precision. When declaring a variable that will store the result of a division operation, it is best to use a data type that can store decimal values, such as Decimal.

When you need to perform a calculation on a single operand (e.g., doubling a value), you can use the following operators, each of which performs a calculation and then assigns a value:

▲ +=

▲ —=

▲ *=

▲ /=

▲ \=

▲ ^=

For example, to add the amount entered in txtAmtIncrease to the variable intTotal, you use this code:

```
intTotal += CInt(txtAmtIncrease.Text)
```

The longhand way to write this code is:

```
intTotal = intTotal + CInt(txtAmtIncrease.Text)
```

2.4.2 Using Comparison Operators

You were briefly introduced to the If...Else...End If statement earlier in this chapter. You learned that it tests a Boolean expression, which is either True or False. That could be a Boolean variable, as you have already seen, or it could be the result of a comparison operation. The comparison operators are equal (=), greater than (>), less than (<), greater than or equal to (>=), less than or equal to (<=), and not equal (<>). There are also two special comparison operators for working with objects, Is and IsNot, which we'll look at when we talk about objects, a little later in this book. The Like operator is used to compare a string to a pattern. The Like, Is, and IsNot operators are beyond the scope of this chapter.

You usually use a comparison operator with an If statement. For example, you might need to test whether a value is greater than 0. To do so, you would use code similar to the following:

```
If intMyValue > 0 Then
    MsgBox("Value is over 0")
Else
    MsgBox("Value is 0 or less")
End If
```

When you use a comparison operator with a string, the result depends on the value of the Option Compare compiler option. The Option Compare compiler option has two possible values:

▲ **Binary:** When Option Compare is set to Binary, two strings are compared, based on their binary values. For example, when using the ASCII character set, A=65, B=66, and a=91. Therefore A<B<a.

▲ **Text:** When Option Compare is set to Text, two strings are compared as case-insensitive text. For example, A=a and A<B.

2.4.3 Managing the Order of Precedence

A complex expression has several operations that are performed in a single expression and can be used to combine multiple lines of code in a program into one line of code. A complex expression can contain arithmetic operations or logical operations.

For example, 7 + 5 * 2 is a complex expression that contains two arithmetic operations; each operation could be performed in its own equation on separate lines of code. Operations are placed one after the other in an expression. The result of one operation becomes the operand for the next operation. This means that the result of 5 * 2, which is 10, becomes part of the next operation, which is 7 + 10.

Visual Basic determines the order in which it performs operations by using operator precedence. For example, 7 + 5 * 2 could be evaluated two ways: The first way is 7 + 5 = 12 and then 12 * 2 = 24. The other way is 5 * 2 = 10 and then 7 + 10 = 17. Operator precedence requires that multiplication be performed before addition. Therefore, Visual Basic evaluates this as 7 + 5 * 2 = 17.

A common programming error is to create an expression without paying attention to the operator precedence and incorrectly assume the order in which Visual Basic will evaluate the expression. The result is that your program generates an unexpected value when evaluating the expression. For example, you may expect 7 + 5 * 2 = 24 when Visual Basic evaluates this expression as 17.

Visual Basic uses the following operator precedence, in this order:

▲ Exponentiation (^) and NOT
▲ Negation (−) and AND
▲ Multiplication(*), division (/), and OR
▲ Integer division (\)
▲ Modulus arithmetic (Mod)
▲ Addition (+) and subtraction (−)

▲ String concatenation (&)

▲ Equals (=), less than (<), greater than (>), less than or equal to (<=), and greater than or equal to (>=)

When an expression contains two operations that are at the same level in terms of operator precedence, Visual Basic evaluates the expression from left to right. The left operation is performed first, followed by the second operation, the third operation, and so on, until all the operations are performed.

You can use parentheses around equations in an expression to specify your own operator precedence. Visual Basic performs an operation within parentheses before performing other operations in the expression. You can place parentheses within parentheses, such as (7 * (5 + 2)). The operation in the innermost parentheses is performed first, followed by the operation in the next outer parentheses. After performing the operation within the parentheses, Visual Basic replaces that equation with the value returned from the operation, such as (7 * 7).

You can use both values and names of variables to form a complex expression. Visual Basic replaces variable names with the value stored in the variable before performing the operation in the expression.

Let's say that you need to calculate local and state sales tax for a product price. The local sales tax is assigned to the decLocalSalesTaxRate variable, and the state sales tax is assigned to the decStateSalesTaxRate variable. The price of the product is assigned to the decProductPrice variable. The expression to calculate the total amount the customer pays for the product is decProductPrice + (decProductPrice * decLocalSalesTaxRate) + (decProductPrice * decStateSalesTaxRate). Remember that operations contained within parentheses are performed first, before operations outside the parentheses. This means that the local sales tax is calculated first and then the state sales tax is calculated. The final operation adds together the product price and both sales taxes to arrive at the amount of money the customer pays for the product.

Parentheses must be balanced. For every open parenthesis, you must have a close parenthesis. It is easy to balance parentheses if you have a simple expression; however, you can easily lose track of open and close parentheses in complex expressions that contain many sets of parentheses inside other sets of parentheses. Fortunately, the Visual Studio code editor reports an unbalanced number of parentheses. If you are missing an open parenthesis, Visual Studio displays the error "End of statement expected." If you are missing a close parenthesis, it displays the error ") expected".

Sometimes, combining operations into one expression makes the line of code confusing for you to read. If it is confusing to read, you should either rewrite it so it is simpler to understand or document it by using a comment. Confusing code can be difficult to debug. So, even though the compiler would have no trouble understanding it, you should make sure humans can decipher it easily as well.

FOR EXAMPLE

The Importance of Order of Precedence

Say that you are helping another programmer create a payroll application. The program must calculate an employee's total pay. An employee must be paid 1.5 times his or her normal wage for hours over 40 in a week. You have declared the following constants and variables:

```
Const OTPAY = 1.5D
Const OTPAYTHRESHOLD = 40I
Dim decWage, decPayTotal As Decimal
Dim intHours As Integer
```

The other programmer has written the following code:

```
If intHours > 40 Then
    decPayTotal = intHours - OTPAYTHRESHOLD * _
        decWage * OTPAY
    decPayTotal += decWage * OTPAYTHRESHOLD
Else
    decPayTotal = decWage * OTPAY
End If
```

When you test the code, you realize that decPayTotal is being set to the wrong value when overtime hours are worked. For example, when an employee who makes $10.00 per hour works 50 hours a week, the total generated is $−150.00 instead of the expected value of $550.00.

You examine the code and realize that the problem is caused by a misunderstanding of the order of precedence. You modify the code as follows to ensure that the subtraction occurs before the multiplication:

```
If intHours > 40 Then
    decPayTotal = (intHours - OTPAYTHRESHOLD) * _
        decWage * OTPAY
    decPayTotal += decWage * OTPAYTHRESHOLD
Else
    decPayTotal = decWage * OTPAY
End If
```

You realize that the code needs to be documented to ensure that you and other programmers understand the code in the future. You therefore add the following documentation:

```
If intHours > 40 Then
    'Calculate the overtime pay for hours over 40
    decPayTotal = (intHours - OTPAYTHRESHOLD) * _
        decWage * OTPAY
```

(Continued)

```
            'Calculate the regular pay and add it to the
            'overtime pay
            decPayTotal += decWage * OTPAYTHRESHOLD
    Else
            decPayTotal = decWage * OTPAY
    End If
```

SELF-CHECK

- Give examples of when you would use a modulo operator.
- Give examples of when you would use the <> comparison operator.
- Write a complex expression and use parentheses to manage the order of precedence. Perform the calculations to see how the parentheses affect the results.

SUMMARY

In this chapter, you have learned how to declare and use variables, constants, and enumerations. You have learned about variables, data types, and variable declaration. You have also learned about data type conversion. In addition, you have learned how to declare and use constants and enumerations and how to ensure that the compiler considers a literal to be of a specific type. You have learned how to use arithmetic and conditional operators and to manage the order of precedence of complex expressions.

KEY TERMS

Accessibility	Bitwise operator
Arithmetic operator	Byte
As	Comparison operator
Assignment operator	Compiler option
Base 2	Concatenation
Base 10	Constant
Binary	Conversion function
Bit	Data type
Bit shift operator	Data type character

Dim	Operand
Enumerated type	Operator
Enumeration	Order of precedence
Exponentiation	Petabyte (PB)
Gigabyte (GB)	Precision
If...Then statement	Reference
Initialize	Reserved word
Kilobyte (KB)	Scope
Lifetime	Terabyte (TB)
Logical operator	Undeclared variable
Megabyte (MB)	Unicode
Memory	Validate
Modulo	Variable
Narrowing conversion	Widening conversion

ASSESS YOUR UNDERSTANDING

Go to www.wiley.com/college/petroutsos to evaluate your knowledge of variables, constants, and operators.

Measure your learning by comparing pre-test and post-test results.

Summary Questions

1. Which of the following terms defines what code within a current module can access a variable?
   (a) accessibility
   (b) data type
   (c) lifetime
   (d) scope

2. Which of the following lists units of measurement in order, from smallest to largest?
   (a) bit, byte, kilobyte, megabyte, gigabyte, terabyte, petabyte
   (b) byte, bit, petabyte, kilobyte, megabyte, gigabyte, terabyte
   (c) bit, byte, kilobyte, megabyte, gigabyte, terabyte, petabyte
   (d) byte, petabyte, terabyte, bit, kilobyte, megabyte, gigabyte

3. Which of the following data types can you use to store a value that includes a decimal point?
   (a) Long
   (b) Byte
   (c) Single
   (d) UShort

4. Which of the following variable declarations correctly declares a variable of type Decimal?
   (a) Dim decMyVar@
   (b) Dim decMyVar!
   (c) Dim decMyVar#
   (d) Dim decMyVar&

5. Which assignment statement would you use to assign a literal value to a variable declared as follows?

   ```
   Dim strCode As String
   ```

   (a) strCode = Hello
   (b) strCode = "Hello"

(c) strCode = 'Hello'

(d) strCode = [Hello]

6. Setting Option Strict = On causes an error to occur if a narrowing conversion is attempted implicitly. True or False?

7. Which of the following functions rounds fractional values to the nearest whole number?

   (a) CDec

   (b) CDbl

   (c) CLng

   (d) CSng

8. Validating user input is necessary only when Option Strict is set to Off. True or False?

9. Option Strict is On. Which of the following would you use to assign a literal value to a variable declared as follows?

   ```
   Dim cCode As Char
   ```

   (a) cCode = "b"c

   (b) cCode = 'b'c

   (c) cCode = "b"

   (d) cCode = 'b'

10. Option Strict is On. Which of the following is a valid constant declaration?

    (a) Const Discount1 As Decimal

    (b) Const Discount1 =. 10

    (c) Const Discount1 .10D

    (d) Const Discount1 As Decimal = .10

11. Which data type cannot be used to define an enumeration?

    (a) UInteger

    (b) Integer

    (c) Short

    (d) Byte

12. Which operator performs multiplication on and then changes the value of the left-hand operand?

    (a) *

    (b) *=

    (c) =*

    (d) **

13. Which operator is used to determine whether two values are not equivalent?

    (a) !=

    (b) NOT

(c) NOT EQUAL

(d) <>

14. The statement 7 + 5 / 2 evaluates to 6. True or False?

Applying This Chapter

1. You are writing an application to track items you have sold on eBay. You need to be able to track the following information:

    (a) Product name

    (b) Buyer name

    (c) Buyer address

    (d) Sale price

    (e) Whether the sale was a Buy It Now

    (f) Feedback you received (Good, Neutral, or Poor)

    Identify the data type you will use for each. Explain why. Write a variable declaration for each.

2. You wrote a program, compiled it using default compiler options, and tested it. You receive a number of data conversion errors. List the steps you should take to resolve the errors and prevent them from reoccurring in the future.

3. You are writing a program that converts measurements from English to metric units. Describe how you could use constants in the program. Describe how you could use an enumeration.

4. You are writing a program that performs the following:

    (a) Calculates the average weekly sales.

    (b) Calculates commission as 10% of total weekly sales.

    (c) Calculates a bonus as 5% of the average weekly sales.

    The user will input the total weekly sales. Write the code to perform these three calculations. Use variables and constants. Make sure to validate data and perform narrowing conversions, if necessary.

Fixing Programs by Declaring Variables

You are trying to fix a program written by another programmer. The program has a large number of problems. Some values are not being calculated correctly. You notice that the Option Explicit compiler option is set to Off. Discuss how this could lead to the types of errors you are seeing. How will setting Option Explicit to On help you locate and fix the errors?

Optimizing Data Storage I

You are developing a program that will perform calculations on many whole numbers between −5000 and 5000. You need to select a data type for these variables. Discuss the implications of using Short, Integer, and Long data types. Consider memory use and performance.

Optimizing Data Storage II

You are developing a program that will perform calculations on fractional numbers between −0.000001 and 9999.000001. Discuss the implications of using Single, Double, and Decimal data types. Consider memory use, precision, and performance.

Data Type Conversion

You are debugging a program that performs a number of calculations, based on values entered by a user. The program frequently reports data type conversion errors. Also, some calculations lose precision. Discuss the steps you should take to correct the problems.

Using Constants for Consistency

You are developing an application that performs a number of calculations and reports the results to users. You want to ensure that each time a user receives a result, it is worded the same way. You also want to ensure that some values used in the calculations, such as the values used in formulas, are always specified to the same precision. Discuss how constants can help you meet your objective.

Improving Code Readability

You are trying to fix a program written by another programmer. The program is difficult to understand. Variables are letters of the alphabet, literal expressions are hard coded into expressions, and there are many complex expressions. Identify the steps you can take to improve the program's readability and discuss how they will help you find and fix the problems.

3

MANAGING PROGRAM FLOW

Starting Point

Go to www.wiley.com/college/petroutsos to assess your knowledge of programming flow, control statements, and debugging.
Determine where you need to concentrate your effort.

What You'll Learn in This Chapter

▲ The role pseudocode and flowcharts play in designing program flow
▲ Decision-making statements
▲ Statements that perform an operation multiple times
▲ Visual Studio debugging tools

After Studying This Chapter, You'll Be Able To

▲ Use pseudocode to describe program flow
▲ Identify flowchart symbols
▲ Create a program that includes If…Then…Else and Select Case decision-making statements
▲ Create a program that performs repetitive tasks, using For…Next, Do While…Loop, Do Until…Loop, and While…End While statements
▲ Use Visual Studio debugging tools to locate and fix logic errors

INTRODUCTION

When you write a program, you need to tell the computer exactly what you want it to do, using step-by-step instructions. In this chapter, you'll learn how to break down what a program should do into steps and write code that describes those steps to the compiler. In the first section, you'll learn about two important tools that help you describe what a program needs to do. In the second section, you'll learn how to write code that makes decisions. In the third section, you'll learn how to write code that performs repetitive tasks. In the fourth section, you'll learn how to use Visual Studio tools to find and fix problems in code.

3.1 Describing a Program, Using Algorithms and Flowcharts

When you write a program, that program must perform some task. It might be a real-world business task, such as managing payroll or processing orders. Or it might be a program that provides entertainment, such as a game. In either case, the program will perform a large number of tasks, and for each of them, you must provide a very specific set of instructions.

Before you begin to write code, you need a clear understanding of the tasks the program must perform: the requirements and the steps it should take to perform them. The steps a program must take to perform a task is known as the program's **flow.** You can design a program's flow by using algorithms and flowcharts.

3.1.1 Writing Algorithms Using Pseudocode

An **algorithm** is a step-by-step description of a procedure. Writing an algorithm allows you to think about the logic of a program without worrying about the syntax of the programming language.

You can think of an algorithm as being like a recipe:

1. Put 1 tablespoon of oil in a frying pan.
2. Heat the oil on the stove at low temperature.
3. Break three eggs into a bowl.
4. Beat the eggs with a whisk.
5. Add cheese.
6. Add seasonings.
7. Add the egg mixture to the frying pan.
8. Cook on both sides.

You write an algorithm by using pseudocode. As the word suggests, *pseudocode* is like code but different. In fact, **pseudocode** is a description of the program flow, written in the language you speak. When you write pseudocode, you usually keep the sentences short and to the point.

You clearly define each step that must be taken to perform the task. For example, suppose you need to write a program that accepts a person's hourly wage and calculates the person's pay. For the sake of this example, let's assume a withholding rate of 20%. The algorithm for this procedure is as follows:

1. Declare variables for Wage, HoursWorked, GrossPay, WithholdingAmount, and NetPay.
2. Declare a constant for WithholdingPercent and set it equal to 20%.
3. Input Wage.
4. Input HoursWorked.
5. Set GrossPay = Wage * HoursWorked.
6. Set WithholdingAmount = GrossPay * WithholdingPercent.
7. Set NetPay = GrossPay − WithholdingAmount.
8. Output NetPay.

There are different ways you could write this pseudocode. For example, you could write step 5 as "Multiply Wage by HoursWorked and store the result in GrossPay." However, the point of writing an algorithm is to describe the program's logic, not to worry about language.

3.1.2 Using Flowcharts

A **flowchart** is a graphical representation of a program's logic. You can draw a flowchart on paper or using a flowcharting tool such as Microsoft Visio. There are even flowcharting objects available in Microsoft Office.

FOR EXAMPLE

Creating an Algorithm and Flowchart

Say that you are writing a program that will calculate a company's gross sales and revenue. Sales and expenses are logged in a database, by month. You need to create an algorithm and a flowchart for the program.

You write the following algorithm:

1. Get sales data from the database.
2. Add the sales data for each of the 12 months to calculate gross sales.
3. Output gross sales.
4. Get expense data from the database.
5. Add expense data for each of the 12 months to calculate total expenses.
6. Subtract total expenses from gross sales to calculate revenue.
7. Output revenue.

You draw the flowchart shown in Figure 3-1 to represent the solution.

Figure 3-1

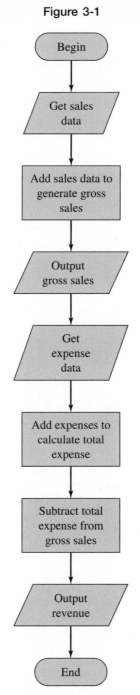

A revenue flowchart.

Figure 3-2

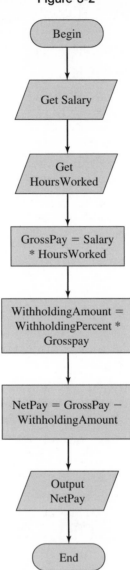

A simple flowchart.

When you draw a flowchart, you should use industry-standard shapes to represent each step in the process. You usually draw the flow from top to bottom or from left to right. Arrows connect the shapes to define the flow. Figure 3-2 shows the algorithm from the preceding section drawn as a flowchart.

The oval is a terminator and marks the beginning and end of the flow. The parallelograms are used to represent input and output. The rectangles are used to represent a process. You will be introduced to other shapes later in the chapter.

SELF-CHECK

- Compare an algorithm with a flowchart.
- Compare pseudocode and code.
- Write the algorithm for the process of calculating the perimeter and area of a rectangle.
- Draw a flowchart for the process of applying a discount of 25% to the price of an item and outputting the discounted price.

3.2 Writing Code That Makes Decisions

An application needs a built-in capability to test conditions and take a different course of action, depending on the outcome of the test. Visual Basic provides three such decision structures:

▲ If…Then
▲ If…Then…Else
▲ Select Case

In this section we'll first look at the If…Then statement. Next, we'll examine how to write more complex logic by using If…Then…Else. After that, we'll look at logical operators and examine how to use them to test for multiple conditions. Finally, we'll look at the Select Case statement to see how it can be used to make some code easier to read.

3.2.1 Using the If…Then Statement

The **If…Then statement** tests a condition. If the condition is true, the program executes the statement(s) that follow the Then clause of the statement. If the condition is false, the application continues with the statement following the End If keyword.

The If structure can have a single-line or a multiple-line syntax. To execute one statement conditionally, you use the single-line syntax, as follows:

```
If condition Then statement
```

You can also execute multiple statements by separating them with colons:

```
If condition Then statement: statement: statement
```

Here's an example of a single-line If statement:

```
If xpdate.Month > 12 Then xpYr = xpYr + 1: xpMonth = 1
```

You can break this statement into multiple lines by using End If, as shown here:

```
If  xpDate.Month  >  12  Then
     xpYr = xpYr + 1
     xpMonth = 1
End If
```

Some programmers prefer the multiple-line syntax of the If...Then statement, even if it contains a single statement. The block of statements between the Then and End If keywords form the body of the conditional statement, and you can have as many statements in the body as needed.

Notice that after a True condition is found, Visual Basic executes the associated statements. If the statement evaluates to False, the program skips the statements inside the If block and continues executing with the statement immediately after End If.

Let's look at another example. This time we'll use a flowchart to illustrate the design. Suppose you want to apply a 25% discount to a product's sales price. However, you do not want the product to sell for less than its wholesale price. One way to solve this problem is illustrated in Figure 3-3.

Notice that we're using two new symbols here: the decision symbol that represents the If statement and a connector symbol that brings the two branches (True and False) together.

The code for this is as follows:

```
Dim DiscPrice, Price, WholesalePrice As Decimal
Price = CDec(txtPrice.Text)
WholesalePrice = CDec(txtWPrice.Text)
DiscPrice = Price * .25
If DiscPrice >= WholesalePrice Then Price = DiscPrice
txtNewPrice.Text = CStr(Price)
```

3.2.2 Using the If...Then...Else Statement

A variation of the If...Then statement is the **If...Then...Else statement,** which executes one block of statements if the condition is true and another block of statements if the condition is false. The syntax of the If...Then...Else statement is as follows:

```
If  condition  Then
     statementblock1
Else
     statementblock2
End If
```

Visual Basic evaluates the condition. If it's true, Visual Basic executes the first block of statements and then jumps to the statement following the End If statement. If the condition is false, Visual Basic ignores the first block of statements and executes the block following the Else keyword.

Figure 3-3

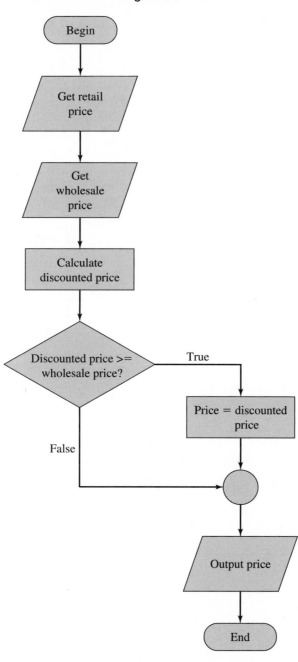

A conditional flowchart.

A third variation of the If...Then...Else statement uses several conditions, with the ElseIf keyword:

```
If  condition1  Then
     statementblock1
ElseIf  condition2  Then
     statementblock2
ElseIf  condition3  Then
     statementblock3
Else
     statementblock4
End If
```

You can have any number of ElseIf clauses. This is known as a **nested If...Then...Else statement.** The conditions are evaluated from the top, and if one of them is true, the corresponding block of statements is executed. The Else clause is executed if none of the previous expressions is true. Here is an example of a nested If...Then...Else statement:

```
score = InputBox("Enter  score")
If  score  <  50  Then
     Result  =  "Failed"
ElseIf  score  <  75  Then
     Result  =  "Pass"
ElseIf  score  <  90  Then
     Result  =  "Very  Good"
Else
     Result  =  "Excellent"
End If
MsgBox  R3esult
```

The flowchart for this code is shown in Figure 3-4.

The order of the comparisons is vital in an If...Then structure that uses ElseIf statements. Had you written the previous code segment with the first two conditions switched, like the following segment, the results would be quite unexpected:

```
If  score  <  75  Then
     Result  =  "Pass"
ElseIf  score  <  50  Then
     Result  =  "Failed"
ElseIf  score  <  90  Then
     Result  =  "Very  Good"
Else
     Result  =  "Excellent"
End If
```

Figure 3-4

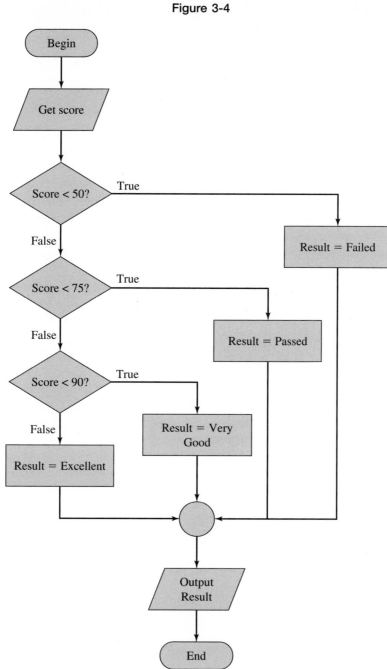

A nested If...Then...Else statement.

Let's assume that the score is 49. The code would compare the score variable to the value 75. Because 49 is less than 75, it would assign the value "Pass" to the variable Result, and then it would skip the remaining clauses. Thus, a student who scored a 49 would pass the test! You need to be extremely careful and test your code thoroughly if it uses multiple ElseIf clauses.

3.2.3 Using the Select Case Statement

An alternative to the efficient but difficult-to-read code of the multiple ElseIf structure is the **Select Case structure,** which compares the same expression to different values. The advantage of the Select Case statement over multiple If...Then...ElseIf statements is that it makes the code easier to read and maintain. The Select Case structure tests a single expression, which is evaluated once at the top of the structure. The result of the expression is then compared with several values; if it matches one of them, the corresponding block of statements is executed. Here's the syntax of the Select Case statement:

```
Select Case expression
Case value1
     statementblock1
Case value2
     statementblock2
  .
  .
  .
Case Else
     StatementblockN
End Select
```

The following is a practical example based on the Select Case statement:

```
Dim Message As String
Select Case Now.DayOfWeek
Case DayOfWeek.Monday
     message = "Have a nice week"
Case DayOfWeek.Friday
     message = "Have a nice weekend"
Case Else
     message = "Welcome back!"
End Select
MsgBox(message)
```

In this code example, the expression that's evaluated at the beginning of the statement is the weekday, as reported by the DayOfWeek property of the date type. It's a numeric value, but its possible settings are the members of the DayOfWeek enumeration, and you can use the names of these members in your code to make it easier to read. The value of this expression is compared with the values that follow each Case keyword. If they match, the block of statements up to the next Case keyword is executed, and the program skips to the statement following the End Select statement. The block of the Case Else statement is optional and is executed if none of the previous Case values matches the expression. The first two Case statements take care of Fridays and Mondays, and the Case Else statement takes care of the weekdays.

Some Case statements can be followed by multiple values, which are separated by commas. The following code example shows how this coding technique can be used to have the same action occur if the day of the week is Tuesday, Wednesday, Thursday, or Friday:

```
Select Case Now.DayOfWeek
Case DayOfWeek.Monday
    message = "Have a nice week"
Case DayOfWeek.Tuesday, DayOfWeek.Wednesday, _
    DayOfWeek.Thursday, DayOfWeek.Friday
    message = "Welcome back!"
Case DayOfWeek.Friday, DayOfWeek.Saturday, _
    DayOfWeek.Sunday
    message = "Have a nice weekend!"
End Select
MsgBox(message)
```

Monday, Friday, weekends, and weekdays are handled separately by three Case statements. The second Case statement handles multiple values (all weekdays except for Monday and Friday). Monday is handled by a separate Case statement. This structure doesn't contain a Case Else statement because all possible values are examined in the Case statements. The DayOfWeek method can't return another value.

3.2.4 Using Logical Operators

A program's flow might depend on evaluating multiple conditions. For example, suppose you are writing an order entry application. You need to charge a special handling fee if an item weighs over 2 pounds and is being shipped outside the continental United States. For this, you need to create an If statement with two Boolean values that are linked together with a logical operator.

A **logical operator** compares two Boolean values and returns True or False, depending on the result. Table 3-1 summarizes Visual Basic's logical operators.

The operators Not, And, and Or are relatively straightforward. The Xor operator returns true if one of its operands is true and the other one is false.

The AndAlso and OrElse operators are similar to the And and Or operators except that they provide short-circuit evaluation. In **short-circuit evaluation,** Visual Basic is allowed to stop evaluating operands if it can deduce the final result without them. For example, consider the expression A AndAlso B. If Visual

Table 3-1: Logical Operators

Operator	Purpose	Example	Result
Not	Logical or bitwise NOT	Not A	True if A is false
And	Logical or bitwise AND	A And B	True if A and B are both true
Or	Logical or bitwise OR	A Or B	True if A or B or both are true
Xor	Logical or bitwise exclusive OR	A Xor B	True if A or B but not both are true
AndAlso	Logical or bitwise AND with short-circuit evaluation	A AndAlso B	True if A and B are both true
OrElse	Logical or bitwise OR with short-circuit evaluation	A OrElse B	True if A or B or both are true

Basic evaluates the value A and discovers that it is false, the program knows that the expression A AndAlso B is also false no matter what value B has, so it doesn't need to evaluate B.

Whether the program evaluates both operands doesn't matter much if A and B are simple Boolean variables. However, assume that they are time-consuming functions, as shown in the following code:

```
If TimeConsumingFunction("A") AndAlso _
    TimeConsumingFunction("B") Then
```

For example, the TimeConsumingFunction function might need to look up values in a database or download data from a web site. In that case, not evaluating the second operand might save a lot of time.

Just as AndAlso can stop evaluation if it discovers that one of its operands is false, the OrElse operand can stop evaluating if it discovers that one of its operands is true. The expression A OrElse B is true if either A or B is true. If the program finds that A is true, it doesn't need to evaluate B.

Because AndAlso and OrElse do the same thing as And and Or but sometimes faster, you might wonder why you would ever use And and Or. The main reason is that the operands may have side effects. A **side effect** is some action a routine performs that is not obviously part of the routine. For example, suppose that the NumEmployees function opens an employee database and returns the number of

FOR EXAMPLE

Using AndAlso

Say that you are creating an order entry application. The shipping fee is calculated based on the weight of a package. A package that weighs under 1 ounce is charged a flat rate for each region. Packages over 1 ounce but under 1 pound are charged a rate per ounce, based on the destination region. Packages over 1 pound are charged a rate per pound, based on the destination region. There are three regions. Orders from in-state customers are subject to sales tax. Other orders are not.

You decide to use the following:

▲ An If...Then statement to test for in-state customers.
▲ A Select Case statement to test for the destination region.
▲ An If...Else statement within each case to apply shipping charges based on weight.

You write the following code:

```
Dim strState As String
Dim region As RegionEnum
Dim intWeightOz, intWeightLbs As Integer
Dim decTotal, decTax, decShipping As Decimal
'Code to set values
If strState = "CA" Then
    decTax = ApplySalesTax(decTotal)
End If
Select Case region
Case RegionEnum.West
    If intWeightLbs < 1 And intWeightOz < 1 Then
        decShipping = .70
    ElseIf intWeightLbs < 1 And intWeightOz >= 1 Then
        decShipping = intWeightOz * .07
    Else
        decShipping = intWeightLbs * .2
    End If
Case RegionEnum.Central
    If intWeightLbs < 1 And intWeightOz < 1 Then
        decShipping = .90
    ElseIf intWeightLbs < 1 And intWeightOz >= 1 Then
        decShipping = intWeightOz * .09
    Else
        decShipping = intWeightLbs * .15
    End If
```

(continued)

```
     Case RegionEnum.East
         If intWeightLbs < 1 And intWeightOz < 1 Then
             decShipping = 1.00
         ElseIf intWeightLbs < 1 And intWeightOz >= 1 Then
             decShipping = intWeightOz * .1
         Else
             decShipping = intWeightLbs * .25
         End If
     End Select
     decTotal += decTax
     decTotal += decShipping
```

You run the application and test your procedure. The resulting form is shown in Figure 3-5.

Another programmer reviews your code and suggests changing the And operators to AndAlso. You do some research and realize that AndAlso is slightly more efficient because it evaluates the second condition only if necessary.

employee records, leaving the database open. The fact that this function leaves the database open is a side effect. Now, suppose that the NumCustomers function similarly opens the customer database, and then consider the following statement:

```
     If (NumEmployees() > 0) AndAlso _
         (NumCustomers() > 0) Then
```

Figure 3-5

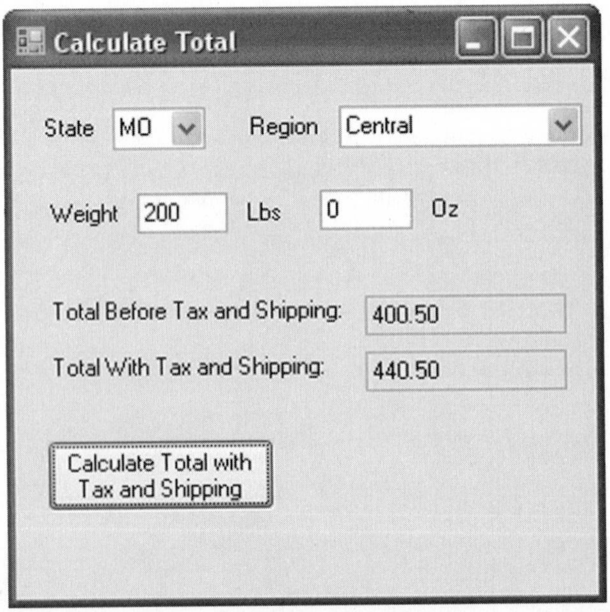

A running order entry application.

After this code executes, you cannot be certain which databases are open. If NumEmployees returns 0, the AndAlso operator's first operand is false, so it doesn't evaluate the NumCustomers function, and that function doesn't open the customer database. The AndAlso and OrElse operators can improve application performance under some circumstances. However, to avoid possible confusion and long debugging sessions, you should not use AndAlso or OrElse with operands that have side effects.

SELF-CHECK

- Compare using a nested If...Else statement to using a Select Case statement. Give examples of where each is appropriate.
- Discuss the benefits and drawbacks of using the OrElse operator instead of the Or operator. Give examples of where each is appropriate.

3.3 Repeating Yourself

A **loop structure** allows you to execute one or more lines of code repetitively. Many tasks consist of operations that must be repeated over and over, and loop structures are an important part of any programming language. Visual Basic supports the following loop structures:

▲ For...Next
▲ Do...Loop
▲ While...End While

3.3.1 Using a For...Next Loop

The **For...Next loop** is one of the oldest loop structures in programming languages. The For...Next loop requires that you know how many times the statements in the loop will be executed. It loop uses a variable (called the loop's *counter*) that increases or decreases in value during each repetition of the loop. Figure 3-6 shows the general flow of a For...Next loop.

The For...Next loop has the following syntax:

```
For counter = start To end [Step increment]
    statements
Next [counter]
```

Figure 3-6

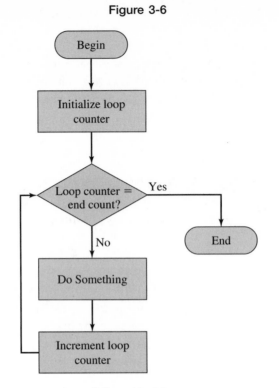

A For...Next loop.

The keywords in the square brackets are optional. The arguments *counter, start,* end, and *increment* are all numeric. The loop is executed as many times as required for the counter to exceed the end value.

In executing a For...Next loop, Visual Basic completes the following steps:

1. Sets *counter* equal to *start.*
2. Tests to see whether *counter* is greater than *end*. If so, it exits the loop. If *increment* is negative, Visual Basic tests whether *counter* is less than *end*. If it is, it exits the loop.
3. Executes the statements in the block.
4. Increments *counter* by the amount specified with the *increment* argument. If the *increment* argument isn't specified, increments *counter* by 1.
5. Repeats the statements.

increment can be positive or negative. The default *increment* value is 1. The following is an example of a For...Next loop with the default increment:

```
Dim WeeklySales As Decimal = 0
Dim i As Integer
```

```
For i = 1 to 7
    WeeklySales += GetDailySales(i)
Next
```

This code executes seven times (or until i is greater than 7). If *increment* is negative, the counter value is decremented until it is less than the end value. Here's an example:

```
Dim i As Integer = 100
For i = 100 to 0 Step -1
    ListStudentsWithScore(i)
Next
```

This code executes 101 times (or until i is less than 0).

You can adjust the value of the counter from within the loop. The following is an example of an **endless (or infinite) loop:**

```
For i = 0 To 10
    Debug.WriteLine(i)
    i = i - 1
Next i
```

This loop never ends because the loop's counter, in effect, is never increased. (If you try this, press Ctrl+Break to interrupt the endless loop.) However, just because you can do something doesn't mean you should. Changing the counter value within the For...Next loop can lead to bugs. A **bug** is an error in the program.

3.3.2 Using Do Until...Loop and Do While...Loop

The **Do...Loop statement** executes a block of statements for as long as a state remains the same. The basic flowchart for a Do...Loop statement is shown in Figure 3-7.

Figure 3-7

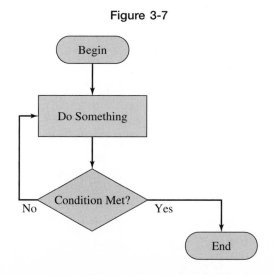

A Do...Loop statement flowchart.

There are two variations of the Do...Loop statement, and both use the same basic model. A loop can be executed either while the condition is true or until the condition becomes true. These two variations use the keywords While and Until to specify how long the statements are executed. To execute a block of statements while a condition is true, you use the following syntax:

```
Do While condition
    statement-block
Loop
```

For example, suppose you want to add additional items to a list of tasks until the estimated time to complete exceeds eight hours (i.e., 480 minutes). You implement this functionality as follows:

```
Dim intEstTime As Integer
Do While intEstTime <= 480
    txtTasks.Text = txtTasks.Text & " " _
        & GetNextTask()
    intEstTime += GetTaskTime()
Loop
```

To execute a block of statements until the condition becomes true, you use the following syntax:

```
Do Until condition
    statement-block
Loop
```

You can implement the previous example as a Do Until loop by changing the conditional operator, as shown here:

```
Dim intEstTime As Integer
Do Until intEstTime > 480
    txtTasks.Text = txtTasks.Text & " " & GetNextTask()
    intEstTime += GetTaskTime()
Loop
```

It is vital to keep in mind that the code inside the Do Until...Loop statement always executes at least once. You also need to ensure that the exit condition can be reached. A loop that has an impossible exit condition is called an *infinite loop*. One cause of an infinite loop in using a Do...Loop with a counter variable is forgetting to increment the counter. For example, consider the following loop:

```
Dim i As Integer = 1
Do Until GetNextEmployee(i) = -1
    CalculatePaycheck(i)
Loop
```

The same paycheck is calculated over and over because the value of i never changes. To resolve this problem, you change the code as follows:

```
Dim i As Integer = 1
Do Until GetNextEmployee(i) = -1
    CalculatePaycheck(i)
    i += 1
Loop
```

Notice that you increment the counter after calculating the paycheck. If you increment it before calculating the paycheck, you skip the first employee's paycheck.

3.3.3 Using the While...End While Loop

The **While...End While loop** executes a block of statements as long as a condition is true and has the following syntax:

```
While condition
    statement-block
End While
```

If the condition is true, all statements are executed. When the End While statement is reached, control is returned to the While statement, which evaluates the condition again. If the condition is still True, the process is repeated. If the condition is False, the program resumes with the statement following End While.

The basic flow of a While...End While statement is shown in Figure 3-8.

The example prompts the user for numeric data. The user can type a negative value to indicate that he or she is done entering values and terminate the loop.

```
Dim number, total As Double
number = 0
While number => 0
    total = total + number
    number = InputBox("Please enter another value")
End While
```

You must always initialize the variable used to test the condition before beginning the loop. This is sometimes called **priming** the variable. You assign the value 0 to the number variable before the loop starts because this value isn't negative and it can't affect the total. Another technique is to precede the While statement with an InputBox function to get the first number from the user.

Figure 3-8

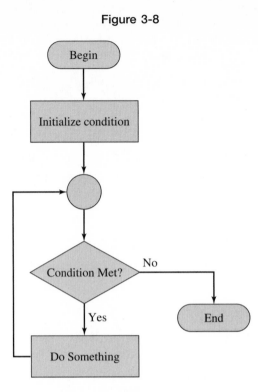

A While...End While statement.

3.3.4 Ducking Out Before a Loop Is Over

The **Exit statement** allows you to exit prematurely from a block of statements in a control structure, from a loop, or even from a procedure. Going back to the previous example, suppose you do not want the user to be able to enter another number after the total has reached 1,000. One way to do this would be to use the Exit statement, which has the following syntax:

```
Exit { Do | For | Function | Property | Select | Sub | Try
| While }
```

You use one of the keywords following it to indicate which structure you should exit. For example, to exit a While loop, you use the following code:

```
Dim number, total As Double
number = 0
While number => 0
    total = total + number
    If total > 1000 Then Exit While
    number = InputBox("Please enter another value")
End While
```

FOR EXAMPLE

Using a While...End While Loop

Say that you are writing an order fulfillment application. You are writing the code to display onscreen the items ordered and the quantity, price, and extended price for each. The following functions have already been created:

▲ OpenItemList

▲ GetItemName

▲ GetItemPrice

▲ GetQuantity

▲ NextItem

When there are no more items in the order, the NextItem function returns −1. Otherwise, it returns 0.

You decide to use a While…End While loop to process the data. You write the following code:

```
OpenItemList()
While NextItem() <> -1
    TextItem.Text = TextItem.Text & GetItemName()
    TextItem.Text = TextItem.Text & " " _
        & GetItemPrice()
    TextItem.Text = TextItem.Text & " " _
        & GetItemQuantity()
    TextItem.Text = TextItem.Text & " " _
        & GetItemPrice() * GetItemQuantity()
End While
```

When you test the code, you find that the first item in the list is not being printed. You realize that the While statement tests the condition first before executing the code. You revise the code to use a Do…Loop statement, as follows:

```
OpenItemList()
Do Until NextItem = -1
    TextItem.Text = TextItem.Text & GetItemName()
    TextItem.Text = TextItem.Text & " " _
        & GetItemPrice()
    TextItem.Text = TextItem.Text & " " _
        & GetItemQuantity()
    TextItem.Text = TextItem.Text & " " _
        & GetItemPrice() * GetItemQuantity()
Loop
```

The code now executes correctly.

This code causes the loop to terminate if the user enters a negative number or if the total exceeds 1,000. Another way to meet a similar requirement is to use the logical operator And or AndAlso, discussed earlier in the chapter. To do so, you write the following code:

```
Dim number, total As Double
number = 0
While number => 0 AndAlso total <= 1000
    total = total + number
    number = InputBox("Please enter another value")
End While
```

SELF-CHECK

- Compare the various types of loops. Give an example of when each would be appropriate.
- Explain the dangers of infinite loops and how to avoid them.
- Give an example of a situation in which you would use the Exit statement.

3.4 Debugging Code

Debugging is an essential part of any development project because it helps you find errors in code and in logic. Visual Studio has a sophisticated debugger built right into the development environment.

This section looks at some of the debugging features available in Visual Studio. You'll learn how to set breakpoints in your code to stop execution at any given point, how to watch the value of a variable change, and how to control the number of times a loop can execute before stopping. All these can help you determine just what is going on inside code.

3.4.1 Understanding Types of Errors

The errors caused by a computer program (regardless of the language in which the program is written) can be categorized into three major groups: design-time errors, runtime errors, and logic errors.

Correcting Design-Time Errors

Design-time errors, which are the easiest type of error to find and fix, occur when you write a piece of code that does not conform to the rules of the language

Figure 3-9

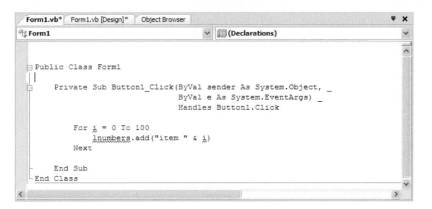

Code with design-time errors.

in which you're writing. They are easy to find because Visual Studio tells you not only where they are but also what part of the line it doesn't understand. Design-time errors, also called **syntax errors,** occur when the Visual Basic compiler cannot recognize one or more statements that you have written. Some design-time errors are simply typographical errors (e.g., a mistyped keyword). Others are the result of missing items (e.g., undeclared or untyped variables).

A program with as few as one design-time error cannot be compiled and run; you must locate and correct the error before you can continue. The event code shown in Figure 3-9 was typed into the Click event of a button named Button1. Note the three squiggly lines under various parts of this brief code (under the two instances of the variable i and under the term lbNumbers). Each one of those squiggly lines represents a design-time error. To determine what the errors are, you locate the Task List window in the IDE and bring it forward. The Error List dialog (see Figure 3-10) displays the errors from the code in Figure 3-9.

Figure 3-10

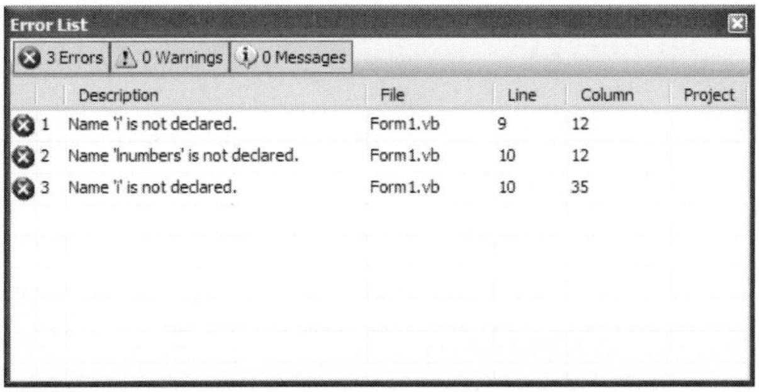

	Description	File	Line	Column	Project
1	Name 'i' is not declared.	Form1.vb	9	12	
2	Name 'lnumbers' is not declared.	Form1.vb	10	12	
3	Name 'i' is not declared.	Form1.vb	10	35	

An error list for design-time errors.

Figure 3-11

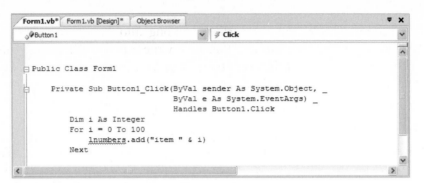

Code with an error fixed.

You can determine which squiggly blue line corresponds to which design-time error in the Error List dialog by double-clicking the error in the Error List dialog. The corresponding error is then selected in the code window. Note that two of the errors are the same: They state, "The name 'i' is not declared." These errors are telling you that you've referenced a variable named i, but you have not declared it. To fix these two errors, you need to modify the code as shown in Figure 3-11.

The only error remaining now is "The name 'lbNumbers' is not declared." You have either forgotten to add the control named lbNumbers to the form or you have named it something different.

Understanding Runtime Errors

Runtime errors are harder to locate than design-time errors because Visual Studio doesn't give you any help in finding an error until it occurs in a program. Runtime errors occur when a program attempts something illegal, such as accessing data that doesn't exist or a resource to which it doesn't have the proper permissions. These types of errors can cause a program to crash, or hang, unless they are handled properly.

Runtime errors are much more difficult to find and fix than design-time errors. Runtime errors can take on dozens of different shapes and forms. Here are some examples:

- ▲ Attempting to open a file that doesn't exist
- ▲ Trying to log in to a server with an incorrect username or password
- ▲ Trying to access a folder for which you have insufficient rights
- ▲ Accessing an Internet URL that no longer exists
- ▲ Dividing a number by zero
- ▲ Entering character data where a number is expected (and vice versa)

As you can see, runtime errors can occur because of an unexpected state of the computer or network on which the program is running, or they can occur simply because the user has supplied the wrong information (e.g., an invalid password, a bad filename). You can therefore write a program that runs fine on your own computer and all the computers in your test environment but fails on a customer site because of the state of that customer's computing resources.

Understanding Logic Errors

The third type of error, the **logic error,** is often the most difficult type to locate because it might not appear as a problem in the program at all. If a program has a logic error, the output or operation of the program is simply not exactly as you intended it. The problem could be as simple as an incorrect calculation or having a menu option enabled when you wanted it disabled. Quite often, logic errors are discovered by users after the application has been deployed.

Logic errors also occur at runtime, so they are often difficult to track down. A logic error occurs when a program does not do what the developer intended it to do. For example, you might provide the code to add a customer to a customer list, but when the end user runs the program and adds a new customer, the customer is not there. The error might lie in the code that adds the customer to the database; or perhaps the customer is indeed being added, but the grid that lists all the customers is not being refreshed after the add-customer code, so it merely appears that the customer wasn't added.

As another example, suppose that you allow end users to manually type the two-letter state code of each customer address that they enter into the program. One of the functions of the program might be to display a map of the United States that shades the states based on the number of customers within each state. Your code uses a Select Case to highlight a state. There is no default condition. The code also enters the customer information into a database without validating the state's value. How do you suppose your shaded map will display customers with invalid state codes? These customers will not be displayed on the map at all.

Later, the manager of the department calls you and says, "The Total Customers Entered report for last month tells me that 7,245 customers were entered into our system. However, the Density Map report shows only 6,270 customers on it. Why don't these two reports match?" This example involves a design decision to allow the end user to type the two-digit state code—and that decision has led to a major logic error: the fact that two reports from the same system give different results for the number of customers entered into the system for the same time period.

Here is an actual Visual Basic .NET code snippet that produces a logic error:

```
Private Sub Button1_Click(ByVal sender _
   As System.Object, ByVal e As System.EventArgs) _
```

```
Handles Button1.Click
   Dim i As Integer
   i = 1
   Do While i > 0
       i += 1
   Loop
End Sub
```

This example has an integer variable set to 1 and incremented by 1 in a loop. Each time the loop iterates, the number gets bigger. The loop will continue to iterate as long as the variable is greater than 0. See any problem with this? The problem is that the value of the variable will always be greater than 0, so the loop will never terminate. This is called an *infinite loop,* and it's a very common error. Of course, this loop isn't exactly infinite; after two billion iterations, an overflow will occur, and that is a good indication of what happened.

Logic errors are often discovered by the users of an application, although rigorous testing reveals most of them. When such an error is reported, you must debug the application: You need to locate the statements that produce the error and fix them. Discovering the statements responsible for a logic error is usually much more difficult than fixing those statements.

3.4.2 Desk Checking Logic

Debugging an application should actually start when you are designing the program flow. After you write the algorithm for a procedure, you should walk through it using a pencil and paper to make sure it works as you intended. This process is called **desk checking.**

To desk check an algorithm, you supply sample values and walk through the algorithm, performing the calculations. To see how this works, let's go back to the algorithm example from the beginning of this chapter:

1. Declare variables for Wage, HoursWorked, GrossPay, WithholdingAmount, and NetPay.
2. Declare a constant for WithholdingPercent and set it equal to 20%.
3. Input Wage.
4. Input HoursWorked.
5. Set GrossPay = Wage * HoursWorked.
6. Set WithholdingAmount = GrossPay * WithholdingPercent.
7. Set NetPay = GrossPay − WithholdingAmount.
8. Output NetPay.

To desk check this algorithm, you perform each step, using sample values for the variables. You document the expected value for each variable after the

Table 3-2: Desk Checking Values

Step	Wage	HoursWorked	GrossPay	WithholdingAmount	NetPay
1	0	0	0	0	0
2	0	0	0	0	0
3	$10.00	0	0	0	0
4	$10.00	35	0	0	0
5	$10.00	35	$350.00	0	0
6	$10.00	35	$350.00	70	0
7	$10.00	35	$350.00	70	$280.00

step completes. Table 3-2 shows how to desk check the algorithm, but you could use a pencil and scratch paper just as easily.

You test expected input values and unexpected input values to try to find potential problems in the algorithm. For example, what if the user entered a negative number for hours worked? Table 3-3 shows the result.

As you can see, not testing the input value of HoursWorked causes a logic error.

3.4.3 Setting Breakpoints

When trying to debug a large program, you might find that you want to debug only a section of code; that is, you might want your code to run up to a certain point and then stop. This is where **breakpoints** come in handy: They cause execution of code to stop anywhere a breakpoint is set. You can set breakpoints

Table 3-3: Desk Checking an Invalid Value

Step	Wage	HoursWorked	GrossPay	WithholdingAmount	NetPay
1	0	0	0	0	0
2	0	0	0	0	0
3	$10.00	0	0	0	0
4	$10.00	−20	0	0	0
5	$10.00	−20	−200.00	0	0
6	$10.00	−20	−200.00	−40.00	0
7	$10.00	−20	−200.00	−40.00	−240.00

anywhere in code, and the code will run up to that point and stop. Note that execution of the code stops before the line on which a breakpoint is set.

Before you begin setting breakpoints, you should display the Debug toolbar in the development environment because this will make it easier to quickly see and choose the debugging options you want. You can do this in one of two ways. You can either right-click an empty space on the current toolbar and choose Debug in the context menu or select View, and then Toolbars, and then Debug.

You can set breakpoints when you write code, and you can also set them at runtime by switching to the code and setting a breakpoint at the desired location. You cannot set a breakpoint while a program is actually executing a section of code, such as the code in a loop, but you can when the program is idle and waiting for user input.

When the development environment encounters a breakpoint, execution of the code halts, and the program is considered to be in **break mode.** While the program is in break mode, a lot of debugging features are available. In fact, a lot of debugging features are available to you *only* while a program is in break mode.

You can set a breakpoint by clicking the gray margin next to the line of code on which you want to set the breakpoint. When a breakpoint is set, you see a solid red circle in the gray margin, and the line is highlighted in red. When you are done using a particular breakpoint, you can remove it by clicking the solid red circle. Figure 3-12 shows a breakpoint set.

At some point you might want to debug code in a loop, such as a loop that reads data from a file. You know that the first *x* number of records are good, and it is time-consuming to step through all the code repetitively until you get to what you suspect is the bad record. You can set a breakpoint inside the loop and then set a hit counter on it. The code inside the loop then executes the number of times specified in the hit counter and then stops and places you in break mode. This can be a real time saver. You can also set a condition on a breakpoint, such as when a variable contains a certain value or when the value of a variable changes.

Figure 3-12

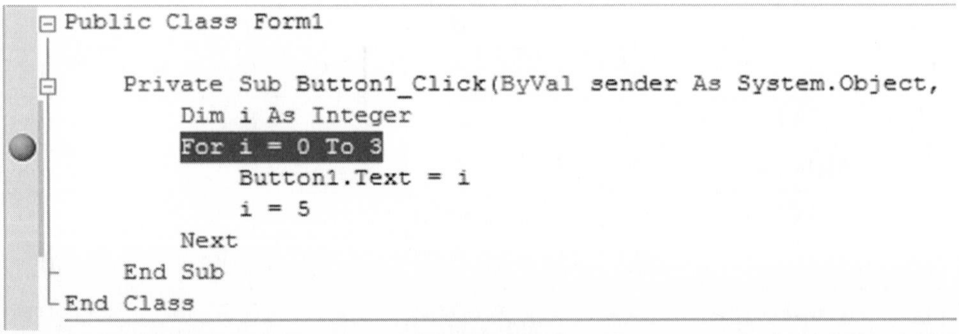

```
Public Class Form1

    Private Sub Button1_Click(ByVal sender As System.Object,
        Dim i As Integer
        For i = 0 To 3
            Button1.Text = i
            i = 5
        Next
    End Sub
End Class
```

A breakpoint.

Figure 3-13

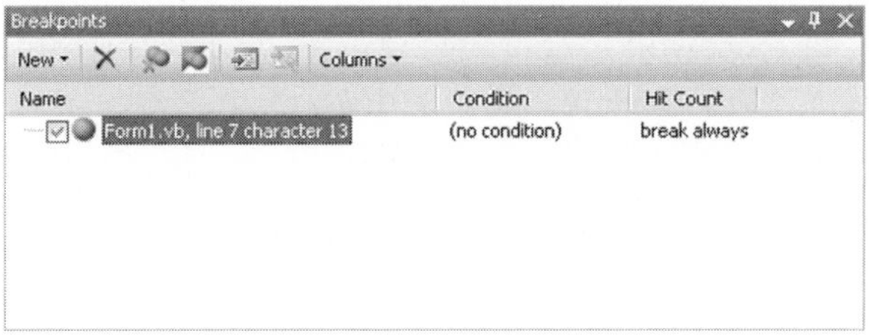

The Breakpoints window.

You can display the Breakpoints window, if the tab is not shown, in the bottom-right of the IDE by clicking the Breakpoints icon on the Debug toolbar or by opening the Debug menu and selecting Windows and then Breakpoints. The Breakpoints window shows what line of code the current breakpoint is at, any conditions it has, and the hit count, if applicable, as shown in Figure 3-13.

3.4.4 Stepping Through Code

When debugging an application, it is helpful to be able to step through the code line by line. On the Debug toolbar, three icons are of particular interest (see Figure 3-14):

▲ **Step Into:** When you click this icon, you can step through the code line by line. This includes stepping into any function or procedure that the code calls and working through it line by line.

▲ **Step Over:** This works in a similar way to Step Into, but it enables you to pass straight over the procedures and functions; they still execute, but all in one go. You then move straight on to the next line in the block of code that called the procedure.

▲ **Step Out:** This icon allows you to jump to the end of the procedure or function that you are currently in and to move to the line of code after

Figure 3-14

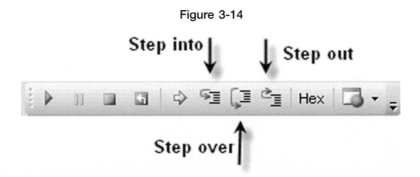

The Step Into, Step Over, and Step Out icons.

the line that called the procedure or function. This is handy when you step into a long procedure and want to get out of it. The rest of the code in the procedure is still executed, but you do not step through it.

One more really useful button is worth adding to the toolbar: Run to Cursor. You can place your cursor anywhere in the code following the current breakpoint where execution has been paused and then click the Run to Cursor icon. The code between the current breakpoint and where the cursor is positioned is executed, and execution stops on the line of code where the cursor is located.

To add this button, you right-click any empty area of the toolbar and choose Customize from the context menu. In the Customize dialog, you click the Commands tab and then select Debug from the Categories list. In the Commands list, you select Run to Cursor. After you select Run to Cursor, you drag its icon from the Commands list onto the Debug toolbar to form a group of icons, as shown in Figure 3-15, and then click the Close button to close the Customize dialog box.

Figure 3-15

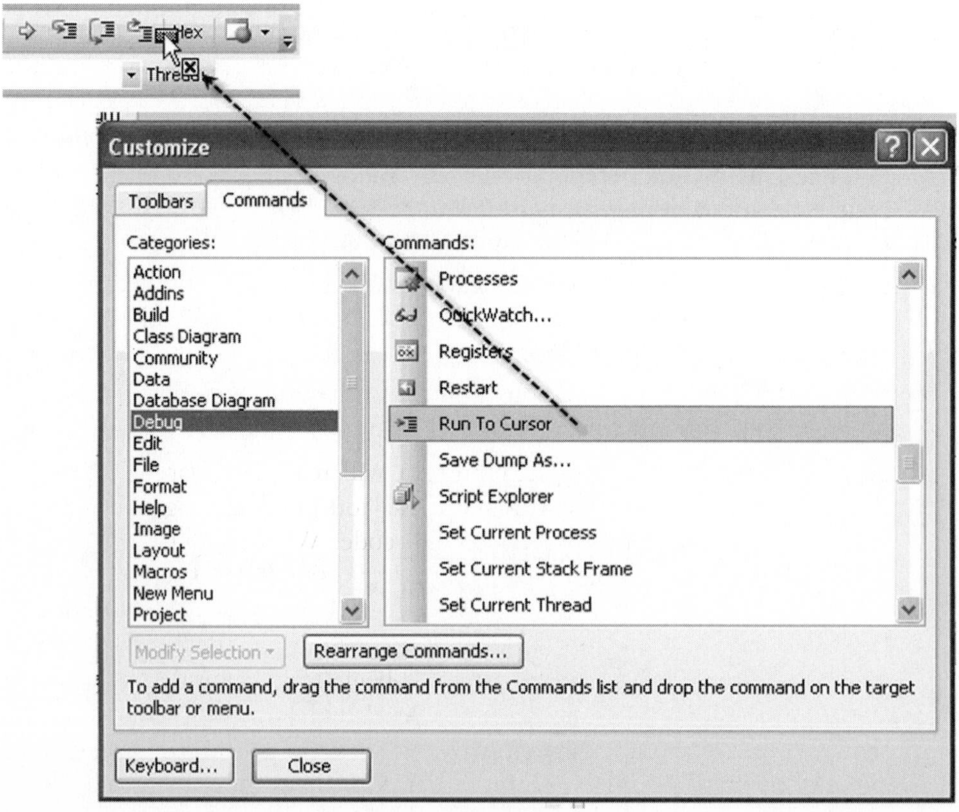

The Run to Cursor icon.

3.4.3 Watching the Inner Workings of a Program

You can use the Watch window to watch variables and expressions easily while the code is executing; this can be invaluable when you are trying to debug unwanted results in a variable. You can even change the values of variables in the Watch window, and you can add as many variables and expressions as needed to debug your program. You can therefore watch the values of your variables change without intervening.

You can add and delete a variable or an expression to the QuickWatch dialog box only when a program is in break mode. Therefore, before you run a program, you need to set a breakpoint before the variable or expression you want to watch. When the breakpoint has been reached, you can add as many watch variables or expressions as needed.

The Locals window is similar to the Watch window except that it shows all variables and objects for the current function or procedure. The Locals window also lets you change the value of a variable or an object, and the same rules that apply to the Watch window apply here (i.e., the program must be paused before a value can be changed). The text for a value that has just changed also turns red, making it easy to spot the variable or object that has just changed.

The Locals window is great if you want a quick glance at everything that is going on in a function or procedure, but it is not very useful for watching the values of one or two variables or expressions. This is because the Locals window contains all variables and objects in a procedure or function. Therefore, if you have a lot of variables and objects, you have to scroll through the window constantly to view the various variables and objects. This is where the Watch window comes in handy; it lets you watch just the variables you need.

FOR EXAMPLE

Debugging with the Locals Window

Say that you are writing an application that will read data from a file and perform a series of calculations on the data. You create an algorithm and desk check your logic. Next, you write the code. When you use the same set of values you used to desk check your logic, the code generates a different result. You realize that there is probably a logic error in your code.

You set a breakpoint in the loop and set watches on the variables you want to study. Next, you start debugging and begin to step through the code. You believe the problem is that a variable is being set to the wrong value. You use the Locals window to modify the value and step through the code again. This time, the result is correct. You stop debugging and make the necessary change in the code.

SELF-CHECK

- Compare design-time errors, runtime errors, and logic errors. Give an example of each.
- Describe how desk checking can help you avoid errors in code.
- Describe how setting a breakpoint can help you debug a program.
- Compare the Watch window and the Locals window and describe a situation in which you would use each.

SUMMARY

In this chapter, you have learned how to write code to describe the logical flow of a process. You have learned how to use algorithms and flowcharts to design a program's flow. You have also learned how to write code that makes decisions and how to write code that performs repetitive tasks, using loops. You have also learned how to test and debug programs.

KEY TERMS

Algorithm	If…Then…Else statement
Breakpoint	Logic error
Break mode	Logical operator
Bug	Loop structure
Debugging	Nested If…Then…Else statement
Design-time error	Priming
Desk checking	Pseudocode
Do…Loop statement	Runtime error
Endless (or infinite) loop	Select Case structure
Exit statement	Short-circuit evaluation
Flow	Side effect
Flowchart	Syntax error
For…Next loop	While…End While loop
If…Then statement	

ASSESS YOUR UNDERSTANDING

Go to www.wiley.com/college/petroutsos to evaluate your knowledge of programming flow, control statements, and debugging.
Measure your learning by comparing pre-test and post-test results.

Summary Questions

1. Which of the following is a step-by-step description of a process written in pseudocode?
   (a) algorithm
   (b) flowchart
   (c) control of flow

2. Which of the following is a graphical depiction of a program's flow?
   (a) algorithm
   (b) control of flow
   (c) flowchart
   (d) UML diagram

3. Which of the following statements is true about the If...Then statement?
   (a) The If...Then statement can include only a single condition.
   (b) The If...Then statement can include multiple statements on a line.
   (c) The If...Then statement should always include an Else clause.

4. Multiple Else blocks can execute when you have a nested If...Then...Else statement. True or False?

5. A Select Case statement compares the same expression to different values. True or False?

6. A logical operator compares two Boolean values and returns either True or False.

7. Which type of loop requires that you know the number of times the loop must execute before the loop begins?
   (a) Do...Loop
   (b) For...Next
   (c) While...End While

8. Which type of loop executes at least once and continues to execute until the defined condition becomes true?
   (a) Do Until...Loop
   (b) Do While...Loop
   (c) For...Next
   (d) While...End While

9. A While…End While loop always executes at least once. True or False?

10. What statement would you use to cause the flow to exit a Do…Loop and resume execution at the first statement after the Do…Loop?

   (a) Exit Loop

   (b) GoTo End

   (c) Exit Do

   (d) GoTo Loop

11. A logic error is also called a syntax error. True or False?

12. Which type of error results in a hang or an exception during execution?

   (a) design-time error

   (b) logic error

   (c) runtime error

   (d) syntax error

13. Logic errors are often discovered by end users. True or False?

14. Desk checking is performed after you write code. True or False?

15. You can set a hit counter on a breakpoint to cause a program to pause after a loop executes a specific number of times. True or False?

16. Which debugging option would you use to execute each statement in a function or procedure?

   (a) Run to Cursor

   (b) Step Into

   (c) Step Out

   (d) Step Over

17. You can only add only a single expression to the Watch window. True or False?

Applying This Chapter

1. You are writing an application that will calculate annual savings account interest. Savings account interest is accrued monthly at 3%. Draw a flowchart to illustrate the program flow. What type of loop will you use when you create the code?

2. You are writing an application that will accept a user's sex and weight and return the recommended daily calorie intake, based on four different weight ranges for each sex. Write an algorithm for the problem. Which decision statements will you use when you create the code?

3. You are writing a program that converts measurements from English to metric units. Describe the importance of writing an algorithm and desk checking values before writing code.

4. You have written the code for an application that will calculate annual savings account interest (see Question 1). The program is generating an unexpected result. Describe how you will use Visual Studio debugging tools to resolve the problem.

YOU TRY IT

Writing and Desk Checking an Algorithm

You need to create a program that accepts the length of three sides of a triangle and determines whether the triangle is equilateral (i.e., all sides are equal), isosceles (i.e., two sides are equal), or scalene (i.e., no two sides are equal). It must also output the triangle's circumference. Write an algorithm to meet the requirements. Desk check the algorithm with values for all three types of triangles. Write the Visual Basic code, using TextBox controls for the input and output values.

Creating a Flowchart and Deciding on a Conditional Structure

You need to create a program that outputs weather advisories based on temperature and humidity. A heat advisory should be issued if the temperature is over 90 with humidity over 50%. A heat advisory should also be issued if the temperature is over 100, regardless of humidity. A cold advisory should be issued if the temperature is below 32 degrees, regardless of humidity. If no advisory is in effect, the program should output "Weather is nice." Create a flowchart to meet the requirements. Write the Visual Basic code, using TextBox controls for the input and output values.

Deciding on a Loop Structure

You are writing a program that must calculate the average high temperature over a week, a month, and a year. Data will be input to the program, using a GetDailyHighTemp function. The function accepts an Integer value between 1 and 365. How would you write this code using For…Next loops? How would you write this code using Do Until loops?

Locating and Fixing Runtime Errors

You are trying to fix a program written by another programmer. The program has a Calculate button that performs several calculations on two values entered in TextBox controls. The calculations are performed inside a While loop. When you enter 0 in both TextBox controls, the loop executes infinitely. Describe how you can determine the cause of the problem.

4

SAVING TIME WITH REUSABLE CODE

Starting Point

Go to www.wiley.com/college/petroutsos to assess your knowledge of functions, methods, object-oriented programming, and error handling. *Determine where you need to concentrate your effort.*

What You'll Learn in This Chapter

▲ Functions and procedures
▲ Variable scope and lifetime
▲ Object-oriented concepts and terminology
▲ .NET Framework objects
▲ Structured exception handling

After Studying This Chapter, You'll Be Able To

▲ Create functions and procedures to facilitate code reuse
▲ Pass arguments by value and by reference
▲ Identify the scope and lifetime of a variable
▲ Determine the most appropriate place to declare a variable
▲ Instantiate and use objects to reduce the amount of code you need to write
▲ Define and implement an exception-handling strategy to catch and handle exceptions

INTRODUCTION

As you design programs, you find that in many cases, a program needs to perform the same task over and over again or in response to different events. You also discover that certain tasks must be performed by multiple programs. These situations present opportunities to create code that can be reused by a program or by different programs. In the first section, you'll learn how to create functions and procedures that can be called from different places in a program. In the second section, you'll learn more about object-oriented programming and you'll be introduced to some important .NET Framework objects. In the final section, you'll learn how to use the Exception object to implement exception handling in an application.

4.1 Segmenting Code with Functions and Subprocedures

You are now ready to consider more complex programs that carry out a variety of activities. Creating projects for more complex situations requires that you use the Julius Caesar approach to programming: Divide and conquer! This means that instead of trying to think about the entire project all at one time, you should divide it up into pieces that are more easily programmed. You have already been doing this with the Visual Basic event procedures that you have been writing for controls on your forms. Each event procedure carries out a piece of the project, thus dividing the project into small pieces. For example, when you write an event procedure for the Click event of a button, you are taking care of that part of the overall project without having to worry about other controls and events.

   In this section, you'll learn how to create and use general procedures to divide a program into small chunks that are easier to debug and that can often be reused to reduce the amount of code you need to write. You will learn the difference between a function and a subprocedure. You will also learn how to pass information into and out of a procedure. Finally, you'll learn how to manage the scope and lifetime of variables.

4.1.1 Using General Procedures

Although event procedures are extremely useful in creating projects, each is associated with a particular event, and unless you remove the word Private that precedes an event procedure, the procedure is not available to other forms. There are likely to be many situations in which you will want to write code that is not associated with a particular event or that will be available to multiple forms or both. To do this, you need to use general (rather than event) procedures.

   A **general procedure** tells a project how to carry out a specific task that is not associated with an event. General procedures are general because they are not associated with any specific event or control and can be invoked by any part of a project allowed by their scope. General procedures must be defined in the Declaration region of the form class and then invoked elsewhere on the form. **Invoking,** or **calling,** a general procedure involves referring to it in another general or event procedure and causing its code to execute. For example, if you wrote a general procedure called FindMax to find the maximum value in a list, you could use FindMax in the code whenever you wanted it to find the maximum value. In comparison, an event procedure reacts to some event caused by the user or by the system.

General procedures are a form of **reusable code** because they can be invoked repeatedly throughout a project or saved and added to other projects where a specific task is required. Rather than writing the same code over again in each location, you could create a general procedure that is invoked every time you want to do the same task. For example, the general procedure FindMax mentioned earlier could be used in several different places in a project to find the maximum value in a list. It could also be saved and used in other projects where it is necessary to find the maximum value in a list.

Another reason for using a general procedure is to reduce the complexity of event procedures. Instead of placing all the input, output, and logic in an event procedure, it is possible to place some or all of the logic in one or more general procedures and then call the general procedures from the event procedure. This is another way of dividing up the work that can enable you to separately test and debug parts of an event procedure.

4.1.2 Types of General Procedures

There are two types of general procedures that the user can write and include in a project: subprocedures (also called subroutines) and function procedures. Figure 4-1 shows the relationship between event procedures and the two types of general procedures.

A **function procedure** (or more simply, a **function**) is similar to the built-in functions you have used. **Arguments** (i.e., data values passed from the calling procedure

Figure 4-1

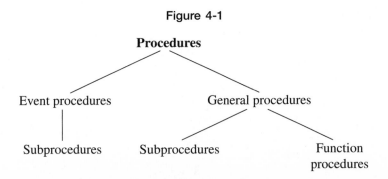

The relationship between general and event procedures.

to the called procedure) are passed to it and are processed to compute a single value that is returned through its name. The value returned is known as the **return value.** The FindMax general procedure discussed earlier should be written as a function because a single value—the maximum value in the list—is returned.

On the other hand, a **subprocedure** (hereafter referred to simply as a **sub**) is similar to an event procedure in that it is a unit of code that performs a specific task within a program but returns no value. Like an event procedure, a general subprocedure begins with the word Sub plus a name and ends with End Sub. Although it returns no value, a sub can have arguments passed to it, the values of which can be changed in the sub and passed back to the calling procedure. For example, a sub to sort a list of names will have the list and the number of names in the list passed to it, and those names will be rearranged in the sub and passed back. Figure 4-2 shows the primary purposes of subs and functions.

Note in Figure 4-2 that two of the arguments passed to the sub are modified by it, and one is not. It is possible for none, some, or all of the arguments to be modified by the sub. On the other hand, although it is possible to modify the arguments of a function, this is not its primary purpose, so none are modified in this example.

Whether to create a function or a sub depends on whether a single value is to be returned. If it is, then a function should be used; otherwise, a sub should be used. For example, if you are creating a general procedure that calculates the sales tax on an item and returns only the sales tax, you should create a function. However, if you are creating a procedure that changes the font of all controls on

Figure 4-2

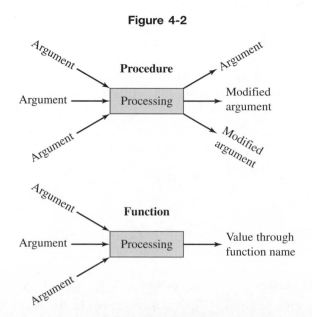

The primary purposes of subs and functions.

the form, that procedure does not return a value. Therefore, you should create a sub. Similarly, if you are creating a procedure that returns a city and state, based on a zip code, you should create a sub with three arguments: one that is not modified and two that are modified.

Designing a general procedure is much like designing an event procedure: You must decide what you want it to do, what the input and desired output are, and what logic is required to convert the input into the desired output. Input for a general procedure is usually through the arguments that pass values to it, but it is possible to use other forms of input. Similarly, output for a function is usually through its return value, and output from a sub is usually through the arguments. However, in both cases, it is possible to use other forms of output. Pseudocode is very important for developing the logic of a function or sub.

4.1.3 Adding Subs and Functions

To work with subs and functions, you must first add them to a project and then invoke them. To add a function or sub, you go to the end of any event or general procedure in the code window and press the Enter key to open a line. Then you enter the word Function or Sub plus the procedure name and press the Enter key to create the first and last lines of the general procedure. Next, you must include the list of parameters that will be used in the general procedure between the parentheses in the first line. **Parameters** are name and **type specifiers** (i.e., the keywords that define the parameters' data types) of data being passed to and from the general procedure. They are separated by commas and must include the data type in the same way as declaration statements do, using the As keyword.

The **Function definition statement** includes the name of the function followed by the list of parameters, with type specifiers. Also, because the name of the function returns a value, the name must be declared as a data type. The general form of the Function definition statement is as follows:

```
Function FuncName(param1 As type, _
    param2 As type,...) As type
```

For example, the Function definition statement for a function to accept two string parameters and return the number of characters in the longest string would look like this:

```
Function intMost(strWrd1 As String, strWrd2 As _
    String) As Integer
```

Note that this example uses a data type prefix for the function. This is done because functions return a value of a specific type, and using the data type prefix tells what type value will be returned. It is important to note that the parameter types and the type of the function don't have to be the same. In the example shown here, the parameters are Strings, and the value returned is an Integer.

An important rule for creating functions is that a function must return a value. You can ensure this by assigning a value to a function name or using a **Return statement.** In the first case, this means that the function name would appear on the left side of an assignment statement. For example, the following statement would assign a value to the function name in the intMost function example (and thus return the value stored in intLongWord to the calling procedure):

```
intMost= intLongWord
```

In the second case, the variable that contains the value to be returned must be included in the Return operation. For example, the following statement would return the value of intLongWord in the case of the intMost function:

```
Return(intLongWord)
```

Failure to assign a value to the function name or to return the value results in the function not returning a value.

Because a function returns a value, it is usually used on the right side of an assignment statement. Here's an example:

```
intNumChar = intMost("The Sun Also Rises", _
    "A Farewell to Arms")
```

The general form of the Sub definition statement is similar to that of the function definition statement, with the keyword Sub instead of Function:

```
Sub SubName (parameter1 as type, _
    parameter2 as type,...)
```

Note that there is no data type definition for a sub because it returns no value through the name. In fact, the name of a sub has no meaning other than to link the Sub definition statement to the statement invoking the sub. Because no value is returned through the sub name, it is incorrect to define a data type for the sub. For example, the following is the Sub procedure definition statement for a sub named Reverse that includes two parameters, decFirst and decSecond:

```
Sub Reverse(ByRef decFirst as Decimal, _
    ByRef decSecond as Decimal)
```

4.1.4 Invoking a Function or Sub

You invoke a function that you have written the same way you invoke a Visual Basic built-in function—by placing it on the right side of an assignment statement or by including it in any statement that would use a variable, such as a Debug.Writeline statement. In any case, you invoke the function by referring to the function name with the arguments in parentheses (where *arg1*, *arg2*, . . . , *argn* are the arguments passed to the function):

```
variable = functionName(arg1, arg2, ..., argn)
```

For example, if you have created the intMost function described earlier, you would write the following statement to invoke this function with two string variables (strOne and strTwo) and display the result in a text box (txtMostLetters):

```
txtMostLetters.Text = intMost(strOne, strTwo)
```

Note that here we are using implicit conversion to convert the return value of Integer to the String data type expected by the Text property. Another option would have been to use the CStr conversion function.

On the other hand, you invoke a sub by referring to its name and arguments in a separate line of code, with the arguments listed after the name, separated by commas. The arguments are enclosed in parentheses in the same way as they are with functions. The following is the general form for calling a sub:

```
subName(arg1, arg2,..., argn)
```

For example, assume that you have created the sub called Reverse, mentioned earlier, to reverse the values in two Decimal data type variables, decFirst and decSecond. After this sub is invoked, the variable decFirst is equal to the old value of decSecond, and decSecond is equal to the old value of decFirst. You would invoke Reverse as follows:

```
Reverse(decFirst, decSecond)
```

Matching Parameters and Arguments

The parameters in Function and Sub definition statements must match the arguments that appear in the statement that invokes the function or sub, in terms of position, number, and data type. That is, the first argument must match the first parameter, the second argument the second parameter, and so on. Similarly, the number of parameters should match the number of arguments. Finally, the data type of a parameter should match the data type of the corresponding argument. This is required because the parameters and arguments constitute the links between the definition statement and the statement invoking the function or sub.

You can define some parameters as optional by placing the **Optional keyword** in front of the corresponding parameter. If it is used, all parameters listed after the first Optional keyword must be optional, too. You must also identify a default value for any optional parameters. For example, to create a function that accepts a first name, a last name, and an optional middle initial, you declare the function as follows:

```
Function GetSalary(ByVal EmployeeFirstName As _
    String, ByVal EmployeeLastName As String, _
    Optional ByVal EmployeeMiddleInitial As _
    String = "")
```

For example, if there are three required parameters in a Sub definition statement, with the first two being Integer data types and the last one being a String data

Figure 4-3

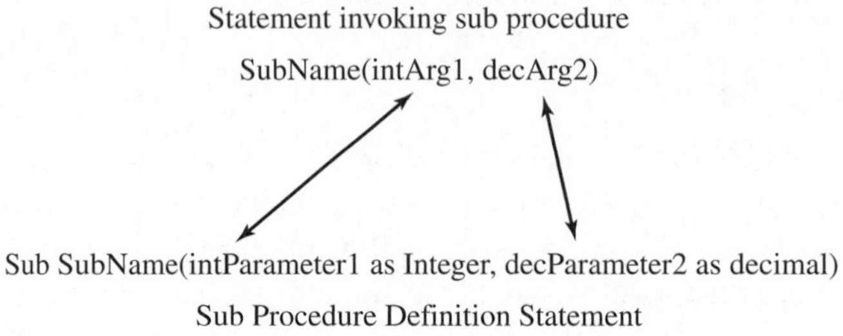

Statement invoking sub procedure

SubName(intArg1, decArg2)

Sub SubName(intParameter1 as Integer, decParameter2 as decimal)

Sub Procedure Definition Statement

The relationship between Sub and parameters.

type, then there must be three arguments in the statement invoking the sub, with the first two being integers and the third one being a string.

Figure 4-3 shows the relationship between the Sub definition statement and the statement that invokes the sub. In this figure, the name of the sub (SubName) must be the same in the statement that invokes the sub and in the Sub definition statement. Also, the number of arguments must match the number of parameters, and their types must match. That is, the first argument (*arg1*) must be an Integer data type, and the second argument (*arg2*) must a Decimal data type.

This type of argument/parameter matching holds for functions as well. This is shown in Figure 4-4 for a function that has one Integer parameter and one Decimal parameter and returns a Single data type value.

You have undoubtedly noticed in the examples so far that the variable names used as parameters in the functions and subs are not the same as the names used in the argument list. The reason for this is that the parameter names are local variables in the sub or function to which the values of the corresponding arguments are passed from the arguments in the invoking sub or function. This means that the same sub and function can be used with different arguments as long as the arguments match the parameters. For example, you could use the

Figure 4-4

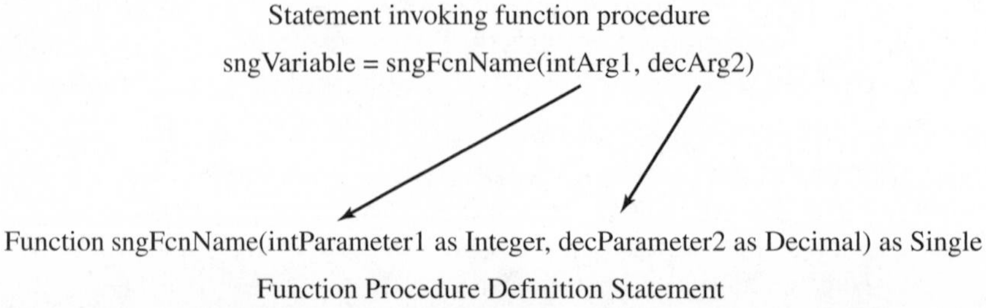

Statement invoking function procedure

sngVariable = sngFcnName(intArg1, decArg2)

Function sngFcnName(intParameter1 as Integer, decParameter2 as Decimal) as Single

Function Procedure Definition Statement

The relationship between a Function definition statement and a statement that invokes a function.

Reverse sub shown earlier to reverse another pair of Decimal values by calling it with a different set of arguments, as shown here:

```
Reverse(decMySalary, decYourSalary)
```

Passing by Value or by Reference

As mentioned earlier, parameters in functions and subs are local variables that correspond to arguments passed in the invoking statement. These values can be passed in one of two ways: by value or by reference.

Passing by value means that argument values are passed into a sub or function but not passed out; that is, the passing is a one-way street, and the arguments are protected from being changed in the sub or function. When a parameter is defined as being passed by value in a sub or function, it becomes a local variable in the sub that is initialized to the value of the corresponding argument. In essence, it is a local copy of the argument that cannot leave the sub. An argument that is passed by value can be a variable, a constant, or a literal value.

On the other hand, **passing by reference** means that the argument in the calling procedure and the parameter in the sub or function occupy the same memory location. When a parameter variable is modified within the sub, the corresponding argument variable is also modified. The argument/parameter pair creates a two-way communication link between the sub or function and the statement that invokes it. Changes to a parameter inside the procedure are communicated back to the corresponding variable outside the procedure. You must use a variable when passing an argument by reference.

Let's look at a code example that demonstrates the difference between passing by reference and passing by value. In this example, we'll look again at the earlier example of creating a procedure that returns a city and state based on a zip code. Here is the procedure declaration:

```
Sub LocateCityAndState(ByVal ZipCode As Integer, _
    ByRef city As String, ByRef state As String)
    Select Case ZipCode
        Case 95120
            city = "San Jose"
            state = "California"
        Case 60601
            city = "Chicago"
            state = "Illinois"
    End Select
End Sub
```

Of course, only a subset of the zip codes you would need to support is shown, but you get the idea. Now let's look at the code to call the sub:

```
Dim strCity As String
Dim strState As String
```

```
Dim intZipCode As Integer

intZipCode = CInt(txtZipCode.Text)
LocateCityAndState(intZipCode, strCity, strState)
txtCity.Text = strCity
txtState.Text = strState
```

In this example, if a user entered 95120 into txtZipCode and then caused the code to execute, the txtCity.Text property would be set to "San Jose", and the txtState.Text property would be set to "California". This is because the variables strCity and strState are passed by reference. Therefore, they can be changed by the code in the Sub.

Passing by value is preferred when there is no need to communicate to the corresponding argument changes to variables inside a procedure. This is almost always the case with a function because the name of the function is assigned to the result of processing in the function. On the other hand, it is often useful to pass variables by reference in subs. For example, in the Reverse sub discussed earlier, passing by reference would be required to change the values of the arguments.

Passing by value is the default way to pass arguments when using Visual Basic. This is indicated by the fact that whenever a sub or function is created, the keyword, ByVal, is automatically inserted prior to every parameter in the sub or Function definition statement, as shown here:

```
Function intGetTotal(ByVal param1 As Integer) _
    As Integer
```

For this reason, the arrows in Figure 4-3 and Figure 4-4 are one way from the invoking statements to the procedure definition statements. Although passing by value is the default method, it is easy to change to passing by reference by simply changing the procedure definition, as in this example:

```
Sub Reverse(ByRef decOne As Decimal, ByRef decTwo _
    As Decimal)
```

4.1.5 Scope and Lifetime

Variables declared in a procedure are referred to as **local** or **procedure-level variables,** and they are protected from being accessed by other procedures. Within a procedure, it is possible to declare **block variables** in a block of statements, such as a decision block or a loop. Block variables are only "known" within that block, but local variables are known everywhere in the procedure.

You can also declare a local variable to be static. A **static variable** is one that retains its value between executions of a procedure. The period of execution over which a variable retains its value is known as its **lifetime.** Normally, a local variable is reset to its default value between events, but when it is declared static, the variable retains its value until the project is terminated. The form of the static declaration statement is:

```
Static variable as type
```

Figure 4-5

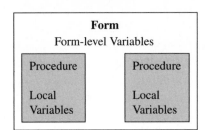

Variable scope.

Outside a procedure, variables can be declared as form-level variables such that all event procedures that are a part of the form are aware of them. This concept is shown in Figure 4-5 for a single form where both procedures know about the form-level variables.

If the same variable is declared at both the form level and the procedure level, the procedure-level declaration overrides the form-level declaration. It is therefore important to avoid double-declaring variables.

If multiple forms need to know about a variable, then this needs to be declared at the project level, using a module. These variables are known as **global variables.** Procedures can also be made available to all the modules in a project by using a module. These are known as **global procedures.** You can also declare constants and enumerations in the module to make them available to all forms in a project.

The **module** is a section of pure code that is known to all forms in a project. It contains only declarations and general procedures—no controls or event procedures. Figure 4-6 shows the concept of scope for global, form-level, and

Figure 4-6

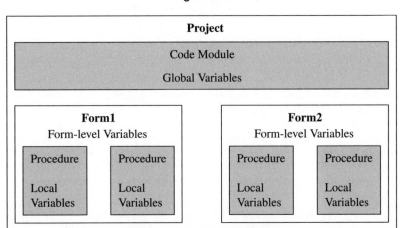

The scope of global variables.

procedure-level variables. In each case, the elements below a variable declaration know about those variables. That is, procedures know about the form-level variables, and the forms and procedures all know about the global variables. This is a way of protecting variables from inadvertent contamination.

You add a module to a project by selecting Project and then Add Module menu and then selecting the Module template. The module has a .vb extension, just like the forms you have already added. The only indication that a module has been added is the addition of the module name to the Solution Explorer window, beneath any existing forms, and the appearance of a blank code window with the module filename in the title bar. As with any other object, you can rename a module in the Properties window, and it is saved along with other files when you save all files.

The actual declaration of global variables occurs in the Declarations area of the module between the Module and End Module blocks. Initially, this is the procedure in the module, so it is the one that is automatically displayed when you add the module or select it from the Solution Explorer window. Declaring a variable globally is just like declaring it at the form level or control level, except that you use the keyword Public instead of the keyword Dim in the declaration. The general form for globally declaring variables is:

```
Public varName1 As type
```

For example, if you wanted to declare an Integer data type variable intNumMembers so that it would be known to all forms and procedures in a project, you would use the following statement in a module:

```
Module Module1
    Public intNumMembers as Integer
End Module
```

You can also declare a Public variable inside a form to allow it to be referenced by other forms. A variable declared as Public at the form level can be accessed using the syntax:

```
formName.variablename
```

In this case, *formName* is a variable that holds a reference to a form. You'll learn more about references later in the chapter.

Although declaring variables globally is necessary for multiple forms to know about them, declaring a variable globally means that any changes to that variable in a procedure changes it everywhere in the project. In other words, you must be careful when you change a global variable because the change may have far-reaching effects.

When global variables are declared globally in the module, it is not necessary or even useful to declare them again in a general procedure or an event procedure. In fact, if a global variable is declared again in any type of procedure, all values are zeroed out when the procedure is executed, and the procedure will not know about the contents of the global variables. For this reason, after a variable is declared globally, declaring the same variable locally in a procedure is generally a bad idea and could lead to bugs that are difficult to isolate and fix.

Why pass variables to a general procedure rather than just declare everything as global variables? There are two reasons for passing variables instead of using global variables. First, if you use global variables instead of passing variables, there is the possibility of inadvertently changing a global variable within a procedure. Second, if you use global variables instead of passing variables, subs or functions cannot be used in multiple locations in the project. You use the same technique for declaring a global function, sub, constant, or enumeration: You simply precede the declaration with the Public keyword. For example, to declare the Reverse sub as a global sub, you use this declaration:

```
Public Sub Reverse(ByRef num1 As Integer, _
    ByRef num2 As Integer)
```

FOR EXAMPLE

Dividing a Program into Functions and Procedures

Say that you are writing a program that will calculate total sales and average sales per region for a specific time period and report the region with the highest average sales and the region with the lowest average sales. Sales data is stored in a file. Two forms in the application require these calculations.

You decide to create a function named GetTotalSales that returns a data type of Decimal. The function will accept two ByVal parameters of type Date. You create a Code module and declare the function as follows:

```
Public Function GetTotalSales(ByVal startDate As _
    Date, ByVal endDate As Date) As Decimal
```

You also create a sub named GetAverageSales that accepts two ByVal parameters and three ByRef parameters. You declare the function in the code module as follows:

```
Public Sub GetAverageSales(ByVal startDate As _
    Date, ByVal endDate As Date, ByRef AverageSales _
    As Decimal, ByRef LowSalesRegion As String, _
    ByRef HighSalesRegion As String)
```

(Continued)

You call the functions from the btnSalesData_Click event procedure, using the following code:

```
Dim decTotalSales As Decimal
Dim decAverageSales As Decimal
Dim strLowSales As String
Dim strHighSales As String

decTotalSales = _
    GetTotalSales(CDate(txtStartDate.Text), _
    CDate(txtEndDate.Text))
GetAverageSales(CDate(txtStartDate.Text), _
    CDate(txtEndDate.Text), _decAverageSales, _
    strLowSales, strHighSales)
```

The code works as expected. In another form, you want to use the GetAverageSales sub to report only decAverageSales. You want to avoid declaring variables that will not be used. You change the sub procedure definition as follows:

```
Public Sub GetAverageSales(ByVal startDate As _
    Date, ByVal endDate As Date, ByRef AverageSales _
    As Decimal, Optional ByRef LowSalesRegion _
    As String = "", Optional ByRef HighSalesRegion _
    As String="")
```

SELF-CHECK

- Identify a situation in which you would create a function.
- Identify a situation in which you would create a sub that has only parameters passed by value.
- Identify a situation in which you would create a sub that has only parameters passed by reference.
- Describe the purpose of a Code module.

4.2 Object-Oriented Programming

Why is it necessary to understand objects? Objects are the fundamental concept behind an entire programming methodology known as **object-oriented programming (OOP).** OOP arose from the need to model real-world objects in simulation programs. This methodology is easier to work with because it is more intuitive than traditional programming methods, which divide programs into hierarchies and separate data from programming code.

To understand why objects are extremely valuable programming tools, it is necessary to understand that all programs consist of data that requires processing and procedures for processing that data. As long as the data and procedures remain the same, the program works; however, if either the data or the procedures change, the program may not work. OOP transforms programming by binding data and procedures in objects. A primary advantage of objects is that once created, they can be reused many times. Users can combine objects with relative ease to create new systems and extend existing ones. Around us is a world made of objects, so the use of objects to create information systems provides a natural approach to programming.

4.2.1 Visual Basic Objects

If you think about it, you have been using many objects already. The controls that you add to a form can be called visual objects (i.e., objects that can be seen on the screen). These visual objects include data in the form of the property values that you set. They also include program code both in the event procedures that you write and in the methods that are built in with the control. Finally, what sets controls apart from other objects is that they usually have a graphical user interface that allows the user to interact with the control object by causing events.

As you may have noticed, however, Visual Basic is not restricted to visual objects; objects that are not displayed onscreen can also be used. In very general terms, the term *object* can refer to almost any piece of data or code in an application, including variables, controls, and procedures. For example, a variable that has been declared as a String data type is actually an instance of an object class called String. The String variable can hold data such as the current variable value and the length of the string held in the Length property. The String variable can also execute several methods, such as the Insert method, which inserts a string value at a specified index position in this String variable, or the Start method, which determines whether the beginning of the String variable matches a specified string of characters. In general, nonvisual objects cannot be accessed by the user. They only appear in lines of program code.

In fact, Visual Basic comes with a huge library of objects that you can include and use in programs. In addition, Visual Basic enables you to create and use your own objects. Commonly referred to as **application objects,** these are objects that you as a programmer can use to improve the efficiency of a project. Like visual objects, application objects have both properties and methods.

4.2.2 OOP Concepts

To work with objects in Visual Basic (or any other computer language), it is necessary to understand some basic concepts. First, an object can be anything about

Figure 4-7

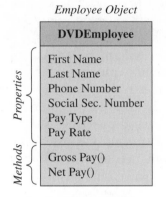

Employee Object

An Employee object.

which you want to capture information—things, people, places, events, and even ideas. For example, an object that is important to a payroll application is the Employee object. Objects include properties and methods. Properties contain data that describes information about an object. Data such as the employee's last and first names, phone number, Social Security number, pay time, and pay rate may be stored as properties of the Employee object. Methods correspond to actions that the object can perform. An Employee object could include methods such as GrossPay and NetPay. A model of such an Employee object is shown in Figure 4-7.

In order to create an object, you must first create a class. A *class* is a template with data and procedures from which objects are created. Every object is associated with a class. The class defines the properties, methods, and events that can be used by consumers of the class. It also provides an implementation of the properties and methods. All the actual work in creating an object is accomplished in creating the class; you create an object by defining it to be an instance of a class. A class often includes **member variables,** which are variables that have a scope and limited to code within the class itself. The relationship between a class, an object, and an instance is illustrated in Figure 4-8.

An example of a visual class is a form that you create: You can use it to create new forms with the same characteristics as the class form. Similarly, the controls in the toolbox are classes from which you can create instances on a form.

All object-oriented languages, including Visual Basic, incorporate three important concepts, known as the "pillars of OOP." The first pillar, encapsulation, refers to how well the language hides the internal implementation of an object. It should never be possible to work with member variables directly; they

Figure 4-8

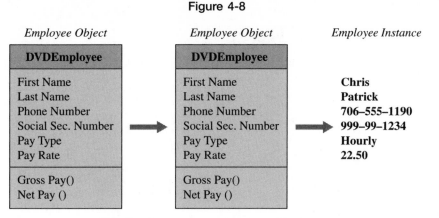

The Employee class, object, and instance.

must be addressed through the object's properties and methods. Encapsulation is also known as **data hiding** or **information hiding**. This implies a **black-box view** of an object, in which the programmer does not need to know what is going on inside the object but only needs to know how to work with the object's methods and properties. For example, you have been using text boxes without knowing exactly how the Text property displays the string onscreen; you just know that it does.

The second pillar in OOP, inheritance, refers to the capability to create classes that descend from other classes—so-called subclasses. Inheritance is key in allowing for code reuse. This capability makes it easier to build a new class by having it inherit properties and methods from another class. With inheritance, a class usually has an "is-a" relationship with its heir. For example, suppose the payroll application needs to support two types of employees—hourly and salaried. Both of the types of employees will inherit certain properties and methods from a more general type of employee. In this relationship, the higher-level class, such as Employee, is known as the **parent class,** and the subclass, DVDEmployee, is known as the **child class.** The child class is said to *inherit* all properties and methods from the parent class. This relationship is illustrated in Figure 4-9.

The third pillar of OOP is polymorphism. Using polymorphism, you can create child classes that perform the same functions found in the parent class, but the child class may perform one or more of those functions in a different way. For example, the DVDEmployee class will inherit the GrossPay method from the more general Employee class. With Polymorphism, you can redefine the GrossPay method in the DVDEmployee class so that a new DVD employee can, say, receive overtime for more than 35 hours instead of the standard

Figure 4-9

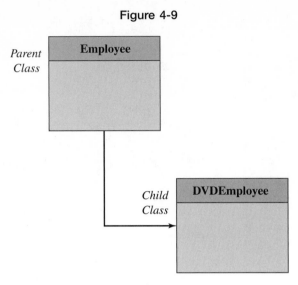

Inheritance.

40 hours per week. An example of this type of polymorphism is illustrated in Figure 4-10.

4.2.3 Namespaces

As mentioned earlier, a huge number of object classes are provided as part of the .NET Framework. The **.NET Framework Class Library (FCL)** is a compre-

Figure 4-10

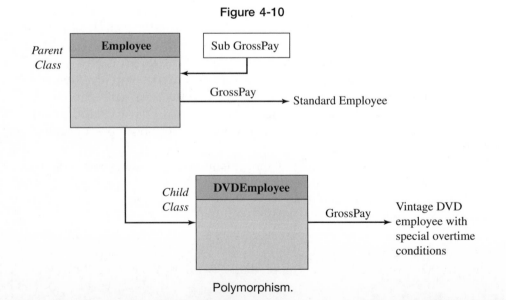

Polymorphism.

hensive, object-oriented collection of reusable types that you can use in applications. Like your local library, the .NET FCL is organized into categories and subcategories. For example, your local library may be organized into sections such as fiction, nonfiction, and periodicals. Further, the fiction section may have various subsections, such as mystery, romance, science fiction, and others. This not only helps the library to organize the volumes and allows you to find the volumes more easily, but it also allows you to make a distinction between books that have the same title but are of different types. (One thing to note is that the .NET FCL is the .NET Framework library and not the Visual Basic library. This means that the .NET FCL is available for all .NET-compatible languages and not just Visual Basic.)

In the .NET FCL, the categories are known as namespaces. Formally, a **namespace** is a logical naming scheme that the .NET Framework uses to group related types, classes, and objects under a distinct umbrella. For example, the System.Data namespace includes classes that may be used for database manipulation. A namespace allows you to uniquely identify a class, even if a class with the same name is available in multiple namespaces.

When you start creating a Visual Basic project, several namespaces are referenced automatically. To see some of these, you can open a project in Visual Studio, open the View menu, select Class View, and click the plus (+) sign next to the References folder. You should see a list of .NET FCL namespaces that can be referenced by a project similar to the one shown in Figure 4-11.

Figure 4-11

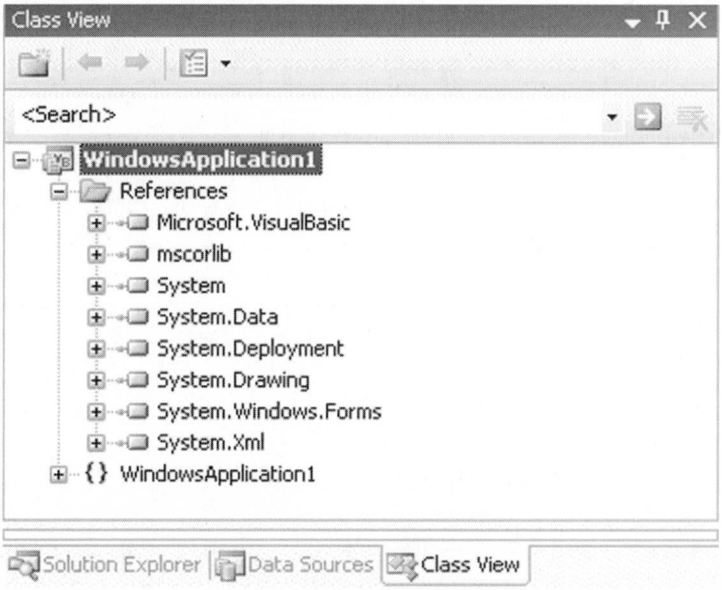

Default references.

Some common namespaces that may be referenced in an application are described as follows in the Visual Studio help system:

▲ **System:** This namespace contains fundamental classes and base classes that define commonly used value and reference data types, events and event handlers, interfaces, attributes, and processing exceptions.

▲ **System.IO:** This namespace contains classes that are used for input and output operations, such as StreamReader and StreamWriter.

▲ **System.Data:** This namespace consists mostly of the classes that constitute the ADO.NET architecture. The ADO.NET architecture enables you to build components that efficiently manage data from multiple data sources, such as a database.

▲ **System.Drawing:** This namespace provides access to GDI+ basic graphics functionality.

▲ **System.Windows.Forms:** This namespace contains classes for creating Windows-based applications that take advantage of the user interface features available in the Microsoft Windows operating system.

▲ **System.XML:** This namespace provides standards-based support for processing XML.

Besides the namespaces that are already included in a project, you can use additional namespaces from the .NET FCL. To do this, you use the **Imports keyword.** For example, if you want to use an object from the System.Collections namespace, which contains interfaces and classes that define various collections of objects, you include the following statement in your code:

```
Imports System.Collections
```

You can then declare in the program objects that are instances of classes within this namespace.

Other namespaces can exist and be used besides those that are defined as part of the .NET FCL. For example, every executable file you create with Visual Basic automatically contains a namespace with the same name as your project. Each object that you create within the project will then be included in this namespace. For example, if you define an object within a project named MyNewProject, the executable file, MyNewProject.exe, contains a namespace called MyNewProject. This particular namespace is known as the **root namespace.**

As you create classes of your own, you can also create your own custom namespaces in which to group them. This is easy to do: You simply create them in a single project that you name using the desired namespace title. For instance, if you create your class in a program that you call MyClasses, this creates a corresponding root namespace of the same name that you can include in any of your projects.

4.2.4 Declaring and Using Objects

After a class is created, the next steps are to declare an object, using the class name as the data type, and to use that object. Objects can be declared at any level, just like variables, with one major difference: The **New keyword** is used to denote an object as a new object from a class rather than as a variable declaration. Using the New keyword to create an instance of an object is called **instantiation.** The following is the general form of this declaration statement:

```
Dim objectname As New classname
```

For example, you use the following statement to declare an object called objShowingEmp of the class DVDEmployee:

```
Dim objShowingEmp As New DVDEmployee
```

If a class with the same name exists in multiple namespaces used by a project, you need to declare the object by using the **fully qualified name.** The fully qualified name includes the namespace. For example, this is the fully qualified name of the Form object:

```
System.Windows.Forms.Form
```

It is a class named Form in the System.Windows.Forms namespace.

You can also declare an object variable and instantiate it later. For example, you might want to declare a form-level variable of type DVDEmployee but not actually create an instance of the variable until an event procedure is executed. To do so, you simply use an assignment statement with the New keyword, as follows:

```
Dim objShowingEmp As DVDEmployee
objShowingEmp = New DVDEmployee
```

Some classes also allow you to pass arguments when instantiating an object of that class. For example, DVDEmployee might allow you to pass an employee ID. In this case, you could instantiate the object as follows:

```
objShowingEmp = New DVDEmployee(intEmployeeID)
```

One important point to remember is that a variable that has been declared as a specific class or of the generic Object type does not actually store the object instance. Instead, it stores a **reference** (i.e., a pointer to the location in memory) to the data. This means you can have multiple object variables, all referencing the same object in memory, as in the following example:

```
Dim objEmp1 As DVDEmployee
Dim objEmp2 As New DVDEmployee
objEmp1 = objEmp2
```

In this example, objEmp1 and objEmp2 reference the same instance of the object.

After an application object has been declared, its properties are used in much the same way as those of visual objects. That is, properties are assigned values, and variables are assigned object properties. Also, an application's object methods are used to process data and return values, in a manner similar to that used by visual objects.

4.2.5 Using Shared Classes

A **shared class** is a class that you can use without instantiating it. The .NET FCL includes several shared classes. One of them is the Math class, which has a number of methods that allow you to perform common calculations, such as trigonometric functions, determining a square root, truncating and rounding numbers, and determining the larger or smaller of two integers. It also defines the constants pi and e, which are accessed as properties. To access a method or property of a shared class, you use the class name, a period, and the method name. For example, to retrieve the lower of two values stored in variables val1 and val2, you execute this:

```
Lower = Math.Min(val1, val2)
```

FOR EXAMPLE

Using Objects

Say that you are working on a team to develop an application that models chemical research data. Another programmer has given you an assembly that includes two classes: a shared class named Elementals that includes a number of functions that return data about elements and a standard class named Compound that is used to track data about a specific compound. The two classes are in the namespace Chemistry.

To make the classes available to a project, you execute this statement:

```
Imports Chemistry
```

Next, you declare a form-level variable of type Compound, using this statement:

```
Private cmpResearch As Compound
```

In a procedure that uses the two classes, you instantiate the cmpResearch variable and access the shared Elementals class directly:

```
cmpResearch = New Compound
cmpResearch.CompoundName = txtCompound.Text
dblSpecificGravity = _
    Elementals.GetSpecificGravity(cmpResearch)
```

In this example, the Compound object implements a property named CompoundName of type String, and the Elementals class implements a method named GetDensity that accepts a Compound object and returns a Double.

- Which pillar of OOP prevents you from accessing a member variable directly?
- Describe a situation in which you would use the Imports statement.
- Assume that AccountingFormulas is a class with a method named ProfitMargin. You execute profit margin by using this code:

```
AccountingFormulas.ProfitMargin
```

What do you know about the AccountingFormulas class?

4.3 Catching Errors Before They Catch You

A good deal of the code you will write will likely be designed to handle errors. More than half of a professional application's code validates data and handles possible errors. Most error-handling code is never executed. Users aren't supposed to enter a discount percentage that exceeds 100 percent or a future birth date. These things aren't supposed to happen, and they might never happen. However, you must validate the discount's value from within your code and not proceed with your calculations until the user supplies a valid value. Note that a valid value is not necessarily the correct value, but there's nothing you can do about that. Consider an application that performs static calculations. The individual parameters supplied by the user might be correct, but when they're combined, the calculations might fail (i.e., the calculations might produce results that don't make sense). No parameter is in error, but the parameters are incompatible with one another. For example, they might result in a division by zero, the calculation of the square root of a negative value, and so on. Your task is to detect this condition in your code and allow users to revise their data rather than allow the application to crash.

The situation just described can't be handled with data validation because you discover a problem with the data only after you attempt to use it in some calculations. Another type of error you can't prevent with data validation is an error caused by the hardware itself. The disk might be full when you attempt to save a large file, or the drive you're accessing might be disconnected. When your application runs into a situation like this, it should be able to detect the error and handle it.

4.3.1 About Exceptions

To handle errors that surface at runtime, you use structured exception handlers. Exceptions that are handled from within the application's code are called **handled**

Figure 4-12

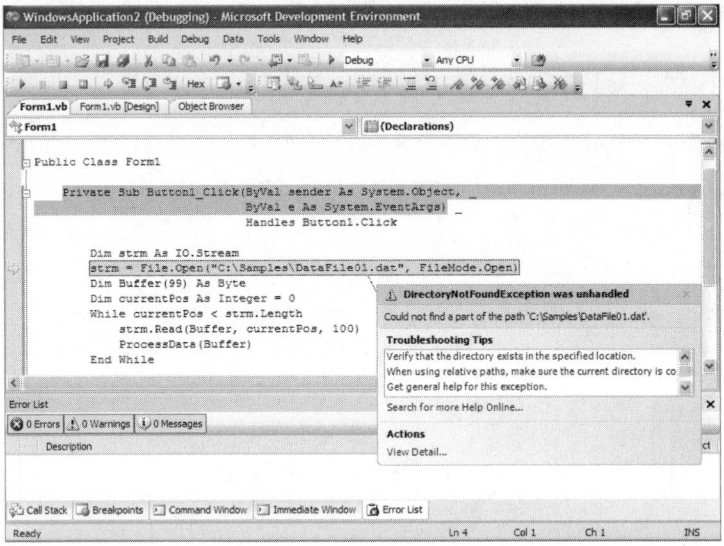

An exception message in the IDE.

exceptions, and they result in robust applications. Exceptions that are not handled from within code are called **unhandled exceptions,** and they lead to program crashes. (In effect, the Common Language Runtime [CLR] handles these errors in a rather crude manner.)

Figure 4-12 shows an example of an exception message. This is the dialog box that appears when you are running a program in the IDE. The statement that is in error is highlighted, and a box with the error's description appears. The troubleshooting tips that appear in this dialog box provide hints as to what might have caused the exception and, in many cases, suggestions about how to correct the error.

If the same error were to be encountered by a user running your program, the dialog box would look slightly different, as shown in Figure 4-13.

Normally, the Details section of the dialog box isn't shown, but Figure 4-13 shows the type of information that is displayed if the user clicks Details. If you scroll the Details text to the right, you see the number of the line in the source code that caused the runtime exception. Note that this dialog box gives the user the opportunity to continue the program. In some rare cases, this might be desirable, but in most cases, you probably do not want users attempting to continue after a program exception has occurred. Think about it: Your program has just encountered some form of data that it cannot handle correctly, and now it is asking the user whether it should attempt to ignore that bad data and continue. It is difficult to predict what type of further problems might result as the program continues on and attempts to handle the bad data. Most likely, further

Figure 4-13

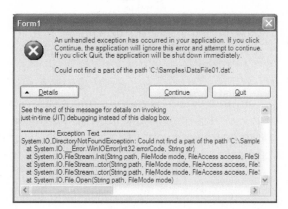

An unhandled exception message at runtime.

exceptions will be generated as the subsequent lines of code attempt to deal with the same unexpected data.

If you don't want your users handling an exception that the program generates, you have to handle it yourself. The Visual Basic error-handling model allows you to do just that. An **error handler** is a section of Visual Basic code that allows you to detect exceptions and take the necessary steps to recover from them. Let's look at some exception-handling code examples.

The exception dialog boxes shown in Figures 4-12 and 4-13 were generated by a statement that attempts to open a file that doesn't exist:

```
strm = File.Open("C:\Samples\DataFile01.dat", _
    FileMode.Open)
```

Sometimes, the description of the error isn't this obvious. Consider the following, which also results in a runtime exception:

```
Private Sub Button2_Click(ByVal sender As _
    System.Object, ByVal e As System.EventArgs) _
    Handles Button2.Click
    Dim s As String
    s = "answer"
    Label1.Text = s.Substring(10, 1)
End Sub
```

This code is attempting to display the 11th character in the string "answer", using the Substring method of the String class. Because the word *answer* contains only 6 characters, an exception is generated. You can examine the exact phrasing of the exception to learn as much as possible about this particular error:

```
An unhandled exception of type
'System.ArgumentOutOfRangeException' occurred in
mscorlib.dll
```

```
Additional information: Index and length must refer
to a location within the string.
```

You should always thoroughly read the exceptions that a program generates. Their purpose is to give you a brief description of the condition that caused the error, and of course you need to know that before you can figure out how to handle the error. The first thing to notice is the fact that this message refers to this runtime error as an unhandled exception. This means that the line of code that generated this error is not contained within an exception-handling block.

The second interesting piece of information is that this exception is of type System.ArgumentOutOfRangeException. What's important to note about this is that the different types of errors can be classified in groups. This is important when you realize that the .NET Framework exception-handling mechanism follows the same object-oriented design principles that the rest of the .NET Framework follows.

An exception creates an instance of an object, and that object is a descendent of class Exception. The previous error message is telling you that the Exception object instance generated is of class (i.e., type) System.ArgumentOutOfRangeException, which is a descendent of class Exception.

The "additional information" block gives some specific notes on the nature of the error: It tells you that the index and length parameters of the Substring method must both lie within the boundaries of the string. In this case, you attempted to retrieve the 11th character of a 6-character string, which was clearly outside the boundary.

4.3.2 Structured Exception Handling

The following code is the same defective code statement you saw earlier, but with a simple **exception handler** wrapped around it:

```
Private Sub Button2_Click(ByVal sender As _
    System.Object, ByVal e As System.EventArgs) _
    Handles Button2.Click
    Dim s As String
    s = "answer"
    Try
        Label1.Text = s.Substring(10, 1)
    Catch
        Label1.Text = "error"
    End Try
End Sub
```

This code attempts to do the same thing as the preceding code, but this time, the faulty Substring statement is wrapped inside a **Try...Catch...End Try block.** This block is a basic exception handler. Using a Try...Catch...End Try block is known as **structured exception handling.** If any of the code after the Try statement generates an exception, program control automatically jumps to the code after the Catch statement. If no exceptions are generated in the code under the

Try statement, the Catch block is skipped. When this code is run, System.Argu-
mentOutOfRangeException is generated, but now the code does not terminate
with a message box. Instead, the text property of Label1 is set to the word "error",
and the program continues.

The following code handles the same error in a slightly different way:

```
Private Sub Button2_Click(ByVal sender As _
    System.Object, ByVal e As System.EventArgs) _
    Handles Button2.Click
    Dim s As String
    s = "answer"
    Try
        Label1.Text = s.Substring(10, 1)
    Catch oEX As Exception
        Call MsgBox(oEX.Message)
    End Try
End Sub
```

In this example, the exception generates an instance of the Exception class and
places that instance in a variable named oEX. Having the exception variable is
useful because it can give you the text of the exception, which is displayed in a
message box in this case. Of course, displaying the exception message in a message box is pretty much the same thing that your program does when an unhandled exception is generated, so it's doubtful that you would do this in your own
program. However, you could log the exception text to the event log or a custom error file. Using the Call statement is an alternative way to call a subprocedure (in this case, the MsgBox sub).

Note that the exception handlers do not differentiate between types of errors.
If any exception is generated within the Try block, the Catch block is executed.
You can also write exception handlers that handle different classes of errors, as
shown in the following code:

```
Private Sub Button3_Click(ByVal sender _
    As System.Object, ByVal e As System.EventArgs) _
    Handles Button3.Click
    Try
        Label1.Text = lbStates.SelectedItem.ToString
    Catch oEX As System.NullReferenceException
        Call MsgBox("Please select an item first")
    Catch oEX As Exception
        Call MsgBox("Some other error:" _
            & oEX.Message)
    End Try
End Sub
```

This code attempts to read the selected item in a ListBox control named lbStates
and display it as the caption of a Label control. If no item is selected in the list
box, System.NullReferenceException is generated, and you use that information

to tell the user to select an item in the list box. If any other type of exception is generated, this code displays the text of that error message. In the list of exceptions, the more specific exception handler comes first, and the more general exception handler comes last. You should code all your multiple Catch exception handlers this way so that they are handled in the correct order. If you put your more general Catch handlers first, they will execute first and override the more specific handlers. Also note that the variable oEX is reused in each of the exception blocks, which is possible because the Catch statement actually serves as a declaration of that variable, and the oEX variable has a local scope only within the Catch block.

Note that because the exception instance is declared in each Catch block, it has scope only within that block. The following code is illegal for scoping reasons:

```
Private Sub Button3_Click(ByVal sender As _
    System.Object, ByVal e As System.EventArgs) _
    Handles Button3.Click
    Try
        Button3.Text = lbStates.SelectedItem.ToString
    Catch oEX As System.NullReferenceException
        Call MsgBox("please select an item first")
    Catch oEX As Exception
        Call MsgBox("some other error")
    End Try
    MsgBox(oEX.message)
End Sub
```

The final MsgBox is not valid because the oEX variable that it attempts to display is not in scope at this point in the procedure. The scope of the two oEX variables is restricted in their Catch blocks.

You can avoid the NullReferenceException altogether by making sure the user has selected an item on the ListBox control with a few statements like the following:

```
If lbStates.SelectedItems.Count = 0 Then
    MsgBox _
        ("Please select a state on the States list!")
    Exit Sub
End If
```

This If statement doesn't attempt to process the state unless the user has already selected a state in the lbStates control. If the user has not selected a state, the event handler is terminated, without taking any action.

4.3.3 Using a Finally Block

When an exception is generated and handled by a Catch statement, the code execution is immediately transferred to the first relevant Catch exception handler block and then continues on out of the Try...Catch...End

Try block. Sometimes, it might be necessary to perform some cleanup before moving out of the exception-handling block. Consider the following procedure:

```
Sub ReadFromATextFile(cFilename as String)
    Dim s As StreamReader
    Dim cLine As String
    Dim bDone As Boolean = False
    lbresults.Items.Clear()
    s = New StreamReader(cFilename)
    Try
        While Not bDone
            cLine = s.ReadLine()
            If cLine Is Nothing Then
                bDone = True
            Else
                Call lbresults.Items.Add(cLine)
            End If
        End While
        s.Close()
    Catch oEX as Exception
        Call MsgBox("some error occurred")
    End Try
End Sub
```

This method uses an instance of the **StreamReader class** (a class used to read from a file) to attempt to read the contents of a text file and put the results into a ListBox control, line by line. Most of the reading code is wrapped within a generic exception handler. If an exception is encountered in the main loop, the s.Close() line will in all likelihood not be executed. This means that the file stream will never be properly closed, possibly leading to problems.

Fortunately, there is an additional type of block available in exception handlers that specifically allows you to avoid this type of problem. This block is called the **Finally block.** The code within a Finally block always executes, whether an exception is generated or not. The code that follows is the same as the method you saw earlier but has now been modified to wrap the s.Close method inside a Finally block:

```
Protected Sub ReadFromATextFile(cFilename as string)
    Dim s As StreamReader
    Dim cLine As String
    Dim bDone As Boolean = False
    lbresults.Items.Clear()
    s = New Streamreader(cFilename)
    Try
        While Not bDone
            cLine = s.ReadLine()
            If cLine Is Nothing Then
```

```
            bDone = True
        Else
            Call lbresults.Items.Add(cLine)
        End If
    End While
Catch oEX as Exception
    Call MsgBox("some error occurred")
Finally
    s.Close()
End Try
End Sub
```

Here, you see that any exception within the file-reading loop will be handled with a message box and then the StreamReader object will be closed inside the Finally block. This close statement runs whether the code within the Try...Catch block succeeds or fails. It allows you to guarantee that certain resources are properly disposed of when they are no longer needed.

One thing you need to be cautious of is closing in the Finally block resources that have not been opened. You should always check to make sure an object variable contains a valid reference before attempting to use it. When an object variable does not contain a valid reference, it is set to Nothing. In the previous example, if the StreamReader object is instantiated inside the Try block, you need to test to ensure that s contains a valid object reference. To do so, you execute this:

```
If s Is Not Nothing Then
    s.Close()
End If
```

If you attempt to execute a method on an object that has not been instantiated, a NullReferenceException occurs.

FOR EXAMPLE

Using Structured Error Handling

Say that you are writing a function that must open a file, read data from the file, and perform a calculation on the data. You identify that a number of possible errors might occur, including a missing file, invalid data in the file, or errors caused by the combination of data values used in a calculation. You decide to use structured error handling.

You enclose the code inside a Try block with three Catch clauses: a specific clause to catch file I/O exceptions, a specific clause to catch a divide-by-zero exception, and a general clause to catch the Exception object. Your code looks like this:

```
Try
    'Code to read file
    'Code to calculate data
    'Code to close file
Catch objEx As Exception
    'Code to handle general exception
Catch objEx As System.IO.IOException
    'Code to handle file i/o exception
Catch objEx As System.DivideByZeroException
    'Code to handle DivideByZeroException
End Try
```

You test the exception-handling functionality by moving the file to a different location. The exception-handling code for the general exception executes, but the code for the I/O exception does not. You realize that the Catch clauses are in the wrong order, so you change the code as follows:

```
Try
    'Code to read file
    'Code to calculate data
    'Code to close file
Catch objEx As System.IO.IOException
    'Code to handle file i/o exception
Catch objEx As System.DivideByZeroException
    'Code to handle DivideByZeroException
Catch objEx As Exception
    'Code to handle general exception
End Try
```

You test the exception-handling functionality again. This time, you realize that if a divide-by-zero exception occurs, the file is left open. You modify the exception-handling code to add a Finally block and move the code to close the file to the Finally block:

```
Try
    'Code to read file
    'Code to calculate data
Catch objEx As System.IO.IOException
    'Code to handle file i/o exception
Catch objEx As System.DivideByZeroException
    'Code to handle DivideByZeroException
Catch objEx As Exception
    'Code to handle general exception
Finally
    'Code to close file
End Try
```

SELF-CHECK

- Describe why exception-handling code is important.
- Compare the Catch block and the Finally block.
- Identify the scope of the variable that references the Exception object.

SUMMARY

In this chapter, you have learned how to write code that is reusable and that can handle unexpected events that generate exceptions. You have learned to segment code by using subprocedures and functions. You have also learned how to use classes instantiated as objects and shared classes to perform procedures that are common to multiple applications. You have also learned how to write robust code, using structured exception handling.

KEY TERMS

Application object	Imports keyword
Argument	Information hiding
Black-box view	Instantiation
Block variable	Invoke
Call	Lifetime
Child class	Local variable
Data hiding	Member variable
Error handler	Module
Exception handler	Namespace
Finally block	.NET Framework Class Library
Fully qualified name	New keyword
Function	Object-oriented programming (OOP)
Function definition statement	Optional keyword
Function procedure	Parameter
General procedure	Parent class
Global procedure	Passing by reference
Global variable	Passing by value
Handled exception	Procedure-level variable

Reference

Return statement

Return value

Reusable code

Root namespace

Shared class

Static variable

StreamReader class

Structured exception handling

Sub

Subprocedure

Try...Catch...End Try block

Type specifier

Unhandled exception

ASSESS YOUR UNDERSTANDING

Go to www.wiley.com/college/petroutsos to evaluate your knowledge of functions, methods, OOP, and error handling.
Measure your learning by comparing pre-test and post-test results.

Summary Questions

1. In which code region of a form do you define a general procedure?
   (a) within the Form class Declaration region
   (b) within the Form class event procedure where it is called
   (c) within the Form class Events region
2. Which of the following is a characteristic of a function but not a sub?
   (a) It accepts arguments.
   (b) It has a return value.
   (c) It can be made public.
   (d) It can include optional parameters.
3. Which of the following are name and type specifiers of data being passed
   to and from a procedure?
   (a) arguments
   (b) return values
   (c) parameters
4. When calling a function, the function name should appear on the right
   side of an assignment statement. True or False?
5. The Optional keyword can be used with any parameter in the parameter
   list. True or False?
6. You cannot pass literal values by reference. True or False?
7. What type of variable retains its value between calls to a procedure but
   cannot be accessed outside that procedure?
   (a) block
   (b) local
   (c) static
   (d) global
8. All objects in Visual Basic are visual objects. True or False?
9. A class implements encapsulation. Which of the following cannot be
   accessed by a program that creates an instance of the class?
   (a) member variables
   (b) methods
   (c) properties

10. Which of the following is used to group related classes and provide a unique naming scheme?

    (a) library

    (b) foundation class

    (c) parent class

    (d) namespace

11. You can only instantiate objects at the form level. True or False?

12. You can use the Math class without instantiating an object. True or False?

13. A carefully constructed and tested program does not need error-handling code. True or False?

14. Which block contains the code that should be executed only if an exception occurs?

    (a) Catch

    (b) Exception

    (c) Finally

    (d) Try

15. A Finally block executes before the appropriate Catch block. True or False?

Applying This Chapter

1. You are writing an application that will calculate the volume and surface area of a cylinder. Product packaging designers will use the application to design labels and determine the dimensions of cylindrical product packaging. Why should you create Volume and SurfaceArea functions? How will you define these functions? How can you ensure a consistent value of pi across all procedures that need it?

2. You are writing a procedure that will accept a string and encrypt it, using a simple alphabetic replacement strategy. What type of procedure should you create? How should you pass the String argument?

3. You are writing a function that allows users to specify a file path, opens the file, and reads data from it, using a StreamReader. The data is numeric, and the function also performs calculations on the data. You want to allow users to specify a different file path if the file cannot be opened. You want to handle all other exceptions by reporting the error message. You do not want the application to terminate. How should you implement exception handling?

YOU TRY IT

Designing Procedures

You need to create a program that accepts the length of three or four sides of a shape, determines whether the shape is an equilateral triangle (i.e., all sides are equal), an isosceles triangle (i.e., two sides are equal), a scalene triangle (i.e., no two sides are equal), a rectangle, or a square. It must also output the shape's circumference. What procedures will you create and how will you pass arguments?

Creating Global Functions or Objects

You need to create a program that reads bank account data from a database, accepts deposits and withdrawals, and calculates interest. Compare the benefits of creating a BankAccount class with the benefits of defining global procedures.

Designing Exception Handling

You are writing a program that allows users to select an item from a list and then calculates the price of that item, based on data the application retrieves from a live service. Think about the types of errors that can occur. Which errors will you want to handle by using structured exception handling? Which will you handle in other ways? Will you create a Catch clause for the general Exception object? Will you need a Finally clause?

5
USING ARRAYS AND COLLECTIONS

Starting Point

Go to www.wiley.com/college/petroutsos to assess your knowledge of arrays and collections.
Determine where you need to concentrate your effort.

What You'll Learn in This Chapter

▲ One-dimensional arrays
▲ Sorting and searching arrays
▲ Two-dimensional arrays
▲ ArrayList and Hashtable objects

After Studying This Chapter, You'll Be Able To

▲ Select the best control structure for performing an operation on tabular data
▲ Declare and initialize an array
▲ Populate an array
▲ Sort an array
▲ Perform operations using an array
▲ Store tabular data in an array
▲ Select an appropriate class for processing list data
▲ Use the ArrayList and Hashtable objects

INTRODUCTION

Many programs require the programmer to work on lists and tables of data. This chapter begins with a look at how you can use arrays to store and process list data in memory. Next, it looks at the procedures you use to process list data. The next section focuses on how to process tables of data. The final section examines two classes that can be used for working with lists: the ArrayList class and the Hashtable class.

5.1 Arrays

Many programming situations require that you work with lists of data. You might need to display a list, sort a list, or calculate a value based on the values in a list. In programming terms, a list of data values is known as an **array**. In this section, you'll learn ways to store an array in memory and procedures for accessing its values.

5.1.1 About Arrays

Arrays provide a way of working with lists in memory. You can input items into the list, initialize them to some value, process them to find the sum and average of numeric values, find the largest or smallest item in a list, look up an item in a list, or rearrange a list in alphabetical or numerical order. It is important to note that an array can store only one type of data. For example, an array can store String data or Decimal data, but not both.

Arrays hold multiple values or strings by giving each value or string a number that defines its position in the list or table. This number is known as the **index** or **subscript** of the array element. Table 5-1 shows an array of values. As you can see, the index value starts at 0 and counts up.

The name of the array in Table 5-1 is decPrices. The Decimal type array values are designated as decPrices(0), decPrices(1), decPrices(2), and so on, where the numbers in parentheses after the variable names are the index values. That is, the index for the first decPrices value is 0, the second is 1, and so on. When

Table 5-1: Array Indexes and Values

Index	Value
decPrices(0)	3.35
decPrices(1)	9.50
decPrices(2)	12.80
decPrices(3)	7.62

you want to refer to an element of an array, you must always give the index value for that element.

In summary, each item in an array is identified by two things:

1. The name of the array
2. The position of the item in the array (i.e., its index), which must be an Integer constant, variable, or expression.

5.1.2 Declaring an Array

Before using an array, you must declare it so that Visual Basic knows that it is a list of variables and not a single-value variable. An array has the same scoping and lifetime rules as other variables.

You declare arrays the same way as any other type of variable, except that you declare the maximum number of elements the array can contain. The following is the general form of a fixed-size array declaration statement for a list array:

```
Dim ArrayName(max_index_value) As data_type
```

This declaration statement defines the upper limit on the index for the array, with the lower limit being 0 by default. An array with the lowest limit set to 0 is a **zero-based array.** Attempting to reference an element with an index outside the specified limits results in a Subscript Out of Range error. For example, if the decPrices array discussed earlier has an upper limit on the index of 99, then the declaration would be as follows:

```
Dim decPrices(99) as Decimal
```

Note that this allows a total of 100 prices to be stored, with the index starting at 0. An array that has an upper bound declared is known as a **bounded array.** Although all values of an array of a numeric data type are automatically set to 0 when it is declared, it may be necessary to initialize all values to some other value. You can do this by using a For…Next loop, as follows:

```
For intCounter = 0 to 99
    decPrices(intCounter) = -1.0
Next
```

You can also initialize an array when you declare it. To do so, you surround the element values with curly braces, as follows:

```
Dim decMoney() As Decimal = _
    {10.00, 20.00, 30.00, 40.00}
```

Notice that you do not need to specify an upper limit. Visual Basic sets the upper limit based on the number of values in the initialization list.

It is possible to change the upper limit on the subscript of an array by using the **ReDim statement.** Reducing the size of an array to match the actual number of elements needed is a good way to conserve memory within a computer. For the decPrices example, if the maximum required number of elements is determined to be only 50, you could resize the array by using the following ReDim statement:

```
ReDim decPrices(49)
```

When an array is redimensioned, as shown here, the data is lost unless you use the ReDim Preserve statement. For example, if data has been stored in the decPrices array that is being redimensioned, you can save it with the following statement:

```
ReDim Preserve decPrices(49)
```

You can use the ReDim Preserve combination to declare a **dynamic array** (i.e., an array that has no upper limit on the array size). This is useful if you have no idea how large the array may become. For example, if you initially dynamically declared the array decPrices() with no upper limit, like this, you can use the ReDim Preserve statement to increase the upper limit each time a new element is added to the array:

```
Dim decPrices() as Decimal
```

5.1.3 Inputting Values to an Array

After you have declared an array, you can either input or assign values to it. An important rule about input to an array is that inputting data to an array must always be done one element at a time. It is not possible to input an entire array in one operation. Inputting a value into a single element of an array is just like inputting a value into a single-value variable, except that you must include the index for the array element. For example, to use an input box to input a value to decPrices(3), which was declared earlier as an array of the Decimal data type, you use this statement:

```
decPrices(3) = CDec(InputBox("Please input a price"))
```

Although you can input data into a single element of the array, many times you need to load the data from another source, such as a file or database. For that reason, loops are usually used to input the entire array, one element at a time. If the number of elements to be input is known, a For...Next loop can be used. However, this is not a good way to input array elements if the number of elements may change or is unknown. A more realistic situation is one in which an unknown number of array values are input from a sequential access file. A sequential access file is one that is read from beginning to end. When you don't know the number of elements in advance, you can use a Do Until loop to input values to the array. For example, the following code reads data from a file and inputs it into an array named decPrices:

```
Private Sub frmArrayInput_Load(ByVal sender As _
    Object, ByVal e As EventArgs) Handles MyBase.Load
    Dim strMyPath As String
```

```
        Dim intNumPrices As Integer
        intNumPrices = 0
        strMyPath = CurDir()
        FileOpen(5, strMyPath + "\Prices.txt", _
            OpenMode.Input)
        Do Until EOF(5)
            ReDim Preserve decPrices(intNumPrices)
            Input(5, decPrices(intNumPrices))
            intNumPrices = intNumPrices + 1
        Loop
    End Sub
```

The intNumPrices variable contains the current index. As you can see, it starts at 0 and is incremented each time through the loop. First, you redimension the loop, using the Preserve statement. Next, you input the value directly from the file, using the Input statement. The loop ends when the end of file (EOF) condition is met.

5.1.4 Displaying an Array

After an array is input and stored in memory, you can then display it in a List-Box control or other control by using a For...Next loop. For example, in the btnDisplay_Click event procedure, you can use a For...Next loop to display the contents of the decPrices array by adding them to a list box

```
    Private Sub btnDisplay_Click(ByVal sender As _
        Object, ByVal e As EventArgs) _
        Handles btnDisplay.Click
        Dim intCounter As Integer
        Dim intNumPrices As Integer
        intNumPrices = decPrices.GetUpperBound(0)
        For intCounter = 0 To itNumPrices
            lstPrices.Items.Add(decPrices(intCounter))
        Next
    End Sub

    Private Sub btnClear_Click(ByVal sender As Object, _
        ByVal e As EventArgs) Handles btnClear.Click
        lstPrices.Items.Clear()
    End Sub
```

You can use the GetUpperBound method of the Array object to determine the upper bound of the array. In this case, you can store that value in intNumPrices and use it for the exit condition of the For...Next loop. The list in a ListBox control is stored in the Items property. You add an item to the Items property by calling the Add method. An example of the program's output is shown in Figure 5-1.

You can also code the Clear button to clear the list stored in the ListBox control's Items property.

Figure 5-1

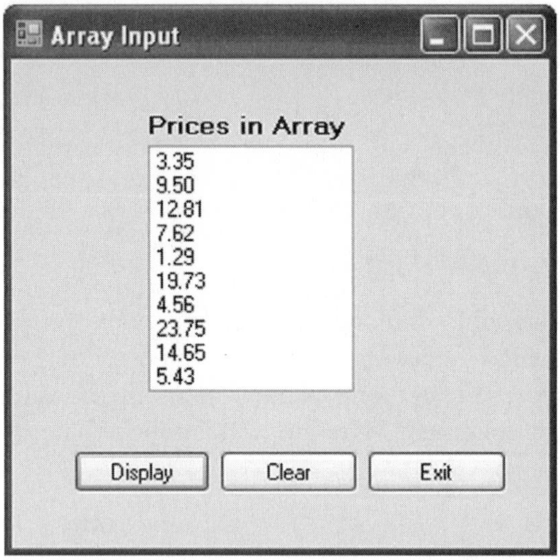

Result of displaying an array of prices.

5.1.5 Using For...Next and For Each Loops

As you have probably already noticed, processing arrays often requires the use of a For...Next loop. In fact, working with arrays is a very important use for For...Next loops. The Integer counter variable in a For...Next loop matches up very well with the Integer index values of the array elements. To iterate through each element in an array, you can use a For...Next loop with starting and ending values that match the declared lower and upper limits of the array index values. If the actual number of array elements is less than the declared number (which is a common occurrence), the index value of the last used array value can be used in the For...Next loop instead of the declared upper limit. For example, even though the Scores array presented earlier had all of its elements initialized to -1, if the last index of an element that actually is used is only 25, then this would be the For...Next loop to process the array:

```
For intCounter = 0 to 25
```

Another loop construct that is very useful for working with arrays is the **For Each loop.** With this type of loop, it is not necessary to know the maximum number of elements in the array because each element will be processed in order. The For Each loop has the following form:

```
For Each variable in ArrayName
    'array processing using variable
Next
```

The variable in the For Each statement is of the same data type as the array identified by ArrayName. For example, you can declare each element in the sngScores array to be equal to −1.0 by using a For Each loop, as shown here:

```
Dim sngScores(100) As Single
Dim sngValue As Single
For Each sngValue in sngScores
    sngValue = -1.0
Next
```

Note that the variable needs to be the same data type as the array. This variable is used to carry out all the processing, and there is no need to refer to the array subscript to identify each value in the array. The variable in the For Each loop, sngValue in this case, sequentially takes the place of each element of the array in the processing or initialization. This type of loop continues to work even when the size of the array is changed.

The primary shortcoming of the For Each loop is that it processes every element in the array up to the declared maximum number of elements. This can cause problems when there are empty elements in the array that are processed by the For Each loop. The For Each loop should be used to process an array only if the size of the array has been redimensioned to be equal to the actual number of elements in the array. Otherwise, many "empty" array elements or array elements initialized to default values may be processed, leading to potentially incorrect results.

FOR EXAMPLE

Using an Array

Say that you are writing an application that will be used to enter and track travel expenses. You decide to store the expense amount and the expense description in two separate arrays: the first of type Decimal and the second of type String. You declare two dynamic arrays at the form level, using the following code:

```
Dim arExpenses() As Decimal
Dim arExpDesc() As String
```

You use the following code to redimension and populate the array:

```
Dim intXUpperBound As Integer
If arExpenses Is Nothing Then
    intXUpperBound = 0
Else
    intXUpperBound = arExpenses.GetUpperBound(0) + 1
```

(Continued)

```
End If
ReDim Preserve arExpenses(intXUpperBound)
ReDim Preserve arExpDesc(intXUpperBound)
arExpenses(intXUpperBound) = CDec(txtExpAmt.Text)
arExpDesc(intXUpperBound) = txtDescription.Text
```

You use the following code to display each item and its amount in a ListBox control.

```
Dim iCounter As Integer
For iCounter = 0 to arExpenses.GetUpperBound(0)
    lstExpenses.Items.Add(arExpDesc(iCounter) & _
        " - " & arExpenses(iCounter)
Next
```

You consider whether a For Each loop would simplify the code and decide that because you are dealing with two parallel arrays, a For Each loop would not be appropriate.

SELF-CHECK

- Identify a situation in which you would create a bounded array.
- Identify a situation in which you would create a dynamic array.
- Describe the difference between using a For...Next loop and using a For Each loop to retrieve data from an array.

5.2 Processing Arrays

Inputting data into an array is only the first step in using it. Arrays are good at handling a large number of processing activities, including summing and averaging the values in an array, finding the largest or smallest value in a list, working with multiple lists, finding a particular value in a list, and sorting a list into a desired order.

In this section, we'll start by discussing summing and averaging values. Next, we'll look at how to find the minimum and maximum value in an array. Finally, we'll look at two ways to sort an array: by using a bubble sort and by using the Array.Sort method.

5.2.1 Summing and Averaging Values

When you have an array of values, it is very easy to sum and average them by using a For…Next or For Each loop to add each array element to the sum. To calculate the average, you divide the sum by the number of elements. This is shown in the following code example:

```
Private Sub btnSumAverage_Click(ByVal sender As _
    Object, ByVal e As EventArgs) _
    Handles btnSumAverage.Click
    Dim decSum As Decimal, intNumPrices As Integer
    Dim decAverage, decOnePrice As Decimal
    decSum = 0
    For Each decOnePrice In decPrices
        decSum = decSum + decOnePrice
        intNumPrices += 1
    Next
    If intNumPrices > 0 Then
        decAverage = decSum / intNumPrices
    Else
        MsgBox("No values to average!")
        Exit Sub
    End If
    txtSum.Text = CStr(decSum)
    txtAverage.Text = CStr(decAverage)
End Sub
```

This example uses a For Each loop to compute the sum. It also increments intNumPrices to keep track of the number of elements in the array. Note that the average is computed by dividing the sum by intNumPrices because this value is the actual absolute number of elements in the array. You need to ensure that intNumPrices is not 0 before you try to divide by it. Attempting to divide by zero is a very common error. The output from running this procedure is shown in Figure 5-2.

Instead of keeping track of intNumPrices, you could have used the GetUpperBound method. However, you would have had to add 1 to account for the value at element 0.

5.2.2 Finding the Largest and Smallest Values in an Array

A common operation in working with lists is finding the largest or smallest value (i.e., a numeric value or a character string) in the list. For numeric values, it is obvious what *larger* and *smaller* mean, but what about for character strings? For character strings, the alphabetical ordering holds; that is, the letter A is smaller than the letter B because it comes first in the alphabetical ordering. Similarly, lowercase letters come after uppercase letters, and numeric digits come before the alphabetical characters. The sort order of characters is

Figure 5-2

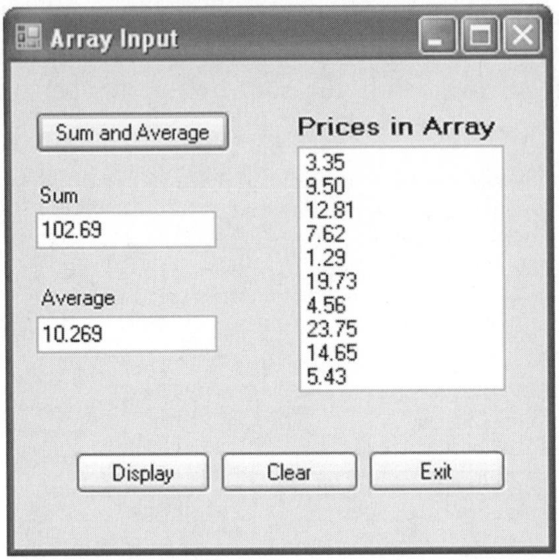

A form to compute the sum and average of array values.

known as the **collating sequence,** and it includes all 256 characters that Visual Basic recognizes for the Char data type. You can see the complete collating sequence by entering and running the code shown here in the Form_Load event for a new project (you will need to display the Immediate window to see the values):

```
Private Sub frmCollate_Load(ByVal sender As Object, _
    ByVal e As EventArgs) Handles MyBase.Load
    Dim intCounter As Integer
    For intCounter = 0 To 255
        Debug.Write(Chr(intCounter))
    Next
End Sub
```

This code uses the **Chr** function to convert the Integer values of the For...Next counter variable into the corresponding characters. To reverse this operation and find the position of a particular character in the collating sequence, you use the **Asc** function with the character as the argument of the function. For example, try executing the following:

```
Debug.Writeline Asc("A")
```

The number 65 is shown in the Immediate window.

Regardless of whether you are working with characters or numbers, finding the largest value in an array requires that each item in the list be compared to the currently known largest value. If an item in the list is larger than the currently known largest value, the item in the list becomes the largest known value. This comparison process continues until all items in the list have been compared to the currently known largest value, at which time the comparisons end, and the largest value is known. The pseudocode for this logic is shown here:

```
Begin procedure to find largest value
    Set largest value to first item in list
    Repeat beginning with second item to last item
        If item in list > largest value then
            Largest value = item in list
        End decision
    End repeat
    Display largest value
End procedure
```

To find the smallest value, you simply reverse the direction of the inequality from greater than to less than.

Note that the largest value is initialized to the first item in the list and then compared to every item in the list, starting with the second item. The largest value must be compared to something, and the first item in the list is a convenient value to use. To see how this works, assume that you have an array of 10 prices, and you want to find the largest value. If you walk through the pseudocode shown earlier for these prices, the results are as follows:

```
Set Largest = decPrices(0) = $3.35
Set intCounter = 1
Is decPrices(1) = $9.50 > $3.35? Yes, so Largest =
decPrices(1) = $9.50
Is decPrices(2) = $12.81 > $9.50? Yes, so Largest =
decPrices(2) = $12.81
Is decPrices(3) = $7.62 > $12.81? No, so no change
Is decPrices(4) = $1.29 > $12.81? No, so no change
Is decPrices(5) = $19.73 > $12.81? Yes, so Largest =
decPrices(5) = $19.73
Is decPrices(6) = $4.56 > $19.73? No, so no change
Is decPrices(7) = $23.75 > $19.73? Yes, so Largest =
decPrices(7) = $23.75
Is decPrices(8) = $14.65 > $23.75? No, so no change
Is decPrices(9) = $5.43 > $23.75? No, so no change
End of array, so Largest = $23.75
```

To implement this procedure in Visual Basic, you can use a file of 10 prices (Prices.txt) and code a button to find the largest value (btnFindMax) and a text box (txtMaxPrice) to display the largest value in the array, with a corresponding label added. The code for the btnFindMax_Click event procedure is shown

Figure 5-3

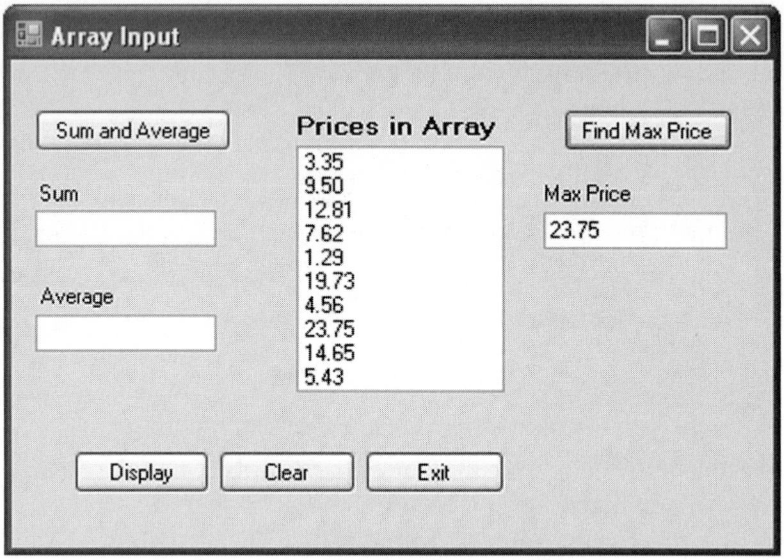

A form to find the maximum value.

here, and the result of clicking the Display and FindMax buttons is shown in Figure 5-3:

```
Private Sub btnFindMax_Click(ByVal sender As _
    Object, ByVal e As System.EventArgs) _
    Handles btnFindMax.Click
    Dim decLargest As Decimal
    Dim DecOnePrice As Decimal
    decLargest = decPrices(0)
    For Each DecOnePrice In decPrices
        If DecOnePrice > decLargest Then
            decLargest = DecOnePrice
        End If
    Next
    txtMaxPrice.Text = CStr(decLargest)
End Sub
```

5.2.3 Sorting an Array with Bubble Sort

Sorting an array is a frequent operation in processing data. This operation is similar to finding the maximum (or minimum) value in an array or finding an element in the array because it involves **pairwise comparisons** (i.e., comparisons of two values in an array). However, it goes further by also requiring repositioning of array elements. To help you understand the sorting process, this section uses a list of 10 prices, Prices(), which is shown in Figure 5-4.

Figure 5-4

Prices(0)	$3.35
Prices(1)	$9.50
Prices(2)	$12.81
Prices(3)	$7.62
Prices(4)	$1.29
Prices(5)	$19.73
Prices(6)	$4.56
Prices(7)	$23.75
Prices(8)	$14.65
Prices(9)	$5.43

The Prices array.

There are a variety of algorithms for sorting lists, but we will use a sort procedure that is not very fast but is easy to understand. Called the **bubble sort**, this sorting process uses a For...Next loop to compare each array element to the next one, and if they are out of order, it reverses them. For example, if the Prices() array is being ordered from smallest to largest, the Prices(0) element is compared to Prices(1). Because Prices(0) is less than Prices(1), no changes are made. Next, Prices(1) is compared to Prices(2), and once again, no changes are made. Next, Prices(2) is compared to Prices(3), and because Prices(2) is greater than Prices(3), they are reversed. The result of this reversal is shown in the leftmost set of prices in Figure 5-5, along with the remaining comparisons and reversals for the array.

Note in Figure 5-5 that, including the reversals of Prices(2) and Prices(3), which are not shown, there are five reversals of array elements due to a price being higher than the next price in the list. Note also that after this loop, the largest value is at the bottom, but the array is not completely sorted. Even though this sorting algorithm is called the bubble sort because the lowest values bubble their way to the top of the list, in actuality, the largest values sink to their relative positions at the bottom of the list on each pass through the loop.

Figure 5-5

Prices(0)	$3.35	$3.35	$3.35	$3.35	$3.35
Prices(1)	$9.50	$9.50	$9.50	$9.50	$9.50
Prices(2)	$7.62	$7.62	$7.62	$7.62	$7.62
Prices(3)	$12.81	$1.29	$1.29	$1.29	$1.29
Prices(4)	$1.29	$12.81	$12.81	$12.81	$12.81
Prices(5)	$19.73	$19.73	$4.56	$4.56	$4.56
Prices(6)	$4.56	$4.56	$19.73	$19.73	$19.73
Prices(7)	$23.75	$23.75	$23.75	$14.63	$14.63
Prices(8)	$14.65	$14.65	$14.65	$23.75	$5.43
Prices(9)	$5.43	$5.43	$5.43	$5.43	$23.75

Comparisons and the reversal process after the first reversal.

To completely sort the array, the comparison-reversal loop must be repeated as many times as necessary to sort the array. How do you know when the array is sorted? Note that if no reversals are made in the comparison-reversal loop, the array is sorted. This indicates that you need a loop to repeat the comparison-reversal loop until no reversals are made. This is a situation in which you use nested loops, with the outer loop being a Do Until loop and the inner loop being a For...Next loop. The pseudocode for this process is as follows:

```
Begin Sort procedure
    Repeat until no reversals made
        Repeat for each pair of values
            If value > next value then
                Reverse values
            End decision
        End repeat
    End repeat
End Procedure
```

To implement this pseudocode in Visual Basic, you need to address several programming issues:

1. How do you handle the For...Next loop and decisions to carry out the pairwise comparisons on array elements?
2. How do you reverse two array elements?
3. How do you handle the nested Do Until and For...Next loops so that the array is repeatedly searched until no reversals have been made?

Pairwise Comparisons

To carry out the pairwise comparisons for the Prices() array with index values that run from 0 to intNumPrices − 1 (where intNumPrices is the number of prices in the array), the For...Next loop runs from the first array element to the next to last, with each element being compared to the one that follows it. Because you are not processing every element in the array, you cannot use the For Each loop. Note that the loop stops at the next-to-last array element because there is no next element after the last one. If the last element of the array has index intNumValues − 1, the index for the next-to-last array element is intNumPrices − 2. This means that the first statement of the For...Next loop is:

```
For intCounter = 0 to intNumPrices - 2
```

Using the intCounter variable for the Prices() array, the current value is Prices(intCounter), and the next value is Prices(intCounter + 1). This means that the pairwise comparisons are of the following form:

```
If Prices(intCounter) > _
    Prices(intCounter + 1) Then
```

If the comparison is found to be true, and the two array elements are out of order, they should be reversed. The code that performs the loop and comparison is as follows:

```
For intCounter = 0 To intNumList - 2
    If decList1(intCounter) > _
        decList1(intCounter + 1) Then
        Reverse(decList1(intCounter), _
            decList1(intCounter + 1))
    End If
Next
```

Using a sub to reverse the array elements is an example of reducing the complexity of code. Even though you do not yet know the logic that will go into the sub, you can write the statement to invoke it and handle creating the sub later.

Reversing the Values in an Array

The key to the sorting process is being able to reverse two array elements when they are found to be out of order. Reversing two array elements is not as simple as just setting one element equal to the other. For example, these two statements do not reverse two string array elements:

```
strList(intCounter)     = strList(intCounter + 1)
strList(intCounter + 1) = strList(intCounter)
```

In fact, all these two statements can accomplish is setting the two array elements to the same value—the original value of strList(intCounter + 1). For this reason, you need to use a variable to carry out the reversal, as shown in Figure 5-6 for Prices(3) and Prices(4), which are initially out of order.

In step 1 of the reversal process, the temporary variable is set equal to Prices(3). In step 2, Prices(3) is set equal to Prices(4). Finally, in step 3, Prices(4) is set equal to the temporary variable. In the process, the value of Prices(3) is

Figure 5-6

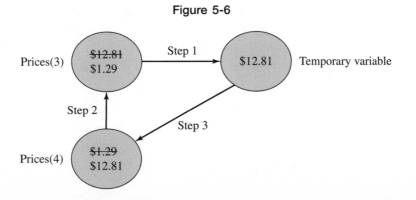

Using a variable to reverse the values in an array.

changed to $1.29, and the value of Prices(4) is changed to $12.81. In each case, the old value for the array element is replaced by the new value, as shown by the values being struck out. This process can be generalized by replacing Prices(3) and Prices(4) with Prices(intCounter) and Prices(intCounter + 1).

The following Reverse sub handles reversing two elements in the For...Next loop:

```
Sub  Reverse(ByRef decFirst As  Decimal,  _
     ByRef decSecond As Decimal)
     Dim decTemp As Decimal
     decTemp = decFirst
     decFirst = decSecond
     decSecond = decTemp
End  Sub
```

It is not necessary to use arrays in the sub because two specific array elements—Prices(intCounter) and Prices(intCounter + 1)—are passed by reference to the array. They match the decFirst and decSecond parameters in the Sub definition statement. Note that the parameters in the Reverse sub are passed by reference because you are going to change their values and want this information passed back to the calling sub. Finally, the temporary variable, decTemp, is declared as a Decimal data type local variable.

Repeating the For...Next Loop Until an Array Is Sorted

The last issue to be dealt with in the sorting process is using nested loops with a Do Until outer loop that repeats a For...Next inner loop until the array is sorted. You already know that the sample array will be sorted when there are no reversals in the For...Next loop, so you can use this fact to terminate the Do Until outer loop. One way to do this is to use a Boolean variable called blnNoReversal that is set to False before the Do Until loop and then reset to True within the Do Until before the start of the For...Next loop. Within the For...Next loop, if any reversals occur, blnNoReversal is set to False. If blnNoReversal is still True after the For...Next loop, there were no reversals; the Do Until loop can be terminated, and the array is sorted. The assignment of blnNoReversal to False before the Do Until loop ensures that the Do Until loop will complete at least one repetition. The pseudocode for this process is as follows:

```
Begin Sort procedure
     Repeat until no reversals made
          If value > next value then
               Reverse values
          End decision
     End repeat
End procedure
```

The corresponding Visual Basic code for the complete Sort sub that will go in the Code module is shown here:

```
Sub Sort(ByRef decList1() As Decimal, _
    ByRef strList2() As String, _
    ByVal intNumList As Integer)
    Dim blnNoReversal As Boolean, intCounter As _
        Integer
    blnNoReversal = False
    Do Until blnNoReversal
        blnNoReversal = True
        For intCounter = 0 To intNumList - 2
            If decList1(intCounter) > _
                decList1(intCounter + 1) Then
                Reverse(decList1(intCounter), _
                    decList1(intCounter + 1))
                ReverseStr(strList2(intCounter), _
                    strList2(intCounter + 1))
                blnNoReversal = False
            End If
        Next
    Loop
End Sub
```

Note that the parameters decList1(), strList2(), and intNumList are defined to match the arguments in the statement that invokes the sub—Prices, strPartID, and intNumPrices. Also, because the Prices() array is being used to sort both the Prices() and strPartID() arrays, whatever is done to the Prices() array should also be done to the strPartID() array. This requires a second sub called ReverseStr to reverse the String data type strPartID() array because the Reverse sub was created to reverse Decimal data type elements. The ReverseStr sub looks exactly like the Reverse sub for Decimal type data variables except that the decFirst, decSecond, and decTemp variables are String data type instead of Decimal type. Finally, to check the status of the Boolean variable blnNoReversal, you do not need to use an equal operator to compare it to True; Boolean variables are already True or False, so you can use the statement If blnNoReversal to check the status.

5.2.4 Sorting with Array Object Methods

Now that you have some understanding of how a general procedure works for sorting arrays, it's time to look at how to use the Sort method of the Array class. This method can be used to sort one list array or two list arrays, based on values in one of the arrays. In the first case, the statement has the following form (where the array name is in the parentheses):

```
Array.Sort(list1)
```

For example, to sort just the Prices array, the statement would be as follows:

```
Array.Sort(Prices)
```

For two arrays, they are both enclosed in the parentheses, with the first array controlling the order of the sorting. So in this case, you want to sort both Prices and strPartID based on the order of Prices, so the statement would be as follows:

```
Array.Sort(Prices, strPartID)
```

Because the Sort method of the Array class is based on much faster sorting methodology than the bubble sort, it would be able to sort much bigger lists in much less time than the routine you created. In addition to the Sort method, the Array class has a very fast search method, a method to reverse the order of the array, and a number of other methods, all of which can be found in online help.

FOR EXAMPLE

Processing Arrays

Say that you are writing an application to analyze sales data. You need to find the sale with the highest total, and you need to output sales, sorted by region and by total. You also need to output the total sales per region. Sales data is stored in a two arrays: strRegion() is an array of type String that stores the region. decTotal() is an array of type Decimal that stores the amount of the sale.

You decide to use the Array.Sort method to sort the two arrays by region and by total. You write the following code:

```
Array.Sort(decTotal, strRegion)
For intCounter = 0 to decTotal.GetUpperBound(0)
    lstByTotal.Items.Add _
        decTotal(intCounter) & " " _
        & strRegion(intCounter)
Next
txtHighestSale.Text = strRegion(intCounter - 1) & _
" " & decTotal(intCounter - 1)
Array.Sort(strRegion, decTotal)
For intCounter = 0 to decTotal.GetUpperBound(0)
    lstByRegion.Items.Add _
        strRegion(intCounter) & " " _
        & decTotal(intCounter)
Next
```

This code outputs the two sorted lists and the maximum sale.

Next, you need to output the sales totals for each region. You can do this easily by using a For...Next loop because the list is currently sorted by region. To do so, you add the following code:

```
Dim strThisRegion As String
Dim decPerRegionTotal As Decimal
strThisRegion = strRegion(0)
For intCounter = 0 to decTotal.GetUpperBound(0)
    If strThisRegion = strRegion(intCounter) Then
        decPerRegionTotal += decTotal(intCounter)
    Else
        lstTotalByRegion.Items.Add(strThisRegion & _
            ": " & _decPerRegionTotal)
        decPerRegionTotal = decTotal(intCounter)
        strThisRegion = strRegion(intCounter)
    End If
Next
lstTotalByRegion.Items.Add(strThisRegion & _
    ": " & decPerRegionTotal)
```

In this code, you initialize the strThisRegion variable to be the first region in the strRegion array. Then you execute a For...Next loop, using an If...Then...Else statement to check whether the region is the same. If it is, you add the total. If it isn't, you reset the total to that of the first element associated with the new region and you reinitialize strThisRegion to the new region name.

You test the code with the values shown in Table 5-2. The results of the test are shown in Figure 5-7.

Table 5-2: Sample Values

Region	Amount
West	400
Central	320
East	250
East	600
Central	750
Central	200

(Continued)

Figure 5-7

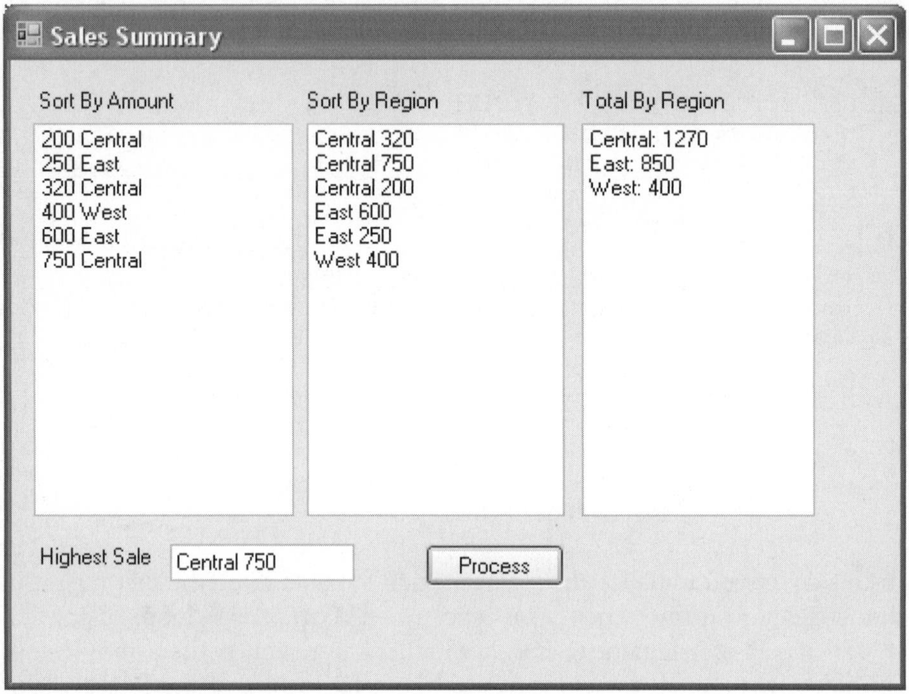

Sort By Amount	Sort By Region	Total By Region
200 Central	Central 320	Central: 1270
250 East	Central 750	East: 850
320 Central	Central 200	West: 400
400 West	East 600	
600 East	East 250	
750 Central	West 400	

Highest Sale `Central 750`   [Process]

Results Generated by Running the Code.

SELF-CHECK

- Describe how you would find the maximum value in an array of Integer values.
- Describe how a bubble sort works.
- Describe the advantages of using the Array class's Sort method instead of performing a bubble sort.

5.3 Multidimensional Arrays

Now that you have worked with one-dimensional arrays of lists of items, you're ready to consider situations in which a two-dimensional array or table is needed. There are many situations in business where tables are used, including tables of intercity shipping charges, income tax tables, tables of unemployment statistics by month and city, and many more. We'll wrap up the section with a quick overview of arrays that have more than two dimensions.

5.3.1 Declaring Two-Dimensional Arrays

Two-dimensional arrays share many characteristics with one-dimensional arrays, so much of this discussion is an extension of the earlier part of this chapter. The first thing to note is that for a two-dimensional array, you need two index values or subscripts for the array, with the first giving the row position and the second giving the column position.

To declare a two-dimensional array (i.e., a table), you must provide the maximum row and column index values. The following is the general form for declaring a table array:

```
Dim ArrayName(max_row_index, max_column_index) _
    As var_type
```

For example, if the maximum row index is 10 and the maximum column index is 20 for an array that will hold Single data type values, the declaration statement is as follows:

```
Dim sngNumberTable(10, 20) As Single
```

Like lists, table arrays start both the row and column index values at 0; therefore, in the example, sngNumberTable will hold 11 rows and 21 columns, for a total of $11 \times 21 = 231$ elements. To illustrate, assume that you have a table of revenues for products and regions (in millions of dollars) for a computer company, as shown in Table 5-3.

If you wanted to store this information in a two-dimensional array, you would first declare the maximum row index in the first position and then the maximum column index in the second position. You would do this as follows:

```
Dim decRevenue(2,3) as Decimal
```

As in list arrays, the index values for the first row and first column are 0. In Table 5-3, the revenue for PCs in the Northeast region is in the element decRevenue(0,0) because PCs is the first row and Northeast is the first column.

Table 5-3: Product Revenues by Title (in Millions of Dollars)

Product	Northeast	Southeast	Midwest	West
PCs	53.5	62.1	27.1	41.5
Storage	24.7	23.5	27.3	20.3
Memory	15.1	11.3	17.9	20.7

Likewise, the element decRevenue(2,3) gives the revenue for memory in the West region. Each element of the table is uniquely defined by its row and column position.

5.3.2 Input for Two-Dimensional Arrays

All the methods for handling input with lists also work for tables. The most commonly used method of input for tables is a nested For...Next loop, where the outer loop is used to input the rows of an array and the inner loop is used to input the columns. This means that all the elements of the first row are input first, followed by all the elements of the second row.

For example, in the product revenues table example, the statements necessary to read the revenue data from a file on an item-by-item basis for each row in the frmRevenue_Load event procedure are shown here:

```
Private decRevenue(2, 3) As Decimal
Private Sub frmRevenue_Load(ByVal sender As Object, _
    ByVal e As EventArgs) Handles MyBase.Load
    Dim intProduct As Integer, intRegion As Integer
    FileOpen(10, CurDir() + "\revenue.txt", _
        OpenMode.Input)
    For intProduct = 0 To 2
        For intRegion = 0 To 3
            Input(10, decRevenue(intProduct, _
                intRegion))
        Next intRegion
    Next intProduct
End Sub
```

This example includes a form-level declaration of the decRevenue array. The input assumes that revenue.txt has only one value per line. The Input statement reads all of the first row, then all of the second row, then all of the third row, as shown in Table 5-4. If you reverse the row and column counters in the For...Next loop, the order of input reads all of the first column, then all of the second column, and so on through all four columns.

Table 5-4: Revenue Data

	intRegion = 0	intRegion = 1	intRegion = 2	intRegion = 3
Read first	53.5	62.1	27.1	41.5
Read second	24.7	23.5	27.3	20.3
Read third	15.1	11.3	17.9	20.7

5.3.3 Processing Two-Dimensional Arrays

As in one-dimensional arrays, data manipulation on two-dimensional arrays is performed on an element-by-element basis. Although you have performed these operations with a single For Each loop for list arrays, tables often require nested For...Next loops, especially if all values in the array are involved in the operation. For Each loops are inappropriate because you need to specify exactly which element of the table is being input or processed.

For example, suppose you want to know the total revenues by product and by region. To make these calculations, you need to use nested For...Next loops to cover all elements. Assume that you have a form with three buttons—one for product totals, one for regional totals, and one to exit the project—and a list box for output (see Figure 5-8).

To find the product totals, you need to sum across the rows and add the sum to the list box with an appropriate message. To find the regional totals, you need to sum down columns, adding the sums to the list box. The code window to do this is as follows:

```
Private Sub btnProduct_Click(ByVal sender As Object, _
    ByVal e As EventArgs) Handles btnProduct.Click
    Dim decProductSum As Decimal
    Dim intProduct As Integer
    Dim intRegion As Integer
    lstSums.Items.Clear()
    lstSums.Items.Add("Sums by Product")
```

Figure 5-8

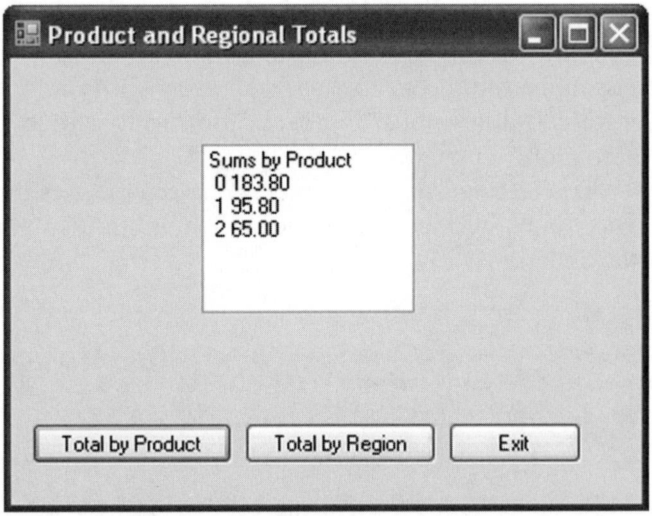

Results of finding sums by product.

```
       For intProduct = 0 To 2
           decProductSum = 0
           For intRegion = 0 To 3
               decProductSum = decProductSum + _
               decRevenue(intProduct, intRegion)
           Next intRegion
           lstSums.Items.Add(Str(intProduct) & " " & _
               CStr(decProductSum))
       Next intProduct
   End Sub
   Private Sub btnRegion_Click(ByVal sender As Object, _
       ByVal e As EventArgs) Handles btnRegion.Click
       Dim decRegionSum As Decimal
       Dim intProduct As Integer
       Dim intRegion As Integer
       lstSums.Items.Clear()
       lstSums.Items.Add("Sums by Region")
       For intRegion = 0 To 3
           decRegionSum = 0
           For intProduct = 0 To 2
               decRegionSum = decRegionSum + _
                   decRevenue(intProduct, intRegion)
           Next intProduct
           lstSums.Items.Add(Str(intRegion) & " " _
               & CStr(decRegionSum))
       Next intRegion
   End Sub
```

5.3.4 Arrays with More Than Two Dimensions

In some situations, you need to model data by using more than two dimensions. For example, you might need to process data for a three-dimensional space such as a cube. The same basic process applies to an array with multiple dimensions as to an array with two dimensions: You declare the array with an upper boundary for each dimension.

Suppose you are creating a game in which a character moves through a three-dimensional space and captures objects worth a number of points. You could declare the array as follows:

```
Const SpaceLength As Integer = 99
Const SpaceWidth As Integer = 199
Const SpaceDepth As Integer = 199
Dim intSpacePoints(SpaceLength, SpaceWidth, _
    SpaceDepth) As Integer
```

This array would store 4,000,000 elements (100 × 200 × 200). To populate the array, you would use three nested loops: one for each dimension. In this example, you are using a function named GetPoints to determine the point value of a specific element. The code to populate the array is as follows:

```
Dim intLength As Integer
Dim intWidth As Integer
Dim intDepth As Integer
For intLength = 0 to SpaceLength
    For intWidth = 0 to SpaceWidth
        For intDepth = 0 to SpaceDepth
            intSpacePoints(intLength, intWidth, _
                intDepth) = GetPoints()
        Next
    Next
Next
```

You retrieve values and process array data by using a similar strategy as for two-dimensional arrays. However, the loops are nested three deep instead of two deep. For example, to retrieve the number of points at 20, 15, 75, you use this code:

```
intPoints = intSpacePoints(20, 15, 75)
```

Therefore, to retrieve all the points of every coordinate along the length of 20, you use this code:

```
Dim intLength As Integer
Dim intWidth As Integer
Dim intDepth As Integer
For intWidth = 0 to SpaceWidth
    For intDepth = 0 to SpaceDepth
        intSpacePoints(20, intWidth, _
            intDepth) = GetPoints()
    Next
Next
```

FOR EXAMPLE

Processing Two-Dimensional Arrays

Say that you are writing an application to analyze expense data. Each expense has an amount, a project ID, and a category associated with it. You decide to use a two-dimensional array to process this data. There are 10 projects and 8 categories. You declare the array as follows:

```
Dim arrProjectExpense(9, 7) As Decimal
```

(Continued)

You need to find the total expense for each project. You write the following code:

```
Dim intProject, intCategory As Integer
Dim decProjectExpense As Integer
For intProject = 0 to 9
    decProjectExpense = 0
    For intCategory = 0 to 7
        decProjectExpense += _
            arrProjectExpense(intProject, _
            intCategory)
    Next
    lstTotalByProject.Items.Add(" Project " & _
        intProject & " " & decProjectExpense)
Next
```

SELF-CHECK

- Compare a two-dimensional array with a table.
- Explain why nested loops are used to process a two-dimensional array.

5.4 Using Collections

As your learned earlier in this chapter, when you declare an array, you actually create an instance of the Array class. The .NET Framework includes two other powerful classes for working with lists: the ArrayList class and the Hashtable class. In this section we'll look at both of them.

5.4.1 The ArrayList Class

The **ArrayList class,** which is part of the Collections namespace, allows you to create objects that act like smart arrays (i.e., arrays that know how to perform operations such as sorting and reversing their order). An ArrayList object includes properties and methods that can make it easier to work with than regular arrays. Among other things, it is easier to load, sort, and search an ArrayList object than an array.

Some properties and methods available with the ArrayList class are listed in Table 5-5 and Table 5-6, as they are discussed in the Visual Studio Help documentation. ArrayList objects are fairly flexible in that they can store lists of any type—simple data types, user-defined variables, and even other objects.

Table 5-5: ArrayList Properties

Property	Description
Capacity	Gets or sets the number of elements that the ArrayList can contain.
Count	Gets the number of elements actually contained in the ArrayList.
Item	Gets or sets the element at the specified index.

To put this list into an ArrayList, you first need to create an instance of an ArrayList object from the ArrayList class. For example, to declare an instance of an ArrayList to store the price data, you use the following command:

```
Dim PriceArray As New ArrayList()
```

PriceArray is now an ArrayList object. You can use ArrayList properties and methods to work with the data that will eventually be stored there.

5.4.2 The Hashtable Class

Another useful class provided in the .NET Framework Class Library (FCL) is the **Hashtable class.** A Hashtable object lets you store items in a list similarly to an ArrayList object, but with Hashtable, you give a unique name to each element

Table 5-6: ArrayList Methods

Method	Description
Add	Adds an object to the end of the ArrayList.
Clear	Removes all elements from the ArrayList.
Contains	Determines whether an element is in the ArrayList.
Insert	Inserts an element into the ArrayList at the specified index.
Remove	Removes the first occurrence of a specific object from the ArrayList.
RemoveAt	Removes the element at the specified index of the ArrayList.
Reverse	Reverses the order of the elements in the ArrayList or a portion of it.
Sort	Sorts the elements in the ArrayList or a portion of it.

you store. Then when you want to access a specific element, you can simply refer to its name rather than searching for the appropriate index. The name assigned to each element is actually converted and stored as a number called a *hash*. When you associate a hash with each record, searching the list is more efficient. For example, assume that you want to store a list of prices in a Hashtable in which each price can be identified by a part identifier. To do this, you first need to declare a new instance of the Hashtable class, as follows:

```
Dim Parts As Hashtable() = New Hashtable
```

You can then add members to the Parts Hashtable, using the Add method. For each part, you enter the part identifier as the key and the price as the value that is stored there. For example, you could enter several members as follows:

```
Parts.Add("V23-5W", 3.35)
Parts.Add("X37-3K", 9.59)
:
Parts.Add("R13-8W", 5.43)
```

You can now retrieve any of the entered parts by simply using the part identifier as a key. For instance, to assign the price for the part with an identifier of X37-3K to a Decimal type variable, you can use this:

```
decPrice = Parts("X37-3K")
```

Like ArrayList, Hashtable exposes some other useful properties and methods. For example, you can use the Count property to ascertain the number of members currently in the table:

```
intNumofParts = Parts.Count()
```

You can also edit a value at a specific key:

```
Parts("R13-8W") = 5.45
```

You can remove all items by using the Clear method or remove a specific entry as follows:

```
Parts.Remove("V23-5W")
```

FOR EXAMPLE

Using a Hashtable

Say that you are writing an application that will be used to store and process employee salary information. Each employee is identified by a Social Security number. The payroll application will use the employee's Social Security number to access the employee's salary. You decide to use a Hashtable to store the employee salary information. You use the employee's Social Security number as the key.

You declare the Hashtable as follows:

```
Dim htSalaries As New Hashtable
```

You write the following code to allow users to enter employee data:

```
htSalaries.Add(txtSSN.Text, txtSalary.Text)
```

You write the following code to retrieve the salary of a specific employee, assuming that strSSN contains the employee's Social Security number:

```
decSalary = CDec(htSalaries(strSSN))
```

SELF-CHECK

- Describe how using an ArrayList can make it easier to process list data.
- Identify a situation in which a Hashtable is appropriate.

SUMMARY

In this chapter, you've learned how to process data by using arrays and collections. You've learned how to declare, populate, and retrieve data from a single-dimensional array. You've also learned how to find the minimum value, find the maximum value, add the values in an array, and sort arrays. You've learned how to use two-dimensional arrays to manage tabular data, and you've learned how to use classes in the System.Collections namespace.

KEY TERMS

Array	For Each loop
ArrayList class	Hashtable class
Asc function	Index
Bounded array	Pairwise comparison
Bubble sort	ReDim statement
Chr function	Subscript
Collating sequence	Two-dimensional array
Dynamic array	Zero-based array

ASSESS YOUR UNDERSTANDING

Go to www.wiley.com/college/petroutsos to evaluate your knowledge of arrays and collections.

Measure your learning by comparing pre-test and post-test results.

Summary Questions

1. The first value in any array is identified with a subscript of 1. True or False?

2. Which of the following statements would you use to change the upper boundary of an array without deleting its contents?

   (a) Dim arrMyArray(10)

   (b) Dim Preserve arrMyArray(10)

   (c) ReDim arrMyArray(10)

   (d) ReDim Preserve arrMyArray(10)

3. Which of the following statements would you use to set the value of the second element in the strNames array declared below to "Steve"?

   ```
   Dim strNames(50) As String
   ```

   (a) strNames(2) = "Steve"

   (b) strNames(1) = "Steve"

   (c) strNames.Add ("Steve", 2)

   (d) strNames.AddAt("Steve", 1)

4. Which method is used to determine the index number of the last element in an array?

   (a) GetUpperBound

   (b) GetLastIndex

   (c) UpperBound

   (d) LastIndex

5. You can use a For Each loop only if you know the index of the last element in an array. True or False?

6. You can use a For Each loop to calculate the sum of all the elements in an array. True or False?

7. The sort order for character data is known as the collating sequence. True or False?

8. A bubble sort is the only algorithm you can use to sort an array. True or False?

9. You are performing a bubble sort of an index named intAge(). You are using the following For...Next loop:

```
For intCounter = 0 to intAge.GetUpperBound(0) - 1
    'Pairwise comparison goes here
Next
```

Which statement would you use to perform the pairwise comparison?

(a) If intAge(intCounter) > intAge(intCounter − 1)

(b) If intAge(intCounter) > intAge(intCounter + 1)

(c) If intAge(intCounter) > intAge(intAge.GetUpperBound(0))

10. When performing a bubble sort, you need to use a variable to reverse the order of elements in the array. True or False?

11. When performing a bubble sort, you use a For...Next loop nested inside a Do Until loop. True or False?

12. Which statement can you use to easily sort the values in the following array?

```
Dim intScores(500) As Integer
```

(a) ArrayList.Sort(intScores)

(b) intScores.Sort()

(c) Array.Sort(intScores)

13. A two-dimensional array can store data of two different data types. True or False?

14. Which control structure would you use to input data into a two-dimensional array?

(a) Nested For Each loop

(b) Nested For...Next loop

(c) For Each loop

(d) For...Next loop

15. You can use either a For Each loop or a For...Next loop to summarize the row values in a two-dimensional array. True or False?

16. An array can have no more than two dimensions. True or False?

17. The ArrayList class allows you to retrieve an element's value by a key value. True or False?

18. The Collections namespace includes the Hashtable and ArrayList classes. True or False?

Applying This Chapter

1. You are writing an application that will allow users to enter the number of hours required to complete each task of a project. Each project has a

different number of tasks. The application will summarize the number of hours for each task. What are the benefits of using a dynamic array? What statement would you use to increase the size of the array? What advantage would you gain by using a Hashtable?

2. You are writing a procedure that will read customer names and the balance due from a file. There are 100 customers in the file. You want to be able to sort the data by customer name and by balance due. How will you declare the arrays? How will you read data into the arrays? How will you sort the arrays?

3. You are writing a procedure that will output the number of times the value 4 appears in a single-dimensional array that stores 2,000 values. What code will you use?

4. You are writing a program that tracks the date on which each patient receives specific vaccines. You need to be able to identify patients who are past due for a vaccine. Each patient receives four different vaccines. How will you structure the data in memory? What type of loop will you use to determine which patients need vaccines?

Declaring, Populating, and Using Arrays

You need to create a program that allows users to enter an item code, a quantity, and a cost per item for an order and that outputs the total for the order. Write the declaration for the data structures you will use to store the data. Write the code you will use to input the data. Assume that you are getting the data from TextBox controls. Write the code for determining the order total.

Sorting Arrays

You need to create an accounting program that allows users to enter withdrawal and deposit information. You need to be able to sort the withdrawal and deposit information by date. How will you structure the data? What is the easiest way to sort the data?

Processing Tabular Data

You are writing a program that allows members of the Human Resources department to analyze the salaries of employees across each department. You need to be able to generate a report that shows the minimum, average, and maximum salary for each department. The output should be placed in three different ListBox controls. If a department has fewer than numEmployees, the value at that index is 0. How will you store employee salary data? Write the procedure to obtain the data you need. Assume the constants numDepartments and numEmployees.

6

HANDLING USER INPUT AND FORMATTING OUTPUT

Starting Point

Go to www.wiley.com/college/petroutsos to assess your knowledge of user interface design and string manipulation.
Determine where you need to concentrate your effort.

What You'll Learn in This Chapter

▲ Types of controls
▲ Tab order and shortcut keys
▲ Dynamic controls
▲ String manipulation methods
▲ Number formatting
▲ Date formatting

After Studying This Chapter, You'll Be Able To

▲ Choose the best control to meet a design requirement
▲ Design a form that meets usability requirements
▲ Apply formatting to numeric output
▲ Determine how to format and display dates
▲ Set tab order and identify shortcut keys
▲ Create resizable forms
▲ Add controls to a form at runtime
▲ Develop a strategy for working with String data
▲ Compare strings
▲ Manipulate strings
▲ Validate user input
▲ Use the Format function
▲ Use Date properties and methods

INTRODUCTION

Although the code that drives an application is important, the user interface is critical. In this chapter, we'll begin by looking at selecting controls and designing forms that meet business and usability requirements. In the next section, we'll examine string manipulation and formatting concerns. In the final section, we'll look at formatting numeric and date variables.

6.1 Building an Intuitive User Interface

As the name suggests, the **user interface** incorporates the parts of a program that the user interacts with. A user interface that is easy for a user to understand and navigate is critical to a program's success. This section introduces you to some commonly used Windows controls and looks at some guidelines for choosing the right controls. Next, you'll learn how you can easily allow a user to use the keyboard to navigate through the controls on a form. After that, you'll learn how you can create a resizable form. The section concludes with a look at adding controls to a form at runtime.

6.1.1 Choosing the Right Controls

The .NET Framework includes a large number of controls you can use to create a user interface. While a discussion of all these controls is beyond the scope of this book, we examine a few commonly used controls and discuss situations in which they would be appropriate.

With all the controls to choose from, how do you know which ones to use? The first step in building an application is to analyze the application's requirements. As with creating programming logic, these requirements provide the key to selecting the best controls to add to a form.

Before selecting controls, you should make a list of the information that must be displayed on the form and the information that must be input by the user. You should include a description of the information, such as whether it is text or a graphic, how large it is, and whether it must be allowed to grow dynamically. For data that will be input by the user, you should include whether the user will type the data in, select a value from a predefined list, or enter the data from a file. You should also list other characteristics of the data, including the following:

▲ Will the data fit on a single line, or will the user enter multiple lines?
▲ If the user will select from a list, will the choice be **mutually exclusive** (i.e., the user can select only one item) or will multiple selections be allowed?
▲ Is the data being entered confidential?

▲ Is the data a simple value, an ordered list, or structured data?

▲ If the data is being input, are there business and technical rules that define its validity?

After you have answered all these questions about each data element displayed or input on the form, you are ready to start selecting controls.

Controls for Selecting Options

In many situations, you need to allow users to select from a list of items. A number of controls are available that enable users to select one or more items. To choose which is most appropriate, you should answer the following questions:

▲ Are the choices mutually exclusive?

▲ Is there a large or a small number of choices?

▲ Will the choices change over time?

▲ Can the user enter a different choice than those shown?

When designing your user interface, you can choose to either display a set of RadioButton controls or CheckBox controls or allow users to select from a list. If there are only a few choices, you might use RadioButton or CheckBox controls. If there are a large number of items, you are better off using one of the list controls.

RadioButton controls present the user with mutually exclusive choices. For example, an application that allows you to manage service requests might use RadioButton controls to reflect the status of the request as Pending, Dispatched, or Closed (see Figure 6-1).

You control which radio buttons are mutually exclusive by grouping them on a GroupBox control. The Text property of the GroupBox control provides a label for the radio button group.

CheckBox controls present selections from which the user can choose zero or more items. As with RadioButton controls, you usually use a CheckBox control

Figure 6-1

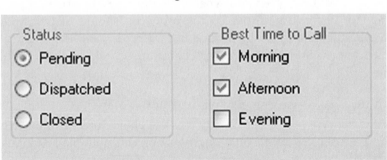

RadioButton and CheckBox controls.

Figure 6-2

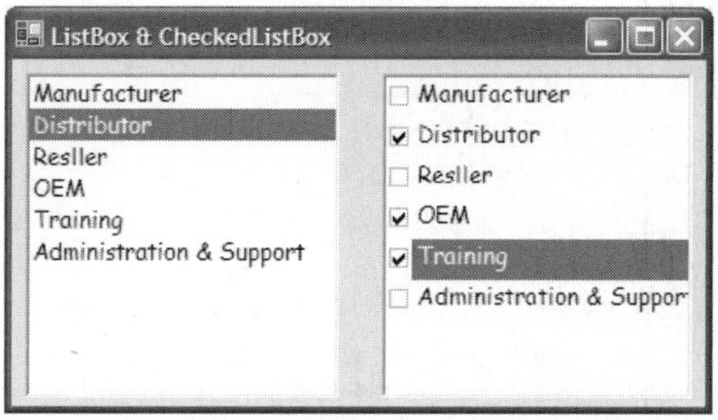

ListBox and CheckListBox controls.

if there are only a few possible choices. For example, in the service request application, you might use a CheckBox control to set whether a good time to call is morning, afternoon, and/or evening.

The ListBox, CheckedListBox, and ComboBox controls present lists of choices from which the user can select one or more. ListBox and CheckedListBox controls are illustrated in Figure 6-2. The ListBox control occupies a programmer-specified amount of space on the form and is populated with a list of items. If the list of items is longer than can fit on the control, a vertical scrollbar appears automatically. The CheckListBox control is a variation of the ListBox control. It is identical to the ListBox control, but a check box appears in front of each item. The user can select any number of items by checking the boxes in front of them.

To add items at design time, you locate the Items property in a control's Properties window and click the ellipsis button. The String Collection Editor window pops up; in it, you can add the items you want to display on the list. Each item must appear on a separate text line, and blank text lines will result in blank lines on the list. These items will appear on the list when the form is loaded, but you can add more items (or remove existing ones) from within your code at any time. The items appear in the same order as entered using the String Collection Editor window unless the control has its Sorted property set to True, in which case the items are automatically sorted, regardless of the order in which you specify them.

A ComboBox control also contains multiple items, but it typically occupies less space onscreen than a ListBox or CheckedListBox control. The ComboBox control is an expandable ListBox control: The user can expand it to make a selection and collapse it after the selection is made. The real advantage of the ComboBox control is that the user can enter new information in the ComboBox rather than being forced to select from the items listed.

Three types of ComboBox controls are available in Visual Basic 2005. The value of the control's DropDownStyle property, whose available values are shown in Table 6-1, determines which box is used. The three styles are shown in Figure 6-3.

Table 6-1: Styles of the ComboBox Controls

Value	Effect
DropDown (default)	This control is made up of a drop-down list and a text box. The user can select an item from the list or type a new one in the text box.
DropDownList	This control is a drop-down list from which the user can select one of the items but can't enter a new one.
Simple	This control includes a text box and a list that doesn't drop down. The user can select from the list or type in the text box.

Controls for Entering Text

Two controls allow users to enter text: the TextBox control and the RichTextBox control. Which of these controls you choose depends on the formatting requirements for the text and whether the text should be treated like a password.

The TextBox control is the primary mechanism for displaying and entering text and is one of the most common elements of the Windows user interface. The TextBox control is a small text editor that provides all the basic text-editing facilities, including inserting and selecting text, scrolling if the text doesn't fit in the control's area, and even exchanging text with other applications through the **Clipboard**.

Figure 6-3

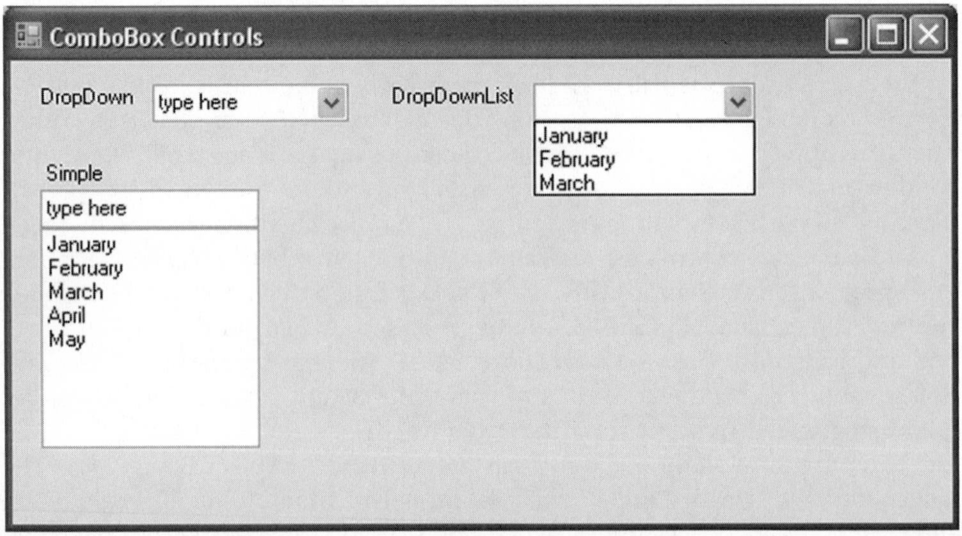

ComboBox styles.

Figure 6-4

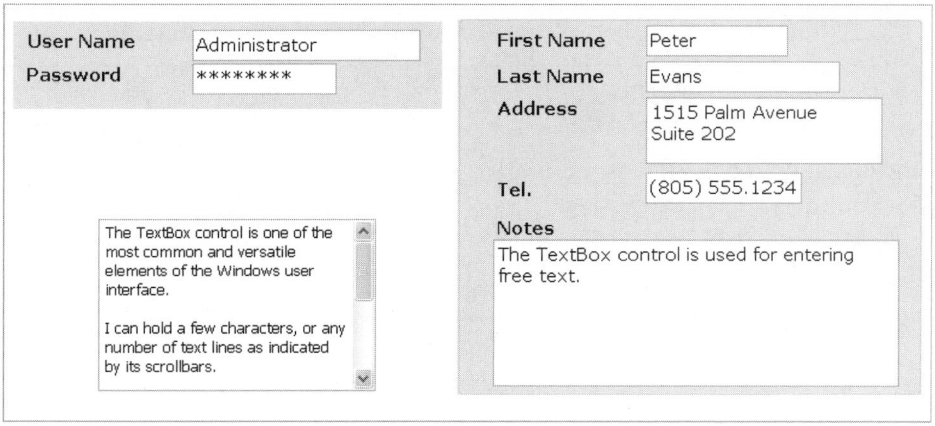

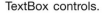

TextBox controls.

The Clipboard is a Windows feature that allows you to copy and paste data within an application and between applications. The TextBox control can be used for entering and editing single lines of text, such as a number or a password, or an entire text file. Figure 6-4 shows a few typical examples. All the boxes in Figure 6-4 contain text: Some contain a single line and some contain several lines. The scrollbars you see in some text boxes are part of the control. You can specify which scrollbars (vertical and/or horizontal) will be attached to the control, and they will appear automatically whenever the control's contents exceed the visible area of the control.

The RichTextBox control is effectively the core of a full-blown word processor. It provides all the functionality of a TextBox control; gives users the ability to mix different fonts, sizes, and attributes; and offers precise control over the margins of the text (see Figure 6-5). You can even place images in your text on a RichTextBox control (although you don't have the kind of control over the embedded images that you have with Microsoft Word).

The fundamental property of the RichTextBox control is its RTF property. Similarly to the Text property of the TextBox control, this property is the text displayed on the control. Unlike the Text property, however, which returns (or sets) the text of the control but doesn't contain formatting information, the RTF property returns the text along with any formatting information. Therefore, you can use the RichTextBox control to specify the text's formatting, including paragraph indentation, font, and font size or style.

RTF, which stands for **Rich Text Format,** is a standard for storing formatting information along with text. The beauty of the RichTextBox control for programmers is that they don't need to supply the formatting codes. The control provides simple properties that turn the selected text into bold, change the alignment of the current paragraph, and so on. The RTF code is generated internally

Figure 6-5

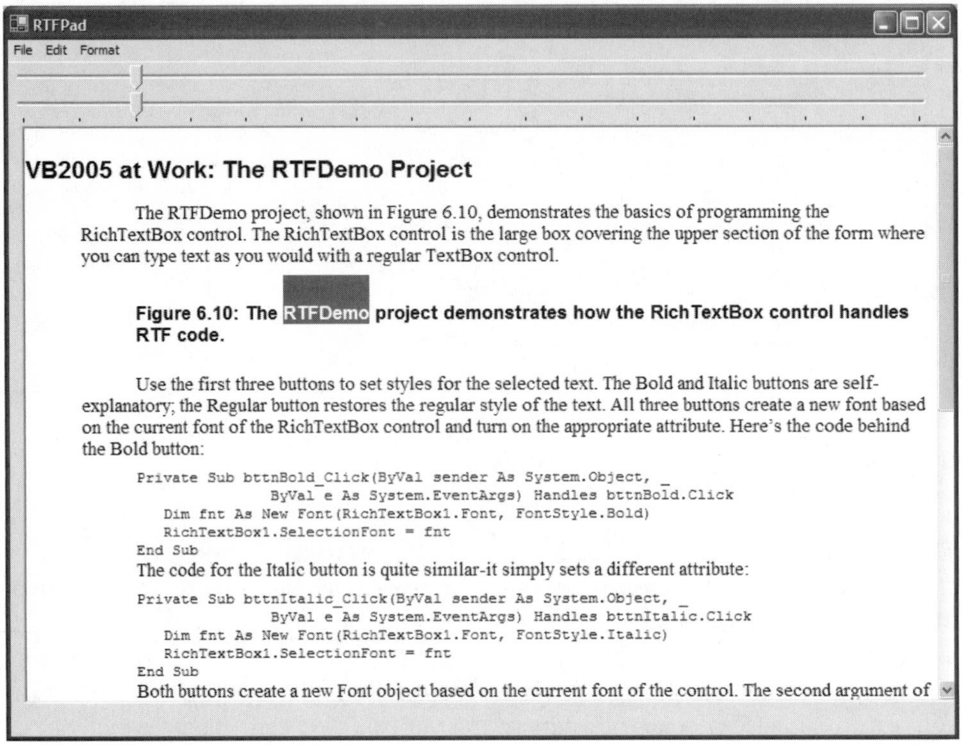

A RichTextBox control.

by the control and used to save and load formatted files. It's possible to create elaborately formatted documents without knowing the RTF language.

TreeView and ListView Controls

The items of a ListBox control can be sorted, but they have no particular structure. For instance, a list with city and state names should be structured so that each city appears under the corresponding state name. In a ListBox control, you can indent some of the entries, but the control itself can't impose or maintain any structure on its data. The TreeView and ListView controls address the shortcomings of the ListBox control.

Figure 6-6 shows the TreeView and ListView controls used in tandem. What you see in Figure 6-6 is **Windows Explorer,** a utility for examining and navigating a hard disk's structure. The left pane, where the folders are displayed, is a TreeView control. The folder names are displayed in a manner that reflects their structure on the hard disk. You can expand and contract certain branches and view only the segment(s) of the tree structure you're interested in.

Figure 6-6

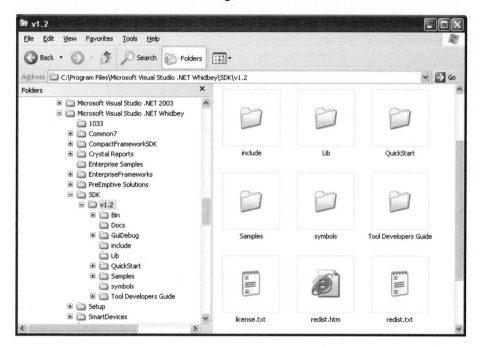

Windows Explorer is made up of a TreeView (left pane) and a ListView (right pane) control.

The right pane of Windows Explorer is a ListView control. The items on the ListView control can be displayed in four different ways (i.e., as large icons, as small icons, as a list, or as a grid). They are the various views you can set through the View menu in Windows Explorer. Although some people prefer to look at the contents of the folders as icons, the more useful view is the Details view, which displays filenames as well as the attributes of the files. In the Details view, the list can be sorted according to any of its columns, making it very easy for the user to locate any item based on various criteria (e.g., file type, size, creation date).

The TreeView control implements a data structure known as a **tree,** which is the most appropriate structure for storing hierarchical information. The organizational charts of most companies use a tree structure. Every person reports to another person above him or her, all the way to the president or CEO. Figure 6-7 depicts a possible organization of continents, countries, and cities as a tree. Every city belongs to a country, and every country belongs to a continent. In the same way, every computer file belongs to a folder that may belong to a higher-level folder. You can't draw large tree structures on paper, but it's possible to create a similar structure in the computer's memory without size limitations. Each item in a tree like the one in Figure 6-7 is called a **node.** Nodes can be nested to any level. The top node is the **root** of the tree, and the subordinate nodes are called **child nodes.** If you try to visualize this structure as a real

Figure 6-7

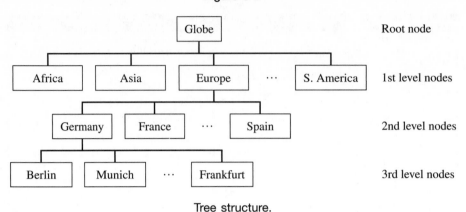

Tree structure.

tree, you can think of it as upside-down, with the branches emerging from the root. The end nodes, which don't lead to any other nodes, are called **leaf nodes.**

To locate a city in the tree structure in Figure 6-7, you must start at the root node and select the continent to which the city belongs. Then you must find the country (in the selected continent) to which the city belongs. Finally, you can find the city you're looking for.

You can also start with a city and find its country. The country node is the city node's parent node. Notice that there is only one route from a child node to its parent node, which means you can instantly locate the country or continent of a city. The same data shown in Figure 6-7 is shown in Figure 6-8 on a TreeView control. Only the nodes we're interested in are expanded. A plus sign indicates that the corresponding node contains child nodes. To view them, you click the plus sign button to expand the node.

The tree structure is ideal for data with **parent/child relationships** (i.e., relationships that can be described as "belongs to" or "owns"). The continents/countries/cities data is a typical example. The folder structure on a hard disk is

Figure 6-8

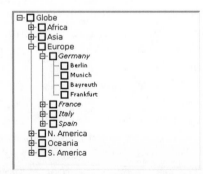

The tree of Figure 6-7, implemented with a TreeView control.

another typical example. Any given folder is the child of another folder or the root folder. If you need a method to traverse the folder structure of your hard disk quickly and conveniently, you should probably store the folders in a Tree-View control, just like Windows Explorer. This approach is not only efficient, it also provides the most suitable interface for this type of information.

The ListView control implements a simpler structure, known as a **list.** A list's items aren't structured in a hierarchy. They are all on the same level and can be traversed serially, one after the other. You can also think of a list as an array but with more features. A list item can have subitems and can be sorted according to any column, like the Details view in Windows Explorer. For example, you can set up a list of customer names (i.e., the list's items) and assign a number of subitems to each customer (e.g., a contact, an address, a phone number). Figure 6-9 shows a Windows folder mapped on a ListView control. Each file is an item, and its attributes are the subitems. As you already know, you can sort this list by filename, size, file type, and so on. All you have to do is click the header of the corresponding column. You can also display the list of files in different views: as icons, as a list of filenames only, or as a report (which is the view shown in Figure 6-9).

The TreeView and ListView controls are commonly used along with the ImageList control. The ImageList control is a very simple control for storing images so they can be retrieved quickly and used at runtime. You populate the

Figure 6-9

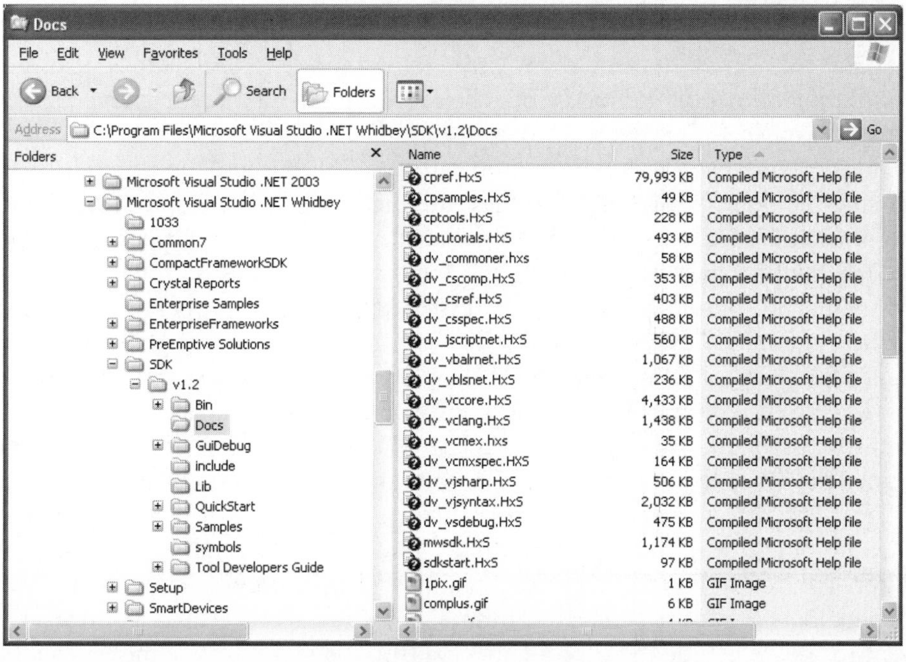

A ListView control.

ImageList control with images, usually at design time, and then you recall them by using an index value at runtime.

6.1.2 Configuring Keyboard Navigation

Allowing users to navigate a form by using the keyboard is a very important issue for designing practical user interfaces, especially for data entry forms. You shouldn't force your users to switch between the keyboard and the mouse all the time. You should follow Windows standards (i.e., the Enter key for the default button, the Tab key to move from one control to the next) and use short-cuts to make sure your application can be used without the mouse.

When you design an application, you can specify in which order the controls receive the focus when the Tab key is pressed (called the **tab order**) with the help of the TabOrder property. Each control has its own TabOrder setting, which is an integer value. When the Tab key is pressed, the focus is moved to the control whose tab order immediately follows that of the current control.

The tab order need not be the same as the physical order of the controls on the form, but controls that are next to each other in the tab order should typically be placed next to each other on the form as well to provide intuitive navigation.

In a TextBox control, you might want the Tab key to insert a Tab character in the text of the control instead of navigating to the next control. To make this possible, you set the control's AcceptsTab property to True (the default value is False). If you do this, users can still move to the next control in the tab order by pressing Ctrl+Tab. Notice that the AcceptsTab property has no effect on other controls. Users may have to press Ctrl+Tab to move to the next control while a TextBox control has the focus, but they can use the Tab key to move from any other control to the next one.

Most forms have a default button, and users can cause its event to fire by pressing the Enter key. Otherwise, they are forced to take their hands off the keyboard, use the mouse to click a button and then return to the keyboard—or press the Tab button repeatedly to move the focus to one of the buttons. You configure the default button by setting the form's AcceptButton property.

In a multiline TextBox control, you want to be able to use the Enter key to change lines. The default value of this property is True, so pressing Enter creates a new line on the control. If you set it to False, users can still create new lines in the TextBox control, but they have to press Ctrl+Enter. If the form contains no default button, the Enter key creates a new line, regardless of the AcceptsReturn setting.

You can activate a **shortcut key** at runtime by pressing the shortcut character while holding down the Alt key. Shortcut keys can be defined for Label controls, Button controls, or other controls that have a read-only Text property. When defined for a Button control, a shortcut key causes the Button control's Click event to fire. When defined for a Label control, the shortcut key moves the focus to the corresponding Label control, but because labels can't receive the focus, the focus is moved immediately to the next control in the tab order, which is the adjacent TextBox control. For this technique to work, you must make sure all controls are properly arranged in the tab order.

To add shortcut keys for the most common fields, you need to determine which of the fields will have their own shortcut keys and which will be used for that purpose. To create a shortcut, you insert the & symbol in front of the character you want to act as a shortcut for each Label control.

If you want to display a & symbol on a control, you prefix it with another & symbol. To display the string "Tom & Jerry" on a Label control, for example, you assign the string "Tom && Jerry" to its Text property.

6.1.3 Anchoring and Docking Controls

A common issue in form design is the design of forms that are properly resized. You might design a nice form for a given size, and when it's resized at runtime, the controls are all clustered in the top-left corner. A TextBox control that covered the entire width of the form at design time suddenly "cringes" on the left when the user drags out the window. If the user makes the form smaller than the default size, part of the TextBox is invisible because it's outside the form. You can attach scrollbars to the form, but that doesn't really help; who wants to type text and have to scroll the form horizontally? It makes sense to scroll vertically because you get to see many lines at once, but if the TextBox control is wider than the form, you can't read entire lines.

The Anchor property lets you **anchor** a control (i.e., attach one or more edges of the control to corresponding edges of the form). The anchored edges of the control maintain the same distance from the corresponding edges of the form. When you anchor a control to the left side of the form, the distance between the control's left side and the form's left edge remains the same. This is the default behavior of the controls. If you dock the right side of the control to the right side of the form, as you resize the width of the form, the control is moved so that its distance from the right side of the form remains fixed—you can even push the control out of the left edge of the form. If you anchor two opposite sides of the control (i.e., top and bottom, left and right), the control is resized, and the docking distances of both sides remain the same. Finally, if you anchor all four sides, the control is resized along with the form.

To see how this works, you can try an example of anchoring a control. Place a TextBox control on a new form and then open the control's Anchor property in the Properties window. You see a little square within a larger square and four pegs that connect the small control to the sides of the larger box (see Figure 6-10). The large box is the form, and the small one is the control. The four pegs are the anchors, which can be either white or gray. The gray anchors denote a fixed distance between the control and the form. By default, the control is placed at a fixed distance from the top-left corner of the form. When the form is resized, the control retains its size and its distance from the top-left corner of the form.

Figure 6-10

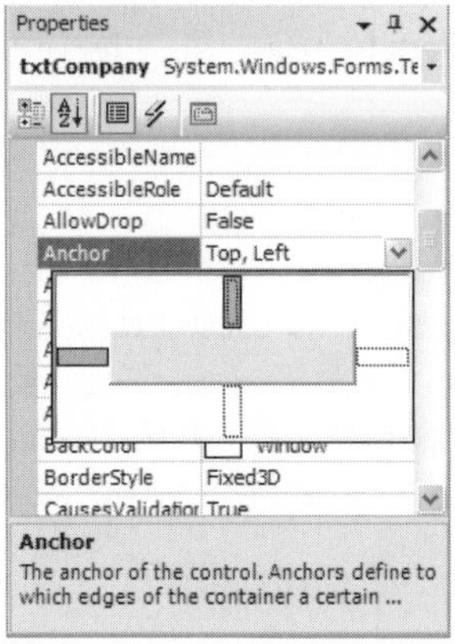

Anchor Property settings.

There is a small problem even when using the Anchor property: If you make the form very narrow, there is no room for both buttons across the form's width. The simplest way to fix this problem is to impose a minimum size for the form. To do so, you must first decide the form's minimum width and height and then set the MinimumSize property to these values.

In addition to the Anchor property, most controls expose the Dock property, which determines how a control will **dock** on the form (i.e., attach to one or more edges of the form and grow or shrink with the form). The default value of this property is None. To see this, you can create a new form, place a TextBox control on it, and then open the control's Dock property. The various rectangular shapes are the settings of the property (see Figure 6-11. If you click the mid-

Figure 6-11

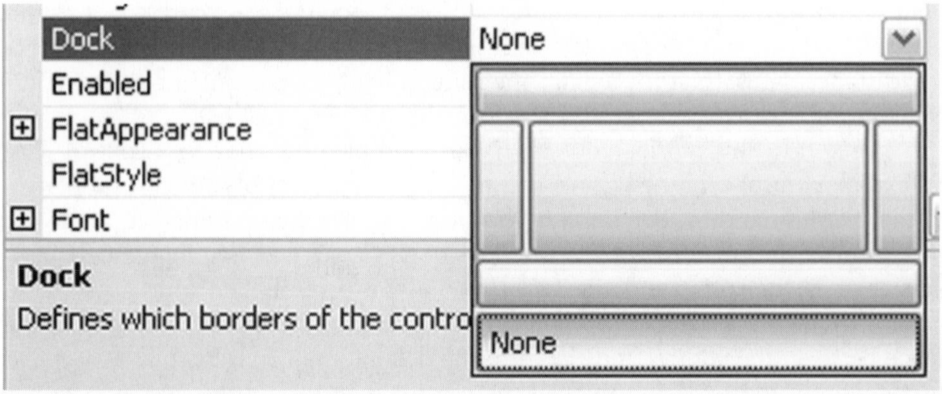

Setting the Dock property.

dle rectangle, the control will be docked over the entire form: It will expand and shrink both horizontally and vertically to cover the entire form. This setting is appropriate for simple forms that contain a single control, usually a TextBox control, and sometimes a menu.

6.1.4 Dynamic Controls

In some situations, you don't know in advance how many instances of a given control might be required on a form. For example, you might need to enable certain features of an application, depending on the current state of the application or the user's privileges. In these situations, it is possible to design dynamic forms that are populated at runtime.

The simplest approach is to create more controls than you'll ever need and set their Visible property to False at design time. At runtime, you can display the controls by switching their Visible property to True. As you know already, quick-and-dirty methods are not the most efficient ones. You must still rearrange the controls on the form to make the form look nice at all times. The proper method to create dynamic forms at runtime is to add and remove controls on your form as needed, using the techniques discussed in this section.

Just as you can create new instances of forms, you can also create new instances of any control and place them on a form. The Form object exposes the **Controls collection,** which contains all the controls on the form. This collection is created automatically as you place controls on the form at design time, and you can access the members of this collection from within code. It is also possible to add new members to the collection or remove existing members.

The Controls collection is also a property of any control that can host other controls, known as a **container control.** Many of the controls that come with Visual Basic 2005 can host other controls. The Panel control and the GroupBox controls are examples of container controls. The Panel control belongs to the form's Controls collection. The element that corresponds to the Panel control provides its own Controls collection, which lets you access the controls on the panel. If a panel is the third element of the Controls collection, you can access it with this expression:

```
Me.Controls(2)
```

To access the controls on this panel, you use the following Controls collection:

```
Me.Controls(2).Controls
```

The Controls collection exposes members for accessing and manipulating the controls at runtime. The Add method is used to add a new element to the Controls collection. In effect, it adds a new control on the current form or container control. The Add method accepts a control as an argument and adds it to the collection. Its syntax is as follows, where *controlObj* is an instance of a control:

```
Me.Controls.Add(controlObj)
```

The **Me keyword** references the current form. To place a new Button control on the form, you declare and instantiate a variable of the Button type, set its properties, and then add it to the Controls collection:

```
Dim bttn As New Button
bttn.Text = "New Button"
bttn.Left = 100
bttn.Top = 60
bttn.Width = 80
Me.Controls.Add(bttn)
```

You use the Remove method to remove an element from the Controls collection. It accepts as an argument either the index of the control to be removed or a reference to the control to be removed (i.e., a variable of the Control type that represents one of the controls on the form). These two forms of the Remove method have the following syntax:

```
Me.Controls.Remove(index)
Me.Controls.Remove(controlObj)
```

The Count property returns the number of elements in the Controls collection. You use the following expression to give the number of controls on the current form:

```
Me.Controls.Count
```

Notice that if there are container controls, the controls in the containers are not included in the count. For example, if a form contains a Panel control, the controls on the panel aren't included in the value returned by the Count property. The Panel control, however, has its own Controls collection.

The Clear method removes all the elements of the Controls array and effectively clears a form.

FOR EXAMPLE

Designing a User Interface

Say that you are designing a user interface for an application that will be used to submit an auto insurance application. The form accepts the following information:

▲ First name
▲ Middle initial
▲ Last name
▲ Date of birth
▲ Driver's license number
▲ Sex

Figure 6-12

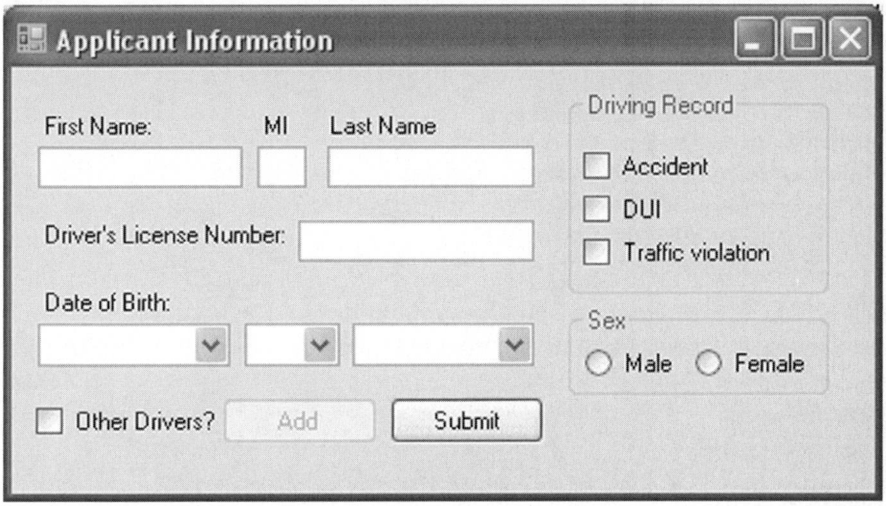

An insurance application form.

▲ Whether the applicant has had a ticket, an accident, or a driving under the influence conviction

▲ Whether there are other drivers in the household (If there are other drivers, the same information must be entered for each other driver. There are no limits to the number of additional drivers.)

The insurance agent should be able to select a month, a date, and a year between 1900 and 16 years prior to the current year from a list when entering the birth date to prevent entering invalid birth dates.

You decide to use TextBox controls for the First Name, Middle Initial, Last Name, and Driver's License Number fields. You decide to use ComboBox controls for each element of the date. You set the DropDownStyle property to Drop-DownList. You use RadioButton controls in a GroupBox for Sex and CheckBox controls in another GroupBox for the driving record information. You add an additional CheckBox control to the form that allows the user to check whether there are additional drivers. If there are, an Add button is enabled. When the user clicks the Add button, you dynamically create a Panel control and add the necessary controls to the Panel control's Controls collection in code. Then you add the Panel control to the form's Controls collection. You set the form's Auto-Size property to True. The form is shown in Figure 6-12.

The code is as follows:

```
Private Sub btnAdd_Click(ByVal sender As System. Object, _
    ByVal e As System.EventArgs) Handles btnAdd.Click
    Static iNextDriverY As Integer = 190
```

(Continued)

```
Static iNextDriverX As Integer = 2
Static iNumDrivers = 1

Dim tx As TextBox
Dim lb As Label
Dim gb As GroupBox
Dim rb As RadioButton
Dim ck As CheckBox
Dim cb As ComboBox
Dim pnl As New Panel
Dim arrMonths() As String = {"January", _
    "February", "March", "April", "May", _
    "June", "July", "August", "September", _
    "October", "November", "December"}
Dim i As Integer
iNumDrivers += 1

pnl.Top = iNextDriverY
pnl.Left = iNextDriverX
pnl.AutoSize = True
pnl.BorderStyle = BorderStyle.Fixed3D
Me.Controls.Add(pnl)

lb = New Label
lb.Text = "First Name"
lb.Top = lbFirstD1.Top
lb.Left = lbFirstD1.Left
lb.Width = lbFirstD1.Width
lb.Height = lbFirstD1.Height
pnl.Controls.Add(lb)

lb = New Label
lb.Text = "MI"
lb.Top = lbMID1.Top
lb.Left = lbMID1.Left
lb.Width = lbMID1.Width
lb.Height = lbMID1.Height
pnl.Controls.Add(lb)

lb = New Label
lb.Text = "Last Name"
lb.Top = lbLastD1.Top
lb.Left = lbLastD1.Left
lb.Width = lbLastD1.Width
lb.Height = lbLastD1.Height
pnl.Controls.Add(lb)

lb = New Label
lb.Text = "Driver's License Number"
```

```
lb.Top = lbDLND1.Top
lb.Left = lbDLND1.Left
lb.Width = lbDLND1.Width
lb.Height = lbDLND1.Height
pnl.Controls.Add(lb)

lb = New Label
lb.Text = "Date of Birth"
lb.Top = lbDOBD1.Top
lb.Left = lbDOBD1.Left
lb.Width = lbDOBD1.Width
lb.Height = lbDOBD1.Height
pnl.Controls.Add(lb)

tx = New TextBox
tx.Top = txtFirstD1.Top
tx.Left = txtFirstD1.Left
tx.Width = txtFirstD1.Width
tx.Height = txtFirstD1.Height
tx.Name = "txtFirstD" & iNumDrivers
pnl.Controls.Add(tx)

tx = New TextBox
tx.Top = txtMID1.Top
tx.Left = txtMID1.Left
tx.Width = txtMID1.Width
tx.Height = txtMID1.Height
tx.Name = "txtMID" & iNumDrivers
pnl.Controls.Add(tx)

tx = New TextBox
tx.Top = txtLastD1.Top
tx.Left = txtLastD1.Left
tx.Width = txtLastD1.Width
tx.Height = txtLastD1.Height
tx.Name = "txtLastD" & iNumDrivers
pnl.Controls.Add(tx)

tx = New TextBox
tx.Top = txtDLND1.Top
tx.Left = txtDLND1.Left
tx.Width = txtDLND1.Width
tx.Height = txtDLND1.Height
tx.Name = "txtDLND" & iNumDrivers
pnl.Controls.Add(tx)

cb = New ComboBox
cb.Name = "cboDOBMonD" & iNumDrivers
cb.Top = cboDOBMonD1.Top
```

(Continued)

```
cb.Left = cboDOBMonD1.Left
cb.Width = cboDOBMonD1.Width
cb.Height = cboDOBMonD1.Height
cb.Items.AddRange(arrMonths)
pnl.Controls.Add(cb)

cb = New ComboBox
cb.Name = "cboDOBDayD" & iNumDrivers
cb.Top = cboDOBDayD1.Top
cb.Left = cboDOBDayD1.Left
cb.Width = cboDOBDayD1.Width
cb.Height = cboDOBDayD1.Height
For i = 1 To 31
    cb.Items.Add(i)
Next

pnl.Controls.Add(cb)

cb = New ComboBox
cb.Name = "cboDOBYearD" & iNumDrivers
cb.Top = cboDOBYearD1.Top
cb.Left = cboDOBYearD1.Left
cb.Width = cboDOBYearD1.Width
cb.Height = cboDOBYearD1.Height
For i = 1900 To Today.Year - 15
    cb.Items.Add(i)
Next

pnl.Controls.Add(cb)

gb = New GroupBox
gb.Text = "Driving Record"
gb.Top = gbRecordD1.Top
gb.Left = gbRecordD1.Left
gb.Width = gbRecordD1.Width
gb.Height = gbRecordD1.Height
pnl.Controls.Add(gb)

ck = New CheckBox
ck.Text = "Accident"
ck.Top = ckAccidentD1.Top
ck.Left = ckAccidentD1.Left
ck.Width = ckAccidentD1.Width
ck.Height = ckAccidentD1.Height
ck.Name = "ckAccidentD" & iNumDrivers
gb.Controls.Add(ck)

ck = New CheckBox
ck.Text = "DUI"
ck.Top = ckDUID1.Top
```

```
ck.Left = ckDUID1.Left
ck.Width = ckDUID1.Width
ck.Height = ckDUID1.Height
ck.Name = "ckDUID" & iNumDrivers
gb.Controls.Add(ck)


ck = New CheckBox
ck.Text = "Traffic Violation"
ck.Top = ckTicketD1.Top
ck.Left = ckTicketD1.Left
ck.Width = ckTicketD1.Width
ck.Height = ckTicketD1.Height
ck.Name = "ckTicketD" & iNumDrivers
gb.Controls.Add(ck)


gb = New GroupBox
gb.Text = "Sex"
gb.Top = gbSexD1.Top
gb.Left = gbSexD1.Left
gb.Width = gbSexD1.Width
gb.Height = gbSexD1.Height
pnl.Controls.Add(gb)


rb = New RadioButton
rb.Text = "Male"
rb.Top = rbMaleD1.Top
rb.Left = rbMaleD1.Left
rb.Width = rbMaleD1.Width
rb.Height = rbMaleD1.Height
rb.Name = "rbMaleD" & iNumDrivers
gb.Controls.Add(rb)


rb = New RadioButton
rb.Text = "Female"
rb.Top = rbFemaleD1.Top
rb.Left = rbFemaleD1.Left
rb.Width = rbFemaleD1.Width
rb.Height = rbFemaleD1.Height
rb.Name = "rbFemaleD" & iNumDrivers
gb.Controls.Add(rb)


If iNumDrivers Mod 4 = 0 Then 'Add another column
    iNextDriverX = pnl.Right + 2
    iNextDriverY = 22
Else
    iNextDriverY = pnl.Bottom + 2
End If
End Sub
```

(Continued)

```
Private Sub ckOthers_CheckedChanged(ByVal sender As _
    System.Object, ByVal e As System.EventArgs) Handles _
    ckOthers.CheckedChanged
        If ckOthers.Checked = True Then
            btnAdd.Enabled = True
        End If
End Sub
```

Figure 6-13 shows the form after you click Add four times. As you can see, the form can support four drivers vertically before another column is added. One potential drawback is that, depending on the screen resolution, this form will eventually be bigger than the screen. Of course, most households don't have more than a few drivers, so this might not be an important issue.

Figure 6-13

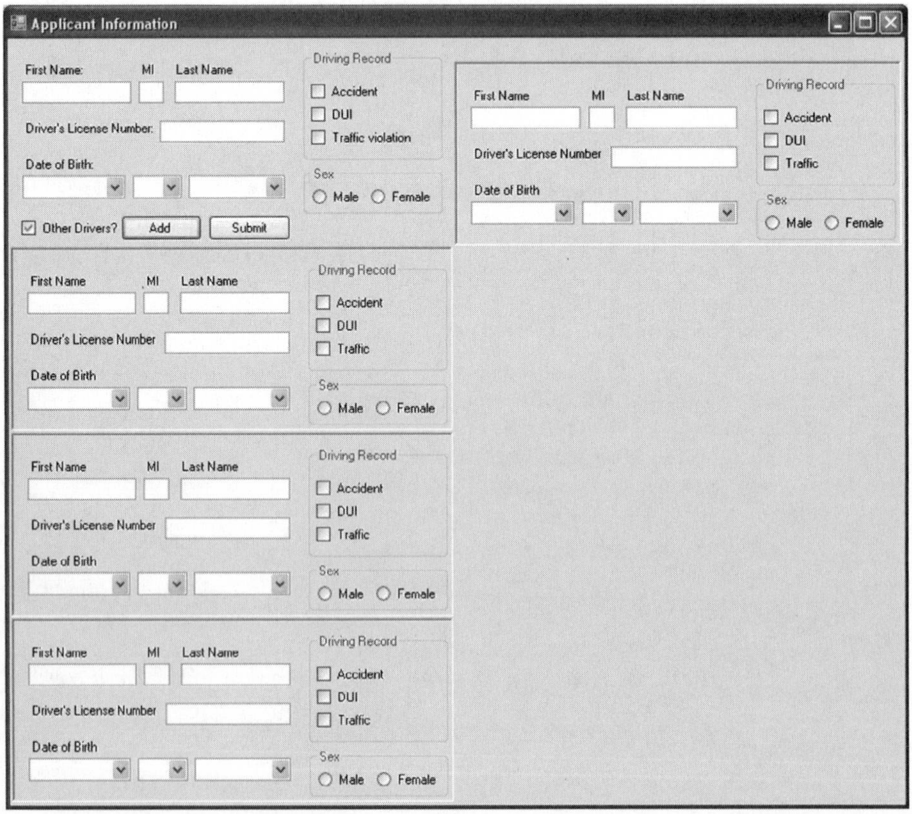

The Applicant Information form after you add room for four other drivers.

6.2 Manipulating and Formatting Strings

You can think of a sString as being like an array of characters. You can retrieve individual characters from a string, compare one string against another, **concatenate** (join together) strings, and add characters to a string. In this section, we'll look some of the methods available for manipulating strings.

6.2.1 The String Class

The String class implements the String data type, which is one of the richest data types in terms of the members it exposes. To create a new instance of the String class, you simply declare a variable of the String type. You can also initialize it by assigning a text value to the corresponding variable:

```
Dim title As String = "Hello"
```

The String class exposes two properties and a number of methods. We'll take only a brief look at a few of the methods. Let's look first at the properties.

The Length property returns the number of characters in the string and is read-only. To find out the number of characters in a string variable, you use the following statement:

```
chars = myString.Length
```

The Chars property is an array of characters that holds all the characters in the string. You use this property to read individual characters from a string, based on their location in the string. The index of the first character in the chars array is 0. The Chars property is read-only, and you can't edit a string by setting individual characters.

The following code rejects strings (presumably passwords) that are fewer than six characters long and don't contain a special symbol:

```
Private Function ValidatePassword(ByVal password As String) _
    As Boolean
```

```
        If password.Length < 6 Then
            MsgBox _
            ("Password must be at least 6 characters.")
            Return False
        End If
        Dim i As Integer
        Dim valid As Boolean = False
        For i = 0 To password.Length - 1
            If Not Char.IsLetterOrDigit _
                (password.Chars(i)) Then
                    Return True
            End If
        Next
        MsgBox("The password must contain at least" _
            & " one character that is not a letter or" _
            & " a digit.")
        Return False
    End Function
```

The code checks the length of the user-supplied string and makes sure it's at least six characters long. If it's not, the program issues a warning and returns False. Then it starts a loop that scans all the characters in the string. Each character is accessed by its index in the string. If one of them is not a letter or digit—in which case the IsLetterOrDigit method returns False—the function terminates and returns True to indicate a valid password. If the loop is exhausted, the password argument contains no special symbols, and the function displays another message and returns False.

6.2.2 Changing a String's Case

You might at some point need to store a string value in either uppercase or lowercase. If such a case, you can use the ToUpper method to convert the string to uppercase. You can use the ToLower method to convert the string to lowercase.

6.2.3 Comparing Strings

The Compare method is a shared method that compares two strings and returns a negative value if the first string is less than the second, a positive value if the second string is less than the first, and 0 if the two strings are equal. The Compare method is **overloaded** (i.e., has multiple versions that accept different arguments), and the first two arguments are always the two strings to be compared.

The simplest form of the method accepts two strings as arguments:

```
String.Compare(str1, str2)
```

The following statements return the values shown in bold below each:

```
Debug.WriteLine(String.Compare( _
    "the quick brown fox", _
    "THE QUICK BROWN FOX"))
-1
Debug.WriteLine(String.Compare( _
    "THE QUICK BROWN FOX", _
    "the quick brown fox"))
1
Debug.WriteLine(String.Compare( _
    "THE QUICK BROWN FOX", _
    "THE QUICK BROWN FOX"))
0
```

By default, a case sensitive comparison is made. In the first example, a-1 is returned because the ASCII codes for the lower case letters are less than the ASCII codes for the uppercase characters. The following form of the method accepts a third argument, which is a True/False value and determines whether the search will be case sensitive (if True):

```
String.Compare(str1, str2, case)
```

Another form of the Compare method allows you to compare segments of two strings; its syntax is as follows:

```
String.Compare(str1, index1, str2, index2, length)
```

The index1 and index2 parameters are the starting locations of the segment to be compared in each string. The two segments must have the same length, which is specified by the last argument. If you want to specify a case-sensitive search, you append yet another argument and set it to True.

The EndsWith and StartsWith methods return True if the string ends or starts with a user-supplied substring. The syntax of these methods is as follows:

```
found = str.EndsWith(string)
found = str.StartsWith(string)
```

Notice that the comparison performed by the StartsWith method is case sensitive. If you don't care about the case, you can convert both the string and the substring to uppercase, as in the following example:

```
If name.ToUpper.StartsWith("VIS") Then ...
```

This If clause is true, regardless of the case of the name variable.

The IndexOf and LastIndexOf methods locate a substring in a larger string. The IndexOf method starts searching from the beginning of the string, and the LastIndexOf method starts searching from the end of the string. Each of these methods returns an integer, which is the order of the substring's first character in the larger string; the order of the first character is 0.

To locate a single character in a string, you use the following forms of the IndexOf method:

```
str.IndexOf(Char)
str.IndexOf(Char,  startIndex)
str.IndexOf(Char,  startIndex,  endIndex)
```

The startIndex and the endIndex arguments delimit the section of the string where the search will take place.

To locate a string, you use the following forms of the IndexOf method:

```
str.IndexOf(String)
str.IndexOf(String,  startIndex)
str.IndexOf(String,  startIndex,  endIndex)
```

The last three forms of the IndexOf method search for an array of characters in the string:

```
str.IndexOf(Char())
str.IndexOf(Char(),  startIndex)
str.IndexOf(Char(),  startIndex,  endIndex)
```

The following statement returns the position of the string "Visual" in the text of the TextBox1 control or will return -1 if the string isn't contained in the text:

```
Dim pos As  Integer
pos  =  TextBox1.IndexOf("Visual")
```

Both of these methods perform a case-sensitive search, taking into consideration the current locale. To make case-insensitive searches, you use uppercase for both the string and the substring. The following statement returns the location of the string "visual" (or "VISUAL", "Visual", or even "vISUAL") within the text of TextBox1:

```
Dim pos As  Integer
pos  =  TextBox1.Text.ToUpper.IndexOf("VISUAL")
```

The expression TextBox1.Text is the text on the control, and its type is String. First, you apply the method ToUpper to convert the text to uppercase and then you apply the IndexOf method to this string to locate the first instance of the word "VISUAL."

6.2.4 Changing String Variables

The String class includes a number of methods for modifying the contents of a String variable. However, behind the scenes, when you change the contents of a String variable, you are really copying the new value to a new instance of the String variable. Let's look at some of these methods.

Concat

The Concat method concatenates two or more strings and forms a new string. The simpler form of the Concat method has the following syntax and it is equivalent to the & operator:

```
newString = String.Concat(string1, string2)
```

This statement is equivalent to the following:

```
newString = string1 & string2
```

A more useful form of the same method concatenates a large number of strings stored in an array:

```
newString = String.Concat(strings())
```

To use this form of the method, you store all the strings you want to concatenate in a string array and then call the Concat method, as shown in this code segment:

```
Dim strings() As String = {"string1", "string2", _
    "string3", "string4"}
Dim longString As String
longString = String.Concat(strings())
```

If you want to separate the individual strings with special **delimiters** (i.e., characters that separates items in a list), you append the delimiters to each individual string before concatenating them. Or you can use the Join method discussed later in this section. The Concat method simply appends each string to the end of the previous one.

Insert

The Insert method inserts one or more characters at a specified location in a string and returns the new string. The following is the syntax of the Insert method is:

```
newString = str.Insert(startIndex, subString)
```

startIndex is the position in the *str* variable, where the string specified by the second argument will be inserted. The following statement inserts a dash between the second and third characters of the string "CA93010":

```
Dim Zip As String = "CA93010"
Dim StateZip As String
StateZip = Zip.Insert(2, "-")
```

The StateZip string variable will become "CA-93010" after the execution of these statements.

Joining Two or More Strings

This method joins two or more strings and returns a single string that has a separator between the original strings. Its syntax as follows following, where *separator* is the string that will be used as a separator, and *strings* is an array containing the strings to be joined:

```
newString = String.Join(separator, strings)
```

If you have an array of several strings and you want to join a few of them, you can specify the index of the first string in the array and the number of strings to be joined with the following form of the Join method:

```
newString = String.Join(separator, strings, _
    startIndex, count)
```

The following statement creates a full path by joining folder names:

```
Dim path As String
Dim folders() As String = {"My Documents", _
    "Business", "Expenses"}
path = String.Join("/", folders)
```

The value of the path variable after the execution of these statements is as follows:

```
My Documents/Business/Expenses
```

Splitting Strings

Just as you can join strings, you can split long strings into smaller ones. To do so, you use the Split method, whose syntax is as follows, where *delimiters* is an array of characters and *str* is the string to be split:

```
strings() = String.Split(delimiters, str)
```

The string is split into sections that are separated by any one of the delimiters specified with the first argument. These strings are returned as an array of strings. The *delimiters* array allows you to specify multiple delimiters, which makes it a great tool for isolating words in a text. You can specify all the characters that separate words in text (e.g., spaces, tabs, periods, exclamation marks) as delimiters and pass them along with the text to be parsed to the Split method.

The following statements isolate the parts of a path, which are delimited by a backslash character.

```
Dim path As String = _
    "c:\My Documents\Business\Expenses"
Dim delimiters() As Char = {CChar("\")}
Dim parts() As String
Dim s As String
```

```
parts = path.Split(delimiters)
For Each s In parts
     Debug.WriteLine(s)
Next
```

If you execute this code, it displays the following:

```
c:
My Documents
Business
Expenses
```

If the path ends with a slash, the Split method returns an extra empty string. You should either make sure the string doesn't start or end with a delimiter or ignore the elements of the parts array that hold empty strings.

Notice that the parts array is declared without a size. It's a one-dimensional array that will be dimensioned automatically by the Split method, according to the number of substrings separated by the specified delimiter(s). The second half of the code iterates through the parts of the path and displays them on the Output window.

Removing Characters

The Remove method removes a given number of characters from a string, starting at a specific location, and returns the result as a new string. Its syntax is as follows, where *startIndex* is the index of the first character to be removed in the *str* variable and *count* is the number of characters to be removed:

```
newString = str.Remove(startIndex, count)
```

For example, to remove the first five characters of a string named strLocSpecProductCode, you use this code:

```
strProductCode = strLocSpecProductCode.Remove(0, 5)
```

Replacing Characters

The Replace method replaces all instances of a specified character (or substring) in a string with a new one. It creates a new instance of the string, replaces the characters as specified by its arguments, and returns this string, where *oldChar* is the character in the *str* variable to be replaced and *newChar* is the character to replace the occurrences of *oldChar*:

```
newString = str.Replace(oldChar, newChar)
```

You can also specify strings instead of characters as arguments to the Replace method. The string after the replacement is returned as the result of the method. The following statements replace all instances of the tab character with a single space:

```
Dim txt, newTxt As String
Dim vbTab As String = vbCrLf
txt = "some text with two tabs"
newTxt = txt.Replace(vbTab, " ")
```

You can change the last statement to replace tabs with a specific number of spaces—usually three, four, or five spaces—by entering the spaces as literal characters inside the quotation marks.

FOR EXAMPLE

Manipulating Strings

Say that you are building an application for managing auto insurance policies. The application has two forms. The first form accepts input about the drivers on the policy. The drivers' names are entered as First Name, Middle Initial, Last Name, using separate TextBox controls, because that is the way the data is stored in the database. After the user clicks the Submit button, another form should display. This form should include each driver's name in a ListBox control. It should also include a CheckedListBox control named clbOptions that lists the insurance choices available. The insurance choices are stored in a comma-delimited file.

You use the following code to join the three parts of the name together:

```
Dim strNameParts(2) As String
Dim strFullName As String
strNameParts(0) = strFirstName
strNameParts(1) = strMiddleInitial
strNameParts(2) = strLastName
strFullName = String.Join(" ", strNameParts)
```

You use the following code to add the insurance choices to the CheckedListBox control:

```
Dim delimiters() As Char = {CChar(",")}
Dim strCoverageChoices() As String
Dim s As String
strCoverageChoices = strOptions.Split(delimiters)
For Each s in strCoverageChoices
    clbOptions.Items.Add(s)
Next
```

This code assumes a variable named strOptions that stores the complete list of coverage options.

- Compare the Concat method with the Join method.
- Identify a situation in which using the Split method is appropriate.
- Describe the effect of the following code:

```
String.Compare(str1, str2, false)
```

6.3 Formatting Output

Sometimes you need to output numeric and date data formatted a specific way. In this section, we'll look at the Format function. Next, we'll look at using the Date data type properties to format how a Date value is output.

6.3.1 The Format Function

To control the form of numeric items in output, you need to use the Format function, which has the following syntax:

```
Format(expression, format)
```

The *expression* variable is any valid expression that is to be formatted, and the *format* variable is any valid format expression. A **format expression** is a string value that identifies the format that should be used to display the value. The more commonly used numeric format expressions are shown in Table 6-2, where each format expression is enclosed in quotation marks in the Format function. Note that the Format function has no effect on nonnumeric variables. For example, to format a number as currency with two decimal places, the expression would be "currency"; to format it as a percentage, the expression would be "percent". These formats can also be abbreviated as "c" for currency and "p" for percentage.

For example, to format the value stored in decTaxes and display it in the txtTaxes text box as currency, you use this code:

```
txtTaxes.text = Format(decTaxes, "currency")
```

If you do not include the format expression, the Format function returns the same result as the CStr function.

6.3.2 Formatting Date Values

When you declare a variable of type Date, you are actually creating an instance of the DateTime class. Date and time values are stored internally as Double numbers. The integer part of the value corresponds to the date, and the fractional part corresponds to the time.

Table 6-2: Numeric Format Expressions

Format Expression	Abbreviation	Result
Currency	"c" or "C"	Displays a number with a dollar sign, a thousands separator, and two digits to the right of the decimal point.
Fixed	"f" or "F"	Displays a number with at least one digit to the left and two digits to the right of the decimal point.
Standard	"s" or "S"	Displays a number with a thousands separator and at least one digit to the left and two digits to the right of the decimal point.
Percent	"p" or "P"	Displays a number multiplied by 100, with a percent sign (%) on the right and two digits to the right of the decimal point.
Scientific	"e" or "E"	Uses standard scientific notation.

Initializing and Inputting Dates

To initialize a DateTime variable, you supply a date value enclosed in a pair of pound symbols. If the value contains time information, you separate it from the date part with a space. Here's an example:

```
Dim date1 As Date = #4/15/2005#
Dim date2 As Date = #4/15/2005 2:01:59#
```

If you have a string that represents a date and you want to assign it to a DateTime variable for further processing, you use the DateTime class's Parse and ParseExact methods. The Parse method parses a string and returns a date value if the string can be interpreted as a date value. Let's say your code prompts the user for a date that it then uses in date calculations. The user-supplied date is read as a string, and you must convert it to a date value:

```
Dim sDate1 As String
Dim dDate1 As DateTime
sDate1 = InputBox( _
    "Please enter a date after 1/1/2002")
Try
    dDate1 = System.DateTime.Parse(sDate1)
    ' use dDate1 in your calculations
Catch exc As Exception
    MsgBox("You've entered an invalid date")
End Try
```

The Parse method converts a string that represents a date to a DateTime value, regardless of the format of the date. You can enter dates such as "1/17/2005", "Jan. 17, 2005", or "January 17, 2005" (with or without the comma).

DateTime Properties

The DateTime class exposes a number of properties that allow you to display a part of the date. We'll look at some of them here.

The Date property returns the date from a date/time value and sets the time to midnight. Say that you use the following statements:

```
Dim date1 As DateTime
date1 = Now()
Debug.WriteLine(date1)
Debug.WriteLine(date1.Date)
```

Something like the following values then appear in the Output window:

```
5/29/2001 2:30:17 PM
5/29/2001 12:00:00 AM
```

The DayOfWeek property returns the day of the week (i.e., a number from 1 to 7). The DayOfYear property returns the number of the day in the year (i.e., an integer from 1 to 365, or 366 for leap years).

The Hour, Minute, Second, and Millisecond properties return the corresponding time part of the date value, passed as an argument. For example, say that you place these statements in a button's Click event handler and execute them when the current time is 1:32:27 p.m.:

```
Debug.WriteLine("The current time is " _
    & Date.Now.ToString)
Debug.WriteLine("The hour is " & Date.Now.Hour)
Debug.WriteLine("The minute is " & Date.Now.Minute)
Debug.WriteLine("The second is " & Date.Now.Second)
```

The following is then shown on the Output window:

```
The current time is 13:35:22.0527552
The hour is 13
The minute is 35
The second is 22
```

The Day, Month, and Year properties return the day of the month, the month, and the year of a DateTime value. The Day and Month properties are numeric values, but you can convert them to the appropriate string (the name of the day or month) with the WeekDayName and MonthName functions. The WeekDayName function accepts as an argument the number of the day (i.e., a value from 1 to 7) and returns the name of the corresponding day of the week. The MonthName function accepts as an argument the month (i.e., a value from 1 to 13) and returns the corresponding month name. You can use the value 13 with a 13-month calendar (applies to non-U.S. or non-European calendars). Otherwise, MonthName returns an empty string when 13 is passed as the argument. The functions also accept a second optional argument that is a true/false value and indicates whether the function should return the abbreviated name (if True) or full name (if False). The WeekDayName function accepts a third optional argument, which determines the first day of the week. You can set this argument to one of the members of the FirstDayOfWeek enumeration. By default, the first day of the week is Sunday.

The TimeOfDay property returns the time from a date/time value. The following statement returns a value like the one shown in bold after the statement:

```
Debug.WriteLine(Now().TimeOfDay)
14:35:44.4589088
```

Comparing Dates

Compare is a shared method that compares two date/time values and returns an integer value that indicates the relative order of the two values. The syntax of the Compare method is as follows, where *date1* and *date2* are the two values to be compared:

```
order = System.DateTime.Compare(date1, date2)
```

The method returns an integer, which is −1 if *date1* is less than *date2,* 0 if they're equal, and 1 if *date1* is greater than *date2.*

Getting Information About Dates

DaysInMonth is a shared method that returns the number of days in a specific month. Because February contains a variable number of days, depending on the year, the DaysInMonth method accepts as arguments both the month and the year:

```
monDays = System.DateTime.DaysInMonth(year, month)
```

To find the number of days in February 2009, you use the following expression:

```
FebDays = System.DateTime.DaysInMonth(2009, 2)
```

IsLeapYear is a shared method that returns a true/false value that indicates whether the specified year is a leap year:

```
Dim leapYear As Boolean
leapYear = System.DateTime.IsLeapYear(year)
```

Adding and Subtracting Intervals

Various methods add specific intervals to a date/time value. Each method accepts the number of intervals to add (e.g., days, hours, milliseconds) to the current instance of the DateTime class. These methods are AddYears, AddMonths, AddDays,

AddHours, AddMinutes, AddSeconds, AddMilliseconds, and AddTicks. A **tick** is 100 nanoseconds and is used for really fine timing operations. To add 3 years and 12 hours to the current date, you use the following statements:

```
Dim aDate As Date
aDate = Now()
aDate = aDate.AddYears(3)
aDate = aDate.AddHours(12)
```

If the argument is a negative value, the corresponding intervals are subtracted from the current instance of the class. The following statement subtracts 2 minutes from a date variable:

```
aDate = aDate.AddMinutes(-2)
```

Formatting Dates for Output

The ToString method converts a date/time value to a string, using a specific format. The DateTime class recognizes numerous format patterns. The syntax of the ToString method is as follows, where *formatSpec* is a format specification:

```
aDate.ToString(formatSpec)
```

The "D" date format, for example, formats a date value as a long date, and the following statement returns the string shown in bold below the statement:

```
Debug.Writeline(#9/17/2005#.ToString("D"))
```
Saturday, September 17, 2005

The following examples format the current date, using all the standard format patterns. An example of the output produced by each statement is shown in bold under each statement:

```
Debug.WriteLine(now().ToString("d"))
```
2/16/2004
```
Debug.WriteLine(now().ToString("D"))
```
Monday, February 16, 2004
```
Debug.WriteLine(now().ToString("f"))
```
Monday, February 16, 2004 1:55 AM
```
Debug.WriteLine(now().ToString("F"))
```
Monday, February 16, 2004 1:55:36 AM
```
Debug.WriteLine(now().ToString("g"))
```
2/16/2004 1:55 AM
```
Debug.WriteLine(now().ToString("G"))
```
2/16/2004 1:55:36 AM
```
Debug.WriteLine(now().ToString("m"))
```
February 16
```
Debug.WriteLine(now().ToString("r"))
```
Mon, 16 Feb 2004 01:55:36 GMT

```
Debug.WriteLine(now().ToString("s"))
2004-02-16T01:55:36
Debug.WriteLine(now().ToString("t"))
1:55 AM
Debug.WriteLine(now().ToString("T"))
1:55:36 AM
Debug.WriteLine(now().ToString("u"))
2004-02-16 01:55:36Z
```

FOR EXAMPLE

Managing Dates

Say that you are building the auto insurance application. You need to output the cost of insurance to a Label control. It is stored as a Decimal value, and you want to display it as currency. You also need to create the code to handle the birth date. The code should accept the month, day, and year values from the drop-down lists and store them as a Date value. The code to load the Year list must implement the rule that the dates must be between 1900 and 16 years before the current year. The date entered must be validated to ensure that the driver is at least 16 years old.

You write the following code to display the cost of insurance:

```
lblCost = format(decCost("Currency"))
```

You write the following code to populate the Year ListBox control:

```
Dim intLastYear, i As Integer
intLastYear = Year(AddYears(Now(), -16)
For i = 1900 To intLastYear
    lstYear.Items.Add(CStr(i))
Next
```

You write the following code to validate the birth date:

```
Dim sDate As String
Dim dDate As Date
Dim dSixteen as Date
sDate = lstMonth & " " & lstDay & ", " & lstYear
dDate = System.DateTime.Parse(sDate)
dSixteen = AddYears(Now(), -16)
If System.DateTime.Compare(dSixteen, dDate) _
    >= 0 Then
    'Valid date
Else
    'Driver is not 16
End If
```

SELF-CHECK

- Describe the purpose of the Format function.

- The bDate variable contains your birth date this year. List the steps you would take to determine the day of the week on your birthday in five years. The value should be the name of the day (e.g., Sunday).

- Describe how you would display the current time, without the date. The time should be displayed to minute precision only.

SUMMARY

In this chapter, you've learned how to design a user interface that is effective and easy to use. You've learned how to select the most appropriate control to meet an input or output requirement. You've also learned how to allow users to navigate through a form by using the keyboard. You've been introduced to the Anchor and Dock properties, which allow you to easily create a resizable form. You've seen how to add controls to a form dynamically and how to manipulate variables of type String. You've also learned about formatting numeric and date values.

KEY TERMS

Anchor	Mutually exclusive
Child node	Node
Clipboard	Overloaded
Concatenate	Parent/child relationship
Container control	Root
Controls collection	RTF
Delimiter	Shortcut key
Dock	Tab order
Format expression	Tick
Leaf node	Tree
List	User interface
Me keyword	Windows Explorer

ASSESS YOUR UNDERSTANDING

Go to www.wiley.com/college/petroutsos to evaluate your knowledge of user interface design and string manipulation.

Measure your learning by comparing pre-test and post-test results.

Summary Questions

1. Before selecting the controls to use on a form, you should analyze the input and output requirements. True or False?

2. A CheckBox control is used to support mutually exclusive options. True or False?

3. Which statement correctly describes using the Clipboard with Visual Basic controls??
   (a) Text copied from a TextBox control can only be pasted into another TextBox control.
   (b) Text can only be copied and pasted within the same application.
   (c) You can copy and paste text between controls in the same application or in different applications.

4. When calling a function, the function name should appear on the right side of an assignment statement. True or False?

5. What is a leaf node?
   (a) a node that doesn't have a parent node
   (b) a node that doesn't have any child nodes
   (c) any item in a ListView control
   (d) any item in a TreeView control

6. What character is used to identify a shortcut key?
   (a) /
   (b) %
   (c) ^
   (d) &

7. A control that has its Anchor property set to Left grows and shrinks vertically as the form is resized. True or False?

8. You must declare and instantiate a variable of type Label before you can add it to the Controls collection of a form. True or False?

9. You can change a character in a string by using the Chars property. True or False?

10. Which method allows you to change all the characters in a string to lowercase?
    (a) ToLower
    (b) LowerCase

(c) SetCase

(d) Replace

11. Which method would you use to determine whether the first three characters in a string are "Mr."?

(a) Compare

(b) StartsWith

(c) Equals

(d) Is

12. Which statement is equivalent to executing the following:

```
s = s1 & s2
```

(a) s = String.Parse(s1, s2)

(b) s = String.Add(s1, s2)

(c) s = String.Join(s1, s2)

(d) s = String.Concat(s1, s2)

13. The Insert method can only add a single character to a string. True or False?

14. Which method is used to create a string from multiple strings, with each source string separated by a delimiter?

(a) Parse

(b) Join

(c) Concat

(d) Insert

15. What type of value is returned by the Split method?

(a) a single value of type String

(b) a single value of type Char

(c) an array of type String

(d) an array of type Char

16. The Remove method can remove each instance of a specific character from a string. True or False?

17. Which method can be used to substitute one set of characters for another set of characters in a string?

(a) Remove

(b) Parse

(c) Insert

(d) Replace

18. Which function is used to output the value 40.00% from a variable of type Double?

(a) Format

(b) CDec

    (c) ToString

    (d) Convert

19. What of the following uses the correct syntax for initializing a variable of type Date?

    (a) Dim dStartDate As Date = "5/30/2000"

    (b) Dim dStartDate As Date = {5/30/2000}

    (c) Dim dStartDate As Date = #5/30/2000#

    (d) Dim dStartDate As Date = '5/30/2000'

20. The DayOfWeek property returns a value of type String. True or false?

21. Which method is used to determine whether one date is earlier than another date?

    (a) Equals

    (b) Compare

    (c) IsBefore

22. The DateTime class exposes an IsLeapYear method. True or false?

23. Which method would you use to add 30 days to the current date?

    (a) Add

    (b) AddMonths

    (c) AddDays

24. Which method would you use to display a date using the format Monday, March 12, 2005.

    (a) Format

    (b) CDate

    (c) Parse

    (d) ToString

Applying This Chapter

1. You are writing an application that managers will use to enter performance review information. Managers must be able to rate employee performance in five key areas, based on the four-point scale Excellent, Good, Needs Improvement, and Poor. If any area is marked Poor, a Comments field must display for that area. The interface must also have a Key Accomplishments area. Managers must be able to type key accomplishments for the employee. An employee can have zero or more key accomplishments. What type of control will you use to rate employee performance? How will you display the Comments field? How will you handle the Key Accomplishments area?

2. You are writing an inventory management application. All product IDs must have the format xxx-PRD, where x can be any character. Any

quotation marks in the product description must be changed to a single quotation mark or it will cause problems when it is written to the database. How will you validate the product ID? How will you format the product description?

3. You are writing an accounting application that must report the day of the week when a bill must be paid. If a bill would be due on a Saturday or Sunday, it should consider that bill due on the previous Friday. What code will you use to meet the requirements?

Designing a User Interface and Managing Dates

You are designing an application for a veterinarian. The application will allow the veterinarian to keep track of the pets that belong to each owner. The information it must collect on each pet includes Dog or Cat, Breed, Sex, Spayed/Neutered, Name, Weight, and vaccination information, including the name of the vaccine and the date it was last administered. The owner form should list the owner's name and the name of each pet. A pet form should be displayed, showing each pet's records. The veterinarian must be able to update the information. A list of vaccination reminders should be generated one month before the vaccine will expire. Vaccines expire every three years. The reminder should use the pet's name and the owner's last name as the pet's full name. For example, a pet named Spot with an owner named Miller should be referred to as "Spot Miller."

1. How will you display the data on the main form?
2. What controls will you use for each piece of data displayed on the pet detail form?
3. What code will you use to determine whether a vaccine reminder should be generated?
4. What method will you use to generate the pet's full name?
5. How will you output the pet's weight to include only two digits to the right of the decimal point?

Encrypting a String

You are writing a procedure that will accept a string and encrypt it using a simple alphabetic replacement strategy that replaces each character with the character three lower (using the same case). For example, "d" is replaced with "a", and "Z" is replaced with "W". The three letters at the beginning of the alphabet are replaced with letters at the end of the alphabet. For example, "A" is replaced with "X", and "b" is replaced with "y". Only letters of the alphabet are used. Write the code necessary to perform this task.

7

BUILDING MENUS AND TOOLBARS

Starting Point

Go to www.wiley.com/college/petroutsos to assess your knowledge of menus and toolbars.
Determine where you need to concentrate your effort.

What You'll Learn in This Chapter

▲ Menu design and creation
▲ Toolbar design and creation
▲ Status bar design and creation

After Studying This Chapter, You'll Be Able To

▲ Design a user interface that includes menus and toolbars
▲ Design a menu structure that is easy to navigate
▲ Create menus and associate them with controls
▲ Display menu items dynamically
▲ Create toolbars and design them to enhance usability
▲ Create status bars

INTRODUCTION

Most Windows applications include menus and toolbars that allow users to perform tasks. Many of these applications include menus that are context sensitive and toolbars that are customizable. Some also display status information along the bottom of the window.

This chapter examines some key considerations for adding menus and toolbars to an application. You'll begin by looking at some menu design considerations. Next, you'll learn how to use the MenuStrip control to add a menu to a form. From there, you'll learn how to add dynamic menus, including adding menu items at runtime and using the ContextStrip control to add context-sensitive menus. Finally, you'll learn how to use the ToolStrip control, the StatusStrip control, and the ToolStripContainer control to add toolbars and status bars that the user can later customize.

7.1 Building an Intuitive User Interface

Menus are some of the most common and characteristic elements of the Windows user interface. Despite the visually rich interfaces of Windows applications and the many alternatives, menus are still the most popular means of organizing a large number of options. Many applications duplicate some or all of their menus in the form of toolbar icons, but the menu is a standard fixture of a form. You might allow users to turn toolbars on and off, but typically would not let them do so for the menus.

7.1.1 Designing Menus for Windows Programs

Take a look at just about any program that is available for Windows, and you'll find a menu system. If you compare the menus of two different programs, you'll also see that most menus have a similar look and feel. Figure 7-1 shows the menus of two different Windows programs, Microsoft Word (on the left) and Microsoft Excel (on the right). Notice that several of the menus in both programs have the same name and are positioned near the same location on the menu bar. For example, each program includes a File, Edit, View, Insert, Format, and Tools menu, among others. The standard menus in each program also have similar options. For instance, the File menus for both programs include New, Open, Close, and Save options.

Creating menus that have common options is part of a software design concept known as a **common user interface**, and it provides two major advantages. From a user's perspective, common elements make it easier to learn and use software. When you know how to save a file that you have created using Microsoft Word, you also know how to save a file that you create with Microsoft Excel and most other Windows software. From a programmer's perspective, common elements

Figure 7-1

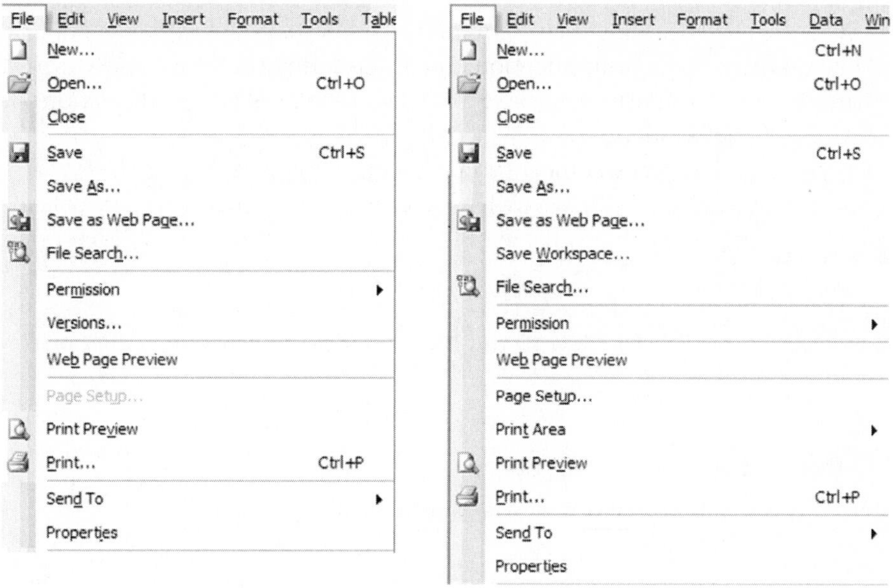

File	Edit	View	Insert	Format	Tools	Table
New...						
Open...					Ctrl+O	
Close						
Save					Ctrl+S	
Save As...						
Save as Web Page...						
File Search...						
Permission					▶	
Versions...						
Web Page Preview						
Page Setup...						
Print Preview						
Print...					Ctrl+P	
Send To					▶	
Properties						

File	Edit	View	Insert	Format	Tools	Data	Win
New...						Ctrl+N	
Open...						Ctrl+O	
Close							
Save						Ctrl+S	
Save As...							
Save as Web Page...							
Save Workspace...							
File Search...							
Permission						▶	
Web Page Preview							
Page Setup...							
Print Area						▶	
Print Preview							
Print...						Ctrl+P	
Send To						▶	
Properties							

Menus in Windows applications.

allow for reuse of controls and code. The code and objects used to save a Microsoft Word file are basically the same as the code and objects used in Microsoft Excel.

You can learn several other characteristics about menus from the examples in Figure 7-1. First, notice how all the options in the File menu are somehow related to working with a file. If you were to browse through other menus, you would find that they are also set up in this way. For example, the Help menu contains options that are all related to obtaining help in using the software, and the Windows menu contains options that are all related to adjusting the Window in which the software appears on the screen.

Second, notice that there are a couple menus that are different in the two programs. For example, Word includes a Table menu that is not available on the Excel menu bar. Likewise, Excel includes a Data menu that is not available on the Word menu bar. Given that the two software applications are created to perform different tasks, it is not surprising that they would each include different menus with different options. Finally, notice that the menus include more than a simple listing of options in text. Graphical icons are incorporated to link the menu option with shortcut buttons available on toolbars. An arrow indicates that a submenu with additional options will appear when the menu item is selected (e.g., the Send To menus in Figure 7-1). The ellipsis (...) is used to indicate that a dialog box will appear when a menu item is selected (e.g., the Open menu in Figure 7-1). Also, shortcut keys are listed to show how a menu option can be executed using the keyboard instead of the mouse.

This brief tour of Windows menu systems provides you with several rules of thumb to keep in mind when adding menus to your Visual Basic programs:

▲ Try to keep main menus similar to the menus in other Windows programs.

▲ Group together related commands under a main menu heading that reflects the overall relationship of those commands.

▲ Use unique menus when necessary but try to keep their use to a minimum.

▲ Use common elements to give the user an idea of what will happen when a menu option is selected.

▲ Use common elements to show the user alternatives for accessing the command on toolbars or from the keyboard.

7.1.2 Designing a Menu System

The first step in designing a menu system is to list the events you want the user to trigger by selecting a menu command. In many cases, this is every event the application needs to handle. Next, you organize the events in terms of whether they are related to common menus, such as File, Edit, View, Window, and Help, or whether they belong under a custom menu title. Some custom menu titles might be Tools, Format, Data, or various others, depending on what the application does. Table 7-1 describes some guidelines for grouping menu items under the common menu titles.

Next, you need to determine whether there should be subgroupings that appear when the mouse rests over a menu item that has an arrow. The organization of menu titles and subgroupings is known as the **menu hierarchy.** A menu item that includes submenu items is sometimes called a **cascading menu** or **fly-out menu.**

Another way to group items is by using separator bars. A **separator bar** is a horizontal line that you add to a menu to create a logical grouping. For example, you might use a separator bar to separate the Save and Save As commands from the New, Open, and Close commands.

Finally, you need to determine which menu items turn features on and off. These menu items need some indicator, such as a check mark or a change in the title, to indicate the feature's current status. Just as with selection controls, some menu selections are mutually exclusive. When this is the case, you should group these menu options together.

7.1.3 The Menu Editor

Menus can be attached only to forms and are implemented through the **MenuStrip control.** The items that make up the menu are ToolStripMenuItem objects. As you

Table 7-1: Common Menu Titles

Menu Title	Types of Events	Examples
File	Events that interact with the file system or that manage the as document a whole	Options such as Open, New, Save, Print, and Exit
Edit	Events that deal with editing the content of a document	Options such as Copy, Cut, Paste, Find, Replace, and Select All
View	Events that manage how the user interface appears	Options for hiding and displaying toolbars and application form elements
Tools	Commands that display a dialog box that allow for customization	Options such as Options and Customize
Window	Events that manage how windows are displayed in a multiple-document interface (MDI) application. An **MDI application** is one that allows you to work with multiple documents, each in a separate window.	Options such as Cascade and Arrange, as well as items to bring a window to the foreground
Help	Events that allow users to display help files or documentation or to access online help.	Options such as About, Help Topics, and Online Help

will see, the MenuStrip control and ToolStripMenuItem objects give you absolute control over the structure and appearance of the menus of an application. The MenuStrip control is a variation of the Strip control, which is the basis of menus, toolbars, and status bars. You will learn in the last part of this chapter how to create toolbars and status bars. For now, we'll focus on designing simple menus.

Creating a menu requires two basic steps:

1. Design the menu visually.
2. Add code to the Click event handler for each menu item.

Depending on the needs of your application, you might want to enable and disable certain commands, add context menus to some of the controls on your form, and so on. Because each item (i.e., command) in a menu is represented by a ToolStripMenuItem object, you can control the application's menus from within your code by manipulating the properties of the ToolStripMenuItem

Figure 7-2

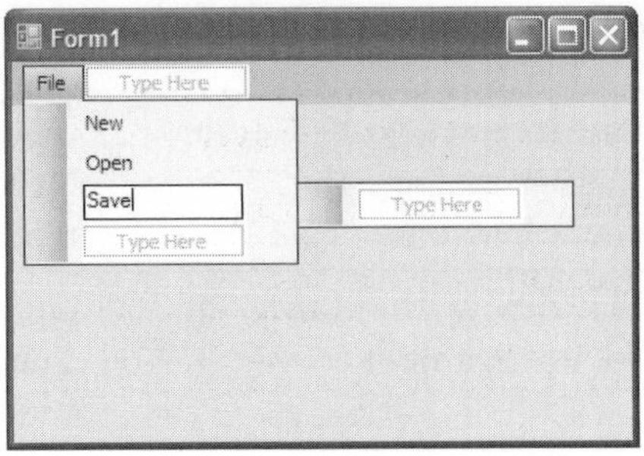

Designing a menu on a form.

objects. Let's start by designing a simple menu, and then we'll look at how to manipulate the menu objects from within code as we go along.

To add a menu to a form, first you double-click the MenuStrip icon on the toolbox. An instance of the MenuStrip control is added to the form, and a single menu command appears on the form, with the caption "Type Here." If you don't see the first menu item on the form right away, you can select the MenuStrip control in the Components tray below the form. You should do as the caption says: Click it and enter the first command's caption, File. To add items under the File menu, you press Enter. To enter another command in the main menu, press Tab. Depending on your action, another box is added, in which you can type the caption of the next command (see in Figure 7-2).

When you hover the pointer over a menu item, a drop-down button appears to the right of the item. You can click this button to select the type of item to place on the menu. You can choose from MenuItem, ComboBox, or TextBox objects. This chapter focuses on menu items, which are by far the most common elements on a menu.

After you enter the remaining items, you should click somewhere on the form. All the temporary items (i.e., the ones with the "Type Here" caption) disappear, and the menu is finalized on the form.

You can insert the items typically seen in a menu by right-clicking the MenuStrip control and choosing Insert Standard Items. A menu bar containing File, Edit, Tools, and Help menus is then inserted, with shortcut and access keys defined and some standard graphics displayed. The menu items this menu contains are described in Table 7-2.

Although these menu items are added, they're not implemented by default. You must add code to the ToolStripItem event procedures for each item.

7.1.4 Using the Items Collection Editor

The most convenient method of editing a menu is to use the Items Collection Editor window, which is shown in Figure 7-3. This isn't a visual editor, but with

Table 7-2: Standard Menu Items

Menu Title	Menu Items
File	New, Open, Save, Save As, Print, Print Preview, Exit
Edit	Undo, Redo, Cut, Copy, Paste, Select All
Tools	Customize, Options
Help	Contents, Index, Search, About

it, you can set all the properties of each menu item without having to switch to the Properties window.

You can select the type of item you want to add to your menu in the top ComboBox of the Items Collection Editor. The default item is the ToolStrip MenuItem, which is a regular menu command. Another common item you can add to a menu is a separator.

The Add button adds to the menu an item of the type specified in the combo box next to it (i.e., a menu item, combo box, or text box). To insert an item at a different location, you add it to the menu and then use the buttons with the arrows to move it up or down. As you add new items, you can set their caption (Text property) and their name (Name property) on the right pane of the editor. You can also set each menu item's font, set the alignment and orientation of the

Figure 7-3

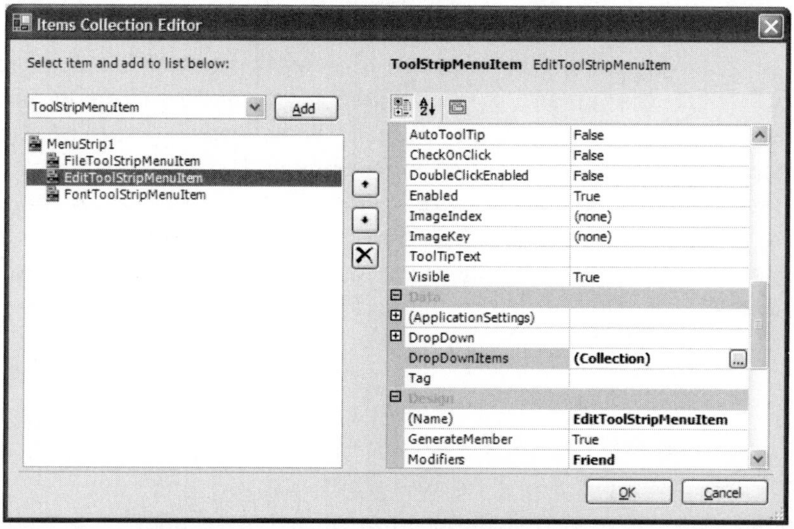

Editing a menu with the Items Collection Editor.

text, and specify an image to be displayed along with the text. To add an image to a menu item, you locate the Image property and click the button with the ellipsis next to it. A dialog box appears, in which you can select the appropriate resource. Notice that all the images you use on your form are stored as resources of the project. You can add all the images and icons you might need in a project to the same resource file and reuse them as you need to. The TextImageRelation property allows you to specify the relative positions of the text and the image. You can also use the DisplayStyle property to select to display text only, images only, or text and images for each menu item.

If a menu item leads to a submenu, you must also specify the submenu's items. You locate the DropDownItems property and click the button with the ellipses next to it. An identical window appears, in which you can enter the drop-down items of the current menu item. Notice that the menu on the form is continuously updated while you edit it in the Items Collection Editor window, so you can see the effects of your changes on the form.

All the items in a menu are objects of the ToolStripMenuItem type, and they expose many properties, including the following, that you can use to set their appearance:

▲ **Checked:** Some menu commands act as toggles, and they are usually checked to indicate that they are on or are unchecked to indicate that they are off. To initially display a check mark next to a menu command, you set its Checked property to True. You can also access this property from within code to change the checked status of a menu command at runtime.

▲ **Enabled:** Some menu commands aren't always available. The Paste command, for example, has no meaning if the Clipboard is empty (or if it contains data that can't be pasted in the current application). To indicate that a command can't be used at the time, you set its Enabled property to False. The command then appears grayed out in the menu, and although it can be highlighted, it can't be activated. The following statements enable and disable the Undo command, depending on whether the TextBox1 control can undo the most recent operation. cmdUndo is the name of the Undo command in the application's Edit menu. The CanUndo property of the TextBox control returns a True/False value that indicates whether the last action can be undone. Here's an example:

```
If TextBox1.CanUndo Then
    cmdUndo.Enabled = True
Else
    cmdUndo.Enabled = False
End If
```

▲ **IsOnDropDown:** If the menu command, represented by a ToolStrip MenuItem object, belongs to a submenu, its IsOnDropDown property is

True. Otherwise, it is False. The IsOnDropDown property is read-only and False for the items of the first level of the menu.

▲ **Visible:** To temporarily remove a command from the menu, you set the command's Visible property to False. The Visible property isn't used frequently in menu design. In general, you should disable a command to indicate that it can't be used at the time (requiring some other action to enable it). Making a command invisible frustrates users, who might try to locate the command in another menu.

7.1.5 Programming Menu Commands

Menu commands are similar to controls. A menu command has certain properties that you can manipulate from within your code, and it triggers a Click event when it's clicked with the mouse or selected with the Enter key. If you double-click a menu command at design time, Visual Basic opens the code for the Click event in the code window. The name of the event handler for the Click event is composed of the command's name followed by an underscore character and the event's name (e.g., Zoom200_Click), as with all other controls.

To program a menu item, you insert the appropriate code in the item's Click event handler. The Exit command's code would be something like this:

```
Sub menuExit(ByVal sender As Object, ByVal e As _
    System.EventArgs) Handles menuExit.Click
    End
End Sub
```

If you need to execute any cleanup code before the application ends, you place it in the CleanUp subroutine and call this subroutine from within the Exit item's Click event handler, like this:

```
Sub menuExit(ByVal sender As Object, ByVal e As _
    System.EventArgs) Handles menuExit.Click
    CleanUp()
    End
End Sub
```

The same subroutine must also be called from within the FormClosing event handler of the application's main form because some users might terminate the application by clicking the form's Close button.

In most cases, you can treat the Click event handler of a ToolStripMenuItem object just like the Click event handler of a Button control.

You can also program multiple menu items with a single **event handler** (i.e., code that runs when an event the procedure is configured to handle occurs). Let's say that you have a Zoom menu that allows the user to select one of several zoom factors. Instead of inserting the same statements in each menu item's Click event handler, you can program all the items of the Zoom menu with a single event handler. To do so, you select all the items that share the same event handler (i.e., click them with the mouse while holding down the Shift key). Then you click the Event button in the Properties window and select the event that you want to be common for all selected items.

The handler of the Click event of a menu item has the following declaration:

```
Private Sub Zoom200_Click(ByVal sender As _
    System.Object, ByVal e As System.EventArgs) _
    Handles Zoom200.Click
End Sub
```

This subroutine handles the menu item 200%, which magnifies an image by 200%. Let's say that the same menu contains the options 100%, 75%, 50%, and 25%; and that the names of these commands are Zoom100, Zoom75, and so on. The common handler for their Click event will have the following declaration:

```
Private Sub Zoom200_Click(ByVal sender As _
    System.Object, ByVal e As System.EventArgs) _
    Handles Zoom200.Click, _Zoom100.Click, _
    Zoom75.Click, Zoom50.Click, Zoom25.Click
End Sub
```

The common event handler wouldn't do you any good unless you could figure out which item was clicked from within the handler's code. This information is in the event's sender argument. You can convert this argument to the ToolStripMenuItem type; then you look up all the properties of the ToolStripMenuItem object that received the event. The following statement prints the name of the menu item that was clicked (if it appears in a common event handler):

```
Debug.WriteLine(CType(sender, ToolStripMenuItem).Text)
```

When you program multiple menu items with a single event handler, you set up a Select Case statement based on the caption of the selected menu item, like the following:

```
Select Case sender.Text
Case "Zoom In"
    'statements to process Zoom In command
Case "Zoom Out"
    'statements to process Zoom Out command
Case "Fit"
    'statements to process Fit command
End Select
```

It's also common to manipulate the ToolStripMenuItem's properties from within its Click event handler. These properties are the same properties you set through the Items Collection Editor dialog box at design time. Menu commands don't have methods you can call. Most menu object properties are toggles. To change the Checked property of the FontBold command, for instance, you use the following statement:

```
FontBold.Checked = Not FontBold.Checked
```

If the command is checked, the check mark will be removed. If the command is unchecked, the check mark will be inserted in front of its name. You can also change the command's caption at runtime, although this practice isn't common.

This method works fine if the setting is global to the form. However, sometimes you need to toggle the state of a menu property based on a text selection. For example, suppose you have a RichTextBox control on the form. When the user displays the Format menu, the Bold item needs to be sensitive to the state of the selected text. You have a choice in how to handle this. You can either set the menu item's Checked property when the text is selected or when the menu that contains the menu items is displayed (i.e., through the Click event of the parent menu).

7.1.6 Defining Access and Shortcut Keys

Opening menus and selecting commands with the mouse can be an inconvenience. When using a word processing program, for example, you don't want to have to take your hands off the keyboard and reach for the mouse. To simplify menu access, Windows forms support access keys and shortcut keys.

Access Keys

Access keys allow the user to open menus by pressing the Alt key and the appropriate letter keys. To open the Edit menu in all Windows applications, for example, you can press Alt+E, so E is the Edit menu's access key. After the menu is open, the user can select a command with the arrow keys or by pressing another key, which is the command's access key. After a menu is open, you don't need to press the Alt key along with the command access key. For example, with the Edit menu open, you can press P to invoke the Paste command or C to copy the selected text.

An application designer designates access keys and marks them with an underline character. The underline under the character E in the Edit menu denotes that E is the menu's access key and that the keystroke Alt+E opens the Edit command. To assign an access key, you insert the ampersand symbol (&) in front of the character you want to use as access key in the ToolStripMenu-Item's Text property.

If you don't designate access keys, Visual Basic uses the first character in each top-level menu as its access key. In this case, the user doesn't see the underline character under the first character but can open the menu by pressing the first character of its caption while holding down the Alt key. If two or more menu items begin with the same letter, the first (leftmost and topmost) menu opens. To open the second item, you would press the access key again.

Because the & symbol has a special meaning in menu design, you can't use it as is in a menu. To actually display the & symbol in a menu item, you need to prefix it with another & symbol. For example, &Drag produces a command labeled Drag with the first character underlined because it's the access key. Drag && Drop creates a command labeled Drag & Drop. Finally, the string &Drag && Drop create a command with the caption Drag & Drop, with the first character underlined because it's the access key.

Shortcut Keys

Shortcut keys are similar to access keys, but instead of opening a menu, a shortcut key runs a command when pressed. It's a good idea to assign shortcut keys to frequently used menu commands so that users can reach them using a single keystroke. A shortcut key is a combination of one or more modifiers (e.g., Alt, Shift, Ctrl) and a keystroke. A keystroke can be a function key and does not need to represent characters that appear in the name. If a keystroke is a function key, you do not need to specify a modifier. The shortcut key can be different from the access key. For example, the usual access key for the Undo command (after the Edit menu is opened with Alt+E) is U, but the usual shortcut key for the Undo command is Ctrl+Z.

To assign a shortcut key to a menu command, you drop down the ShortcutKeys list in the ToolStripMenuItem's Properties window and select a modifier (either the Shift, Control, or Alt key) and a keystroke. You don't have to insert any special characters in the command's caption, nor do you have to enter the keystroke next to the caption. It will be displayed next to the command automatically.

When assigning access and shortcut keys, you should consider well-established Windows standards. Users expect Alt+F to open the File menu, so you shouldn't use Alt+F for the Format menu. Likewise, pressing Ctrl+C universally performs the Copy command, so you shouldn't use Ctrl+C as a shortcut for the Cut command (whose standard shortcut key is Ctrl+X).

FOR EXAMPLE

Designing Menus

Say that you are building an application that will allow users to create party invitations. The application will allow a user to do the following:

- ▲ Write and edit text
- ▲ Add graphics and borders
- ▲ Select 1 of 10 styles
- ▲ Customize a style
- ▲ Create a guest list
- ▲ Import a guest list

▲ Merge a guest list to create customized invitations

▲ Print invitations and envelopes

You add a MenuStrip control and decide to include the standard menu items. You modify the Print command by changing its Text property to Print Invitations. You add a Print Envelopes command within the same subgroup and assign it the shortcut key Ctrl+E. You also include a Guests menu item that includes two commands: Create Guest List and Import Guest List. You decide to handle merge functionality within the File menu's Print commands.

You add a Borders and Graphics menu. You add a Design menu and include items for Borders, Styles, Graphics, and Fonts. You create a custom dialog box for Borders, use the standard Open dialog box for the Graphics item, and use the standard Font dialog box for the Fonts item. You create 10 submenu items beneath Styles to allow users to choose and apply a style. You use the Checked property to indicate which style is applied. For example, if the BlackTie style is applied to the invitation, the following code is added to the mnuBlackTie_Click event:

```
mnuBlackTie.Checked = True
```

SELF-CHECK

- Describe the benefits of using standard items on a menu bar.
- Discuss the benefits of grouping items in a menu beneath a subitem.
- Describe how you can implement a menu item that toggles a feature on and off.
- Describe the importance of knowing which access keys and shortcut keys are commonly used in applications.

7.2 Manipulating Menus at Runtime

Dynamic menus change at runtime to display more or fewer commands, depending on the current status of the program. This section explores three techniques for implementing dynamic menus:

▲ Creating short and long versions of the same menu

▲ Adding and removing menu commands at runtime

▲ Creating context (pop-up) menus

7.2.1 Creating Short and Long Menus

A common technique in menu design is to create long and short versions of a menu. If a menu contains many commands and most of the time only a few of them are needed, you can create one menu that contains all the commands and another that contains the most common ones. The first menu is the long one, and the second is the short one. The last command in the long menu should be Short Menu, and when selected, it should display the short version. The last command in the short menu should be Long Menu, and it should display the long version. The short version omits infrequently used commands and is easier to handle.

One way to implement a long menu and a short menu is to toggle the Visible property of the items that belong in only the long menu during the mnuSize_Click event. The following code shows how you can use this method to implement short and long versions of a Format menu:

```
Private Sub mnuSize_Click(ByVal sender As _
    System.Object, ByVal e As System.EventArgs) _
    Handles mnuSize.Click
    If mnuSize.Text = "Short Menu" Then
        mnuSize.Text = "Long Menu"
    Else
        mnuSize.Text = "Short Menu"
    End If
    mnuUnderline.Visible = Not mnuUnderline.Visible
    mnuStrike.Visible = Not mnuStrike.Visible
    mnuSmallCaps.Visible = Not mnuSmallCaps.Visible
    mnuAllCaps.Visible = Not mnuAllCaps.Visible
End Sub
```

The event procedure simply toggles the Visible property of certain menu commands and changes the command's caption to Short Menu or Long Menu, depending on the menu's current status. Notice that because the Visible property is a True/False value, you don't care about its current status; you simply toggle the current status by using the Not operator.

7.2.2 Adding and Removing Menu Commands at Runtime

Sometimes you need to build dynamic menus, which grow and shrink at runtime. For example, many applications maintain a list of the most recently opened files in their File menu. When you first start the application, this list is empty, and as you open and close files, it starts to grow.

To implement this functionality, you need to create a submenu that will store the items. For this example, that submenu's name is RunTimeToolStripMenu-Item. The submenu will initially be empty. The example appends menu items to the end of the menu and removes items from the bottom of the menu first. To add an item at a specific position, such as at the top of the menu, you would use the Insert method instead of the Add method. This example assumes that the menu items are added when Button control named bttnAddItem is clicked and removed when the bttnRemoveItem Button control is clicked.

```
Private Sub bttnAddItem_Click(ByVal sender As _
    System.Object, ByVal e As System.EventArgs) _
    Handles bttnAddItem.Click
    Dim Item As New ToolStripMenuItem
    Item.Text = "Run Time Option" & _
RunTimeMenuToolStripMenuItem.DropDownItems.Count.ToString
RunTimeMenuToolStripMenuItem.DropDownItems.Add(Item)
    AddHandler Item.Click, _
        New System.EventHandler(AddressOf _
        OptionClick)
End Sub
```

The event procedure first declares and instantiates an instance of Tool-StripMenuItem. It then sets its Text property to a value and adds the item to DropDownItems, which is a property of the RunTimeMenuToolStripMenuItem object. Next, you need to associate an event handler with the menu item. To do so, you use the **AddHandler statement,** which accepts the name of the event (in this case, Item.Click) and the address of an instance of an event handler. You must also create an event handler to handle the Click event for any of these dynamically added menu options. Here's an example of how to do this:

```
Private Sub OptionClick(ByVal sender As Object, _
    ByVal e As EventArgs)
    Dim itemClicked As New ToolStripMenuItem
    itemClicked = CType(sender, ToolStripMenuItem)
    MsgBox("You have selected the item " & _
        itemClicked.Text)
End Sub
```

In this case, you are simply displaying a message box that tells the user which item was clicked. To do so, you need to use the sender property and cast it as a ToolStripMenuItem object, using CType.

The Remove button's code uses the Remove method to remove the last item in the menu by its index, after making sure the menu contains at least one item:

```
Private Sub bttnRemoveItem_Click(ByVal sender As _
    System.Object, ByVal e As System.EventArgs) _
    Handles bttnRemoveItem.Click
    If _
    RunTimeMenuToolStripMenuItem.DropDownItems.Count _
    > 0 Then
        Dim mItem As ToolStripItem
```

```
            Dim items As Integer = _
RunTimeMenuToolStripMenuItem.DropDownItems.Count
        mItem = _
        RunTimeMenuToolStripMenuItem.DropDownItems _
            (items - 1)

RunTimeMenuToolStripMenuItem.DropDownItems.Remove _
        (mItem)
            ' TO REMOVE A MENU ITEM OTHER THAN THE
            ' LAST ONE USE THE FOLLOWING STATEMENT:
            '

        '

RunTimeMenuToolStripMenuItem.DropDownItems.RemoveAt _
        (position)
            '

        ' WHERE position IS THE INDEX OF THE ITEM TO BE
        ' REMOVED IN THE DROP DOWN MENU
        End If
End Sub
```

7.2.3 Creating Context Menus

Nearly every Windows application provides a **context menu** that the user can invoke by right-clicking a form or a control. (It's sometimes called a **short-cut menu** or **pop-up menu**.) A context menu is a regular menu, but it's not anchored on the form. It can be displayed anywhere on the form or on specific controls. Different controls can have different context menus, depending on the operations you can perform on them at the time they are right-clicked.

To create a context menu, you place a ContextMenuStrip control on a form. The new context menu will appear on the form just like a regular menu, but it won't be displayed there at runtime. You can create as many context menus as you need by placing multiple instances of the ContextMenuStrip control on the form and adding the appropriate commands to each one. To associate a context menu with a control on a form, you set the control's ContextMenuStrip property to the name of the corresponding context menu.

Designing a context menu works exactly the same way as designing a regular menu. The only difference is that the first command in the menu is always ContextMenuStrip, and it's not displayed along with the menu. Figure 7-4 shows the same context menu at design time and at runtime.

To edit a context menu on a form, you select the appropriate ContextMenuStrip control at the bottom of the designer. The corresponding context menu appears on the form's menu bar, as if it were a regular form menu. This is temporary, however, and the only menu that appears on the form's menu bar at runtime is the one that corresponds to the MenuStrip control.

Figure 7-4

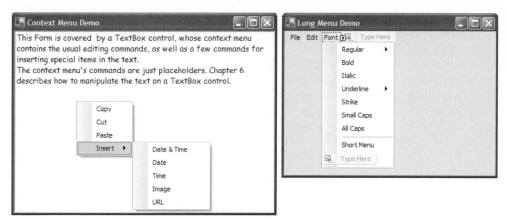

A context menu at design time (left) and runtime (right).

FOR EXAMPLE

Designing Dynamic Menus

Say that you are building an application that will allow users to create party invitations. The application will allow a user to do the following:

▲ Write and edit text
▲ Add graphics and borders
▲ Select 1 of 10 styles
▲ Customize a style
▲ Create a guest list
▲ Import a guest list
▲ Merge a guest list to create customized invitations
▲ Print invitations and envelopes

The form includes a RichTextBox control that displays the invitation and a ComboBox control that contains the names of the guests. Guest information is edited in a separate dialog box.

You decide to create a context menu for the RichTextBox control that includes commands for formatting text. You also decide to create a context menu for the ComboBox control that includes Edit and Remove items. You add two ContextMenuStrip controls to the form and add the appropriate menu items to each.

(Continued)

You also decide to add the last four invitations opened to a Previous Invitations menu item on the File menu. You implement this by using dynamic menus. You add the following code to the mnuOpen_Click event procedure:

```
Private Sub mnuOpen_Click(ByVal sender As Object, _
    ByVal e As System.EventArgs) Handles _
    mnuOpen.Click
        Dim strFileName As String
        OpenFileDialog1.Filter = _
            "Rich Text File (*.rtf) | *.rtf"
        OpenFileDialog1.ShowDialog()
        strFileName = OpenFileDialog1.FileName
        rtbInvite.LoadFile(strFileName)
        Dim Invite As New ToolStripMenuItem
        Invite.Text = strFileName
        mnuPrevious.DropDown.Items.Add(Invite)
        AddHandler Invite.Click, New _
            System.EventHandler(AddressOf Invite_Click)
End Sub
```

You also add the following event handler to handle Click events to the dynamic menu items:

```
Private Sub Invite_Click(ByVal sender As Object, _
    ByVal e As EventArgs)
        Dim itemClicked As New ToolStripMenuItem
        Dim strFileName As String
        itemClicked = CType(sender, ToolStripMenuItem)
        strFileName = itemClicked.Text
        rtbInvite.LoadFile(strFileName)
End Sub
```

SELF-CHECK

- Describe a situation in which it would be appropriate to create short and long versions of a menu.
- List the steps you must take to create a dynamic menu and associate it with an event handler.
- Explain why you would include only commands specific to a control in a pop-up menu.

7.3 Creating Toolbars and Status Bars

Many applications include toolbars as well as menus. **Toolbars** are sets of buttons that can be shown and hidden as a group. They are usually anchored directly under the menu bar or to the left of the form. They contain controls that allow users to perform actions quickly. In most cases, the user can show and hide toolbars to customize the user interface.

An application may also include a status bar. A **status bar** is docked along the bottom of the form and displays dynamic status information about the application. This information might include the page number in a word processing application or the application's state.

7.3.1 Creating a Toolbar

You create a toolbar by adding a ToolStrip control to a form. A **ToolStrip control** is similar to a MenuStrip control in that with it, you add items to an items collection. However, a ToolStrip control supports a wider variety of items, as shown in Table 7-3.

When you add a ToolStrip control to a form, you can select items to add to the toolbar from the drop-down list, as shown in Figure 7-5. If you right-click the ToolStrip control and choose Edit Items, the Items Collection Editor appears. This dialog is very similar to the one you saw for the MenuStrip control: It allows you to add items, delete items, change the order of items, and set item properties.

One key concern when implementing a toolbar using graphical buttons is ensuring that users understand what each item does. Adding a ToolTip to each item can help. A **ToolTip** is a short textual description of the item that appears on the screen when the user rests the mouse over that item. To configure a ToolTip for an item, you set the item's ToolTipText property to a descriptive value. If the AutoToolTip property is set to True and there is no defined ToolTipText property, the Text property of the item will display. You can also control whether ToolTips are shown for items in the entire toolbar by setting ShowItemToolTips for the ToolStrip control. It is True by default, but you can set it to False to prevent ToolTips from being displayed.

ToolStrip items have events just like other controls. You add code to these events to implement the necessary functionality. For example, you add code to the ToolStripButton control's Click event to cause that code to run when the user clicks the button on the toolbar.

7.3.2 Adding a StatusStrip Control

Many applications display status information along the bottom of the window. For example, consider Microsoft Word. By default, it displays status information

Table 7-3: ToolStrip Control Items

Item	Class	Description
Button	ToolStripButton	Similar to a Button control, it can contain both text and an image.
ComboBox	ToolStripComboBox	This item allows you to place a ComboBox control on a toolbar. An example of a ComboBox on a toolbar is the font selection box on Word's Formatting toolbar.
DropDown-Button	ToolStripDropDown-Button	This item is a Button control that includes a drop-down arrow. The AutoShapes button on the Drawing toolbar in Word is an example of a DropDownButton item.
Label	ToolStripLabel	This is an item that can display text, an image, or a hyperlink. It does not have a Click event.
ProgressBar	ToolStripProgressBar	This item allows you to display the progress of an operation on a toolbar.
Separator	ToolStripSeparator	This item allows you to visually group toolbar items.
SplitButton	ToolStripSplitButton	This item includes both a Button control and a drop-down list. The Font Color selection item on Word's Formatting toolbar is an example of a SplitButton item. When the user clicks the button part, the current color is applied. When the user clicks the arrow, the color selection window appears.
TextBox	ToolStripTextBox	This item behaves like a TextBox control.

about the page number, section number, line number on the page, and character number on the line at the bottom of the window.

You can add a **StatusStrip control** to an application to display status information. The StatusStrip control is similar to the MenusStrip and ToolStrip controls in that it has an Items container. You can add the following elements to a StatusStrip control:

▲ StatusLabel
▲ ProgressBar
▲ DropDownButton
▲ SplitButton

Figure 7-5

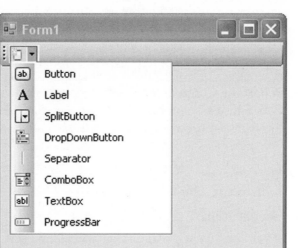

Adding items to a ToolStrip control.

You have already been introduced to the ProgressBar, DropDownButton, and SplitButton items. The StatusLabel item is used to create a panel on the StatusStrip item. By setting the Spring property to True, you can cause the panel to be resized as the form is resized.

7.3.3 Adding a ToolStripContainer Control

If you want to enable users to position multiple toolbars, menus, and status bars along the edges of an application, you can add a ToolStripContainer control. A **ToolStripContainer control** has four containers—one for each edge of the control—that can contain ToolStrip, MenuStrip, and StatusStrip controls. These are the four containers:

▲ **BottomToolStripPanel:** This container positions strips along the bottom edge of the control.
▲ **LeftToolStripPanel:** This container positions strips along the left edge of the control.
▲ **TopToolStripPanel:** This container positions strips along the top edge of the control.
▲ **RightToolStripPanel:** This container positions strips along the right edge of the control.

Each panel has a corresponding property that determines whether the panel is visible. For example, to make the BottomToolStripPanel container of the ToolStripContainer control named Tsc visible, you execute the following:

```
Tsc.BottomToolStripPanelVisible = True
```

Each panel includes a Controls collection. To add a control to a panel, you use the Add method of the Controls collection. You can use Remove, RemoveAt, or RemoveByKey to remove an item from the collection. The RemoveByKey method accepts the name of the control you want to remove.

FOR EXAMPLE

Designing an Application That Uses Toolbars

Say that you are building an application that will allow users to create party invitations. The application will allow a user to do the following:

▲ Write and edit text
▲ Add graphics and borders
▲ Select 1 of 10 styles
▲ Customize a style
▲ Create a guest list
▲ Import a guest list
▲ Merge a guest list to create customized invitations
▲ Print invitations and envelopes

You decide to create toolbars to allow users to perform frequent tasks more easily. You create a Format toolbar that includes commands for formatting selected text, such as Bold, Italic, and Underline. You also create a Standard toolbar and include on it the standard items: New, Open, Save, Print, Cut, Copy, Paste, and Help. Next, you create a Borders toolbar that allows users to change the color, width, and style of borders. Finally, you create a Graphics toolbar that allows users to insert GIFs and change their size.

You use a ToolStripContainer control to allow users to position the toolbars on either the top or the bottom of the form. You allow users to configure the toolbar position through the Customize dialog box. The code for managing the Standard toolbar (tsStandard) is shown here, and the code used to manage the other two toolbars would be similar:

```
Private Sub rbStandardTop_CheckedChanged _
    (ByVal sender As System.Object, _
     ByVal e As System.EventArgs) _
    Handles rbStandardTop.CheckedChanged
```

```
    frmInvite.tsContainer.TopToolStripPanel.Controls.Add _
        (frmInvite.tsStandard)
        frmInvite.tsStandard.Show()

End Sub

Private Sub rbStandardBottom_Click(ByVal sender As _
    Object, ByVal e As System.EventArgs) Handles _
    rbStandardBottom.Click
    frmInvite.tsContainer.BottomToolStripPanel.Controls.Add _
        (frmInvite.tsStandard)
        frmInvite.tsStandard.Show()
End Sub

Private Sub rbStandardHide_Click(ByVal sender As _
    Object, ByVal e As System.EventArgs) Handles _
    rbStandardHide.Click
    frmInvite.tsStandard.Hide()
End Sub
```

You also include a View menu item and implement Toolbars as an item with subitems to allow users to easily hide and show the toolbars by using the Hide and Show method of each toolbar.

You also decide to add a StatusStrip control to the application. It will display the number of invited guests and the number of words in the invitation. You add a StatusLabel control for each item you want to display.

SELF-CHECK

- Describe how toolbars increase the usability of an application.
- Explain why ToolTips are important.
- Describe how you can allow users to hide, show, and manage the position of toolbars.

SUMMARY

In this chapter, you've learned how to design a user interface that includes menus, toolbars, and status information. You've learned how to design and create menu bars. You've also learned how to create dynamic menus and context menus and how to implement toolbars that display ToolTips and can be docked along an edge of a window. You've also learned how to add a status bar to an application.

KEY TERMS

Access key

AddHandler statement

Cascading menu

Common user interface

Context menu

Dynamic menu

Event handler

Fly-out menu

Menu hierarchy

MenuStrip control

Multiple Document Interface (MDI)
application

Pop-up menu

Separator bar

Shortcut key

Shortcut menu

Status bar

StatusStrip control

Toolbar

ToolStrip control

ToolStripContainer control

ToolTip

ASSESS YOUR UNDERSTANDING

Go to www.wiley.com/college/petroutsos to evaluate your knowledge of menus and toolbars.

Measure your learning by comparing pre-test and post-test results.

Summary Questions

1. Using common elements in multiple applications can help users learn an application. True or False?
2. Which menu item should typically be placed under the File menu?
   (a) Copy
   (b) Customize
   (c) Print
   (d) Arrange
3. What type of item do you add to a MenuStrip control to create a menu item?
   (a) ToolStripMenuItem
   (b) ToolStripLabel
   (c) MenuStripMenuItem
   (d) MenuStripItem
4. The Items Collection Editor allows you to write code for menu events. True or False?
5. You create a menu item in the mnuTools menu named mnuOptions that displays a dialog box. In which event do you place code to display the dialog box?
   (a) mnuOptions.MenuClick
   (b) mnuOptions.Click
   (c) mnuTools.MenuClick
   (d) mnuTools.Click
6. A menu's Text property cannot display an ampersand (&). True or False?
7. What shortcut key should you use for the Cut command?
   (a) Ctrl+C
   (b) Alt+C
   (c) Ctrl+X
   (d) Alt+U
8. You are creating a long version and a short version of the Edit menu. You want the Replace item to be visible only in the Long menu version. Which code should you execute when the short menu is enabled?
   (a) Edit.Items("Replace").Hide
   (b) Replace.Enabled = False

    (c) Edit.Items("Replace").Remove

    (d) Replace.Visible = False

9. The AddHandler statement associates the name of an event with the address of the event handler. True or False?

10. You activate a pop-up menu for a specific control by selecting the control and pressing F11. True or False?

11. Which item would you add to a ToolStrip control to create an item that allows users to select the font size from a list that is populated through an items collection?

    (a) ToolStripButton

    (b) ToolStripComboBox

    (c) ToolStripDropDown

    (d) ToolStripSplitButton

12. The only item type you can add to a StatusStrip control is StatusLabel. True or False?

13. Each panel in a ToolStripContainer control can host multiple ToolStrip or StatusStrip controls. True or False?

Applying This Chapter

1. You are writing an application that managers will use to enter performance review information. The information will be saved to a database. It will also be used to generate a performance review document that can be saved to the hard disk and printed. Managers must be able to copy information between the comments fields for different employees and between different fields on the form. Retrieving information from the database sometimes takes several minutes, especially over a slow connection. You want to display progress information when accessing the database.

    (a) How will you ensure that manager can easily learn to use the application?

    (b) What commands will you place on the context menu associated with the Comments fields?

    (c) How can you display status information?

2. You are writing a data analysis and reporting application. The application allows users to perform a number of analysis calculations. Some are primarily used by market research personnel, and others are primarily used by members of the accounting department. You want to allow users to minimize the number of unused commands that are

displayed on the screen. There are also several options available for formatting reports.

(a) What can you do to make the application customizable by the different types of users who use it?

(b) How can you allow users to easily access the last five reports that users created?

3. You have been asked to upgrade an accounting application. The application includes the menu shown in Figure 7-6. New members of the accounting department report that they find the application difficult to use. Most users are familiar with a number of other Windows applications. What changes can you make to help improve the usability of the menu?

Figure 7-6

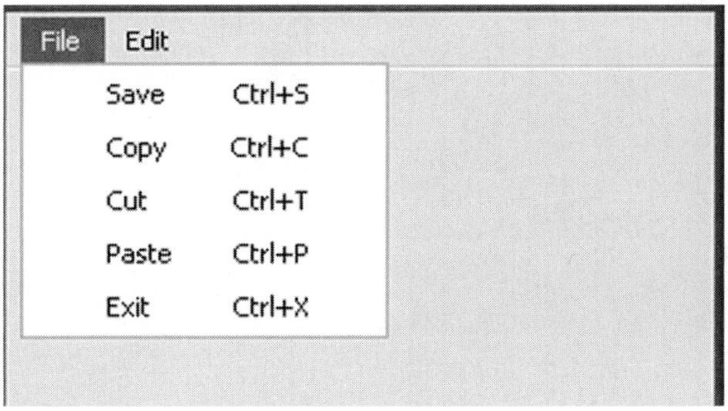

Current menu structure.

YOU TRY IT

Designing Menus and Toolbars

You are designing an application that allows restaurant owners to create menus. Food selections and their nutritional information are retrieved from a database. Restaurant owners arrange the food items, assign prices, and can choose to use the pictures provided by the database or add their own pictures. They can also choose fonts, colors, and borders. Restaurant owners can save menus to a file, open a saved menu, and print the menu.

1. Sketch the menu hierarchy.
2. Which menu items will use the Checked property?
3. Which menu items will display dialogs?
4. Identify the access key and shortcut key for each menu item.
5. What toolbars will you create?
6. Identify the type of ToolStrip control you will use for each item.
7. What steps can you take to make it easier for a new user to learn the application?
8. What information will you display in a Status-Strip control?

8

CREATING YOUR OWN CLASSES

Starting Point

Go to www.wiley.com/college/petroutsos to assess your knowledge of creating classes.
Determine where you need to concentrate your effort.

What You'll Learn in This Chapter

▲ Classes
▲ Properties and methods
▲ Throwing exceptions
▲ Read-only properties
▲ Overloaded methods
▲ Shared methods
▲ Inheritance
▲ Polymorphism
▲ Overriding
▲ Constructors

After Studying This Chapter, You'll Be Able To

▲ Create a custom class module
▲ Create a class that encapsulates functionality
▲ Expose properties and methods
▲ Create and throw exceptions
▲ Create shared methods
▲ Create overloaded methods
▲ Call base class members
▲ Inherit from a base class
▲ Override base class members
▲ Create constructors that initialize variables

INTRODUCTION

Behind every object is a class. When you declare an array, you're invoking the System.Array class, which contains all the code for manipulating arrays. Even when you declare a simple integer variable, you're invoking a class: the System.Integer class. This class contains the code that implements the various properties (such as MinValue and MaxValue) and methods (such as ToString) of the Integer data type. The first time you use an object in code, you're instantiating the class that implements this object. The class's code is loaded into memory, its variables are initialized, and it is ready to execute. The image of the class in memory is said to be an *instance* of the class—that is, it is an object.

You already know how to use classes. Now is the time to find out what goes on behind the scenes when you interact with a class and its members. In this chapter you'll learn how to build your own classes and use them in your projects.

8.1 Defining and Adding Classes

A **class** is a program that doesn't run on its own; it must be used by another application. You use the functionality of a class by creating a variable of the same type as the class and then calling the class's properties and methods through this variable. The methods and properties of the class, as well as its events, constitute the class's **interface.** It's not a visible interface, like the ones you've learned to design so far, because the class doesn't interact directly with the user. Instead, it interacts with the application that uses the class.

In this section, you'll learn the fundamental steps used to create a class and define its interface. This chapter focuses on methods and properties; creating events in a class is beyond the scope of this text.

8.1.1 Using Classes to Combine Code with Data

Classes combine code and data. This simple idea is the very essence of object-oriented programming (OOP).

Meaningful data is processed in specific ways. For example, consider accounting data. You can add or subtract amounts to an account, sum similar accounts, calculate taxes on certain account amounts, and the like. Other types of processing are not valid for this type of data. You never multiply the amounts of two different accounts or calculate logarithms of account balances. Those operations are meaningful with different data but not with accounting data. Because the data itself determines to a large extent the type of processing that will take place on the data, why not "package" the data along with the code for processing it? Classes allow you to do just that.

After you have built a class, you no longer need to write code to process the data; you simply create objects of the class type and call their methods. For example, to transfer an amount from one account to another, you call a method that knows how to transfer the amount. It is up to the method to make sure the amount isn't subtracted from one account unless it has been added to the other account (and vice versa).

To better understand how classes combine code with data, let's take a close look at the Array class. The role of the array is to store sets of data. In addition to holding the data, the Array class also knows how to process it: how to retrieve an element, how to extract a segment of the array, and even how to sort its elements. All these operations require a substantial amount of code. The mechanics of storing data in the array and the code that implements the properties and the methods of the array are hidden from you, the developer. You can instruct an array to perform certain tasks with simple statements. When you call the Sort method, for example, you're telling the array to execute some code that will sort its elements. As a developer, you don't know how the data is stored in the array or how the Sort method works. Some of the operations you can perform with a simple method call are quite complex. Classes abstract many operations by hiding the implementation details, and developers can use them by calling methods.

8.1.2 Building the Minimal Class

Our first example is the Minimal class; we'll start with a class that has minimum functionality and keep adding features to it. You could name this class anything, but it's a good idea to make it suggestive of the class's functionality, so in this case, we'll name it Minimal.

A class might reside in the same file as a form, but it's customary to implement custom classes in a separate module, called a Class module. You can also create a Class project that contains just a class. However, a class doesn't run on its own, and you can't test it without a form. You can create a Windows application, add the class to it, and then test it by adding the appropriate code to the form. After debugging the class, you can remove the test form and reuse the class with any other project.

You create a new class by adding a Class item to a project. You right-click the project's name in the Solution Explorer window and select Add Class from the context menu. In the dialog box that pops up, you select the Class icon and enter a name for the class. For this example, you can set the class's name to Minimal, as shown in Figure 8-1. The code that implements the class resides in the Minimal.vb file, and you'll use the existing form to test the class.

When you open the class by double-clicking its icon in the Project Explorer window, you see the following lines in the code window:

```
Public Class Minimal
End Class
```

Figure 8-1

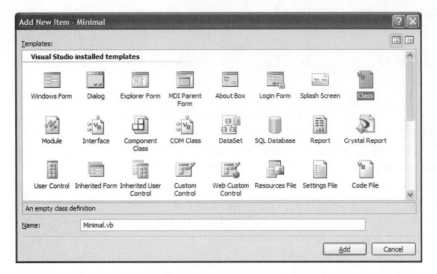

Adding a class item to a project.

At this point, you have a class that you can use in an application. It doesn't do anything, but you can declare it. To do so, you switch back to the Form Designer, add a button to the test form, and insert the following code in its Click event handler:

```
Dim obj1 As Minimal
```

Then you press Enter and type the name of the variable, obj1, followed by a period, on the following line. You see a list of the methods your class exposes already:

```
Equals
GetHashCode
GetType
ReferenceEqual
ToString
```

These methods are provided by the Common Language Runtime (CLR), and you don't have to supply any code for them. To see the kind of functionality these methods expose, you can enter the following lines in the button's Click event handler and then run the application:

```
Dim obj1 As New Minimal
Debug.WriteLine(obj1.ToString)
Debug.WriteLine(obj1.GetType)
Debug.WriteLine(obj1.GetHashCode)
Dim obj2 As New Minimal
Debug.WriteLine(obj1.Equals(obj2))
Debug.WriteLine(Minimal.ReferenceEquals(obj1, obj2))
```

The following lines are then printed on the Immediate window:

```
SimpleClass.Minimal
SimpleClass.Minimal
18796293
False
False
```

The name of the object is the same as its type, which is all the information about the new class that's available to the CLR. The **hash value** of the obj1 variable is an integer value that uniquely identifies the object variable in the context of the current application (it happens to be 18796293, but this is of no consequence).

The next line tells you that two variables of the same type are not equal. But why aren't they equal? You haven't differentiated them at all, yet they're different because they point to two different objects, and the compiler doesn't know how to compare them. All it can do is figure out whether the variables point to the same object. To understand how objects are compared, you can add the following statement after the line that declares obj2:

```
obj2 = obj1
```

When you run the application again, the last statement prints True on the Immediate window. The Equals method checks for **reference equality**; that is, it returns True if both variables point to the same object (i.e., the same instance of the class).

8.1.3 Adding Code to the Minimal Class

Now you can add some functionality to the bare Minimal class. You'll begin by adding two properties and two methods to perform simple text-manipulation tasks. The two properties are called property1 (a string) and property2 (a double). To expose these two members as properties, you can simply declare them as public variables. This isn't the best method of implementing properties, but it really doesn't take more than declaring something as Public to make it available to code outside the class. The following line exposes the two properties of the class:

```
Public property1 As String, property2 As Double
```

The two methods are ReverseString and NegateNumber. The first method reverses the order of the characters in property1 and returns the new string. The NegateNumber method returns the negative of property2. These are two very simple methods that don't accept any arguments; they simply operate on the values of the properties. Methods are exposed as public procedures (i.e., functions or subroutines), just as properties are exposed as public variables. A public procedure or property can be accessed by any **consumer** (i.e., application that declares and instantiates a class) of a class.

To implement the properties and methods, you add the following code:

```
Public Class Minimal
    Public property1 As String, property2 As Double
    Public Function ReverseString() As String
        Return (StrReverse(property1))
    End Function
    Public Function NegateNumber() As Double
        Return (-property2)
    End Function
End Class
```

To test the members you've implemented so far, you switch back to the form and enter the following lines in a new button's Click event handler:

```
Dim obj As New Minimal
obj.property1 = "ABCDEFGHIJKLMNOPQRSTUVWXYZ"
obj.property2 = 999999
Debug.WriteLine(obj.ReverseString)
Debug.WriteLine(obj.NegateNumber)
```

Notice that as soon as you enter the name of the obj variable and the period after it, a complete list of the class's members appears in a list box. The obj variable is of the Minimal type and exposes the public members of the class. You can set and read its properties and call its methods. Your code doesn't see the class's code, just as it doesn't see the code of any of the built-in classes. You trust that the class knows what it is doing and does it right.

8.1.4 Property Procedures

The property1 and property2 properties accept any value, as long as the type is correct and the value of the numeric property is within the acceptable range. But what if the generic properties were meaningful entities, such as email addresses, ages, or zip codes? You should be able to invoke some code to validate the values assigned to the property. To do so, you implement each property as a property procedure.

A **property procedure** is a special type of procedure that contains a Get section and a Set section. The Set section of the procedure is invoked when the application attempts to set the property's value, and the Get section is invoked when the application requests the property's value. The value passed to the property is usually validated in the Set section and, if valid, is stored to a local variable. The same local variable's value is returned to the application when the application requests the property's value from the property's Get section. The following is the implementation of the Age property:

```
Private m_Age As Integer
Property Age() As Integer
    Get
        Age = m_Age
```

```
    End Get
    Set (ByVal value As Integer)
If value < 0 Or value >= 100 Then
    MsgBox("Age must be positive and less than 100")
Else
            m_Age = value
        End If
    End Set
End Property
```

m_Age is the local variable where the age is stored. The m_Age variable is declared as private because you don't want any code outside the class to access it directly; the class uses this variable to store the value of the Age property, and it can't be manipulated directly. The standard naming convention for a variable that cannot be accessed from outside the class is to precede its name with m_. This indicates that it is a member variable. The Age property is, of course, public, so that other applications can set it.

The value argument of the Set procedure represents the actual value that the calling code is attempting to assign to the property. You don't declare this variable; its name is always value, and its type matches the property's type. When a statement like the following is executed in the application that uses your class, the Set section of the property procedure is invoked:

```
obj.Age = 39
```

Because the value is valid, it is stored in the m_Age local variable. Likewise, when a statement like the following is executed, the Get section of the property procedure is invoked, and the value 39 is returned to the application:

```
Debug.WriteLine(obj.Age)
```

FOR EXAMPLE

Creating a Class

Say that you are writing an application for a veterinary office. You decide to create a class that will manage pet information. You decide to expose the following properties:

▲ Name
▲ OwnerName
▲ Weight
▲ Breed
▲ Species

(Continued)

▲ Color

▲ DateOfBirth

▲ Age

You implement the properties as property procedures so that you can validate that data is within range and to ensure that all implementation is encapsulated. You decide to implement the following methods:

▲ AddVaccineInfo

▲ UpdateMedicalHistory

▲ GetDosage

You implement m_VaccinationDates as a HashTable, using the vaccine code as the key. You implement m_MedicalHistory as an array of Strings. However, you know that you can change the implementations of both at a later date because they are encapsulated. You also know that you can change the GetDosage method's implementation if necessary due to changes in recommended dosage levels. You know that none of these changes will affect the application that uses the class. The code for the class is as follows:

```
Public Class Pet

    Private m_Name As String
    Private m_OwnerName As String
    Private m_Weight As Single
    Private m_Breed As String
    Private m_Species As String
    Private m_Color As String
    Private m_DOB As DateTime
    Private m_Age As Integer
    Private m_VaccinationDates As Hashtable
    Private m_MedicalHistory(0) As String

    Public Property Name() As String
        Get
            Return m_Name
        End Get
        Set(ByVal value As String)
            m_Name = value
        End Set
    End Property
    Public Property OwnerName() As String
        Get
            Return m_OwnerName
        End Get
        Set(ByVal value As String)
            m_OwnerName = value
```

```
            End Set
End Property
Public Property Breed() As String
      Get
            Return m_Breed
      End Get
      Set(ByVal value As String)
            m_Breed = value
      End Set
End Property
Public Property Species() As String
      Get
            Return m_Species
      End Get
      Set(ByVal value As String)
            If value = "dog" Or value = "cat" Or _
               value = "bird" Then
               m_Species = value
            Else
                'Handle invalid species
            End If

      End Set
End Property
Public Property Weight() As Single
      Get
            Return m_Weight

      End Get
      Set(ByVal value As Single)
            Select Case Species
                Case "cat"
                    If value > 0 And value < 30 Then
                        m_Weight = value
                    Else
                        'Handle invalid weight
                    End If
                Case "dog"
                    If value > 0 And value < 130 Then
                        m_Weight = value
                    Else
                        'Handle invalid weight
                    End If
                Case "bird"
                    If value > 0 And value < 5 Then
                        m_Weight = value
                    Else
                        'Handle invalid weight
                    End If
```

(Continued)

```
                  End Select
          End Set
  End Property
  Public Property Color() As String
      Get
             Return m_Color
      End Get
      Set(ByVal value As String)
             m_Color = value
      End Set
  End Property
  Public Property DateOfBirth() As DateTime
      Get
             Return m_DOB
      End Get
      Set(ByVal value As DateTime)
             If DateDiff(DateInterval.Year, _
                 value, Now()) < 0 Or _
                 DateDiff(DateInterval.Year, _
                 value, Now()) > 25 Then
                      m_DOB = value
             Else
                 'Handle invalid birth date
             End If
      End Set
  End Property
  Public Property Age() As Integer
      Get
             Return m_Age
      End Get
      Set(ByVal value As Integer)
             m_Age = value
      End Set
  End Property

  Public Sub AddVaccineInfo(ByVal vaccineCode As _
      String, ByVal vaccineDate As Date)
      m_VaccinationDates.Add(vaccineCode, _
          vaccineDate)
  End Sub
  Public Sub UpdateMedicalHistory _
      (ByVal description As String)
      Dim intUpperBound As Integer
      intUpperBound = _
          m_MedicalHistory.GetUpperBound(0)
      If m_MedicalHistory(intUpperBound) Is Nothing _
          Then
          m_MedicalHistory(intUpperBound) = _
              description
      Else
          intUpperBound += 1
```

```
                    ReDim Preserve _
                        m_MedicalHistory(intUpperBound)
                    m_MedicalHistory(intUpperBound) = _
                        description
                End If
            End Sub
            Public Function GetDosage(ByVal medicine As _
                String) As Single
                'Implementation goes here
            End Function

        End Class
```

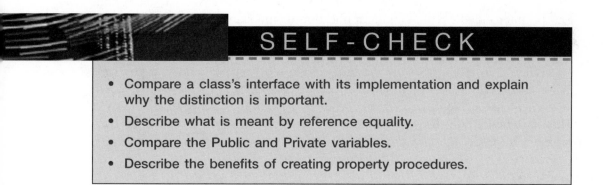

- Compare a class's interface with its implementation and explain why the distinction is important.
- Describe what is meant by reference equality.
- Compare the Public and Private variables.
- Describe the benefits of creating property procedures.

8.2 Implementing Class Members

Now that you know the basic principles of creating a class, it's time to look at some of the issues involved when implementing class members, along with some more advanced techniques. In this section, you'll learn how to handle exceptions in a class, implement read-only properties, use enumerations to make a class easier to use, create class members that can be shared between instances, and overload methods.

8.2.1 Raising Exceptions

There is a problem with the example in the previous section. Remember that a class should interact with the consumer, not with the user. As a developer using the Minimal class in your code, you'd rather receive an exception and handle it from within your code. You should therefore change the implementation of the Age property a little. The property procedure for the Age property throws an InvalidArgument exception if an attempt is made to assign an invalid value to it. You should therefore use the following code:

```
Private m_Age As Integer
Property Age() As Integer
```

```
        Get
            Age = m_Age
        End Get
        Set (ByVal value As Integer)
            If value < 0 Or value >= 100 Then
                Dim AgeException As New _
                    ArgumentException()
                Throw AgeException
            Else
                m_Age = value
            End If
        End Set
    End Property
```

This is a much better technique for handling errors in the class. The exceptions can be intercepted by the calling application, using standard structured exception handling Try…Catch blocks, and developers using your class can write robust applications by handling the exceptions in their code.

When you develop custom classes, you should keep in mind that you can't handle most errors from within a class because you don't know how other developers will use it. You should make your code as robust as you can, but you shouldn't hesitate to throw exceptions for all conditions you can't handle from within your code.

8.2.2 Implementing Read-Only Properties

In this section, you'll make the Minimal class a little more complicated. Age is not usually requested on official documents. Instead, typically, you must furnish your date of birth, from which your current age can be calculated at any time. You can therefore add a BDate property in the Minimal class and make Age a read-only property. To make a property read-only, you simply declare it as ReadOnly and supply the code for the Get procedure only. You therefore need to revise the Age property's code in the Minimal class as follows:

```
Private m_Age As Integer
ReadOnly Property Age() As Integer
    Get
        Age = m_Age
    End Get
End Property
```

Next, you implement the BDate property as shown here:

```
Private m_BDate As DateTime
Property BDate() As DateTime
    Get
        BDate = m_BDate
```

```
      End Get
      Set(ByVal value As Date)
          If Not IsDate(value) Then
              Dim AgeException As New _
                  Exception("Invalid date")
              Throw AgeException
          End If
          If value > Now() Or _
              DateDiff(DateInterval.Year, value, _
                  Now()) >= 120 Then
              Dim AgeException As New Exception _
                  ("Can't accept the birth date " _
                  & "you specified")
              Throw AgeException
          Else
              m_BDate = value
              m_Age = DateDiff(DateInterval.Year, _
                  value, Now())
          End If
      End Set
  End Property
```

Two types of errors can occur when a user sets the BDate property: an invalid date or a date that yields an unreasonable age. First, the code of the BDate property makes sure that the value passed by the calling application is a valid date. If it is not valid, the code throws an exception. If the value variable is a valid date, the code calls the DateDiff function, which returns the difference between two dates in a specified interval—in this case, years. The expression DateInterval.Year is the name of a constant that tells the DateDiff function to calculate the difference between the two dates, in years. The code checks the number of years between the date of birth and the current date. If this difference is negative (which means the person hasn't been born yet) or more than 120 years, the code rejects the value. Otherwise, it sets the value of the m_BDate local variable.

There's still a serious flaw in the implementation of the Age property. Can you see it? The person's age is up-to-date the moment the birth date is entered, but what if you read it back from a file or database three years later? It will still return the original value, which will no longer be the correct age. The Age property's value shouldn't be stored anywhere; it should be calculated as needed. You should therefore revise the Age property's code to calculate the difference between the date of birth and the current date and returns the person's correct age every time it's called:

```
  ReadOnly Property Age() As Integer
      Get
          Age = CInt(DateDiff(DateInterval.Year, _
              m_BDate, Now()))
      End Get
  End Property
```

Now you no longer need the m_Age local variable because the age is calculated when requested. As you can see, you don't always have to store property values to local variables.

You can implement write-only properties with the WriteOnly keyword. This type of property is implemented with a Set section only, but write-only properties are rarely used. An example of a write-only property might be a password. The consumer can set the password using the Password property but cannot retrieve it for security reasons.

8.2.3 Custom Enumerations

You can add a little more complexity to the Minimal class. Because you're storing dates of birth in the class, you can classify a person according to his or her age. To do so, you use an enumeration with the following group names:

```
Public Enum AgeGroup
    Infant
    Child
    Teenager
    Adult
    Senior
    Overaged
End Enum
```

These statements must appear outside any procedure in the class, and you usually place them right after the class declaration. In this example, the name Infant corresponds to 0, the name Child corresponds to 1, and so on. You don't really care about the actual values of the names because the very reason for using enumerations is to replace numeric constants with more meaningful names. You'll see shortly how enumerations are used in both the class and the calling application.

You can add the GetAgeGroup method, which returns the name of the group to which the person represented by an instance of the Minimal class belongs. The name of the group is a member of the AgeGroup enumeration. You add the GetAgeGroup method as follows:

```
Public Function GetAgeGroup() As AgeGroup
    Select Case Age
        Case Is < 36 : Return (AgeGroup.Infant)
        Case Is < 10 : Return (AgeGroup.Child)
        Case Is < 21 : Return (AgeGroup.Teenager)
        Case Is < 65 : Return (AgeGroup.Adult)
        Case Is < 100 : Return (AgeGroup.Senior)
        Case Else : Return (AgeGroup.Overaged)
    End Select
End Function
```

The GetAgeGroup method returns a value of the AgeGroup type. It uses a slightly different version of the Select Case statement than you've seen before. Here, instead of testing for equality, the Is < operator is used. The advantage of using enumerations is that you can manipulate meaningful names instead of numeric constants. This makes your code less prone to errors and far easier to understand.

Because the AgeGroup enumeration was declared as public, it's exposed to any application that uses the Minimal class. To see how you can use the same enumeration in an application, switch to the form's code window, add a new button, and enter the following statements in its event handler:

```
Protected Sub Button3_Click(ByVal sender As Object, _
    ByVal e As System.EventArgs)
    Dim obj As Minimal
    obj = New Minimal()
    obj.BDate = #2/9/1932#
    Debug.WriteLine(obj.Age)
    Dim discount As Single
    If obj.GetAgeGroup = Minimal.AgeGroup.Infant Or _
        obj.GetAgeGroup = Minimal.AgeGroup.Child Then
        discount = 0.4
    End If
    If obj.GetAgeGroup = Minimal.AgeGroup.Senior Then
        discount = 0.5
    End If
    If obj.GetAgeGroup = Minimal.AgeGroup.Teenager _
        Then
        discount = 0.25
    End If
    Debug.WriteLine(discount)
End Sub
```

This routine calculates discounts based on the person's age. Notice that you don't use numeric constants in the code, just descriptive names. Moreover, the possible values of the enumeration are displayed, as needed, in a drop-down list by the IntelliSense feature (see Figure 8-2), and you don't have to memorize

Figure 8-2

AgeGroup enumeration values.

them or look them up as you would with constants. This example is an implementation with multiple If statements, but you could perform the same comparisons with a Select Case statement.

8.2.4 Instance and Shared Methods

Some classes allow you to call some of their members without first creating an instance of the class. The DateTime class, for example, exposes the IsLeapYear method, which accepts a numeric value as the argument and returns a True/False value that indicates whether the year is a leap year. You can call this method through the DateTime (or Date) class without having to create a variable of the DateTime type, as shown in the following statement:

```
If DateTime.IsLeapYear(1999) Then
    'process a leap year
End If
```

A typical example of classes that can be used without an explicit instance is the Math class. To calculate the logarithm of a number, you can use an expression such as this one:

```
Math.Log(3.333)
```

The properties and methods that don't require you to create an instance of the class before you call them are called **shared methods.** Methods that must be applied to an instance of the class are called **instance methods.** By default, all methods are instance methods. To create a shared method, you must prefix the corresponding function declaration with the **Shared keyword,** just as you would a shared property.

When should you create shared methods? If a method doesn't apply to a specific instance of a class, you should make it shared. Let's consider the DateTime class. The DaysInMonth method returns the number of days in the month (of a specific year) that was passed to the method as an argument. You don't really need to create an instance of a Date object to determine the number of days in a specific month of a specific year, so the DaysInMonth method is a shared method and can be called as follows:

```
DateTime.DaysInMonth(2004, 2)
```

The AddDays method, on the other hand, is an instance method. You have a date to which you want to add a number of days and construct a new date. In this case, it makes sense to apply the method to an instance of the class— the instance that represents the date to which you add the number of days.

The SharedMembers project is a simple class that demonstrates the differences between a shared method and an instance method:

```
Public Class SharedMembersClass
    Public strProperty As String
```

```
    Public Function IReverseString() As String
        Return (StrReverse(strProperty))
    End Function
    Public Shared Function SReverseString(ByVal str _
        As String) As String
        Return (StrReverse(str))
    End Function
End Class
```

Both of these methods do the same thing: They reverse the characters in a string. The IReverseString method is an instance method; it reverses the current instance of the class, which is a string. The SReverseString method is a shared method; it reverses its argument.

The instance method acts on the current instance of the class. This means the class must have its strProperty set to a String value before calling the instance method. To test the class, you can add a form to the project, make it the startup object, and add two buttons on it. You use the following code in the two buttons:

```
Private Sub Button1_Click(ByVal sender As _
    System.Object, ByVal e As System.EventArgs) _
    Handles Button1.Click
    Dim testString As String = _
        "ABCDEFGHIJKLMNOPQRSTUVWXYZ"
    Dim obj As New SharedMembersClass()
    obj.strProperty = testString
    Debug.WriteLine(obj.IReverseString)
End Sub
Private Sub Button2_Click(ByVal sender As _
    System.Object, ByVal e As System.EventArgs) _
    Handles Button2.Click
    Dim testString As String = _
        "ABCDEFGHIJKLMNOPQRSTUVWXYZ"
    Debug.WriteLine( _
        SharedMembersClass.SReverseString _
        (testString))
End Sub
```

The code behind the first button creates a new instance of the SharedMembersClass, sets its strProperty value to a string value, and calls its IReverseString method. The second button calls the SReverseString method through the class's name and passes the string to be reversed as an argument to the method.

Another situation in which you would want to create a shared member is when you need to share data across multiple instances of a class. When you instantiate a class, its code is loaded into memory, its local variables are initialized, and then the New subroutine is executed. This happens the first time you instantiate a variable of the class's type. When you instantiate a second instance, a new copy of each local variable is created. The same code acts on different data (i.e., sets of variables), and it appears as if you have multiple instances of the class loaded and running at the same time. Each instance of the class has its own properties, and the values of these properties are local to each instance of the class. Say that you declare two variables of the Minimal type in your application, as follows:

```
Dim obj1, obj2 As Minimal
```

Then you can set their Age properties to different values:

```
obj1.property1 = 10
obj2.property2 = 90
```

The two expressions are independent of one another. There are situations, however, in which you want all instances of a class to see the same property value. Let's say you want to keep track of the users currently accessing your class. You can declare a method that must be called to enable the class, and this method signals that another user has requested your class. This method could establish a connection to a database or open a file. Let's call it the Connect method. Every time an application calls the Connect method, you can increase an internal variable by one. Likewise, every time an application calls the Disconnect method, you can decrease the same internal variable by one. This internal variable can't be private because it will be initialized to zero with each new instance of the class. You need a variable that is common to all instances of the class. Such a variable is called a **shared variable** and is declared with the Shared keyword.

To see how this works, you can add a shared variable, called LoggedUsers, to the Minimal class. It should be read-only. Its value is reported with the Users property, and only the Connect and Disconnect methods can change its value. Here's how you add LoggedUsers:

```
Shared LoggedUsers As Integer
ReadOnly Property Users() As Integer
    Get
        Users = LoggedUsers
    End Get
End Property
Public Function Connect() As Integer
    LoggedUsers = LoggedUsers + 1
    'your own code here
End Function
Public Function Disconnect() As Integer
    If LoggedUsers > 1 Then
        LoggedUsers = LoggedUsers - 1
    End If
    'your own code here
End Function
```

To test the shared variable, you add a new button to the form and enter the following code in its Click event handler:

```
Protected Sub Button5_Click(ByVal sender As Object, _
    ByVal e As System.EventArgs)
    Dim obj1 As New SharedMemberClass
    obj1.Connect()
    Debug.WriteLine(obj1.Users)   'Outputs 1
    obj1.Connect()
    Debug.WriteLine(obj1.Users)  'Outputs 2
    Dim obj2 As New SharedMemberClass
    obj2.Connect()
    Debug.WriteLine(obj1.Users)  'Outputs 3
    Debug.WriteLine(obj2.Users)  'Outputs 3
    Obj2.Disconnect()
    Debug.WriteLine(obj2.Users)  'Outputs 2
End Sub
```

If you run the application, you see the values displayed in the comment after each Debug.WriteLine statement in the Immediate window. As you can see, both obj1 and obj2 variables access the same value of the Users property. Shared variables are commonly used in classes that run on a server and service multiple applications. In effect, they're the class's global variables, which can be shared among all the instances of a class. You can use shared variables to keep track of the total number of rows accessed by all users of the class in a database, connection time, and other similar quantities.

8.2.5 Overloading

One of the strengths of OOP is that it allows you to overload methods. An **overloaded method** is a method that has multiple signatures. A **signature** is a method's contract with the consumer and defines the arguments the method accepts and their data types. After you allow a consumer to use a class, you cannot change the signature of any method, or you will prevent the applications that use that method from working properly. However, you can create additional methods with different signatures.

Suppose that you are creating a class that will calculate various attributes of a room. You want the Perimeter method to accept the room size in both inches and feet and inches. To do so, you create two methods with the following signatures:

```
Public Overloads Function Perimeter(Inches As _
    Double) As Double
End Function
Public Overloads Function Perimeter(Feet As Double, _
    Inches As Double) As Double
End Function
```

This example is a valid overloaded method because one method accepts one argument and the other accepts two arguments. You can also distinguish between methods by passing arguments of different data types. However, you cannot overload methods by creating versions with different argument names. For example, the following signature is not a valid overloaded method for Perimeter:

```
Public Overloads Function Perimeter(Centimeters As _
    Double) As Double
```

Because the arguments passed are identical, the compiler cannot distinguish between this method signature and the first one. Therefore, the class does not compile.

Similarly, you cannot distinguish an overloaded method by using only a different return type. For example, you cannot overload the Perimeter method with the following method:

```
Public Overloads Function Perimeter(Inches As _
    Double) As Integer
```

Once again, the compiler would not be able to determine which version of the method to use when it was called because the consumer might or might not choose to use the return value or might cast the return value to a different data type.

FOR EXAMPLE

Improving the Pet Class

Say that you are writing an application for a veterinary office. You have created a Pet class that includes the following members:

▲ Name
▲ OwnerName
▲ Weight
▲ Breed
▲ Species
▲ Color
▲ Sex
▲ NeuterOrSpay
▲ DateOfBirth
▲ Age
▲ AddVaccineInfo

▲ UpdateMedicalHistory
▲ GetDosage

You decide to make the Age property ReadOnly and implement it as a property that returns a calculated value based on DateOfBirth. The new code is shown here:

```
Public ReadOnly Property Age() As Integer
    Get
            Return DateDiff(DateInterval.Year, _
                DateOfBirth, Now())
    End Get
End Property
```

You decide to create enumerations for Species and Sex, as shown here:

```
Private m_Species As PetSpecies
    Private m_Sex As PetSex
    Public Enum PetSpecies As Integer
        Cat
        Dog
        Bird
    End Enum

    Public Enum PetSex As Integer
        Female
        Male
    End Enum

    Public Property Species() As PetSpecies
        Get
            Return m_Species
        End Get
        Set(ByVal value As PetSpecies)
            m_Species = value
        End Set
    End Property

    Public Property Sex() As PetSex
        Get
            Return m_Sex
        End Get
        Set(ByVal value As PetSex)
            m_Sex = value
        End Set
    End Property
```

You also create an enumeration of the vaccine codes that will be passed to AddVaccineInfo and an enumeration of the drug names that will be passed to GetDosage. These enumerations are too long to show here, but they follow the same format as the ones shown.

(Continued)

You perform range validation within the DateOfBirth and AddVaccineInfo procedures and throw exceptions if an invalid value is entered. The code for this is as follows:

```
Public Property DateOfBirth() As DateTime
    Get
        Return m_DOB
    End Get
    Set(ByVal value As DateTime)
        If DateDiff(DateInterval.Year, value, Now()) _
            < 0 Or DateDiff(DateInterval.Year, value, _
            Now()) > 25 Then
            m_DOB = value
        Else
            Dim ex As New Exception _
                ("Invalid date of birth")
            Throw ex
        End If
    End Set
End Property
Public Sub AddVaccineInfo(ByVal vaccineCode As _
    String, ByVal vaccineDate As Date)
    If DateDiff(DateInterval.Year, vaccineDate, _
        Now()) < 0 Then
        Dim ex As New Exception("Invalid year")
        Throw ex
        ' same year, check date
    ElseIf DateDiff(DateInterval.Year, _
        vaccineDate, Now()) = 0 Then
        If DateDiff(DateInterval.DayOfYear, _
        vaccineDate, Now()) < 0 Then
            'day is in the future
            Dim ex As New Exception("Invalid date")
            Throw ex
        Else
            m_VaccinationDates.Add(vaccineCode, _
              vaccineDate)
        End If
    Else
        m_VaccinationDates.Add(vaccineCode, _
            vaccineDate)
    End If
End Sub
```

You also create three overloaded versions of the UpdateMedicalHistory method. One is for new problems, one is for follow-up visits, and another is for annual exams. The method signatures are as follows:

```
Public Overloads Sub UpdateMedicalHistory(Doctor As _
    String, Date As Date, Comments As String)
End Sub
```

```
Public Overloads Sub UpdateMedicalHistory(Doctor As _
    String, Date As Date, Problem As String, _
    Diagnosis As String, Comments As String)
End Sub

Public Overloads Sub UpdateMedicalHistory(Doctor _
    As String, _FollowUpToVisit As Date, _
    Comments As String, ProblemSolved As Boolean)
End Sub
```

SELF-CHECK

- Discuss why throwing exceptions is a better way to handle errors than displaying a message box when building a class.
- Identify a situation in which a ReadOnly property is appropriate.
- Compare shared methods with instance methods.
- Identify the required differences between overloaded methods.

8.3 Inheritance

The promise of classes, and of object programming at large, is code reuse. The functionality you place in a class is there for your projects, and any other developer can access it as well. However, in order to enhance the code in your class, another developer needs a method to build other classes that are built on your class. This is known as **inheritance.** Before we can discuss inheritance, you need to understand a few terms. A **derived class** (or **child class**) is a class that inherits base functionality from another class. A **base class** (or **parent class**) is the class from which a derived class inherits.

In this section, we'll look at why inheritance is a critical part of OOP. Next, we'll look at how to use inheritance in Visual Basic, including how to add functionality, override functionality, implement polymorphism, and create custom constructors.

8.3.1 The Importance of Inheritance

Inheritance is a technique for reusing and improving code without breaking the applications that use it. The idea is to export the code you want to reuse in a format that doesn't allow editing. If more than two people can edit the same code (or if even a single person is allowed to edit the same code in two different projects), any benefits of code reuse evaporate immediately. The code to be shared must be packaged as a **dynamic link library (DLL),** which exposes all the functionality without the risk of being modified in a haphazard way. A DLL is a file that contains support classes and cannot be executed on its own. Only the original creator of the DLL can edit the code, and it's very likely that this person will make sure that the interface of the class doesn't change. However, you should still be able to enhance the code in different projects. That's where inheritance comes into the picture. Instead of getting a copy of the code, you build classes that inherit one or more classes. The functionality of these base classes can't change. The code in the DLL is well protected, and there's no way to edit the executable code; only the class's functionality is inherited.

It's possible to add new functionality to inherited code or even override some of the existing functionality. You can add new functionality to the code by adding new members to the existing classes or by adding an entirely new class. This doesn't break any existing applications that use the original DLL. You can also override some of the functionality by creating a new method that replaces an existing one. Applications that use the original version of the DLL don't see the new members because they work with the old DLL. Newer projects can make use of the enhanced functionality of the DLL.

Let's look at a simple but quite practical example. A lot of functionality has been built into Windows itself, and it is constantly reused in other applications. The various Windows Forms controls are a typical example. The functionality of the TextBox control is packaged in a DLL (the System.Windows.Forms.TextBox class). Yet many developers enhance the functionality of the TextBox control to address specific application requirements, such as by adding a few statements in the control's Enter and Leave events to change the color of the TextBox control that has the focus.

With Visual Basic, it's possible to write just two event handlers that react to these two events and control the background color of the text box that has the focus. These two handlers handle the corresponding events of all TextBox controls on the form.

A better approach is to design a "new" TextBox control that incorporates all the functionality of the original TextBox control but also changes its background color while it has the focus. The code that implements the TextBox control is hidden from you, but you can reuse it by building a new control that inherits from the TextBox control:

```
Public Class FocusTextBox
Inherits System.Windows.Forms.TextBox
Private Sub FocusedTextBox_Enter(ByVal sender _
    As Object, ByVal e As System.EventArgs) _
    Handles Me.Enter
    Me.BackColor = enterFocusColor
```

```
End Sub
Private Sub FocusedTextBox_Leave(ByVal sender _
    As Object, ByVal e As System.EventArgs) _
    Handles Me.Leave
    Me.BackColor = leaveFocusColor
End Sub
'enterFocusColor implementation
'leaveFocusColor implementation
End Class
```

The two Color variables are properties of the control (implemented with the usual setters and getters) so that different applications can use different colors for the active TextBox control on the form.

With the Inherits statement, you include (i.e., inherit) all the functionality of the original TextBox control without touching the control's code. The inherited class is actually stored in a different file from the rest of the code. Any project that uses the FocusedTextBox control can take advantage of the extra functionality, yet all existing projects will continue to work with the original version of the TextBox control. You can easily upgrade a project to take advantage of the enhanced TextBox control by replacing all the instances of the TextBox control on a form with instances of the new control. Some projects may use the new control yet not take advantage of the new functionality and leave the default colors—in which case the enhanced control behaves just like the original TextBox control.

8.3.2 Inheriting Existing Classes

To demonstrate the power of inheritance, let's extend an existing class: the ArrayList class. The ArrayList class maintains a list of objects that is similar to an array, but it's dynamic. The class you'll develop in this section will inherit all the functionality of ArrayList, plus it will expose a custom method you'll implement here: the EliminateDuplicates method.

You can call the new class myArrayList. The first line in the new class must be the Inherits statement, followed by the name of the class you want to inherit, ArrayList. You need to start a new project, name it CustomArrayList, and add a new class to it, named myArrayList:

```
Class myArrayList
    Inherits ArrayList
End Class
```

If you don't add a single line of code to this class, the myArrayList class exposes exactly the same functionality as the ArrayList class. If you add a public function to the class, it becomes a method of the new class, in addition to the methods of ArrayList.

You need to add the code of the EliminateDuplicates subroutine to the myArrayList class; this subroutine will become a method of the new class:

```
Sub EliminateDuplicates()
    Dim i As Integer = 0
    Dim delEntries As ArrayList
    While i <= MyBase.Count - 2
        Dim j As Integer = i + 1
        While j <= MyBase.count - 1
            If MyBase.Item(i).ToString = _
                MyBase.item(j).ToString Then
                MyBase.RemoveAt(j)
            End If
            j = j + 1
        End While
        i = i + 1
    End While
End Sub
```

This code compares each item with all following items and removes any duplicates. The duplicate items are the ones whose ToString property returns the same value. Notice that the code accesses the members of the ArrayList class through the MyBase object. **MyBase** is a keyword that references the base class, from which the custom class inherits.

In this section, you extended an existing class by writing simple Visual Basic statements that could have appeared in any application. You just inserted the Inherits keyword followed by the name of an existing class on which you wanted to base your class, and provided the implementation of the new functionality. You could also have added properties and methods to the class.

This type of inheritance, in which you inherit an existing class and add new members and/or override existing ones, is called **implementation inheritance.** Implementation inheritance is a powerful feature and can be used in many situations, besides enhancing an existing class. You can design base classes that address a large category of objects and then subclass them for specific objects. The typical example is the Person class, from which you can derive classes such as Contact, Customer, Employee, and so on. Inheritance is used with large-scale projects to ensure consistent behavior across an application.

8.3.3 Inheriting Custom Classes

In the following example, you'll use inheritance to tackle a very real problem. Companies make money by selling products and services. Every company has different requirements. Even two bookstores don't store the same information in their databases. However, there are a few pieces of information that all companies typically use in the process: a product code, a description, and a price. This is the minimum information typically needed.

The specifics of a product can be stored to different tables in a database. If your customer is a bookstore, you'll design tables to store data such as publisher and author names, book descriptions, ISBNs, and the like. You'll also have to write applications to maintain all this information. To use the same module for an electronics store, you would need to create another application for a different type of product, but the table with the basic data would remain the same. In this section, you'll build a custom class for storing products. The application's main form is shown in Figure 8-3.

The most basic class stores the information you'll need for ordering and invoicing applications: the product's ID, its name, and its price. Here's the implementation of a simple Product class:

```
Public Class Product
    Public Description As String
    Public ProductID As String
    Public ProductBarCode As String
    Public ListPrice As Decimal
End Class
```

This class includes the product's barcode because barcodes are usually used in selling products. This class can represent any product for the purposes of

Figure 8-3

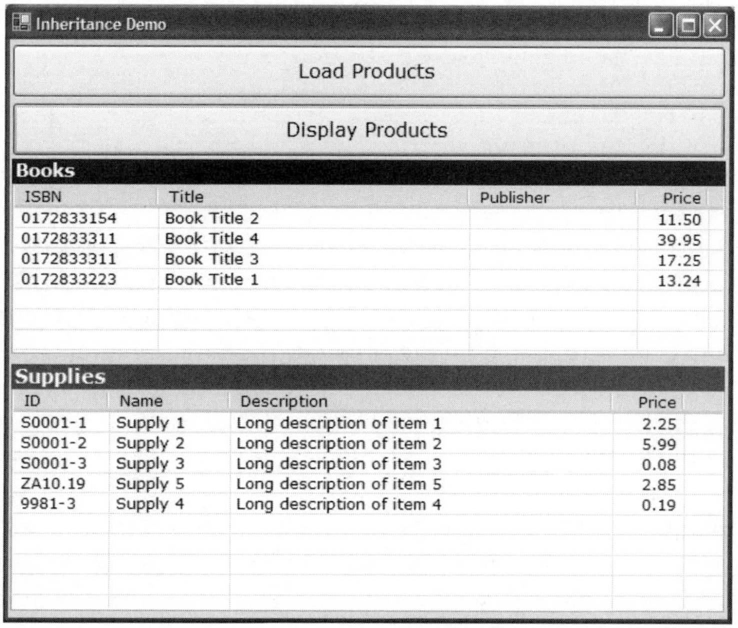

An application's main form.

buying and selling it. Populate a collection with objects of this type, and you're ready to write a functional interface for creating invoices and purchase orders.

Now you must take into consideration the various types of products. To keep the example simple, consider a store that sells books and supplies. Each type of product is implemented with a different class, which inherits from the Product class. The following is a simple class for representing a book:

```
Public Class Book
    Inherits Product
    Public Subtitle As String
    Public ISBN As String
    Public pages As Integer
    Public PublisherID As Long
    Public Author As String
End Class
```

In addition to its own properties, the Book class exposes the properties of the Product class as well. Because the book industry has a universal coding scheme (the ISBN), the product's code is the same as its ISBN. This, however, is not a requirement of the application. You will probably add some extra statements to make sure that the ProductID field of the Product class and the ISBN field of the Book class always have the same value.

The class that represents supplies is as follows:

```
Public Class Supply
    Inherits Product
    Public LongDescription As String
    Public ManufacturerCode As String
    Public ManufacturerID As Long
    Public Function GetPrice() As Decimal
        'Code goes here
    End Function
End Class
```

To make sure that this class can accommodate all pricing policies for a company, you can implement a GetPrice method to return the product's sale price (it can be different at different outlets or for different customers). The idea is that some piece of code accepts the product's list (or purchase) price and the ID of the customer that buys it. This code can perform all kinds of calculations, look up tables in the database, or perform any other action, and it returns the product's sale price: the price that will appear on the customer's receipt. To keep the example very simple, you'll sell with the list price.

You need to write some code to populate a few instances of the Book and Supply classes. The following statements populate a HashTable with books and supplies:

```
Dim Products As New Hashtable
Dim P1 As New Book
```

```
P1.ListPrice = 13.24D
P1.Description = "Book Title 1"
P1.ProductID = "EN0101"
P1.ISBN = "0172833223"
P1.Subtitle = "Book Title 1 Subtitle"
Products.Add(P1.ProductID, P1)
Dim P2 As New Supply
P2.Description = "Supply 1"
P2.ListPrice = 2.25D
P2.LongDescription = "Long description of item 1"
P2.ProductID = "S0001-1"
Products.Add(P2.ProductID, P2)
```

The HashTable is a structure for storing objects along with their keys. In this case, the keys are the IDs of the products. The HashTable can locate items by means of their keys very quickly.

Each item in the Products collection is either of the Book or of the Supply type, and you can determine its type with the following expression:

```
TypeOf Products.Item(key) Is Book ...
```

The following code shows the Display Products button's Click event on the sample application's form:

```
Private Sub Button2_Click(ByVal sender As _
    System.Object, ByVal e As System.EventArgs) _
    Handles bttnDisplay.Click
    Dim key As String
    Dim LI As ListViewItem
    For Each key In Products.Keys
        LI = New ListViewItem
        Dim bookItem As Book, supplyItem As Supply
        If TypeOf Products.Item(key) Is Book Then
            bookItem = _
                CType(Products.Item(key), Book)
            LI.Text = bookItem.ISBN
            LI.SubItems.Add(bookItem.Description)
            LI.SubItems.Add("")
            LI.SubItems.Add _
                (bookItem.ListPrice.ToString _
                ("#,##0.00"))
            ListView1.Items.Add(LI)
        End If
        If TypeOf Products.Item(key) Is Supply Then
            supplyItem = CType(Products.Item(key), _
                Supply)
            LI.Text = supplyItem.ProductID
            LI.SubItems.Add(supplyItem.Description)
            LI.SubItems.Add _
                (supplyItem.LongDescription)
```

```
            LI.SubItems.Add _
                (supplyItem.ListPrice.ToString _
                ("#,##0.00"))
            ListView2.Items.Add(LI)
        End If
    Next
End Sub
```

This code iterates through the items of the collection, determines the type of each item, and adds the product's fields to the appropriate ListView control. You use the CType function to convert the object from the generic base class object type to its actual type. If you do not convert the object using CType, you will not be able to access the properties and methods specific to that type; you will only be able to access the base class members.

It's fairly easy to take advantage of inheritance in your projects. The base class encapsulates the functionality that's necessary for multiple classes. All other classes inherit from the base class, and they add specific members that don't apply to other classes (at least, not all of them do).

8.3.4 Polymorphism

A consequence of inheritance is another powerful OOP technique: **polymorphism,** which is the capability of a base type to adjust itself to accommodate many different derived types. Let's consider some analogies in the English language. Take the word *run*, for example. This verb can be used to describe athletes, cars, or refrigerators; they all run. In different sentences, the same word takes on different meanings. When you use it with a person, it means going a distance at a fast pace. When you use it with a refrigerator, it means that it's working. When you use it with a car, it may take on both meanings. So, in a sense, the word *run* is polymorphic (as are many other English words): Its exact meaning is differentiated according to the context.

To apply the same analogy to computers, think of a class that describes a basic object such as a Shape. This class would be very complicated if it had to describe and handle all shapes. It would be incomplete, too, because the moment you released it to the world, you'd think of a new shape that couldn't be described by the class. To design a class that describes all shapes, you build a very simple class to describe shapes at large, and then you build a separate class for each individual shape: a Triangle class, a Square class, a Circle class, and so on. As you can guess, all these classes inherit from the Shape class. Let's also assume that all the classes that describe individual shapes expose an Area method, which calculates the area of the shape they describe. The name of the Area method is the same for all classes, but it calculates a different formula.

Developers don't have to learn a different syntax of the Area method for each shape; they can declare a Square object and calculate its area with the following statements:

```
Dim shape1 As New Square, area As Double
area = shape1.Area
```

If shape2 represents a circle, the same method will calculate the circle's area:

```
Dim shape2 As New Circle, area As Double
area = shape2.Area
```

You can go through a list of objects derived from the Shape class and calculate their areas by calling the Area method. You do not need to know what shape each object represents—you just call its Area method.

However, if you want to use a loop to calculate the area for the various shapes stored in an ArrayList, this approach presents a problem. Remember that if you declare a variable of a base class type, you can only implement the base class members unless you convert the object to its actual class.

In the following section, you'll build the Shape class, which you'll then extend with individual classes for various shapes. You'll be able to add your own classes to implement additional shapes, and any code written using the older versions of the Shape class will keep working.

Creating the Shape Class

The Shape class will be the base class for all other shapes. This is a very simple class that's pretty useless on its own. Its real use is to expose some members that can be inherited. The base class exposes two methods: Area and Perimeter. Even the two methods don't do much—actually, they do absolutely nothing. They really only provide a naming convention. All classes that will inherit from the Shape class will have an Area method and a Perimeter method. They must provide the implementation of these methods so that all object variables that represent shapes will expose an Area method and a Perimeter method. Here's how you create the Shape class:

```
Class Shape
    Overridable Function Area() As Double
    End Function
    Overridable Function Perimeter() As Double
    End Function
End Class
```

The **Overridable keyword** means that a class that inherits from the Shape class can override the default implementation of the corresponding methods or properties. When a class **overrides** a member, it provides a new implementation for a property or method implemented by the base class. As you will see shortly, it is possible for the base class to provide a few members that can't be overridden in the derived class.

You can implement the classes for the individual shapes. To do so, you add another Class module to the project, name it Shapes, and enter the following code in the module:

```
Public Class Square
    Inherits Shape
    Private sSide As Double
    Public Property Side() As Double
        Get
            Side = sSide
        End Get
        Set
            sSide = Value
        End Set
    End Property
    Public Overrides Function Area() As Double
        Area = sSide * sSide
    End Function
    Public Overrides Function Perimeter() As Double
        Return (4 * sSide)
    End Function
End Class

Public Class Triangle
    Inherits Shape
    Private side1, side2, side3 As Double
    Property SideA() As Double
        Get
            SideA = side1
        End Get
        Set
            side1 = Value
        End Set
    End Property
    Property SideB() As Double
        Get
            SideB = side2
        End Get
        Set
            side2 = Value
        End Set
    End Property
    Public Property SideC() As Double
        Get
            SideC = side3
        End Get
        Set
            side3 = Value
```

```
            End Set
        End Property
        Public Overrides Function Area() As Double
            Dim perim As Double
            perim = Perimeter()
            Return (Math.Sqrt((perim - side1) * _
                (perim - side2) * (perim - side3)))
        End Function
        Public Overrides Function Perimeter() As Double
            Return (side1 + side2 + side3)
        End Function
    End Class

    Public Class Circle
        Inherits Shape
        Private cRadius As Double
        Public Property Radius() As Double
            Get
                Radius = cRadius
            End Get
            Set
                cRadius = Value
            End Set
        End Property
        Public Overrides Function Area() As Double
            Return (Math.Pi * cRadius ^ 2)
        End Function
        Public Overrides Function Perimeter() As Double
            Return (2 * Math.Pi * cRadius)
        End Function
    End Class
```

The Shapes.vb file contains three classes: Square, Triangle, and Circle. All three classes expose their basic geometric characteristics as properties. The Triangle class, for example, exposes the properties SideA, SideB, and SideC, which allow you to set the three sides of the triangle. In addition, all three classes expose the Area and Perimeter methods. These methods are implemented differently for each class, but they do the same thing: They return the area and the perimeter of the corresponding shape. The Area method of the Triangle class is a bit involved, but it's just a formula.

Creating an Abstract Class

The Shape base class and the Shapes derived class work fine, but there's a potential problem: A new derived class that implements a new shape might not override the Area method or the Perimeter method. To make sure that all derived classes implement this method, you can specify the **MustInherit** modifier on the class declaration and the **MustOverride** modifier on the member declaration:

```
Public MustInherit Class Shape
    Public MustOverride Function Area() As Double
    Public MustOverride Function Perimeter() _
        As Double
End Class
```

The MustInherit keyword tells the CLR that the Shape class can't be used as is; it must be inherited by another class, so it is known as an **abstract base class,** an **abstract class,** or a **virtual class.** The MustOverride keyword tells compiler that derived classes (i.e., the classes that will inherit the members of the base class) must provide their own implementation of the two methods.

Notice that there's no End Function statement, just the declaration of the function that must be inherited by all derived classes. If the derived classes can override one or more methods optionally, these methods must be implemented as actual functions. Methods that must be overridden need not be implemented as functions—they're just placeholders for a name.

You can use other modifiers with your classes, such as the **NotInheritable** modifier, which prevents other developers from using your class as a base class. You might want to enhance the Array class by adding a few new members. If you insert the statement Inherits Array in a class, the compiler will complain that the System.Array class can't be inherited. The Array class is an example of a noninheritable class.

The **NotOverridable** keyword can be applied to a method or function to prevent a class that inherits from the base class from overriding that member.

8.3.5 Access Modifiers for Base Classes

You are already familiar with using Private and Public access modifiers to determine whether a member can be accessed by the application that uses the class. When creating a base class, you have two other options for access modifiers: Protected and Protected Friend.

Protected members have scope between public and private, and they can be accessed in the derived class, but they're not exposed to applications using either the parent class or the derived classes. In the derived class, they have a private scope. You use the Protected keyword to mark the members that are of interest to developers who will use your class as a base class but not to developers who will use it in their applications.

The **Protected Friend** modifier tells the CLR that the member is available to the class that inherits the class, as well as to any other class in the same project.

8.3.6 MyBase and MyClass

The MyBase and MyClass keywords let you access the members of the base class and the derived class explicitly. MyBase is an object that lets you access the members of the base class. **MyClass** is an object that references the derived class. To see why they're useful, you can edit ParentClass as shown here:

```
Public Class ParentClass
    Public Overridable Function Method1() As String
        Return (Method4())
    End Function
    Public Overridable Function Method4() As String
        Return ("I'm the original Method4")
    End Function
End Class
```

You override Method4 in the derived class as shown here:

```
Public Class DerivedClass
    Inherits ParentClass
    Overrides Function Method4() As String
        Return("Derived Method4")
    End Function
End Class
```

Next, you switch to the test form, add a button, declare a variable of the derived class, and call its Method4:

```
Dim objDerived As New DerivedClass()
Debug.WriteLine(objDerived.Method4)
```

What do you see if you execute these statements? Obviously, you'll see the string Derived Method4.

So far, all looks reasonable, and the class behaves intuitively. But what if you add the following method in the derived class?

```
Public Function newMethod() As String
    Return (Method1())
End Function
```

This method calls Method1 in the ParentClass class because Method1 is not overridden in the derived class. Method1 in the base class calls Method4. But which Method4 gets invoked? It's the derived Method4. To fix this behavior (assuming that you want to call the Method4 of the base class), you change the implementation of Method1 to the following:

```
Public Overridable Function Method1() As String
    Return (MyClass.Method4())
End Function
```

Now the call to Method1 will return "I'm the original Method 4".

Is it reasonable for a method of the base class to call the overridden method? It is reasonable because the overridden class is newer than the base class, and the compiler tries to use the newest members. If you had other classes inheriting from the DerivedClass class, their members would take precedence.

You use the MyClass keyword to make sure you're calling a member in the same class and not an overriding member in an inheriting class. Likewise, you can use the keyword MyBase to call the implementation of a member in the base class rather than the equivalent member in a derived class.

FOR EXAMPLE

Using Inheritance

Say that you decide to implement the Pet class as a base class and create Cat, Dog, and Bird classes that derive from it. Doing this allows you to implement more species-specific functionality and allows you to more easily expand the program for veterinarians that treat other species. You want to allow for polymorphism to ensure that some routines that are not breed specific can be easily automated (e.g., updating the medical history after an office visit).

You also need the ability to issue vaccination reminders. The logic for issuing reminders depends on the species because the vaccinations are different for each species. However, you also want to be able to automate issuing annual exam reminders, which is not species specific.

You change the Pet class to an abstract class. It includes all the members described earlier, plus two additional methods:

▲ VaccineReminder

▲ AnnualExamReminder

You define VaccineReminder and GetDosage as methods that must be overridden. You define Species, Weight, Breed, and SpayOrNeuter as overridable. The abstract class is as follows:

```
Public MustInherit Class Pet

    Private m_Name As String
    Private m_OwnerName As String
    Private m_Weight As Single
    Private m_Breed As String

    Private m_Color As String
    Private m_DOB As DateTime
```

```
Private m_Age As Integer
Private m_VaccinationDates As Hashtable
Private m_MedicalHistory(0) As String

Private m_Species As PetSpecies
Private m_Sex As PetSex
Private m_Fixed As Boolean

Public Enum PetSpecies As Integer
    Cat
    Dog
    Bird
End Enum

Public Enum PetSex As Integer
    Female
    Male
End Enum

Public Overridable Property SpayOrNeuter() As _
    Boolean
    Get
        Return m_Fixed
    End Get
    Set(ByVal value As Boolean)
        value = m_Fixed
    End Set
End Property

Public Overridable Property Species() As PetSpecies
    Get
        Return m_Species
    End Get
    Set(ByVal value As PetSpecies)
        m_Species = value
    End Set
End Property

Public Property Sex() As PetSex
    Get
        Return m_Sex
    End Get
    Set(ByVal value As PetSex)
        m_Sex = value
    End Set
End Property

Public Property Name() As String
    Get
        Return m_Name
    End Get
    Set(ByVal value As String)
        m_Name = value
```

(Continued)

```
            End Set
        End Property
        Public Property OwnerName() As String
            Get
                Return m_OwnerName
            End Get
            Set(ByVal value As String)
                m_OwnerName = value
            End Set
        End Property
        Public Overridable Property Breed() As String
            Get
                Return m_Breed
            End Get
            Set(ByVal value As String)
                m_Breed = value
            End Set
        End Property

        Public Overridable Property Weight() As Single
            Get
                Return m_Weight

            End Get
            Set(ByVal value As Single)
                Select Case Species
                    Case "cat"
                        If value > 0 And value < 30 Then
                            m_Weight = value
                        Else
                            Dim ex As New Exception _
                                ("Invalid cat weight." & _
            "Please enter a value between .1 and 30")
                            Throw ex
                        End If
                    Case "dog"
                        If value > 0 And value < 130 Then
                            m_Weight = value
                        Else
                            Dim ex As New Exception _
                                ("Invalid dog weight." & _
            "Please enter a value between .1 and 130")
                            Throw ex
                        End If
                    Case "bird"
                        If value > 0 And value < 5 Then
                            m_Weight = value
                        Else
                            Dim ex As New Exception _
                                ("Invalid bird weight." & _
```

```vbnet
                        " Please enter a value between .1 and 5")
                            Throw ex
                        End If
                End Select
        End Set
End Property

Public Property Color() As String
        Get
                Return m_Color
        End Get
        Set(ByVal value As String)
                m_Color = value
        End Set
End Property
Public Property DateOfBirth() As DateTime
        Get
                Return m_DOB
        End Get
        Set(ByVal value As DateTime)
                If DateDiff(DateInterval.Year, value, _
                    Now()) < 0 Or _
                    DateDiff(DateInterval.Year, value, _
                    Now()) > 25 Then
                    m_DOB = value
                Else
                    Dim ex As New Exception _
                        ("Invalid date of birth")
                    Throw ex
                End If
        End Set
End Property
Public ReadOnly Property Age() As Integer
        Get
                Return DateDiff(DateInterval.Year, _
                    DateOfBirth, Now())
        End Get
End Property

Public Sub AddVaccineInfo(ByVal vaccineCode As _
    String, ByVal vaccineDate As Date)
        If DateDiff(DateInterval.Year, vaccineDate, _
            Now()) < 0 Then
            Dim ex As New Exception("Invalid year")
            Throw ex
        ElseIf DateDiff(DateInterval.Year, _
            vaccineDate, Now()) = 0 Then
            ' same year, check date
```

(Continued)

```
                If DateDiff(DateInterval.DayOfYear, _
                    vaccineDate, Now()) < 0 Then
                    'day is in the future
                    Dim ex As New Exception("Invalid date")
                    Throw ex
                Else
                    m_VaccinationDates.Add(vaccineCode, _
                        vaccineDate)
                End If
            Else
                m_VaccinationDates.Add(vaccineCode, _
                    vaccineDate)
            End If
        End Sub
        Public Sub UpdateMedicalHistory(ByVal description _
            As String)
            Dim intUpperBound As Integer
            intUpperBound = _
                MedicalHistory.GetUpperBound(0)
            If m_MedicalHistory(intUpperBound) Is Nothing _
                Then
                m_MedicalHistory(intUpperBound) = _
                    description
            Else
                intUpperBound += 1
                ReDim Preserve _
                    m_MedicalHistory(intUpperBound)
                m_MedicalHistory(intUpperBound) = _
                    description
            End If
        End Sub
        Public Function AnnualExamReminder() As Date
            'Implementation goes here
        End Function
        Public MustOverride Function GetDosage(ByVal _
            medicine As String) As Single
        Public MustOverride Function VaccineReminder() _
            As Date

    End Class
```

You create Dog, Cat, and Bird classes that are derived from Pet. All classes use the base class implementation of the following members:

▲ Name
▲ OwnerName
▲ Weight
▲ Breed
▲ Species

▲ Color

▲ Sex

▲ DateOfBirth

▲ Age

▲ AddVaccineInfo

▲ UpdateMedicalHistory

▲ AnnualExamReminder

The Dog class and the Cat class use the base class implementation of SpayOrNeuter. They also provide their own implementation of the GetDosage method and the VaccineReminder method.

The Cat class also implements an FLKTestDate property that tracks the date of the last feline leukemia test. The Cat class is as follows:

```
Public Class Cat
    Inherits Pet

    Private m_flkTest As Date

    Public Property FLKTestDate() As Date
        Get
            Return m_flkTest
        End Get
        Set(ByVal value As Date)
            m_flkTest = value
        End Set
    End Property

    Public Overrides Function GetDosage(ByVal _
        medicine As String) As Single
        'Cat implementation goes here
    End Function

    Public Overrides Function VaccineReminder() As Date
        'Cat implementation goes here
    End Function
End Class
```

The Dog class also implements a HeartwormTest property that tracks the date of the last heartworm disease test. The Dog class is as follows:

```
Public Class Dog
    Inherits Pet

    Private m_hwTest As Date

    Public Property HeatwormTest() As Date
        Get
```

(Continued)

```
                    Return m_hwTest
                End Get
                Set(ByVal value As Date)
                    m_hwTest = value
                End Set
            End Property

            Public Overrides Function GetDosage(ByVal _
                medicine As String) As Single
                'Dog implementation goes here
            End Function

            Public Overrides Function VaccineReminder() As Date
                'Dog implementation goes here
            End Function
        End Class
```

The Bird class overrides the SpayOrNeuter method and always returns
False. It also implements a WingsClipped method that tracks the date the
bird last had its wings clipped. The Bird class is as follows:

```
    Public Class Bird
        Inherits Pet
        Private m_wingsclipped As DateTime
        Public Property WingsClipped() As DateTime
            Get
                Return m_wingsclipped
            End Get
            Set(ByVal value As DateTime)
                m_wingsclipped = value
            End Set
        End Property

        Public Overrides Property SpayOrNeuter() As Boolean
            Get
                Return False
            End Get
            Set(ByVal value As Boolean)
                MyBase.SpayOrNeuter = False
            End Set
        End Property
        Public Overrides Function GetDosage(ByVal _
            medicine As String) As Single
            'Bird implementation
        End Function

        Public Overrides Function VaccineReminder() As Date
            'Bird implementation
        End Function
        End Class
```

SELF-CHECK

- Describe how inheritance promotes code reuse.
- Identify a situation in which you would want to inherit from a .NET Framework class.
- Discuss the ramifications of inheriting from a custom class, if any.
- Describe how Visual Basic supports polymorphism.
- Compare the Public, Private, Protected, and Protected Friend access modifiers.
- Compare the MyBase and MyClass keywords.

8.4 Object Constructors

Objects are instances of classes, and classes are instantiated with the New keyword. If you declare an object variable without the New keyword, no object will be created, and if you attempt to use this variable later in your code, a Null Reference exception will be thrown. To construct an object, you must first declare it and then set it to a new instance of the class it represents.

When an object is instantiated, its constructor is run. The **constructor** is a special routine that initializes variables and can perform other tasks that prepare the object to be accessed. Each object has a **default constructor,** which accepts no arguments, and it can also have **overloaded constructors** that accept arguments. The arguments are passed when the consumer calls New to instantiate an instance of the object. For example, to construct a rectangle, you can use either of these two statements:

```
Dim shape1 As Rectangle = New Rectangle()
Dim shape2 As Rectangle = New Rectangle(100, 30)
```

The first rectangle has no dimensions; the second one has a width of 100 units and a height of 30 units. This rectangle is instantiated using the default constructor, which is also known as the **parameterless constructor.** The following is the default constructor that is automatically created when you create a class:

```
Public Sub New()

End Sub
```

If you need to add code to the default constructor, you open the class in Code view, select the class name from the left-hand drop-down list, and select New from the right-hand drop-down list.

The second constructor in the preceding code sample is an overloaded constructor, or **parameterized constructor,** which creates a new Rectangle object and initializes its dimensions. Parameterized constructors are implemented with public subroutine with the name New. You can have as many overloaded forms of the New subroutine as needed.

You should add a parameterized constructor for a Contact class. Each contact should have at least a name; here's a parameterized constructor for the Contact class:

```
Public Sub New(ByVal CompanyName As String)
    MyBase.New()
    Me.CompanyName = CompanyName
End Sub
```

The code is quite trivial, with the exception of the statement that calls the MyBase.New subroutine. The reason you must call the New method of the base class is that the base class might have its own constructor, which can't be called directly. You must always insert this statement in your constructors to make sure that any initialization tasks that must be performed by the base class will not be skipped.

The Contact class's constructor accepts a single argument: the company name (this property can't be a blank string). Another useful constructor for the same class accepts two additional arguments—the contact's first and last names—as follows:

```
Public Sub New(ByVal CompanyName As String, _
    ByVal LastName As String, ByVal _
    FirstName As String)
    MyBase.New()
    Me.ContactName = LastName & ", " & FirstName
    Me.CompanyName = CompanyName
End Sub
```

With the two parameterized constructors in place, you can create new instances of the Contact class with statements like the following:

```
Dim contact1 As New Contact("Around the Horn")
```

Or you can use the following:

```
Dim contact1 As New Contact("Hardy", "Thomas")
```

Notice the lack of the Overloads (or Overrides) keyword. Constructors can have multiple forms and don't require the use of Overloads; you just supply as many implementations of the New subroutine as you need.

FOR EXAMPLE

Creating Constructors for the Pet, Dog, Cat, and Bird Classes

You want to minimize the likelihood that a Pet object is instantiated without at least an OwnerName and PetName because those fields are required to retrieve the information from a database. The exception to this is when a new record is created for a pet. In this situation, only the OwnerName and Species might be known when the appointment is first made. Supported species are stored in the base class PetSpecies enumeration.

You create constructors in the child classes that delegate to the base class using the MyBase keyword. The second constructor checks the species before delegating and raises an exception if the wrong species is passed. For example, the following is the code for the constructors of the Dog class:

```
Public Sub New(ByVal OwnerName As String, _
    ByVal PetName As String)
    'Code goes here
    MyBase.New()
End Sub

Public Sub New(ByVal OwnerName As String, _
    ByVal Species As PetSpecies)
    If Species = PetSpecies.Dog
        MyBase.New()
        'Other code goes here
    Else
        Dim ex As New Exception ("Invalid species")
        Throw ex
    End If
End Sub
```

SELF-CHECK

- Discuss the benefit of creating a parameterized constructor.

SUMMARY

In this chapter, you've learned how to create classes to promote code reusability. You've learned how to declare a class and create properties and methods. You've also learned a few advanced topics, such as read-only properties, custom enumerations, shared properties and methods, and overloading. You've learned how to use inheritance, including calling methods on the base class and the derived class, and you've taken a look at constructors.

KEY TERMS

Abstract base class

Abstract class

Base class

Child class

Class

Constructor

Consumer

Default constructor

Derived class

DLL

Hash value

Implementation inheritance

Inheritance

Instance method

Interface

MustInherit

MustOverride

MyBase

MyClass

NotInheritable

NotOverridable

Overloaded constructor

Overloaded method

Overridable

Override

Parameterized constructor

Parameterless constructor

Parent class

Polymorphism

Property procedure

Protected

Protected Friend

Reference equality

Shared keyword

Shared method

Shared variable

Signature

Virtual class

ASSESS YOUR UNDERSTANDING

Go to www.wiley.com/college/petroutsos to evaluate your knowledge of creating classes.

Measure your learning by comparing pre-test and post-test results.

Summary Questions

1. A class is used to separate code from data. True or False?
2. A class can be created in a Class module or a Form module. True or False?
3. Which of the following is a method declaration?
   (a) Public UserName As String
   (b) Private UserName As String
   (c) Public Function GetTotal() As Integer
   (d) Private Function GetTotal() As Integer
4. Which section of a property procedure accepts an argument named value?
   (a) Get
   (b) Set
   (c) Both Get and Set
5. You should not display a message box from within a class method. True or False?
6. A read-only property is a created with a property procedure that has only a Set section. True or False?
7. The following code is added to a class:

```
Public Enum EmployeeType
      Hourly
      Salary
      Contract
End Enum
```

   Where can this enumeration be used?
   (a) only in the consumer
   (b) only in the class
   (c) in both the consumer and the class
8. An instance method can only be called after you instantiate the class. True or False?
9. Which keyword can you use to create two methods in a class that have the same name but accept different numbers of arguments?
   (a) Overrides
   (b) MustInherit
   (c) MustOverride
   (d) Overloads

10. A derived class always implements less functionality than a base class. True or False?

11. Which of the following is the correct way to declare a class that derives from Rectangle?

(**a**) `Class customRect`
        `Inherits Rectangle`
   `End Class`

(**b**) `Class Inherits Rectangle: customRect`
   `End Class`

(**c**) `Class customRect`
        `MustInherit Rectangle`
   `End Class`

(**d**) `MustInherit Rectangle Class customRect`
   `End Class`

12. Which of the following statements correctly describes a derived class?

(**a**) A derived class cannot implement any functionality that is not implemented by the base class.

(**b**) A derived class can implement additional functionality or override functionality implemented by the base class.

(**c**) A derived class must override all methods and properties provided by the base class.

13. Polymorphism is implemented by creating overridable methods and properties in the base class. True or False?

14. Which keyword must be used in an abstract class declaration?

(**a**) MustInherit

(**b**) MustOverride

(**c**) Overridable

(**d**) NotInheritable

15. Which keyword is used to create a function that can be accessed by a derived class but not by a consumer?

(**a**) Private

(**b**) Protected

(**c**) Public

16. Which keyword is used to call a method on a parent class?

(**a**) Me

(**b**) MyBase

(**c**) MyClass

(**d**) Parent

17. You must create a parameterless constructor for each class. True or False?

Applying This Chapter

1. You are creating a class named Product that will be used to store and process inventory and pricing information. The ApplyDiscount method needs to accept a percentage off and apply the discount to the price. Another version of the method needs to accept a percentage off and a lowest possible price and apply the discount only if the threshold is not exceeded. The price can also be set when the object instance is created, but it cannot be modified except by applying a discount.

   (a) How will you create the ApplyDiscount methods?

   (b) How will you implement the Price property?

2. You are creating a class named Trends that will allow an application to perform various calculations on sales data. The sales data is stored in a database and is the same for any instance of the class.

   (a) How will you implement the methods in the Trends class?

   (b) How will you handle errors that occur when performing the calculations?

3. You are creating a game in which players will choose an animal to run an obstacle course. Animals have different characteristics that affect the way they run, climb, jump, and swim. However, all animals accumulate points the same way. You are designing the classes for the game. You want to make it easy to add more animals at a later time.

   (a) How should you design the classes?

   (b) What strategy should you use to expose the Run method?

   (c) What strategy should you use to expose the GetPoints method?

Implementing Classes

You are creating an application to manage inventory for a florist. The florist has three types of inventory: living plants, cut flowers, and nonperishable supplies, such as ribbons and tissue paper. The application must report whether the necessary items to build a specific floral arrangement are available or must be ordered. The shelf life of cut flowers must be considered when determining availability. Price is always a calculated value based on Cost and NumberInStock.

1. Describe the class hierarchy you will create.
2. How will you design the GetAvailability method?
3. How will you expose the Price property?
4. How will you expose the NumberInStock property?

5. Identify at least three other properties you will implement and which class will implement them.
6. Describe how you will modify the application if the florist later begins to also sell chocolates.
7. How will you handle a condition that causes the number in stock to be less than zero?
8. After you finish the application, the florist decides that the application needs to be more flexible in checking for availability. For example, some customers might prefer red roses but settle for any red flowers. Others might settle for roses of any color. How will you modify the interface to support this functionality?

9

ACCESSING DATA

Starting Point

Go to www.wiley.com/college/petroutsos to assess your knowledge of
relational databases and database access techniques.
Determine where you need to concentrate your effort.

What You'll Learn in This Chapter

▲ Relational database fundamentals
▲ Structured Query Language (SQL) fundamentals
▲ ADO.NET data access objects
▲ Data binding

After Studying This Chapter, You'll Be Able To

▲ Identify the features of a well-designed database
▲ Retrieve data to meet business requirements
▲ Insert, update, and delete data
▲ Create an application that accesses a database that uses bound controls

INTRODUCTION

Many applications store data in relational databases. Understanding the fundamental concepts behind relational data and how it is accessed is important to your success as a programmer, especially in a business environment. However, relational database design and implementation is a complex topic that requires much more time and space than we have in this chapter. Therefore, the goal of this chapter is not to make you an expert in relational database programming but to provide you with an overview of the key concepts and procedures.

This chapter begins with a look at relational database concepts. Next, we'll look at SQL, a special language for accessing and writing to a database. Finally, we'll examine the how to access data by using ADO.NET and how to bind relational data to controls.

9.1 Relational Database Fundamentals

Today, most data storage is in the form of databases. For that reason this chapter examines the use of Visual Basic to access databases. To start this discussion, we need to formally define *database*.

9.1.1 Defining *Database*

A **database** stores different types of data in such a way that a user can easily manipulate and retrieve the data. Every database is composed of a series of elements, beginning with fields. A **field** is a single fact or data item; it is the smallest unit of named data that has meaning in a database. Examples of fields include a name, an address, or a phone number on a membership list; a product number in an inventory list; or a price in a price list. Fields are given field names that are used to identify them. A collection of related data that is treated as a unit is referred to as a *record*. Basically, a record is a collection of fields that pertain to a single person, place, or thing. For example, you might have a membership list record that contains numerous fields, including name, phone number, street address, city, state, zip code, and other information of interest.

A related collection of records, all having the same fields, is referred to as a **table.** For example, a table that stores the membership list for a DVD rental application would have a record for each person on the list, with each record referring to a different person but having the same fields. In a table, the records are commonly referred to as the *rows* of the table, and the fields are the *columns* of the table. Figure 9-1 shows the first few records of the Vintage DVDs Members table. Note the rows and columns of this table and that the table includes only the name, phone number, and late fees for each member because this is all the data required. Other tables may contain additional information.

Figure 9-1

	Name	Phone_Number	Late_Fees
⊞	Smith, Joe	706-555-0012	$0.00
⊞	Mullins, Janice	706-555-0777	$1.07
⊞	Smith, Joe	706-555-1234	$0.00
⊞	Randall, Ray	706-555-3214	$3.20
⊞	Arons, Suzy	706-555-3587	$0.00

The Vintage DVDs Members table.

9.1.2 Relational Databases

If you have multiple tables that are related, you have a special type of database known as a **relational database.** This is the most common type of database used today, and it is the type we'll examine in this text. As an example of a relational database, consider the Vintage DVDs database composed of the Members table shown in Figure 9-1, with Name, Phone Number, and Late Fees fields, along with two other tables:

▲ A DVD table of DVD information with fields for the DVD ID and name, the rental price, and the location in the store

▲ A Rental table that contains information about each rental, including fields for the DVD ID number, the phone number of the person renting the DVD, and the date the DVD is to be returned

In this case, the Members table is related to the Rental table through the customer phone number that is common to both tables, and the DVD table is related to the Rental table through the DVD ID number that is common to both tables. Because both the Members table and the DVD table are related to the Rental table, they are also related to each other. These relationships are shown in Figure 9-2.

Figure 9-2

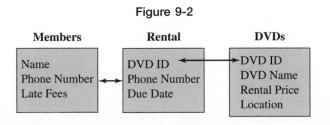

Table relationships.

Why are these particular fields related, rather than some others? It has to do with ensuring that there is no ambiguity about the records being referenced. If you assume that every Vintage DVDs member has a phone and that there is only one membership per household, then the phone number is a unique identifier for each member, with no two members having the same phone number; in database terminology, the phone number is the **primary key** for the Members table. Similarly, the DVD ID is the primary key for the DVD table. In the Rental table, these two keys become what is known as **foreign keys** because they identify records from another table in this database. However, note that each transaction is now uniquely identified by the phone number of the person renting it and the DVD ID of the DVD being rented. Through this relationship, for example, you can find information about the rental status of a DVD or the number of that a person has rented at any one time. In many database packages, the table is automatically sorted on the primary key. For example, Figure 9-1 is arranged in ascending order of telephone numbers because this is its primary key.

9.1.3 Database Management Systems

Databases are maintained by special programs, such as Access and SQL Server. These programs are called **database management systems (DBMSs).** A fundamental characteristic of a DBMS is that it isolates much of the complexity of the database from the developer. Regardless of how each DBMS stores data on disk, you see your data organized in tables, with relationships between tables. To access the data stored in a database and to update the database, you use a special language, **Structured Query Language (SQL).** Unlike other areas of programming, SQL is a truly universal language, and all major DBMSs support it.

9.1.4 Structuring Data

Databases are designed to make data easily retrievable. The purpose of a database is not so much the storage of information as it is quick retrieval. It is important that you structure a database so that it can be queried and modified efficiently.

Let's look at an example. In a database that stores information about books, there is a table with titles, another table with authors, and a table with publishers. The table with the titles contains information such as the title of the book, the number of pages, and the book's description. Author names are stored in a different table because each author might appear in multiple titles. If author information were stored along with each title, you'd be repeating author names. So every time you wanted to change an author's name, you'd have to modify multiple entries in the titles table. Even retrieving a list of unique author names would be a challenge because you'd have to scan the entire database, retrieve all the authors, and then get rid of the duplicate entries.

The reason for breaking the information you want to store in a database into separate tables is to avoid duplication of information. This is a key point in database design. Duplication of information sooner or later leads to inconsistencies in the database. The process of breaking the data into related tables that eliminate all possible forms of information duplication is called **normalization,** and there are rules for normalizing databases. The topic of database normalization is not discussed in this book. However, all it really takes to design a functional database is common sense. After you learn how to extract data from your database's tables by using SQL statements, you'll develop a better understanding of the way databases should be structured.

9.1.5 Exploring a Sample Database

Let's look at the structure of a sample database that comes with both SQL Server 2000 and Access 2003. You can also install the database in SQL Server 2005. The Northwind database stores products, customers, and sales data. We'll discuss the basic objects that make up a database shortly, but it's easiest to explain these objects through examples. Besides, you need to have a good understanding of the structure of this database to follow the examples in the following sections. Unless you understand how data are stored in the tables of the database and how the tables relate to one another, you won't be able to retrieve information from the database or insert new data into it.

The Northwind database is made up of tables, each storing a collection of unique entities (customers, products, and so on). A table that stores products has a column for the product's name, another column for the product's price, and so on. Each product is stored in a different row. As products are added to or removed from the table, the number of rows changes, but the number of columns remains the same; they determine the information stored about each product. The following are the tables in the Northwind database:

▲ **Products table:** The Products table stores information about the products sold by the Northwind Corporation. This information includes the product's name, packaging information, price, and other relevant fields. Each product (or row) in the table is identified by a unique numeric ID. Because the rows of the Products table are referenced by invoices (which are stored in the Order Details table, which is discussed later), the product IDs appear in the Order Details table as well.

▲ **Suppliers table:** Each product has a supplier, too. Because the same supplier can offer more than one product, the supplier information is stored in a different table, and a common field, the SupplierID field, is used to link each product to its supplier (as shown in Figure 9-3). For

Figure 9-3

Suppliers Table

	SupplierID	CompanyName
1	1	Exotic Liquids
2	2	New Orleans Cajun Delights
3	3	Grandma Kelly's Homestead
4	4	Tokyo Traders

Products Table

	productID	ProductName	SupplierID
1	1	Chai	1
2	2	Chang	1
3	3	Aniseed Syrup	1
4	4	Chef Anton's Cajun Seasoning	2
5	5	Chef Anton's Gumbo Mix	2
6	6	Grandma's Boysenberry Spread	3
7	7	Uncle Bob's Organic Dried Pears	3
8	8	Northwoods Cranberry Sauce	3

The relationships between suppliers and products.

example, the products Chai, Chang, and Aniseed Syrup are purchased from the same supplier: Exotic Liquids. Their SupplierID fields all point to the same row in the Suppliers table.

▲ **Categories table:** In addition to having a supplier, each product belongs to a category. Categories are not stored along with product names; they are stored separately, in the Categories table. Again, each category is identified by a numeric value (field CategoryID) and has a name (field CategoryName). In addition, the Categories table has two more columns: Description, which contains text, and Picture, which stores a bitmap. The CategoryID field in the Categories table is the primary key, and the field by the same name in the Products table is the corresponding foreign key.

▲ **Customers table:** The Customers table stores information about the company's customers. Each customer is stored in a separate row of this table, and customers are referenced by the Orders table. Unlike product IDs, customer IDs are five-character strings.

▲ **Orders table:** The Orders table stores information about the orders placed by Northwind's customers. The OrderID field, which is an integer value, identifies each order. Orders are numbered sequentially, so this field is also the order's number. Each time you append a new row to the Orders table, the database automatically generates the value of the new OrderID field. The Orders table is linked to the Customers table through the CustomerID field. By matching rows with identical values in their CustomerID fields in the two tables, you can recombine customers with their orders. Figure 9-4 shows how customers are linked to their orders.

Figure 9-4

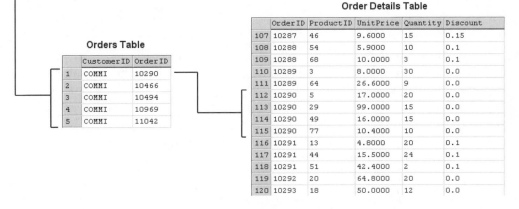

Customers Table

	CustomerID	CompanyName
12	CACTU	Cactus Comidas para llevar
13	CENTC	Centro comercial Moctezuma
14	CHOPS	Chop-suey Chinese
15	COMMI	Comércio Mineiro
16	CONSH	Consolidated Holdings

Orders Table

	CustomerID	OrderID
1	COMMI	10290
2	COMMI	10466
3	COMMI	10494
4	COMMI	10969
5	COMMI	11042

Order Details Table

	OrderID	ProductID	UnitPrice	Quantity	Discount
107	10287	46	9.6000	15	0.15
108	10288	54	5.9000	10	0.1
109	10288	68	10.0000	3	0.1
110	10289	3	8.0000	30	0.0
111	10289	64	26.6000	9	0.0
112	10290	5	17.0000	20	0.0
113	10290	29	99.0000	15	0.0
114	10290	49	16.0000	15	0.0
115	10290	77	10.4000	10	0.0
116	10291	13	4.8000	20	0.1
117	10291	44	15.5000	24	0.1
118	10291	51	42.4000	2	0.1
119	10292	20	64.8000	20	0.0
120	10293	18	50.0000	12	0.0

The relationships between customers, orders, and order details.

▲ **Order Details table:** The Northwind database's Orders table doesn't store any details about the items ordered; that information is stored in the Order Details table (see Figure 9-4). Each order is made up of one or more items; and each item has a price, a quantity, and a discount. In addition to these fields, the Order Details table contains an OrderID column, which holds the ID of the order to which the detail line belongs. The reason details aren't stored along with the order's header is that the Orders and Order Details tables store different entities. The order's header, which contains information about the customer who placed the order, the date of the order, and so on, is quite different from the information you must store for each item ordered.

▲ **Employees table:** This table holds employee information. Each employee is identified by a numeric ID, which appears in the each order. When a sale is made, the ID of the employee who made the sale is recorded in the Orders table.

▲ **Shippers table:** Each order is shipped with one of the three shippers stored in the Shippers table. The appropriate shipper's ID is stored in the Orders table.

FOR EXAMPLE

Defining Relational Data

Sat that you are writing an application for a veterinary office. You are designing the data storage requirements. You need to store client information, including name, phone number, address, and balance due. You also need to store information about each pet, including name, date of birth, weight, and vaccination records. A client might have one or more pets. You must also store information on each appointment a pet has, including the doctor, the date and time of the appointment, a brief description of any procedures that were done or diagnosis that was made, and invoice information for the visit. Charges for a visit are itemized and might include charges for the visit itself, vaccinations, medications, and procedures such as x-rays. An invoice is sometimes, but not always, associated with an appointment.

You decide to store the data in a relational database for which you identify the following tables:

▲ Clients
▲ Pets
▲ Appointments
▲ Charges
▲ Vets
▲ Invoice
▲ Vaccinations

You identify the relationships described in Table 9-1.

Table 9-1: Relationships

Primary Key Table	Foreign Key Table	Key Column
Clients	Pets	ClientID
Clients	Invoice	ClientID
Pets	Appointments	PetID
Pets	Vaccinations	PetID
Invoice	Charges	InvoiceID
Vets	Appointments	VetID

SELF-CHECK

- Describe how a field is related to a record.
- Describe how a relationship is created between two tables.
- Discuss why normalization is important.
- Identify the primary purpose of a DBMS.

9.2 SQL Fundamentals

SQL is a universal language for manipulating tables, and almost every DBMS supports it, so you should invest the time and effort to learn it. You can generate SQL statements with point-and-click operations (by using the Query Builder, a visual tool for generating SQL statements that is included with Visual Studio), but this is no substitute for understanding SQL and writing your own statements.

SQL is a nonprocedural language, which means that SQL doesn't provide traditional programming structures such as IF statements or loops. Instead, it's a language for specifying the operation you want to perform at a high level. The details of the implementation are left to the DBMS.

The SQL statements we are concerned with here are **data manipulation language (DML)** statements, which are used to select and modify data. Most DBMSs also supports **data definition language (DDL) statements,** which are used to define the structure of the database (e.g., creating and modifying tables).

9.2.1 The SELECT Statement

The SELECT statement is used to retrieve data. When you execute a SELECT statement, this is known as executing a **selection query** because it selects and returns data. Depending on the exact statement, it can return either a single value or a table of values, known as a *result set*. In its most basic form, a SELECT statement has the following syntax:

```
SELECT column_list FROM source WHERE filter_criteria
```

SQL is not case sensitive, but it's customary to use uppercase for the SQL statements and keywords. *column_list* is generally the list of column names. *source* is the name of the database table from which you are retrieving data. For example, to retrieve all the company names from the Customers table of the Northwind database, you issue a statement like this one:

```
SELECT CompanyName FROM Customers
```

The DISTINCT keyword eliminates any duplicates from the result set retrieved by the SELECT statement. Let's say you want a list of all countries that have at least one customer. If you retrieve all country names from the Customers table, you'll end up with many duplicates. To eliminate them, you can use the DISTINCT keyword, as shown in the following statement:

```
SELECT DISTINCT CompanyName FROM Customers
```

Filtering Data

The unconditional form of the SELECT statement used in the last few examples is quite trivial. You rarely retrieve data from all rows in a table. Usually, you specify criteria, such as "All companies in Germany," "All customers who have placed three or more orders in the past six months," or even more complicated expressions. To restrict the rows returned by the query, you use the WHERE clause of the SELECT statement. *filter_criteria* provides the condition for selecting rows. For example, to select customers from a specific country, you issue the following statement:

```
SELECT CompanyName FROM Customers WHERE Country = 'Germany'
```

The DBMS retrieves and returns the rows you requested. As you can see, this is not the way you'd retrieve rows with Visual Basic. With a procedural language such as Visual Basic, you'd have to specify the statements to scan the entire table, examine the value of the Country column, and either select or reject the row. Then you would display the selected rows. With SQL, you don't have to specify how the selection operation should take place; you simply specify what you want the database to do for you—not how to do it.

To select customers from multiple countries, you use the OR operator to combine multiple conditions:

```
WHERE Country = 'Germany' OR Country = 'Austria'
```

You can also combine multiple conditions with the AND operator.

You use the IN and NOT IN keywords in a WHERE clause to specify a list of values that a column must match (or not match). They are a form of shorthand notation for multiple OR operators. The following statement, for example, retrieves the names of the customers in all German-speaking countries:

```
SELECT CompanyName FROM Customers
WHERE Country IN ('Germany', 'Austria', 'Switzerland')
```

The BETWEEN keyword lets you specify a range of values and limit the selection to the rows that have a specific column in this range. The BETWEEN keyword is a shorthand notation for an expression like this:

```
column >= minValue AND column <= maxValue
```

For example, to retrieve the orders placed in 2006, you use the following statement:

```
SELECT OrderID, OrderDate, CompanyName FROM Orders, Customers
WHERE Orders.CustomerID = Customers.CustomerID AND
(OrderDate BETWEEN '1/1/2006' AND '12/31/2006')
```

Table 9-2: SQL Wildcard Characters

Wildcard Character	Description
%	Matches any number of characters. For example, The pattern program% finds *program, programming, programmer,* and so on. The pattern %program% locates strings that contain the words *program, programming, nonprogrammer,* and so on.
_ (underscore)	Matches any single alphabetic character. For example, the pattern b_y finds *boy* and *bay* but not *boysenberry.*
[ ]	Matches any single character within the brackets. For example, the pattern Santa [YI]nez finds both *Santa Ynez* and *Santa Inez.*
[^]	Matches any character not in the brackets. For example, the pattern %q[^u]% finds words that contain the character *q* not followed by *u* (which are misspelled words).
[-]	Matches any one of a range of characters. The characters must be consecutive in the alphabet and specified in ascending order (i.e., A to Z, not Z to A). For example, the pattern [a-c]% finds all words that begin with *a, b,* or *c* (in lowercase or uppercase).
#	Matches any single numeric character. For example, the pattern D1## finds *D100* and *D139* but not *D1000* and *D10.*

Pattern Matching Using LIKE

The LIKE operator uses pattern-matching characters (or wildcard characters) to match one or more characters, numeric digits, ranges of letters, and so on. These characters are listed in Table 9-2. You can use the LIKE operator to retrieve all customers with names that start with A by using a statement like the following:

```
SELECT CompanyName FROM Customers WHERE CompanyName LIKE
'A%'
```

To include in a search argument a character that functions as a wildcard character, you enclose it in square brackets. The pattern %50[%]% matches any field that contains the string "50%".

Ordering Results

The rows of a query are not in any particular order. To request that the rows be returned in a specific order, you use the ORDER BY clause, whose syntax is as follows:

```
ORDER BY col1, col2, . . .
```

You can specify any number of columns in the ORDER list. The output of the query is ordered according to the values of the first column (col1). If two rows have identical values in this column, they are sorted according to the second column, and so on. The following statement displays the customers ordered by country and then by city within each country:

```
SELECT CompanyName, ContactName FROM Customers
ORDER BY Country, City
```

By default, results are sorted in ascending order, meaning that the sort order is alphabetical from A to Z for string and character values and from low to high for numeric values. You can use the DESC keyword to cause the data to be sorted in descending order.

Some queries retrieve a large number of rows, but you may be interested in the top few rows only. The TOP N keyword allows you to select the first N rows and ignore the remaining ones. Let's say you want to see the list of the 10 most wanted products. To do so, you would execute this:

```
SELECT TOP 10 ProductName FROM ProductSales
ORDER BY NumberSold DESC
```

Without the TOP keyword, you'd have to calculate how many items from each product have been sold, sort them according to items sold, and examine the first 10 rows returned by the query.

The TOP keyword is used only when the rows are ordered according to some meaningful criteria. Limiting a query's output to the alphabetically top N rows isn't very practical. When the rows are sorted according to items sold, revenue generated, and so on, it makes sense to limit the query's output to N rows.

Retrieving Data from Multiple Tables

It is possible to retrieve data from two or more tables with a single statement; this is actually the most common type of query. When you combine multiple tables in a query, you can use the WHERE clause to specify how the rows of the two tables should be combined. Let's say you want a list of all product names, along with their categories. The information you need is not contained in a single table. You must extract the product name from the Products table and the category name from the Categories table and specify that the ProductID field in the two tables must match. The following statement retrieves the names of all products, along with their category names:

```
SELECT ProductName, CategoryName
```

```
FROM Products, Categories
WHERE Products.CategoryID = Categories.CategoryID
```

Here's how this statement is executed: For each row in the Products table, the SQL engine locates the matching row in the Categories table and then appends the ProductName and CategoryName fields to the result. If a product has no category, then it is not included in the result.

When you retrieve data from multiple tables, the process is known as a **join.** A join specifies how you connect multiple tables in a query. There are four types of joins:

▲ Left outer, or left, join

▲ Right outer, or right, join

▲ Full outer, or full, join

▲ Inner join

You have already seen an example of an inner join. An **inner join** includes only the rows from both tables that match the join condition. In the previous example, these rows would be the ones where the value stored in the CategoryID column in the Products table matched the value in the CategoryID column in the Categories table. The following is another way to write an inner join:

```
SELECT ProductName, CategoryName
FROM Products INNER JOIN Categories
ON Products.CategoryID = Categories.CategoryID
```

The keyword INNER is optional because an inner join is the default type of join performed. Notice that you need to qualify CategoryID with the table name. This is because the CategoryID column appears in both the Products and Categories tables.

You can use a **table alias** (which is like a table nickname) to reduce typing when there are column names duplicated between tables. You define the table alias in the FROM clause and use it in the SELECT, ON, and WHERE clauses. For example, to use table aliases, in the previous example, you would execute this:

```
SELECT ProductName, CategoryName
FROM Products p INNER JOIN Categories c
ON p.CategoryID = c.CategoryID
```

The **left join** displays all the records in the left table and only those records of the table on the right that match certain user-supplied criteria. The **right join** is similar to the left outer join except that all rows in the table on the right are displayed, and only the matching rows from the left table are displayed. The **full join** returns all the rows of the two tables, regardless of whether there are matching rows. In effect, it's a combination of left and right joins. A detailed discussion of outer joins and full joins is beyond the scope of this text.

Performing Calculations

In addition to column names, you can specify calculated columns in the SELECT statement. The Order Details table contains a row for each invoice line. Invoice #10248, for instance, contains four lines (i.e., four items sold), and each detail line appears in a separate row in the Order Details table. Each row holds the number of items sold, the price of the item, and the corresponding discount. To display the line's subtotal, you must multiply the quantity by the price minus the discount, as shown in the following statement:

```
SELECT Orders.OrderID, ProductID,
[Order Details].UnitPrice * [Order Details].Quantity * (1 -
[Order Details].Discount) AS SubTotal
FROM Orders, [Order Details]
WHERE Orders.OrderID = [Order Details].OrderID
```

This statement calculates the subtotal for each line in the invoices issued to all Northwind customers and displays them along with the order number, as shown in Figure 9-5. The order numbers are repeated as many times as there are products in the order (or lines in the invoice).

Figure 9-5

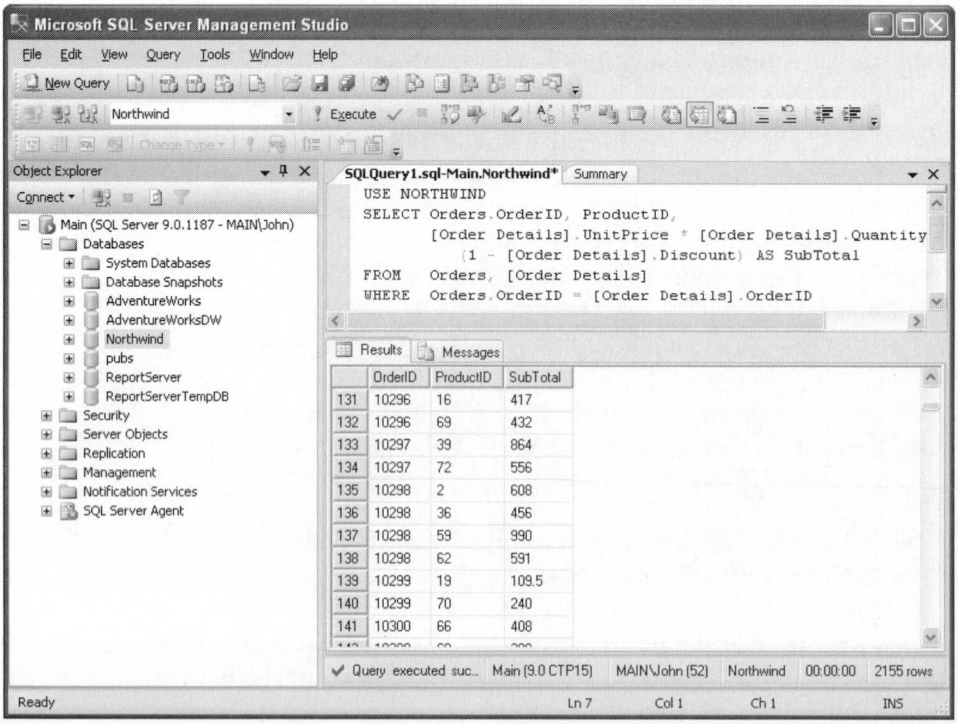

Results of a query to calculate subtotals.

Table 9-3: Aggregate Functions

Function	Description
COUNT	Returns the number (count) of values in a specified column.
SUM	Returns the sum of values in a specified column.
AVG	Returns the average of the values in a specified column.
MIN	Returns the smallest value in a specified column.
MAX	Returns the largest value in a specified column.

You use square brackets around identifiers that have names that contain spaces or other characters that might cause the DBMS to not recognize the name as an identifier. Long lines in a SQL statement can be broken anywhere, and there's no need to insert a line continuation character, as you do with Visual Basic statements. You can shorten the preceding SQL statement by omitting the table name qualifier for the Quantity and UnitPrice fields because their names do not appear in any other table. You can't omit the table qualifier from the OrderID field's name because it appears in both tables involved in the query.

Totaling and Counting

SQL supports some **aggregate functions,** which act on selected fields of all the rows returned by the query. The aggregate functions listed in Table 9-3 perform basic calculations such as summing, counting, and averaging numeric values. An aggregate function accepts field names (or calculated fields) as arguments, and it returns a single value, which is the sum (or average) of all values.

The SUM and AVG functions can process only numeric values. The other three functions can process both numeric and text values.

Aggregate functions are used to summarize data from one or more tables. Let's say you want to know how many of the Northwind database customers are located in Germany. The following SQL statement returns the desired value:

```
SELECT COUNT(CustomerID) FROM Customers WHERE Country =
'Germany'
```

This is a simple demonstration of the COUNT function. If you want to count unique values, you must use the DISTINCT keyword along with the name of the field to count. If you want to find out in how many countries are represented by Northwind customers, you use the following SQL statement:

```
SELECT COUNT(DISTINCT Country) FROM Customers
```

If you omit the DISTINCT keyword, the statement returns the number of rows that have a Country field.

Grouping Rows

Sometimes you need to group the results of a query so that you can calculate subtotals. Let's say you need not only the total revenues generated by a single product but also a list of all products and the revenues they generated. It is possible to use the SUM function to break the calculations at each new product ID, as demonstrated in the following statement. To do so, you must group the product IDs together with the GROUP BY clause:

```
SELECT ProductID,
SUM(Quantity * UnitPrice *(1 - Discount)) AS
[Total Revenues]
FROM [Order Details] GROUP BY ProductID ORDER BY ProductID
```

The preceding statement produces output like this:

```
ProductID     Total Revenues
1             12788.10
2             16355.96
3             3044.0
4             8567.89
5             5347.20
6             7137.0
7             22044.29
```

The GROUP BY clause groups all the rows with the same values in the specified column and forces the aggregate functions to act on each group separately. SQL Server sorts the rows according to the column specified in the GROUP BY clause and starts calculating the aggregate functions. Every time it runs into a new group, it prints the result and resets the aggregate function(s). If you use the GROUP BY clause in a SQL statement, you must be aware that all the fields included in the SELECT list must be either part of an aggregate function or part of the GROUP BY clause. If you use ORDER BY to control the order of the result set, you must also make sure to include only fields that are in the aggregate function or the GROUP BY clause. In addition, the ORDER BY clause must follow the GROUP BY clause.

Let's say you want to change the previous statement to display the names of the products rather than their IDs. The following statement displays product names instead of product IDs. Notice that the ProductName field doesn't appear as an argument to an aggregate function, so it must be part of the GROUP BY clause:

```
SELECT ProductName,
SUM(Quantity *.UnitPrice * (1 - Discount)) AS
[Total Revenues]
FROM [Order Details], Products
```

```
WHERE  Products.ProductID  =  [Order  Details].ProductID
GROUP  BY  ProductName
ORDER  BY  ProductName
```

These are the first few lines of the output produced by this statement:

```
ProductName             Total  Revenues
Alice  Mutton           32698.38
Aniseed  Syrup          3044.0
Boston  Crab  Meat      17910.63
Camembert  Pierrot      46927.48
Carnarvon  Tigers       29171.87
```

The HAVING clause limits the groups that appear in the cursor. In a way, it is similar to the WHERE clause, but the HAVING clause allows you to use aggregate functions. The following statement returns the IDs of the products whose sales exceed 1,000 units:

```
SELECT ProductID, SUM(Quantity) FROM [Order Details]
GROUP BY ProductID HAVING SUM(Quantity) > 1000
```

If you want to include regular restrictions, you can use the WHERE clause as well. To see product names instead of IDs, you add a slightly longer statement that includes the Products table and maps the ProductIDs in the Products table to the ProductIDs in the Order Details table with a WHERE clause:

```
SELECT  Products.ProductName,
[Order  Details].ProductID,
SUM(Quantity)  AS  [Items  Sold]
FROM  Products,  [Order  Details]
WHERE  [Order  Details].ProductID  =  Products.ProductID
GROUP  BY  [Order  Details].ProductID,
Products.ProductName
HAVING  SUM(Quantity)  >  1000
ORDER  BY  Products.ProductName
```

9.2.2 Action Queries

In addition to the selection queries examined so far in this chapter, you can also execute queries that alter the data in the database's tables. These queries are called **action queries,** and they're quite simple compared with the selection queries.

There are three types of actions you can perform against a database: insertions of new rows, deletions of existing rows, and updates (i.e., edits) of existing rows. For each type of action, there's a SQL statement, appropriately named INSERT, DELETE, and UPDATE. Their syntax is very simple, and the only complication is how you specify the affected rows (for deletions and updates). The rows to be affected are specified with a WHERE clause, followed by the criteria discussed with selection queries.

One difference between action and selection queries is that action queries don't return any rows. They return the number of rows affected. Next we'll look at the syntax of the three action SQL statements, starting with the simplest: the DELETE statement.

Deleting Rows

The DELETE statement deletes one or more rows from a table, and its syntax is as follows:

```
DELETE table_name WHERE criteria
```

The WHERE clause specifies the criteria that the rows must meet in order to be deleted. The criteria expression with the DELETE statement is no different from the criteria you specify in the WHERE clause of a selection query. To delete the orders placed before 1998, for example, you use a statement like this one:

```
DELETE Orders WHERE OrderDate < '1/1/1998'
```

If you execute DELETE without a WHERE clause, all rows in the table are deleted.

Inserting New Rows

The INSERT statement is used to insert one or more rows into a table. The syntax of the INSERT statement is as follows:

```
INSERT table_name (column_names) VALUES (values)
```

column_names and *values* are comma-separated lists of columns and their respective values. Values are mapped to their columns by the order in which they appear in the two lists. Notice that you don't have to specify values for all columns in the table, but the *values* list must contain as many items as there are column names in the *column_names* list. To add a new row to the Customers table, you use a statement like the following:

```
INSERT Customers (CustomerID, CompanyName)
VALUES ('FRYOG', 'Fruit & Yogurt')
```

This statement inserts a new row, provided that the FRYOG key isn't already in use. Only two of the new row's columns are set, and they're the columns that can't accept null values. A **null value** is a special value SQL Server assigns when a column does not contain a value. Some columns allow nulls and some do not. You do not need to provide a value for a column that is **identity columns** (i.e., columns with a unique value generated by the DBMS), a column that has a **default constraint** (i.e., a value that is used when one is not included in the INSERT statement), or any other columns that have values that are generated or calculated automatically by the DBMS.

If you want to specify values for all the columns of a new row, you can omit the list of columns. The following statement retrieves a number of rows from the Products table and inserts them into the SelectedProducts table, which has exactly the same structure:

```
INSERT INTO SelectedProducts VALUES (value_list)
```

If the values come from a table, you can replace the VALUES keyword with a SELECT statement:

```
INSERT INTO SelectedProducts
SELECT * FROM Products WHERE CategoryID = 4
```

There are more variations of the INSERT statement, but in this book we use this simplest form, in which you specify both the column names and their values.

Using an UPDATE Statement

The UPDATE statement edits a row's fields, and its syntax is as follows:

```
UPDATE table_name SET field1 = value1, field2 = value2, . . .
WHERE criteria
```

The criteria expression with the UPDATE statement is no different from the criteria you specify in the WHERE clause of a selection query. To change the country from "UK" to "United Kingdom" in the Customers table, for example, you use the following statement:

```
UPDATE Customers SET Country='United Kingdom'
WHERE Country = 'UK'
```

This statement locates all the rows in the Customers table that meet the specified criteria (their Country field is "UK") and change this field's value to "United Kingdom."

FOR EXAMPLE

Creating Queries

Say that you are creating an application for a veterinary office. You are designing the queries you will need to meet business requirements. One requirement is to generate a query for all customers who have unpaid invoices. The Invoices table includes a Paid column, which stores a Boolean value. You want the query to return the name and phone number of the client. You therefore execute the following query:

```
SELECT c.Name, c.Phone, i.InvoiceNumber, i.Amount
FROM Invoices i JOIN Clients c ON i.ClientID =
c.ClientID
WHERE Paid = False
```

(Continued)

Table 9-4: Pets Table

Column	Allow Nulls	Identity	Key
PetID	No	Yes	Primary
Name	No	No	No
Weight	Yes	No	No
Sex	No	No	No
Type	No	No	No
Color	Yes	No	No
OwnerID	No	No	Foreign; relates to Clients
Breed	No	No	No

You also need to create a query that adds a new pet when a client calls to make an appointment. The Pets table is defined as shown in Table 9-4. There are no defaults defined on any of the columns.

You know that you must include Name, Sex, Type, OwnerID, and Breed in the INSERT query. PetID is an identity column that will be generated automatically. The Weight and Color columns allow nulls and can have data added later. You create the following INSERT query:

```
INSERT Pets (Name, Sex, Type, OwnerID)
VALUES (strPetName, strPetSex, strType, strOwnerID)
```

strPetName, strPetSex, strType, and strOwnerID are all variables that store the relevant data.

SELF-CHECK

- Describe the purpose of the WHERE clause in a SELECT query.
- Compare the four different types of joins.
- Describe how you would change the order of a query's results.
- Explain the use of aggregate functions and a GROUP BY clause.
- List reasons you would not need to include a column's value in an INSERT statement.

9.3 Accessing a Database by Using Visual Basic

Now that you have a basic understanding of relational databases and SQL, you are ready to start learning about how to interface with a database by using Visual Basic. Visual Basic classes in the System.Data namespace can be used to retrieve and modify data in a relational database. These classes are an implementation of the ADO.NET architecture. **ADO.NET** defines classes that can be used for accessing a variety of relational databases and other data storage structures.

9.3.1 Data Access Overview

An application uses three basic objects to move data to and from a database: a connection, a data adapter, and a data container such as a DataSet. A connection object defines the connection to the database. It contains information about the database's name and location, any username and password needed to access the data, database engine information, and flags that determine the kinds of access the program will need.

The DataAdapter object defines a mapping from the database to the DataSet. It determines what data is selected from the database and which database columns are mapped to which DataSet columns. The DataSet object stores the data within the application. It can hold more than one table and can define and enforce relationships among the tables. Figure 9-6 shows the relationship between these objects.

When the connection, DataAdapter, and DataSet objects are initialized, the program can call the data adapter's Fill method to copy data from the database into the DataSet. Later, it can call the data adapter's Update method to copy any changes to the data from the DataSet back into the database.

Let's take a closer look at each of these objects and how to use them.

9.3.2 The Connection Objects

A **connection object** manages the application's connection to the database. It allows a data adapter to move data in and out of a DataSet. The different flavors of connection object (e.g., OleDbConnection, SqlConnection, OdbcConnection,

Figure 9-6

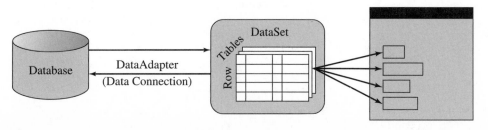

Data access objects.

OracleConnection) provide roughly the same features, but there are some differences.

Some connection objects can work with more than one type of database. For example, the OleDbConnection object works with any database that supports ODBC connections. Generally, connections that work with a specific kind of database (e.g., SqlConnection and OracleConnection) give better performance than others. If you think you might later need to change databases, you can minimize the amount of work required by sticking to features that are shared by all the types of connection objects.

The toolbox window does not automatically display tools for these objects. To add them, you right-click the Toolbox tab where you want them and select Choose Items. Then you check the boxes next to the tools you want to add (e.g., OracleCommand, OdbcConnection) and click OK.

Table 9-5 describes the most useful properties provided by the OleDbConnection and SqlConnection classes.

Table 9-5: Connection Class Properties

Property	Description
ConnectionString	Defines the connection to the database. The connection string includes several fields, separated by semicolons. What fields you must include depends on the database you are accessing.
ConnectionTimeout	Specifies the time the object waits while trying to connect to the database. If this timeout expires, the object gives up and raises an error.
Database	Returns the name of the current database.
DataSource	Returns the name of the current database file or database server.
Provider (OleDbConnection only)	Returns the name of the OLE DB database provider (e.g., "Microsoft.Jet.OLEDB.4.0").
ServerVersion	Returns the database server's version number. This value is available only when the connection is open and may look like "04.00.0000."
State	Returns the connection's current state. This value can be Closed, Connecting, Open, Executing (i.e., executing a command), Fetching (i.e., fetching data), and Broken (i.e., the connection was open but then broke; you can close and reopen the connection).

The following code fragment shows how a program can create, open, use, and close an OleDbConnection object:

```
'To use this Imports statement, add a reference
'to System.Data.
Imports System.Data.OleDb
Public Class Form1
    Private Sub Form1_Load(ByVal sender As _
    System.Object, ByVal e As System.EventArgs) _
    Handles MyBase.Load
        'Create the connection.
        Dim conn As New OleDbConnection( _
        "Provider=Microsoft.Jet.OLEDB.4.0;" & _
        "Data Source= " & _
    """C:\VB Prog Ref\JulyCTPSrc\Ch11\books.mdb"";"_
            & "Persist Security Info=True;" & _
        "Jet OLEDB:Database Password=MyPassword")
        ' Open the connection.
        conn.Open()
        ' Do stuff with the connection.
        '...
        ' Close the connection.
        conn.Close()
    End Sub
End Class
```

9.3.3 The DataAdapter Object

A **DataAdapter** object transfers data between a connection and a DataSet. The DataAdapter object's most important methods are Fill and Update, which move data from and to the database. A DataAdapter object also provides the following properties, which allow you to specify commands to use to access the database:

▲ **DeleteCommand:** The command object that the adapter uses to delete rows.

▲ **InsertCommand:** The command object that the adapter uses to insert rows.

▲ **SelectCommand:** The command object that the adapter uses to select rows.

▲ **UpdateCommand:** The command object that the adapter uses to update rows.

You can create the command objects in a couple ways. For example, if you use the Data Adapter Configuration Wizard to build the adapter at design time, the wizard automatically creates these objects. You can select the adapter and expand these objects in the Properties window to read their properties, including the CommandText property that defines the commands.

You can also create these commands at runtime. If you are using an OleDb-Connection object, you instantiate an OleDbCommand object. If you are using a SQLConnection object, you instantiate a SqlCommand object. In either case, you pass the SQL statement that should be used to perform the command as the constructor object. For example, to create an UpdateCommand object on an OleDbDataAdapter object named da, you execute the following:

```
Dim da As OleDbDataAdapter = New OleDbDataAdapter()
Dim cmd As OleDbCommand
cmd = New OleDbCommand _
    ("UPDATE Customers SET Country=" _
    & "'United Kingdom' WHERE Country = 'UK'")
da.UpdateCommand = cmd
```

9.3.4 The DataSet Object

A **DataSet** object is the flagship object when it comes to holding data in memory. It provides all the features you need to build, load, store, manipulate, and save data similar to that stored in a relational database. It can hold multiple tables that are related with complex parent/child relationships and uniqueness constraints. It provides methods for merging DataSet objects, searching for records that satisfy criteria, and saving data in different ways (e.g., into a relational database). In many ways, it is like a complete database stored in memory rather than on disk.

One of the most common ways to use a DataSet object is to load it from a relational database when the program starts, use various controls to display the data and let the user manipulate it interactively, and then save the changes back into the database when the program ends. For example, the following code loads a DataSet object from a SQL Server database:

```
Dim conn As SqlConnection = _
    New SqlConnection(connectionString)
Dim da As SqlDataAdapter = New SqlDataAdapter
conn.Open()
Dim custCommand As SqlCommand = New SqlCommand _
    ("SELECT * FROM CUSTOMERS")
custCommand.CommandType = CommandType.Text
da.SelectCommand = custCommand

'Fill the DataSet
Dim ds As DataSet = New DataSet("Customers")
da.Fill(ds)
conn.Close()
```

When you create the command object, you can either pass the SQL query to the constructor or use the default constructor and set the CommandText property later. You associate the command with the adapter by setting the adapter's

SelectCommand property because you are performing a selection query. You use the InsertCommand, UpdateCommand, or DeleteCommand properties to perform an action query.

The program can use controls bound to the DataSet object to let the user view and manipulate complex data with little extra programming.

9.3.5 DataTable and Other Objects

The **DataTable** class represents the data in one table within a DataSet. A DataTable contains **DataRow** objects that represent its data, **DataColumn** objects that define the table's columns, constraint objects that define constraints on the table's data (e.g., a uniqueness constraint requires that only one row may contain the same value in a particular column), and objects representing relationships between the table's columns and the columns in other tables. This object also provides methods and events for manipulating rows.

A DataRow object represents the data in one record in a DataTable. This object is relatively simple. It basically just holds data for the DataTable, and the DataTable object does most of the interesting work.

The DataColumn object represents a column in a DataTable. It defines the column's name and data type, and your code can use it to define relationships among different columns.

A **DataView** object represents a customizable view of the data contained in a DataTable. You can use DataView to select some or all of a DataTable's data and display it sorted in some manner without affecting the underlying DataTable.

A program can use multiple DataView objects to select and order a table's data in different ways. You can then bind the DataView objects to controls such as the DataGrid control to display the different views. If any of the views modifies its data (e.g., by adding or deleting a row), the underlying DataTable's data is updated, and any other views that need to see the change are updated as well.

9.3.6 Simple Data Binding

Binding a simple property such as Text to a data source is relatively easy. First, you create a DataSet, DataTable, or DataView object to act as the data source. You can create this object at design time, using controls, or at runtime, using object variables.

If you build the data source at design time, you can also bind the property at design time. To do so, you select the control that you want to bind and open the Properties window. Then you expand the (DataBindings) entry and find the property you want to bind (e.g., Text). Next, you click the drop-down arrow on the right and use the pop-up display to select the data source item

Figure 9-7

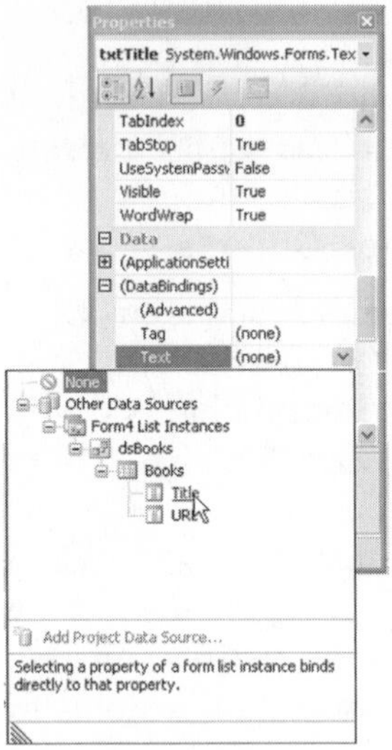

Data binding.

that you want to bind to the property. Figure 9-7 shows the pop-up binding the txtTitle control's Text property to the dsBooks DataSet's Books table's Title field.

At runtime, your code can bind a simple property to a data source by using the control's DataBindings collection. This collection's Add method takes as parameters the name of the property to bind, the data source, and the name of the item in the data source to bind. For example, the following statement binds the txtUrl control's Text property to the dsBooks DataSet's Books table's URL field:

```
txtUrl.DataBindings.Add("Text", dsBooks.Books, "URL")
```

That's all there is to binding simple properties. By itself, however, this binding doesn't provide any form of navigation. If you were to bind the Text properties of a bunch of TextBox controls and run the program, you would see the data for the data source's first record and nothing else. To allow the user to navigate through the data source, you must use a CurrencyManager object.

The CurrencyManager Object

Some controls, such as the DataGrid control, provide their own forms of navigation. If you bind a DataGrid to a DataSet, the user can examine the DataSet's tables, view and edit data, and follow links between the tables. A simpler control, such as a TextBox control, can display only one data value at a time. You must provide some means for the program to navigate through the data source's records. A data source manages its position within its data by using a CurrencyManager object. The **CurrencyManager** object supervises the list of binding objects that bind the data source to controls such as TextBox controls.

The CurrencyManager class raises a PositionChanged event when its position in the data changes. The following code shows how a program can use a CurrencyManager object to let the user navigate through a DataTable:

```
' The data source.
Private m_ContactsTable As DataTable
' The data source's CurrencyManager.
Private m_CurrencyManager As CurrencyManager
Private Sub Form1_Load(ByVal sender As _
    System.Object, ByVal e As System.EventArgs) _
    Handles MyBase.Load
    ' Make a DataTable.
    m_ContactsTable = New DataTable("Contacts")
    ' Add columns.
    m_ContactsTable.Columns.Add("FirstName", _
        GetType(String))
    m_ContactsTable.Columns.Add("LastName", _
        GetType(String))
    m_ContactsTable.Columns.Add("Street", _
        GetType(String))
    m_ContactsTable.Columns.Add("City", _
        GetType(String))
    m_ContactsTable.Columns.Add("State", _
        GetType(String))
    m_ContactsTable.Columns.Add("Zip", _
        GetType(String))
    ' Make the combined FirstName/LastName unique.
    Dim first_last_columns() As DataColumn = { _
        m_ContactsTable.Columns("FirstName"), _
        m_ContactsTable.Columns("LastName") _
        }
    m_ContactsTable.Constraints.Add( _
        New UniqueConstraint(first_last_columns))
    ' Make some contact data.
    m_ContactsTable.Rows.Add(New Object() _
        {"Art", "Ant", "1234 Ash Pl", "Bugville", _
        "CO", "11111"})
    m_ContactsTable.Rows.Add(New Object() _
        {"Bev", "Bug", "22 Beach St", "Bugville", _
        "CO", "22222"})
    m_ContactsTable.Rows.Add(New Object() _
        {"Cid", "Cat", "3 Road Place Lane", _
        "Programmeria", "KS", "33333"})
    m_ContactsTable.Rows.Add(New Object() _
        {"Deb", "Dove", "414 Debugger Way", _
```

```
            "Programmeria", "KS", "44444"})
        m_ContactsTable.Rows.Add(New Object() _
            {"Ed", "Eager", "5746 Elm Blvd", _
            "Bugville", "CO", "55555"})
        m_ContactsTable.Rows.Add(New Object() _
            {"Fran", "Fix", "647 Foxglove Ct", _
            "Bugville", "CO", "66666"})
        m_ContactsTable.Rows.Add(New Object() _
            {"Gus", "Gantry", "71762-B Gooseberry Ave", _
            "Programmeria", "KS", "77777"})
        m_ContactsTable.Rows.Add(New Object() _
            {"Hil", "Harris", "828 Hurryup St", _
            "Programmeria", "KS", "88888"})
        ' Bind to controls.
        txtFirstName.DataBindings.Add("Text", _
            m_ContactsTable, "FirstName")
        txtLastName.DataBindings.Add("Text", _
            m_ContactsTable, "LastName")
        txtStreet.DataBindings.Add("Text", _
            m_ContactsTable, "Street")
        txtCity.DataBindings.Add("Text", _
            m_ContactsTable, "City")
        txtState.DataBindings.Add("Text", _
            m_ContactsTable, "State")
        txtZip.DataBindings.Add("Text", _
            m_ContactsTable, "Zip")
        ' Save a reference to the CurrencyManager.
        m_CurrencyManager = _
            DirectCast(Me.BindingContext _
            (m_ContactsTable), CurrencyManager)
    End Sub

    Private Sub btnFirst_Click(ByVal sender As _
        System.Object, ByVal e As System.EventArgs) _
        Handles btnFirst.Click
        m_CurrencyManager.Position = 0
    End Sub

    Private Sub btnPrev_Click(ByVal sender As _
        System.Object, ByVal e As System.EventArgs) _
        Handles btnPrev.Click
        m_CurrencyManager.Position -= 1
    End Sub

    Private Sub btnNext_Click(ByVal sender As _
        System.Object, ByVal e As System.EventArgs) _
        Handles btnNext.Click
        m_CurrencyManager.Position += 1
    End Sub

    Private Sub btnLast_Click(ByVal sender As _
        System.Object, ByVal e As System.EventArgs) _
```

```
            Handles btnLast.Click
            m_CurrencyManager.Position = _
                m_CurrencyManager.Count - 1
    End Sub

    ' Add a new record.
    Private Sub btnAdd_Click(ByVal sender As _
        System.Object, ByVal e As System.EventArgs) _
        Handles btnAdd.Click
        m_CurrencyManager.AddNew()
    End Sub

    Private Sub btnDelete_Click(ByVal sender As _
        System.Object, ByVal e As System.EventArgs) _
        Handles btnDelete.Click
        If MsgBox( _
        "Are you sure you want to delete this record?", _
            MsgBoxStyle.Question Or MsgBoxStyle.YesNo, _
            "Confirm Delete?") = MsgBoxResult.Yes _
            Then
            m_CurrencyManager.RemoveAt _
                (m_CurrencyManager.Position)
        End If
    End Sub
```

The code begins by declaring the DataTable and CurrencyManager objects. The form's Load event handler builds the DataTable and gives it some data. Next, the event handler uses the DataBindings collections of several TextBox controls to bind them to the fields in the DataTable. The event handler finishes by saving a reference to the DataTable's CurrencyManager. The form's BindingContext property is a collection that contains references to the Binding-ManagerBase objects used by the controls on the form, including the Currency-Manager used by the DataTable. This code passes the DataTable as a parameter to the BindingContext collection to get the table's CurrencyManager. If the data source contained multiple objects (e.g., a DataSet can contain multiple DataTables), you also need to pass the collection a path to the data object that you want to use.

The user can move through the DataTable by clicking the program's navigation buttons, btnFirst, btnPrev, btnNext, and btnLast. The event handlers for these buttons move through the data by adjusting the CurrencyManager's Position property.

When the user clicks the Add button, the btnAdd_Click event handler calls the CurrencyManager's AddNew method to create a new record.

When the user clicks the Delete button, the btnDelete_Click event handler displays a message box, asking if the user really wants to delete the record. If the user clicks Yes, the code uses the CurrencyManager's RemoveAt method to delete the current record.

Figure 9-8 shows this program in action.

Figure 9-8

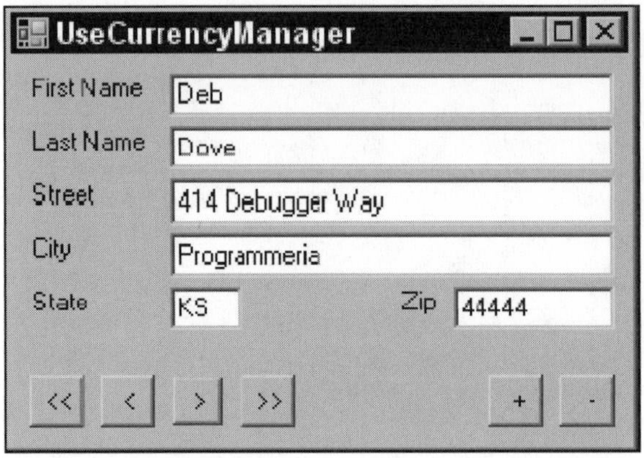

A program that uses the CurrencyManager object.

SELF-CHECK

- Describe the role of the SqlConnection, SqlDataAdapter, SqlCommand, and DataSet objects.
- Describe the steps you should take to bind a control to a DataSet.
- Describe the role of the CurrencyManager.

FOR EXAMPLE

Implementing Data Binding

Say that you are writing an application for a veterinary office. You are retrieving customers with unpaid invoices and need to bind the data to Label controls to allow office assistants to page through the data and contact customers. The data is stored in an Access database.

You create a connection object by using the OleDbConnection class. Next, you create an instance of an OleDbDataAdapter object. You create an OleDbCommand object and set it to the query to retrieve customers with invoices. You set the SelectCommand property of the DataAdapter object to reference the command object. Next, you instantiate a DataSet object and fill it by using the DataAdapter object. Now you are ready to bind the DataSet to the TextBox controls. You add the necessary entries to the DataBindings collection. Finally, you add code to implement the CurrencyManager.

SUMMARY

In this chapter, you've learned about relational database concepts, including fields, records, relationships, and normalization. You've also learned how to perform selection queries by using a SELECT statement and how to perform action queries by using INSERT, UPDATE, and DELETE. Finally, you've learned how to use ADO.NET data objects to bind controls to relational database data.

KEY TERMS

Action query	Field
ADO.NET	Foreign key
Aggregate function	Full join
Connection object	Identity column
CurrencyManager	Inner join
Data definition language (DDL)	Join
Data manipulation language (DML)	Left join
DataAdapter	Normalization
Database	Null value
Database management system (DBMS)	Primary key
DataColumn	Relational database
DataRow	Right join
DataSet	Selection query
DataTable	Structured Query Language (SQL)
DataView	Table
Default constraint	Table alias

ASSESS YOUR UNDERSTANDING

Go to www.wiley.com/college/petroutsos to evaluate your knowledge of relational databases and database access techniques.
Measure your learning by comparing pre-test and post-test results.

Summary Questions

1. A field in a relational database table should store multiple facts. True or False?
2. Which of the following must have a unique value for every record?
   (a) foreign key
   (b) primary key
   (c) neither primary nor foreign key
   (d) both primary and foreign keys
3. You do not need to know how a DBMS stores data on disk in order to read the data into a program. True or False?
4. What is the name of the process that eliminates duplicate data from relational database tables?
   (a) purging
   (b) dereplication
   (c) normalization
   (d) partitioning
5. Which keyword is used to prevent duplicate rows from being included in a result set?
   (a) DISTINCT
   (b) UNIQUE
   (c) WHERE
   (d) NOT IN
6. Which keyword is used to filter a result set by specifying a range of values?
   (a) IN
   (b) LIKE
   (c) BETWEEN
   (d) HAVING
7. Which wildcard character is used to match any number of characters?
   (a) _
   (b) ^
   (c) &
   (d) %

8. Which of the following clauses allows you to sort a result set?
   (a) ORDER BY
   (b) ARRANGE
   (c) GROUP BY
   (d) SORT

9. Which type of join includes only matching rows from both tables?
   (a) left outer join
   (b) right outer join
   (c) full join
   (d) inner join

10. You cannot include calculated columns in a SELECT clause. True or False?

11. Which of the following is an aggregate function that can operate only on numeric values?
    (a) COUNT
    (b) MIN
    (c) TOTAL
    (d) SUM

12. Which of the following statements correctly describes using GROUP BY with ORDER BY?
    (a) The GROUP BY clause must precede the ORDER BY clause.
    (b) The ORDER BY clause must precede the GROUP BY clause.
    (c) The clauses can be in any order.
    (d) You cannot use GROUP BY and ORDER BY in the same SELECT statement.

13. An action query does not return a result set. True or False?

14. A WHERE clause is required with the DELETE statement. True or False?

15. What column values must you define when you execute an INSERT statement?
    (a) All column values except identity columns.
    (b) All column values, including identity columns.
    (c) All column values for which the DBMS cannot automatically generate a value.
    (d) Only the primary key value.

16. Which of the following is a clause of an UPDATE statement?
    (a) UPDATE VALUES SET
    (b) UPDATE SET WHERE
    (c) UPDATE VALUES WHERE
    (d) UPDATE COLUMNS SET

17. Which ADO.NET object can store multiple tables?
    (a) SqlConnection
    (b) OleDbCommand
    (c) DataSet
    (d) SqlDataAdapter

18. Which property is exposed by the OleDbConnection object but not by the SqlConnection object?
    (a) ConnectionString
    (b) Database
    (c) ServerVersion
    (d) Provider

19. Which object exposes an UpdateCommand object?
    (a) SqlCommand
    (b) OleDbDataAdapter
    (c) SqlConnection
    (d) DataSet

20. How can you load data from a selection query into a DataSet?
    (a) Call the Fill method of a DataAdapter object.
    (b) Call the Execute method of a DataSet object.
    (c) Call the Execute method of a Command object.
    (d) Call the Open method of a connection object.

21. You can sort the data in a DataView without affecting the data in the underlying table. True or False?

22. Which property do you set to bind the data in a DataSet to a TextBox control?
    (a) ControlBindings property of the DataSet
    (b) Bindings property of the data adapter
    (c) DataBindings property of the TextBox control

23. The CurrencyManager object is used to allow users to navigate through data that is bound to controls. True or False?

Applying This Chapter

1. You are creating a database to store information about calls to customer service. The database needs to track the caller, the customer service person who took the call, the call date, the problem, and the resolution. You must be able to record the customer's name, phone number, and address. You must also be able to list the customer service person's name and manager in a monthly report. Customers often call multiple times,

Table 9-6: Repairs Table

Column	Nullable	Identity	Default
RepairID	No	Yes	None
EquipmentID	No	No	None
RepairDate	No	No	Current date
ProblemDescription	No	No	No
CostOfMaterials	Yes	No	No
CostOfLabor	Yes	No	No

and when they do, they might speak with the same or a different customer service person.

(a) What tables will you create?

(b) What columns will you include in each table?

(c) What relationships will you create?

2. You are creating a database to track equipment repairs. The Repairs table has the columns described in Table 9-6.

The Equipment table is described in Table 9-7. The EquipmentID is the serial number on the piece of equipment.

You need to create queries to insert new records, update records, and retrieve information about repairs. You can use any values you want to represent actual values.

(a) Write a query to insert information when the item is first brought in for service. Include only the necessary fields.

(b) Write a query to update the item after the repair has been finished. Set the CostOfMaterials and CostOfLabor values.

(c) Write a query to retrieve the total cost of each individual repair.

Table 9-7: The Equipment Table

Column	Nullable	Identity	Default
EquipmentID	No	Yes	None
Name	No	No	None
PurchaseDate	No	No	Current date
Manufacturer	No	No	None

    (d) Write a query to retrieve the total cost of all repairs for each piece of equipment. List the cost of labor, the cost of materials, and the total cost separately.

    (e) Write a query to retrieve the item that was repaired most recently. The output should include the date, equipment ID, and description.

    (f) Modify the query you wrote in item (e) to include the equipment's name, manufacturer, and purchase date.

    (g) What type of join would you perform to return the name, purchase date, and last repair date for all equipment, including equipment that has never been repaired?

3. You are building a Visual Basic application to access a SQL Server database. You plan to use bound TextBox controls to allow users to view data.

    (a) Which class will you use to populate the TextBox controls?

    (b) What code will you use to bind the Category field to txtCategory?

    (c) How will you allow users to navigate between records in the database?

YOU TRY IT

Designing and Accessing Relational Databases

You are designing an application that will be used to track game rentals for a computer and console game store. You need to store information about the games that are in stock, customer contact information, and game rental information. Customers rent games for three days, five days, or a week.

1. Design the tables you will need. Minimize repetitive data storage.

2. Identify the relationships you will need between tables.
3. Write a query to add a game rental entry.
4. Write a query to reduce the number in stock for a specific game.
5. Write a query to mark a game rental as returned.
6. Write a query to retrieve the name of the game that has been rented the most times.

10

PROGRAMMING INPUT AND OUTPUT

Starting Point

Go to www.wiley.com/college/petroutsos to assess your knowledge of input and output concepts and techniques.
Determine where you need to concentrate your effort.

What You'll Learn in This Chapter

▲ File input and output concepts
▲ User-defined types
▲ The FileSystem object
▲ The Graphics object
▲ Printing concepts

After Studying This Chapter, You'll Be Able To

▲ Choose the most appropriate file storage technique
▲ Create a user-defined type
▲ Define a fixed-length record by using a user-defined type
▲ Choose the appropriate method for reading data from a file
▲ Choose the appropriate method for writing data to a file
▲ Use the Graphics object to display shapes, lines, and text on a form
▲ Use the PrintDocument object to allow users to create and print a document
▲ Use the PrintDialog and PrintPreview components to allow users to preview a document before printing it

INTRODUCTION

Most programs enable users to input data from and output data to a file system file. In addition, most programs allow users to print some type of document or report. In this chapter, you'll learn about the concepts behind file input and output. You'll also learn how to input and output data to files by using Visual Basic 2005. Next, you'll learn about output, including how to use the Graphics object to draw to the screen and how to send output to a printer.

10.1 File Input and Output Concepts

Files provide a permanent method of storing large amounts of data that can be input whenever needed for processing into information. Three types of data files are widely used: sequential access files, direct access files, and database files. **Sequential access files** are files for which the data records must be input in the same order in which they were output to the file. **Direct access files** (also known as **random access files**) are files that can be input in any order. Database files are widely used for data storage, but they must be accessed with a database management system.

The format you use to store data and the technique you use to read and write the data depend on both the nature of the data and how it is used in the program. You need to consider whether the program requires that all the data or just a small portion of it be read into memory. You also need to determine how the data is to be mapped to variables in memory or properties in controls.

10.1.1 Sequential Access Files

Data in a sequential access file is stored in the same order in which it is written, and it is read back in that same order. With a sequential access file, it is not possible to access a record of data directly, making it cumbersome to use when the order of processing records on a file differs from the order in which those records are physically stored or when records are being added or deleted during the processing.

The number of **records** (where a record is a collection of one or more data items that are treated as a unit) on a sequential access file is often unknown, but there is an invisible binary marker at the end of the file called the **end of file (EOF) marker.** Although this precludes the use of a For...Next loop for inputting data from a sequential file, it does not affect the use of a Do While loop or a Do Until loop, because these loops can input data until the EOF marker is encountered (or while it has not been encountered).

Delimited Files

A **delimited file** is a type of sequential access file that uses a special character to separate **fields** (i.e., data items) and records in a file. For example, comma-delimited files are commonly used to store spreadsheet data, tabular data, and lists. Tab-delimited files are also common.

Text vs. Binary Files

An important distinction you need to make when writing code to access a file is whether the file is a text file or a binary file. A **text file** is a file that contains only text and is read and written as character or string data. It can be read and written by any text editor, such as Notepad. Text files use character **encoding** to determine how bits are translated to characters. You must read data by using the same encoding that was used to write the data. Most files today use **Unicode encoding** because it has the best support for international characters. Older applications and those than need to support legacy systems use **ASCII encoding.**

A **binary file** is a file that is read and written as bytes. Binary files include multimedia files, such as music and graphic files and files with data stored in proprietary formats.

10.1.2 Direct Access Files

A direct (or random) access file is a type of data file in which data is assumed to be stored as a fixed-length record. Direct access files are so named because the user can access any record on this type of file directly, without going through any other records. The key parameter for a direct access file is the record number. This is a positive integer value that is assigned to the record when it is written onto the file. After a record is written onto a file with a given record number, it can always be identified for processing. The record number of a direct access file is analogous to the subscript on a one-dimensional array, in which each record corresponds to an element in the array. Although the order of the records on a direct access file is the same as the order of their record numbers, a user can write, read, or rewrite any record, regardless of its physical position, by simply specifying its record number.

Pictorially, a direct access file looks as shown in Figure 10-1. Note its similarity to a table in a database file with records and fields. Note also that all records in a direct access file are assumed to have the same fields and to be of the same size.

User-Defined Types

To make sure records are the same size, you need to create a **user-defined type (UDT),** which is a structure that includes multiple variables. All members of the UDT need to have a fixed-length data type.

UDTs in Visual Basic are made up of elements, where each element is declared to be a standard data type (e.g., String, Integer) or a previously declared UDT. UDTs in Visual Basic are much like database records. (In fact, in some programming languages, a UDT is referred to as a *record type*.) For example, a UDT for a college student might include data fields about the student's ID number,

Figure 10-1

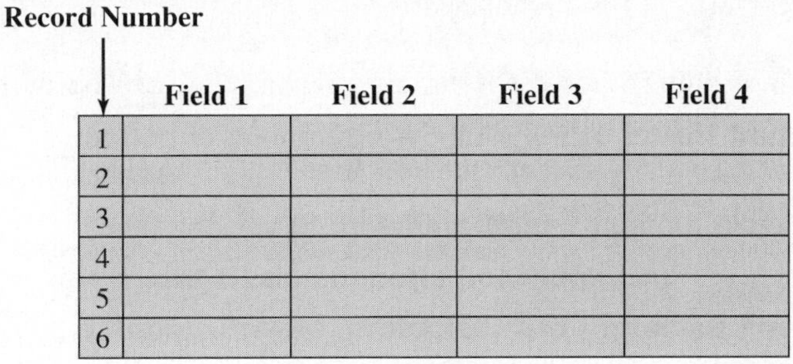

Record Number

	Field 1	Field 2	Field 3	Field 4
1				
2				
3				
4				
5				
6				

A direct access file.

last name, first name, middle initial, and GPA. By creating an array of college student data types, you can store all these different types of information under one name in memory.

Using UDTs is a two-step process. First, you declare the data type and then you declare a variable or an array of that data type in the procedure in which it is going to be used. You cannot use the UDT declaration as the variable; you must declare a variable (or an array) to be of that type and then use it in your code.

In using a UDT, you declare the data type by using the Structure statement. A common place to make this declaration is in a Code module so the UDT will be available throughout the project. The various elements, fields, and methods that make up that data type are then listed. The structure declaration process is terminated with an End Structure statement.

The form of the Structure statement is as follows:

```
Structure UDTname
    Public elementname1 As datatype
    Public elementname2 As datatype
    Public elementnameN As datatype
    Public Sub subname( )
        'sub statements
    End Sub
    Public Function functionname( ) As datatype
        'function statements
    End Function
End Structure
```

For example, the following Structure statement can be used to declare in a Code module the college student data type discussed earlier:

```
Structure CollegeStudent
    Public intIDNumber As Integer
    Public strLastName As String
    Public strFirstName As String
```

```
      Public strMidInit As String
      Public sngGPA As Single
End Structure
```

This UDT is not appropriate for defining a record that can be used for random access because of the variable-length strings. You need to modify it by including the VBFixedString attribute in front of each String, as in the following example:

```
Structure CollegeStudent
    Public intIDNumber As Integer
    <VBFixedString(20)> Public strLastName As String
    <VBFixedString(20)> Public strFirstName As String
    <VBFixedString(1)> Public strMidInit As String
    Public sngGPA As Single
End Structure
```

Although a UDT can be declared at any level, the best place to do so is at the module level. After a UDT has been declared globally in a Code module, it can be used in declaring variables or arrays anywhere in the project, just as any other data type would be used to declare variables. For example, to declare the variable udtOneStudent to be of the type CollegeStudent, you use this statement:

```
Dim udtOneStudent As CollegeStudent
```

Now, the variable udtOneStudent is composed of the same five elements declared for the type CollegeStudent. This structure is shown in Figure 10-2. (Note that the variable prefix for a UDT is udt.)

To refer to the individual elements of the udtOneStudent variable, you use the dot notation—that is, *VariableName.ElementName*. For example, to assign a student name to the strFirstName element of the variable udtOneStudent, you use this statement:

```
udtOneStudent.strFirstName = "George"
```

Similarly, to assign a grade point value to the GPA element, you use this statement:

```
udtOneStudent.sngGPA = 3.12
```

Figure 10-2

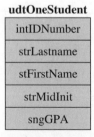

udtOneStudent

| intIDNumber |
| strLastname |
| stFirstName |
| strMidInit |
| sngGPA |

A UDT.

FOR EXAMPLE

Defining a File Storage Strategy

Suppose you are writing an application to track sales leads and create sales correspondence. The application must allow you to store contact information for customers. Each customer is assigned a customer ID, which is a sequential number (with the sequence beginning at 1). This information is stored in a database on a server but must also be available in a local file when the salesperson is traveling. You decide to store the customer information in a fixed-length record so that you can use direct access or sequential access to retrieve the information. You create a UDT for the data.

The application must also track information about each call to a customer. It must track the date of each contact; whether the contact was by phone, email, in person, or direct mail; information about what was discussed; and the amount sold on that call (if any). The information field must be variable in length. You decide to store this information in a tab-delimited file for each customer.

Finally, you decide to allow users to save a text document for each letter. You allow the user to specify the filename when saving the file. You also allow the user to open the file and save it, using a different name, after making modifications. This allows the user to reuse the content of a letter for multiple customers.

SELF-CHECK

- Compare sequential file access and direct file access.
- When you would use a delimited file?
- Identify the requirement for a UDT to be used for direct access.
- Compare a text file and a binary file. Give an example of each.

10.2 Accessing Files by Using Visual Basic

To read and write to files, you need to first locate them in the file system. Next, you need to perform the read or write operation appropriate to your program's needs. Visual Studio provides classes in the System.IO namespace to allow you to perform directory and file operations. However, Visual Basic provides a

FileSystem class that is accessed through the My keyword and is part of the Microsoft.VisualBasic.FileIO namespace that performs file operations more optimally. We focus on the FileSytem object here.

The **My keyword** gives you access to the Computer object, which allows you to access hardware and operating system resources, including the Clipboard, the file system, the system clock, the mouse, the keyboard, and the network.

10.2.1 Reading and Writing Text Files

A text file is a file that can be read using Notepad or any other text editor software. You can write text files from Visual Basic by using the My.Computer. FileSystem.WriteAllText method. The WriteAllText method is an overloaded method that has the following two signatures:

```
Public Sub WriteAllText(ByVal file As String, _
    ByVal text As String, ByVal append As Boolean)

Public Sub WriteAllText(ByVal file As String, _
    ByVal text As String, ByVal append As Boolean, _
    ByVal encoding As System.Text.Encoding)
```

The file parameter accepts the file system path to the file. The text is the String literal or variable to write to the file. If you set append to True, the text is appended to the end of the file. If append is false, the file is overwritten. The encoding parameter determines what encoding should be used. If no encoding is specified, the file is written using UTF-8 encoding (i.e., a Unicode encoding scheme that supports all Unicode characters). You should always read and write a file by using the same encoding value.

You can read a text file by using the My.Computer.FileSystem.ReadAllText method. The method returns a value of type String. Like the WriteAllText method, it has two signatures:

```
Public Function ReadAllText(ByVal file As String) _
    As String

Public Function ReadAllText(ByVal file As String, _
    ByVal encoding As System.Text.Encoding) As String
```

Keep in mind that this method reads all the text in a file to a single variable of type String. This is an appropriate method to use for saving and retrieving documents. It is also appropriate if you can use string processing functions to parse the data.

It is also important to remember to use exception handling with all file processing functions. Any time you must access a file in the file system, a number of things can go wrong, including paths and files not existing, insufficient permissions, or a file being in use by another application.

10.2.2 Reading and Writing Binary Files

You can use the FileSytem object to write data in binary to a file. For example, you might have an array of Byte variables that all need to be written to a file. To do so, you can use the WriteAllBytes method, which has the following syntax:

```
Public Sub WriteAllBytes(ByVal file As String, _
    ByVal data As Byte(), ByVal append As Boolean)
```

You can use the ReadAllBytes method to read the contents of a file and store the results in an array of type Byte.

Remember that a Byte data type is an array of values between 0 and 255. Therefore, although it is appropriate for storing some types of data, it is not appropriate for storing data that needs greater precision or scale.

10.2.3 Reading and Writing Sequential Files

The Microsoft.VisualBasic.FileIO namespace includes a TextFieldParser object that can be used to read and parse a delimited file or a file with fixed-width fields. Reading and parsing such a file requires the following steps:

1. Declare and instantiate an object of type TextFieldParser. Its constructor takes the path to the file.
2. Set the TextFieldType property to either FixedWidth or Delimited.
3. If it's a delimited file, call the SetDelimiters method to set one or more delimiters. If it's a fixed-width file, call the SetFieldWidths method to set the width for each field in the record.
4. Use a Do loop to read each record. The Do loop should terminate when the EndOfData property becomes true. Use the ReadFields function to read all fields in a row and obtain an array of String variables.

A row is terminated with the end-of-line character, which is designated using the VbCrLf (i.e., Visual Basic carriage return line feed) constant.

You can write a sequential file by using the WriteAllText method for each record and setting Append to true. For example, when using a loop, make sure to append the VbCrLf constant.

10.2.4 Reading and Writing Direct Access Files

The My.Computer.FileSystem object does not include methods for direct file access. Instead, you need to use the legacy methods FileOpen, FilePut, and FileGet.

You use the FilePut command to write data to a file. When data or information is being retrieved from a direct access file, you use the FileGet command. Whether you're adding data to or retrieving data from a direct access file, the file must first be opened.

Table 10-1: FileOpen Parameters for a Direct Access File

Parameter	Possible Values	Explanation
FileNumber	1–255 (using the FreeFile function)	Identifies the file in memory.
FileName	Any valid filename	Identifies the file in the file system.
OpenMode.Type	Random	Declares this to be a direct (random) access file.
OpenAccess.Access	Read, Write, or ReadWrite	Determines whether the file is being read from, written to, or both.
OpenShare. ShareMode	Shared, Lock Read, Lock Write, or Lock ReadWrite	Determines the operations restricted on the open file to other processes.
Recordlength	Any positive numeric value greater than 0	The number of bytes required to write a record to storage.

The FileOpen statement for a direct access file has the following form:

```
FileOpen(FileNumber, FileName, OpenMode.Random, _
    OpenAccess.Access, OpenShare.ShareMode, _
    RecordLength)
```

The various parameters for this FileOpen statement are described in Table 10-1.

Rather than having to determine the Recordlength parameter manually, you can rely on the Visual Basic Len function, which returns the number of bytes required to store a variable or record. For example, because Len(udtEmp) returns the number of bytes in the variable udtEmp, which was declared to be an EmpRecord data type, you can use the following statements to open a direct access file to store the employee records created by the employee payroll system discussed earlier:

```
intFileNum = FreeFile()
FileOpen(intFileNum, strFileName, OpenMode.Random, _
    OpenAccess.ReadWrite, OpenShare.Shared, _
    Len(udtEmp))
```

The FileName parameter is equal to strFileName, which must be assigned prior to opening the file. The FileClose(FileNumber) statement is used to close a direct access file. The value used for FileNumber should be the same for both the FileOpen and FileClose commands as well as for other commands that work with the file.

After a direct access file is opened, the next step is to write data on the file. As mentioned earlier, this is accomplished with the FilePut command, which has the following form:

```
FilePut(file number, variable name, record number)
```

where the *record number* parameter is optional. The first record in a file is at record number 1, the second record is at record number 2, and so on. If you omit the record number, the next record after the last FileGet or FilePut command is written. If the length of the data being written is greater than the length specified in the RecordLength clause of the FileOpen function, an error message is generated and needs to be caught with the Try...Catch error-checking mechanism. For example, to write the udtEmployees array to the direct access file opened earlier, the statements are as follows:

```
For intCurrent = 0 To intEmpCntr - 1
    FilePut(intFileNum, udtEmployees(intCurrent), _
        intCurrent + 1)
Next
FileClose(intFileNum)
```

The counter, intCurrent, is increased by one to become the record number because record numbers start with 1, whereas array indices start with 0.

For records on a direct access file to be useful, they must be retrievable. After a direct access file must is opened with the FileOpen statement, the records then are retrieved with the FileGet command, the form of which is shown here:

```
FileGet(file number, variable name, record number)
```

The parameters with FileGet are the same as with the FilePut command. As with the FilePut command, the record number is optional. If you are retrieving records in sequence and the *record number* parameter is omitted, the next record, in order, is retrieved. If you want to retrieve a specific record number, you can pass that record number to the FileGet statement.

If you write a file using FilePut, you must read it using FileGet. You cannot mix methods of reading and writing files.

10.2.5 Interacting with the File System

The FileSystem class includes a number of useful properties and methods for working with files and the file system. Although this chapter does not cover all of them here, this section highlights a few important ones.

The SpecialDirectories Property

In most cases, you store user documents in the user's My Documents folder. You can access this path by using the MyDocuments property of the

FileSystem.SpecialDirectories object. The SpecialDirectories property also gives you access to other user-specific directories, including these:

▲ AllUsersApplicationData
▲ CurrentUserApplicationData
▲ Desktop
▲ MyMusic
▲ MyPictures
▲ Programs
▲ Temp

You can use these directories to construct the path to the directories where you might need to store or retrieve data from files. For example, many applications store configuration settings in the current user's Application Data directory.

Deleting Files

You can delete a file by using the DeleteFile method of the My.Computer.FileSystem class. The DeleteFile method has three overloaded versions. The simplest version allows you to specify only the filename. When this version is used, the file is permanently deleted, and only error messages are shown. The most expansive version allows you to set several different options for deleting the file:

▲ *UIOption:* You set this to AllDialogs to ensure that the user is prompted to confirm the action.
▲ *RecycleOption:* You set this to SendToRecycleBin or DeletePermanently.
▲ *UICancelOption:* This determines the action that will occur if the user cancels the deletion. The default is ThrowException.

You can use the DeleteDirectory method to delete a directory and, optionally, all files within that directory. You can specify the same options as for deleting an individual file. In addition, the DeleteDirectoryOption enumeration allows you to specify whether to throw an exception if there are files in the directory or to delete all files.

Copying and Moving Files

The CopyFile method allows you to copy a file from one directory to another or to a different filename in the same directory. It has four overloaded versions. Each version requires that you specify a source filename and destination filename. In addition, you can select whether to overwrite an existing file with the same name or display a dialog box to allow the user to choose. If you select to display a dialog box, you can specify the action that should occur when the user cancels the operation. When you copy a file, the existing file remains in the source location.

The MoveFile method allows you to move a file to a new location, deleting the original file. It has the same overloaded versions as the CopyFile method.

Creating Directories

You have already seen how to delete a directory. The CreateDirectory method allows you to create a directory at a specific path. There is a single version of this method, and it accepts a String with the path to the new directory.

Checking Whether a Directory or File Exists

You can check whether a directory exists by calling the DirectoryExists method of the FileSystem object. It accepts a String argument, which is the path to the directory.

You can also check whether a file exists by calling the FileExists method of the FileSystem object. Checking whether a directory or file exists before you attempt to access it is a good way to prevent unhandled exceptions or logical errors that result in overwriting data accidentally.

FOR EXAMPLE

Writing Code to Access Files

Suppose you are creating an application to allow users to track sales leads. You have decided to store customer information in a fixed-length record to allow for both sequential and direct access.

You create the following UDT:

```
Structure Customer
    <VBFixedString(20)> Dim CustomerName As String
    <VBFixedString(15)> Dim PhoneNumber As String
    <VBFixedString(25)> Dim Address As String
    <VBFixedString(15)> Dim City As String
    <VBFixedString(2)> Dim State As String
    <VBFixedString(10)> Dim ZipCode As String
End Structure
```

You declare an array of Customer objects named udtCustomers and populate it, using data you retrieve from the database. Next, you write the data to the Customers.txt file in the ApplicationSettings folder, using the following code:

```
Dim filepath As String
filepath = _
My.Computer.FileSystem.SpecialDirectories.
CurrentUserApplicationData()
filepath &= "\customers.txt"
Dim fn As Integer = FreeFile()
```

```
FileOpen(fn, filepath, OpenMode.Random, _
    OpenAccess.ReadWrite, OpenShare.Default, _
    Len(udtCustomers(0)))
Dim cnt As Integer
For cnt = 0 to udtCustomers.GetUpperBounds(0)
    FilePut(fn, udtCustomers(cnt))
Next
FileClose(fn)
```

One dialog of the application displays customer information in an address book format. You need to populate the controls with data from the CustContacts.txt. You load the file into memory, using the following code: (Note that code wraps are due to page width. All calls to CurrentUser-Application data should be on one line.)

```
Dim filepath As String
filepath = _
My.Computer.FileSystem.SpecialDirectories.CurrentUser
ApplicationData()
filepath &= "\customers.txt"
Dim fn As Integer = FreeFile()
FileOpen(fn, filepath, OpenMode.Random, _
    OpenAccess.ReadWrite, OpenShare.Default, _
    Len(udtCustomers(0))
Dim cnt As Integer
Do Until EOF(fn)
    FileGet(fn, udtCustomers(cnt))
    cnt +=1
Next
FileClose(fn)
```

You are storing data about customer communication, using a tab-delimited file. The data has the following format:

customerName, date, type, description, sale amount

You write the data to the custlog.txt file, using the following code:

```
Dim strCustInfo As String
Dim filepath As String
filepath = _
My.Computer.FileSystem.SpecialDirectories.CurrentUser
ApplicationData()
filepath &= "\custlog.txt"
strCustInfo = txtCust.Text & vbTab & _
    Today().ToShortDateString & vbTab & _
    txtType.Text & vbTab & txtComments.Text & vbCrLf
MyComputer.FileSystem.WriteAllText(filepath, _
    strCustInfo, True)
```

(Continued)

You read the data into an array and then use the array to populate the fields on the form. The code to read the data is as follows:

```
Dim tfp As New _
    Microsoft.VisualBasic.FileIO.TextFieldParser _
(My.Computer.FileSystem.SpecialDirectories.
CurrentUserApplicationData _
    () & "\custlog.txt")
tfp.TextFieldType = FileIO.FieldType.Delimited
tfp.SetDelimiters(vbTab)
Dim sValues() As String
Do Until tfp.EndOfData
    sValues = tfp.ReadFields()
    txtCustomer.Text = sValues(0)
    txtDate.Text = sValues(1)
    txtContact.Text = sValues(2)
    txtDetails.Text = sValues(3)
Loop
```

SELF-CHECK

- Compare the WriteAllText method and the WriteAllBinary method.
- Describe the purpose of the TextFieldParser object.
- Identify a situation in which you must use the FilePut method.
- Describe how you can verify whether a file exists before opening it.

10.3 Working with Graphics

Many applications include graphics to help users visualize data or to just provide an aesthetically pleasing interface. In addition, writing the code to print an object relies on understanding how to use the objects in the System.Drawing namespace. This section is not designed to make you an expert in displaying graphics programmatically. Instead, it gives an overview of some of the commonly used objects in the System.Drawing namespace as well as a general understanding of drawing output programmatically.

10.3.1 Introducing GDI+

Visual Basic provides tools for you to create graphics by using an implementation of the Windows graphics design interface (GDI) called GDI+. **GDI+** provides classes that allow you to create vector graphics, draw text, and manipulate graphical images. A **vector graphic** is represented by a set of mathematical properties called *vectors* that define the lines and other properties used to draw the graphic rather than as bitmapped graphics based on a grid of pixels (i.e., the dots used to draw the graphic). **Vectors** describe the graphic's size, properties, and position. Vector graphics are most often used for items that can be represented by line drawings, such as simple pictures and charts. Vector graphics typically incorporate lines, shapes, colors, and text drawn on the background of a control. Because they are mathematically defined, you can resize vector graphics without the loss of quality and resolution that occur when you resize bitmapped graphics. You can use GDI+ to draw graphics on Windows forms and controls.

You can get access to GDI+ basic graphics functionality with the classes that are available in the System.Drawing namespace. Objects created from the Graphics class provide methods for drawing to the forms or controls of a project. The Pen class can be used to draw lines or curves, and the Brush class can be used to fill the interiors of shapes. The System.Drawing namespace also includes other classes that you use to create various shapes, specify the color of graphics, and set the font of the text. To gain access to System.Drawing classes, you need to reference the namespace in your project, using the following statement:

```
Imports System.Drawing
```

You need to be sure to place this statement before the form's class declaration. When the Graphics class is available, there are two main steps involved in creating graphics on a Visual Basic control:

1. Create a Graphics object using the Graphics class.
2. Use the Graphics object as a canvas for drawing lines, shapes, text, or images.

When you want to create and add a Graphics object to a form or another control, you can call the CreateGraphics method of the form or control as shown here:

```
Dim objName As Graphics = _
   controlname.CreateGraphics( )
```

In this case, *controlname* is the name of the control on which the graphic will be displayed, and *objName* is the name of the Graphics object. A form can be used, but the Panel control can be used to group items on a form. Typically, you use panels to divide a form into identifiable groupings of controls. For example, the statement to create a Graphics object named objGraphics on a Panel control named PnlGraphicsDisplay is shown here:

```
Dim objGraphics As Graphics = _
   pnlGraphicsDisplay.CreateGraphics()
```

Figure 10-3

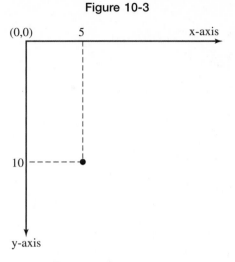

The coordinate system.

10.3.2 The Coordinate System

An important concept when drawing with a Graphics object on a control or form is the coordinate system. The GDI+ **coordinate system** uses a pair of integer values to identify every point of the surface on which the graphic will be drawn. Each pair of values includes an x coordinate and a y coordinate, which together are often expressed as (x,y). The **x coordinate** represents the horizontal distance of a point from the origin. The **y coordinate** represents the vertical position of a point from the origin. Coordinate values are expressed in pixels. For example, the point (5,10) represents a location 5 pixels away along the horizontal, or x, axis and 10 pixels away along the vertical, or y, axis. The coordinate system is shown in Figure 10-3. Notice that the origin of the system, point (0,0), is located on the upper-left corner of the control.

10.3.3 Drawing Graphics

After you have created a Graphics object on a control, you can use its methods to draw various shapes, such as lines, circles, rectangles, or other shapes. The following is a simple example that illustrates how you can work with the Graphics object to make these shapes. To draw the graphics, you can use a Panel control named pnlGraphicsDisplay, with its Height and Width property both set to 300 pixels. The form with the Panel control is shown in Figure 10-4. Note that the panel is distinguished by dashed lines.

To draw the rectangle, you use two drawing objects. The first is the Graphics object, objGraphics, which is declared using the CreateGraphics method of the pnlGraphicsDisplay Panel control. The second is a Pen object created from

Figure 10-4

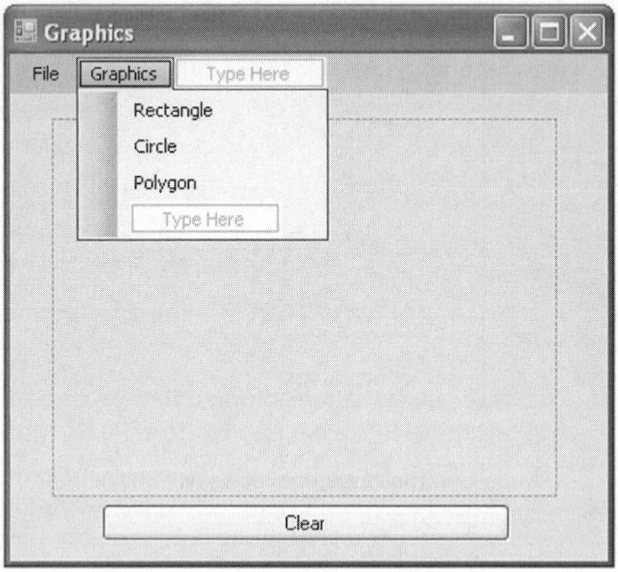

The Panel control.

the Pen class that is used to draw lines and curves. The general syntax for creating a Pen object is as follows:

```
Dim objName as Pen = New Pen(Color.color)
```

The Color object is used here to set the color of the line drawn by the Pen object. For example, the following statement creates a Pen object named objPen that draws in red:

```
Dim objPen As Pen = New Pen(Color.Red)
```

After these objects have been created, you can use the DrawRectangle method of the objGraphics object to draw a rectangle, as shown here:

```
objGraphicsObject.DrawRectangle(objPen, x, y, _
    width, height)
```

In this example, x and y represent the coordinates for the upper-left corner of the rectangle to be drawn. Width and height specify the dimensions of the rectangle. For example, you use this code to draw a 250 × 250-pixel rectangle with the upper-left corner positioned at (25, 25):

```
Private Sub mnuGraphRectangle_Click(ByVal sender As _
    System.Object, ByVal e As System.EventArgs) _
    Handles mnuGraphRectangle.Click
    Dim objGraphics As Graphics = _
        pnlGraphicsDisplay.CreateGraphics()
```

```
        Dim objPen As Pen = New Pen(Color.Red)
        objGraphics.DrawRectangle(objPen, 25, 25, 250, 250)
    End Sub
```

Drawing methods are also available for several common shapes besides rectangles.

Anytime you want to work with the graphics on a control, you need to declare a new Graphics object. For example, you might expect that you could simply use a method of the Panel control to clear the graphics. Instead, you need to declare a Graphics object and then use its Clear method. The code for the Clear button is shown here:

```
    Private Sub btnClear_Click(ByVal sender As _
        System.Object, ByVal e As System.EventArgs) _
        Handles btnClear.Click
        Dim objGraphics As Graphics = _
            pnlGraphicsDisplay.CreateGraphics()
        Dim objColor As Color
        objColor = pnlGraphicsDisplay.BackColor
        objGraphics.Clear(objColor)
    End Sub
```

Note that the Graphics object Clear method clears the control of all graphics and then sets its background to the color specified. In order to set the Panel control back to its original color, you must declare objColor as a Color object and set it to the BackColor property of pnlGraphicsDisplay. The objColor object is then used as the parameter for the Clear method of objGraphics.

You can easily adjust the code to draw a solid circle. In this case, instead of using a line figure, you have drawn a solid object. Technically, this is still a line drawing, but it is now a filled line drawing because of the fill used to make the object solid. To create a filled line drawing, you declare a Graphics object as before, but in this case, instead of using a Pen, you declare a Brush object, which is used to draw solid objects. In general, a Brush object is declared in this manner:

```
    Dim objName As BrushType = New BrushType _
        (Color.color)
```

The SolidBrush type fills the Graphics objects with a single color. Other Brush types exist, such as TextureBrush, which uses an image to fill the interior of a Graphics object. For example, to create a Brush object, you use this statement:

```
    Dim objBrush As SolidBrush = New _
        SolidBrush(Color.Blue)
```

To create a circle, you use the FillEllipse method of the Graphics object instead of the DrawRectangle method. You use Fill methods instead of Draw methods when you want to draw a filled Graphics object. The general format for the FillEllipse method is as follows:

```
    objName.FillEllipse(objBrush, x, y, width, height)
```

The parameters of the FillEllipse method are very much like those of the DrawRectangle method, where the coordinates *x* and *y* specify the upper-left corner of a rectangle, and the *width* and *height* specify the rectangle's dimensions. The object uses the rectangle specified by these values as the boundary in which to draw the ellipse. Because you want to draw a circle, you set the width and height to equal values. For example, to draw a solid blue circle, you use these statements:

```
Dim objBrush As SolidBrush = New _
    SolidBrush(Color.Blue)
objGraphics.FillEllipse(objBrush, 20, 10, 100, 100)
```

As you can see, regular shapes, such as squares, rectangles, and circles, are not too difficult to create using the Draw and Fill methods of the Graphics objects. As it turns out, drawing irregular shapes is only slightly more involved. To draw irregular shapes, you use the FillPolygon method. As you might expect, there is also a DrawPolygon method that is not solid. Both methods require that you provide an array of points that define the location of the corners, or vertices, of the shape. To create this array, you create five Point objects and then assign them to an array called objPolyPoints. Most of the work is in determining the appropriate coordinates for the corners of the shape. The general format for using the FillPolygon method is as follows:

```
objGraphicName.FillPolygon(objBrushName, _
    objPointArrayName)
```

To add text to the Graphics object, you use the DrawString method. The general format for this method is as follows:

```
objGraphicName.DrawString(string, objFontName, _
    objBrushName, x, y)
```

where *x* and *y* are the coordinates of the upper-left corner at which to draw the text. Notice that for each label, coordinates are selected to set the label at an appropriate distance from the shape. For example, to generate an irregular polygon with the points labeled, you use this code:

```
Private Sub mnuGraphPolygon_Click(ByVal sender As _
    System.Object, ByVal e As System.EventArgs) _
    Handles mnuGraphPolygon.Click
    Dim objGraphics As Graphics = _
        pnlGraphicsDisplay.CreateGraphics()
    Dim objBrush As SolidBrush = New _
        SolidBrush(Color.Blue)
    Dim objFont As New Font("Times New Roman", 8)
    Dim objPoint1 As New Point(90, 55)
    Dim objPoint2 As New Point(160, 120)
    Dim objPoint3 As New Point(92, 210)
```

```
Dim objPoint4 As New Point(30, 118)
Dim objPoint5 As New Point(80, 80)
Dim objPolyPoints As Point() = {objPoint1, _
    objPoint2, objPoint3, objPoint4, objPoint5}
objGraphics.FillPolygon(objBrush, objPolyPoints)
objGraphics.DrawString("(90, 55)", objFont, _
    objBrush, 80, 45)
objGraphics.DrawString("(160, 120)", objFont, _
    objBrush, 163, 110)
objGraphics.DrawString("(92, 210)", objFont, _
    objBrush, 82, 215)
objGraphics.DrawString("(30, 118)", objFont, _
    objBrush, 0, 98)
objGraphics.DrawString("(80, 80)", objFont, _
    objBrush, 40, 70)
End Sub
```

Notice that in this code, you have declared the Graphics and Brush objects as before. In addition, you have declared a Font object called objFont. The Font object is used to hold the characteristics of text that will be added to the graphic. The resulting polygon is shown in Figure 10-5.

Table 10-2 summarizes some of the other methods you can use to draw shapes on a VB .NET Graphics object.

Figure 10-5

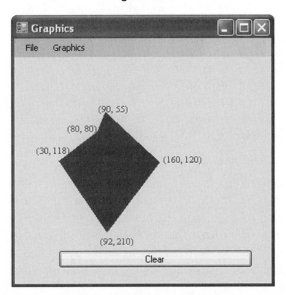

Drawing a labeled polygon.

Table 10-2: Methods of the Graphics Class

Graphic Element	Method	Description	Statement Syntax
Arc	DrawArc	Draws an arc representing a portion of an ellipse specified by a rectangle structure.	`objG.DrawArc(objPen, x, y, width, height, startAngle, sweepAngle)`
Curve	DrawCurve	Draws a curve through a set of points specified by the user.	`objG.DrawCurve (objPen, objPoints)`
Line	DrawLine	Draws a line connecting a pair of coordinate points.	`objG.DrawLine (objPen, x1, y1, x2, y2)`
Pie	DrawPie and FillPie	Draw a wedge of a pie, given a start angle and the size of the wedge, in degrees.	`objG.DrawPie(objPen, x, y, width, height, startAngle, sweepAngle)` `objG.FillPie (objBrush, x, y, width, height, startAngle, sweepAngle)`

FOR EXAMPLE

Using Graphics Objects

Suppose you are building a program to be used by salespeople. You want the program to display a bar graph showing sales over the past year for a selected product. You plan to show sales in 100-unit increments. The product name is selected from a drop-down list and the sales for the last 12 months are retrieved from a database and added to an array named arrSales. Index 0 contains the oldest data. Sales trends indicate that no more than 10,000 of any item is sold in a month.

(Continued)

You add a Panel control to the form and set its width to 240 and its height to 200. You determine that, based on a maximum quantity sold of 10,000, each pixel of height should represent 50 units (10,000/200). Because you want all rectangles to start at the bottom of the graph, you need to calculate the top pixel by subtracting from 200 the sales amount divided by 50. You then need to determine the height (i.e., the distance down) by subtracting the top pixel from 200. The width is much easier. Because you need to display 12 bars and the Panel control is 240 pixels, each bar is 20 pixels wide. You can use a counter to loop through the array and multiply the counter by 20 to obtain the x coordinate (i.e., the leftmost pixel) of each bar.

You add the following code to display the bar graph:

```
Dim arrColors() As Color = {Color.Aqua, _
    Color.BlueViolet, _Color.Coral, Color.Crimson, _
    Color.DarkGreen, Color.DeepPink, _
    Color.DeepSkyBlue, Color.Goldenrod, _
    Color.Honeydew, Color.Khaki, _
    Color.LimeGreen, Color.Magenta}
Dim i As Integer
Dim x, y, h, w As Integer
Dim g As Graphics = Panel1.CreateGraphics()
g.Clear(Me.BackColor)
'Draw rectangles
For i = 0 To 11
    Dim colorBrush As SolidBrush = New _
        SolidBrush(arrColors(i))
    x = i * 20
    y = 200 - (arrSales(i) / 50)
    h = 200 - y
    w = 20
    g.FillRectangle(colorBrush, x, y, w, h)
Next
```

SELF-CHECK

- Describe the role of the Graphics object.
- Compare the DrawEllipse and FillEllipse methods.
- Compare a Pen object and a Brush object.
- Describe the role of a Font object.

10.4 Printing

Most software provides the capabilities of printing output to a printer and previewing what you are going to print before you do so. As usual for common software features, the Visual Basic toolbox provides controls and the .NET Framework Class Library (FCL) provides classes that you can use to add these capabilities to your programs.

10.4.1 The PrintDocument Object

The primary object that is used for printing is the PrintDocument object, and its class is available in the System.Drawing namespace. A PrintDocument object includes properties and methods that allow you to work with and print output. It is basically a Graphics object (it's in the same namespace as the Graphics object), and you can think of the PrintDocument object as a piece of paper on which you draw graphics and text, just as you would on a Panel control or form.

To make sure you have access to the PrintDocument object, you need to add the following line before the class declaration of the form:

```
Imports System.Drawing.Printing
```

A PrintDocument object can cause a PrintPage event to occur. This event occurs whenever the Print method of the PrintDocument object is called. You can write the code that specifies the format of the printed document in the event procedure for the PrintPage event. In general, you should follow four steps when writing text or graphics to the PrintDocument object:

1. Create the item you want to print.
2. Set the location on the document where it should be printed.
3. Select the style, font, color, and so forth of the item you want to print.
4. Use the appropriate method to draw the item on the PrintDocument object.

For example, you use the following code to print employee payroll information:

```
Private Sub objPrintDocument_PrintPage(ByVal sender _
    As Object, ByVal e As PrintPageEventArgs) _
    Handles objPrintDocument.PrintPage
    Dim sngX As Single, sngY As Single
    Dim intEmpCntr As Integer
    Dim sngLeftMargin As Single = e.MarginBounds.Left
    Dim sngRightMargin As Single = _
        e.MarginBounds.Right
    Dim sngTopMargin As Single = e.MarginBounds.Top
    Dim objTitleFont As New Font("Courier New", 14, _
        FontStyle.Bold)
```

```
        Dim objHeadingFont As New Font _
            ("Courier New", 12, FontStyle.Bold)
        Dim objRecordFont As New Font("Courier New", 12)
        Dim objBrush As SolidBrush = New _
            SolidBrush(Color.Black)
        Dim objpen As Pen = New Pen(Color.Black)
        Dim strLine, strName As String, intCounter As _
            Integer
        strLine = "Employees"
        sngX = sngLeftMargin + 10
        sngY = sngTopMargin + 5
        e.Graphics.DrawString(strLine, objTitleFont, _
            objBrush, sngX, sngY)
        ' write column headings
        strLine = "Name" & Space(26)
        strLine = strLine & "Phone" & Space(10)
        strLine = strLine & "Pay Type"
        sngY = sngY + 34
        e.Graphics.DrawString(strLine, objHeadingFont, _
            objBrush, sngX, sngY)
        sngY = sngY + 24
        e.Graphics.DrawLine(objpen, sngX, sngY, _
            sngRightMargin - 10, sngY)
        ' print records
        For intCounter = 0 To intEmpCntr - 1
            strName = _
            Trim(udtEmployees(intCounter).strFName) & _
                " " & _
                Trim(udtEmployees(intCounter).strLName)
            strLine = Spacer(strName, 30)
            strLine = strLine & _
        Spacer(Trim(udtEmployees(intCounter).strPhone _
            ), 15) & Chr(9)
            strLine = strLine & _
                udtEmployees(intCounter).strPaytype _
                & Chr(9)
            sngY = sngY + 24
            e.Graphics.DrawString(strLine, _
                objRecordFont, objBrush, sngX, sngY)
        Next intCounter
        sngY = sngY + 36 ' print total employees
        strLine = "Number of Employees = " & _
            CStr(intEmpCntr)
        e.Graphics.DrawString(strLine, objHeadingFont, _
            objBrush, sngX, sngY)
    End Sub
```

First, notice in this code that the name of the subprocedure is objPrint-Document_PrintPage. Recall from the preceding paragraphs that PrintDocument is an object. You therefore need to instantiate an instance of the object before you can use it. When you add the PrintDocument object to a form, this instantiation is done for you automatically. The preceding code assumes that you added the PrintDocument object to the form. If you add the PrintDocument object through code, you need to declare it, instantiate it, and associate it with an event handler, just as you would any other object.

Also note that in the substatement, you have the parameter e, which is passed as a PrintPageEventArgs object. The Graphics property of this object lets you specify what you want to print.

The first statements in the code of the objPrintDocument_Print subproject are used to declare local variables and objects. The variables sngX and sngY are used as the coordinates for placing things on the PrintDocument object. Using variables instead of simply typing exact values allows you to use equations to determine the next location to draw an item. Several variables, including sngLeftMargin, sngRightMargin, and sngTopMargin, are declared and immediately set to the margin values of the PrintPageEventArgs object. You can use these variables as reference points to ensure that the graphic elements are drawn within the margins of the page. Next, you declare several Font, Brush, and Pen objects that will be used to draw graphics and text on the PrintDocument object. Finally, you declare several processing variables.

The first example of this processing occurs when you print the title of the report. Remember that the first step of the four-step process is to assign the text for the title of the report, Employees, to the String variable strLine. Then, for step 2, you assign coordinate values to the variables sngX and sngY, using the left and top margins for reference. You select the appropriate style for step 3 by choosing the desired Font object that you want to use for the title. Here you use the objTitleFont object that you declared earlier. Finally, you use the DrawString method to draw the word Employees to the PrintDocument object in bold, 14-point, Times New Roman font. With a careful reading of the rest of the code, you see that these same four steps are followed for each item that is drawn to the PrintDocument object. The Spacer function is a user-defined function that returns a string padded at the end so it is a specific length.

There are a few things you should notice in the rest of the code. First, you can set the location of the next item to draw by using the previous location as a reference. You do this by simply adding the appropriate value, representing a distance in pixels to either the sngX variable or the sngY variable. You need to keep in mind that coordinate values are measured in pixels. You should also remember that sngX and sngY represent the location of the upper-left corner of a rectangle in which the item will be drawn. The bottom-left corner of a text item that uses a 14-point font will be approximately 14 pixels farther down the y axis than the upper-left corner. This fact can be important in deciding how much to add when determining the next location.

Second, you can draw graphics as well as text. You add a line under the column headings by using the DrawLine method. Third, because all the records of the udtEmployees array contain similar data, you can use a loop to print these items to the PrintDocument object. Here again, the use of variables for your coordinates comes in handy because you can easily make adjustments each time an item is to be drawn.

10.4.2 Previewing and Printing the PrintDocument Object

To use the PrintDocument object and its PrintPage event, you need to add a few controls to the program. You need to add a Print option and a PrintPreview option to the File menu. You might also decide to add Print and PrintPreview buttons to a toolbar.

You can implement the PrintPreview button by using the PrintPreviewDialog control. You set the UseAntiAlias property to True to help make the text look better onscreen. The code for previewing the document is shown here:

```
Private Sub mnuFilePrintPreview_Click(ByVal sender _
    As System.Object, ByVal e As System.EventArgs) _
    Handles mnuFilePrintPreview.Click
    If PrinterSettings.InstalledPrinters.Count = 0 _
        Then
        MessageBox.Show( _
            "No printers are currently installed", _
            "Print Error", MessageBoxButtons.OK, _
            MessageBoxIcon.Information)
        Exit Sub
    End If
    dlgPreview.document = objPrintDocument
    dlgPreview.ShowDialog()
End Sub
```

You can check whether there are any printers installed by using the PrinterSettings.InstalledPrinters.Count property. If printers are installed, you can set the document property of the PrintPreviewDialog control (here named dlgPreview) to reference the PrintDocument object. Finally, you call the ShowDialog method. The PrintPreviewDialog control is shown in Figure 10-6.

You also need to add a PrintDialog control to allow the user to select a printer. You display the PrintDialog by using its Show method. Its PrinterSettings property includes the printer selected by the user as well as any settings. You can set the PrintDocument object's PrinterSettings property to reference the PrinterSettings property of the PrintDialog control to associate the settings with the document.

Finally, you call the Print method on the PrintDocument object. For example, suppose you have a PrintDialog component named prnDialog and

Figure 10-6

PrintPreviewDialog

The PrintPreviewDialog control.

a PrintDocument component named pDoc. You use the following code to cause the code defined in the PagePrint event of pDoc to run:

```
prnDialog.ShowDialog
pDoc.PrinterSettings = prnDialog.PrinterSettings
pDoc.Print()
```

FOR EXAMPLE

Printing a Document

Suppose you are creating an application to be used by salespeople to display sales reports. You want to allow the salespeople to choose the printer to print to and to choose whether a document should be printed as **landscape** (i.e., longer horizontally) or **portrait** (i.e., longer vertically). The salespeople should be able to create the report on the screen by selecting the products they want to include. A bar graph showing product sales comparisons should be displayed on the screen. That same data should be printed in the report.

You add a PrintDocument object to the form and generate a PrintPage event to print the data as specified by the user. You move the code to draw the bar graph to a subprocedure and pass a reference to a Graphics object and an x and y coordinate to specify where the bar graph should start. When you call it from within PrintPage, you pass the e.Graphics object.

You also add a PrintDialog object to obtain the printer settings, including the name of the printer and the orientation (landscape or portrait). Finally, you add a PrintPreviewDialog object to allow users to preview the report.

SELF-CHECK

- Describe how to use the PrintDocument object.
- Describe the role of the PrintDialog object.
- Describe the role of the PrintPreviewDialog object.

SUMMARY

In this chapter, you've learned about input and output. You've learned how to save data to a file and read data from a file. You've also learned how to output graphics to the screen and how to generate a document to be printed and send it to the printer a user selects.

KEY TERMS

ASCII encoding

Binary file

Coordinate system

Delimited file

Direct access file

Encoding

End Of File (EOF) marker

Field

GDI+

Landscape

My keyword

Portrait

Random access file

Record

Sequential access file

Text file

Unicode encoding

User-defined type (UDT)

Vector

Vector graphic

X coordinate

Y coordinate

ASSESS YOUR UNDERSTANDING

Go to www.wiley.com/college/petroutsos to evaluate your knowledge of input and output concepts and techniques.

Measure your learning by comparing pre-test and post-test results.

Summary Questions

1. You must read a sequential file in the same order in which it was written. True or False?

2. Only random access files include an EOF marker. True or False?

3. What type of sequential access file can include fields of different lengths?
   (a) delimited file
   (b) direct access file
   (c) any text file
   (d) any binary file

4. Only binary files require encoding. True or False?

5. What type of file requires records of a fixed length?
   (a) delimited file
   (b) direct access file
   (c) any text file
   (d) any binary file

6. What keyword is used to define a UDT in Visual Basic?
   (a) Type
   (b) UDT
   (c) Structure
   (d) Struct

7. Which of the following is the fully qualified name of the WriteAllText method?
   (a) My.Computer.FileSystem.WriteAllText
   (b) My.Computer.File.WriteAllText
   (c) My.FileSystem.WriteAllText
   (d) My.File.WriteAllText

8. What data type must you use to read the contents of a file by using the ReadAllBytes method?
   (a) Byte
   (b) Byte Array
   (c) Any numeric data type
   (d) Any UDT

9. What method do you use to read a record from a comma-delimited file, using the objects in the Microsoft.VisualBasic.FileIO namespace?

(a) ReadAllText

(b) Read

(c) FileRead

(d) ReadFields

10. What method must you call before you can call the FileOpen method?

(a) FreeFile

(b) FileGet

(c) FilePut

(d) FileSeek

11. You can use the FileSystem.SpecialDirectories property to retrieve the path to a user's MyPictures folder. True or False?

12. The FileSystem.DeleteFile method always sends documents to the Recycle Bin. True or False?

13. Which of the following can you specify as an option when calling the CopyFile method?

(a) whether to overwrite an existing file that has the same name

(b) whether to delete the source file

(c) whether to move an existing file that has the same name to the Recycle Bin

(d) whether to raise an exception if the file specified does not exist

14. The only way to determine whether a file exists before deleting it is to catch an exception. True or False?

15. Which System.Drawing class is used to draw lines and curves?

(a) Brush

(b) Arc

(c) Pen

(d) Vector

16. The x coordinate measures the distance from the origin along the horizontal axis. True or False?

17. You use the Graphics property of a Panel control as a surface for drawing graphics. True or False?

18. Which method requires you to pass an object of type Brush?

(a) FillEllipse

(b) DrawLine

(c) CreateGraphics

(d) DrawPolygon

19. In which event should you write code that determines how text is printed?
    (a) PrintDocument's Print event
    (b) PrintDocument's PrintPage event
    (c) Printer's Print event
    (d) Printer's PrintPage event

20. Which object should you add to a project to allow a user to choose a printer?
    (a) PrintDocument
    (b) Printer
    (c) PrintPreviewDialog
    (d) PrintDialog

Applying This Chapter

1. You are writing an application in Visual Basic to store user preferences settings in a file. The application will sometimes be stored on a computer where multiple users log on. You want to be sure that the application uses the settings defined by the current user. Most settings are Boolean values. The PreferredURLs setting is a variable-length array of Strings. The settings are written as default values the first time the user launches the application. You want file access to be as optimal as possible.
    (a) What type of file will you create?
    (b) What object and method will you use to write the file?
    (c) What object and method will you use to read the file?
    (d) How will you determine the path to the file?
    (e) How will you determine whether you need to write the default settings to the file?

2. You are writing an application in Visual Basic that will display the number of expenses for each office. The expenses should be broken down by category. You want to provide users with a visual display, using both bar graphs and pie charts. You also want users to be about to print the output.
    (a) How will you color-code each category in the bar chart?
    (b) What method will you use to draw the bars?
    (c) How will you color-code each category in the pie chart?
    (d) What method will you use to draw the pie chart?
    (e) What method will you use to label the charts?
    (f) What object controls the color of the labels?
    (g) How will you allow users to print the graphs?
    (h) How will you allow users to select a printer?
    (i) What can you do to optimize code reuse?

Designing Input and Output

You are creating an application that will be used to design a garden layout. Shapes will be used to represent different types of plants. Users will choose the colors and fills style for the shapes. You need to allow users to save the garden layout to a file or send it to a printer. Users must be able to open and modify a saved design. Users must also be able to view two garden designs side-by-side. Advanced users must be able to open the garden data file in Notepad and modify it there.

1. Describe how you will allow users to design the garden.
2. Describe how you will implement the ability to view garden designs side-by-side.
3. Describe how you will save the data to a file.
4. Describe how you will allow users to print the garden layout.

11

DEPLOYING YOUR APPLICATION

Starting Point

What You'll Learn in This Chapter

▲ Deployment concerns
▲ Private and shared assemblies
▲ XCopy deployment
▲ ClickOnce deployment
▲ Windows Installer deployment
▲ Application dependencies
▲ Configuration files
▲ Types of testing
▲ Conditional compilation
▲ Project properties
▲ Creation of a Windows Installer package

After Studying This Chapter, You'll Be Able To

▲ Plan a deployment of a .NET application
▲ Create and use application and user configuration file settings
▲ Identify the purpose of each phase of application testing
▲ Use conditional compilation to manage differences in code during development and after deployment
▲ Prepare an application for deployment by setting project-level properties
▲ Create a Windows Installer setup program to deploy an application

INTRODUCTION

After you have finished programming and debugging an application on a development computer, you need to deploy it to other computers. Perhaps these will be computers at the company where you work, or you might need to distribute a program on CD or DVD. In this chapter, you'll learn some of the considerations involved in preparing an application to run outside Visual Studio. First, you'll learn some concepts related to deployment and installation. This chapter compares three types of installations supported for applications you build using the .NET Framework 2.0. Finally, you'll learn how to create a setup program.

11.1 Deployment Concepts

One of the last phases in an application's development cycle is the deployment process. While developing, testing, and debugging an application, many developers realize that they must deploy their application to a number of workstations. If you don't think of the deployment process while you're developing an application, you might run into surprises when you attempt to install the application on another machine. In this section, we'll begin with an overview of deployment and installation, defining some key terms and describing how applications and class libraries are configured on a computer.

11.1.1 Deployment and Installation

Deployment is the activity of delivering copies of an application to other computers so that the application runs in the new environment. It is the larger, architectural view for what you may know as an installation or a setup. There is a subtle difference between deployment and installation. **Deployment** is the art of distribution. In other words, deployment is the way in which software is delivered. **Installation,** or **setup,** is the process whereby you load, configure, and install the software. So an installation is what you do to configure the software, and deployment is how you get it where you want it.

Using this terminology, a CD is a **deployment mechanism** (i.e., a medium used to distribute an application), as is the Internet. These two deployment mechanisms have different capabilities. As an example, if installation files are on a CD, you may have all the additional software on which the application depends (e.g., class libraries, help files) on that CD. This would be fine for a CD, but it might not be sufficient for delivery via the Internet. You might also have application configuration settings that differ in the **production environment** (i.e., where the application is run) from the **development environment** (i.e., the computer where you wrote the software). These kinds of considerations are important when you're deciding on your best deployment option. The type of installations you require could also vary by application.

11.1.2 Versioning and Upgrades

Most applications and class libraries need updates as time goes on. New features need to be added to address changes to business requirements. Applications need to be updated to run in an upgraded technical environment. Therefore, developers (especially class library developers) need to identify an application or a class library with a **version number** (i.e., a number that is incremented each time the application is updated). If an application is an upgrade to an existing application, developers need to consider how deploying the new version of the application will affect computers running the existing version. For an executable, this might include the following:

▲ File format conversions for data files
▲ Migration of user settings to the new version
▲ Whether to allow the versions to run side-by-side on the same computer

For a class library, it is also important for developers to ensure that they do not break compatibility with existing consumers. When updating a class library, you as a developer need to make sure to never change an existing interface. You can add new methods, overload methods, add new properties, and change the encapsulated implementation of any member. However, you cannot change the signature of an existing method or property or else applications that are using the current version will not be compatible with the new version.

11.1.3 Assemblies

When you **build** (i.e., compile source code into an executable file) an application or a component, you create an assembly. An **assembly** is a .NET Framework application or class library that has been compiled to run outside the development environment. An application assembly is an executable (.exe) file. A class library assembly is a dynamic link library (.dll) file.

As you have seen, an application includes an executable and often one or more class libraries that have been added to the project as references. One decision you need to make when deploying a class library assembly is whether to deploy it as a private assembly or a shared assembly.

You also need to consider whether to create a strong-named assembly. A **strong-named assembly** has the following:

▲ **Version number:** A version number is incremented each time a new version of the class is released.
▲ **Globally unique identifier (GUID):** A **GUID** is a hexadecimal value that is unique on any computer where the assembly is installed.

▲ **Digital signature:** A **digital signature** is a public key infrastructure (PKI) certificate which guarantees that the executable has not been modified and that it originated from the party who signed the assembly.

A **PKI certificate** is a digital certification that proves an individual's or a company's identity. The certificate includes a **private key** (i.e., a key that is kept protected from unauthorized access) to sign the assembly and a **public key** (i.e., a key that is used to verify the assembly's integrity). When you sign an assembly, you use the private key to create a **hash value** (i.e., a value computed from the assembly's bits). If that hash value changes, you know that the assembly has been modified.

Let's look at the difference between private and shared assemblies.

Private Assemblies

Private assemblies are installed in a directory named Bin located under the application directory. These files are private to the application. There are a few benefits to using private assemblies:

▲ No versioning is required, as long as the assembly is the same version as the one with which the application was built. **Versioning** is the process of incrementing the version number of a class to allow applications to use a version of a class library with which they are known to be compatible.

▲ The private assembly cannot be updated by another application's installation program (at least it is not meant to be).

▲ The application can be deployed using XCopy deployment (i.e., the ability to simply copy and paste files to a location and have them work).

▲ You can make changes to the assembly, and if two different applications use it, you can update one independently from the other.

▲ There is no configuration or signing to do. It just works.

▲ It is great for small utility assemblies and/or application-specific code.

Private assemblies have the following negatives:

▲ When you have multiple applications using one assembly, you have to deploy an assembly with each application.

▲ You would normally have to include the assembly in each setup project where it is used.

▲ Versioning is not enforced as it is in a shared assembly.

▲ The assembly is not strongly named, which means someone could spoof your assembly. **Spoofing an assembly** is a situation in which someone creates an assembly that looks identical to yours and replaces yours with the spoof copy. This spoof copy could do malicious things.

Shared Assemblies

A **shared assembly** is an assembly that can be accessed by multiple applications installed on the same computer. You use a shared assembly for class libraries that need to be accessed by multiple applications.

Using a shared assembly is like going back in time. In Windows 3.1, the main deployment location for shared DLLs was the Windows\System directory. Later developers were advised to have DLLs in the local application path because that made for easier installation and removal. Today, the System directory concept returns in a new guise, called the **Global Assembly Cache (GAC)**. The GAC is a file system directory that is accessible by multiple applications. It is where the .NET Framework looks for classes that are referenced by a project but are not in the application's Bin directory. Before an assembly can be installed in the GAC, you need to make it a strong-named assembly.

The following are the main benefits of a shared assembly:

▲ It is signed and cannot be spoofed.

▲ It has strong versioning support and configuration options.

▲ It is stored in one central location and does not need to be copied to the Bin directory of every application that uses it.

▲ You can have many different versions running side by side.

A shared assembly has the following negatives:

▲ You have to sign the assembly.

▲ You have to be careful not to break compatibility with existing applications, or else you have to configure the different versions.

▲ Configuration can be a nightmare, depending on the requirements.

FOR EXAMPLE

Moving from Development to Deployment

Suppose you are a programmer on a development team responsible for updating your company's accounting program. The current program was written in Visual Basic 6.0 and stored accounting data in a Microsoft Access database. The new program is written using Visual Basic 2005, and it stores data in a SQL Server 2005 database.

The program will use an assembly that will also be used by the company's payroll program, which is currently under development by another team. The assembly will expose classes that implement various business rules. You want to make sure the two programs always use the same version of the assembly.

Your deployment planning must include defining a procedure for migrating the data from the Microsoft Access database to the SQL Server 2005 database. The team must also decide whether you need to upgrade the existing version or allow the two versions to run side-by-side. To make this decision, you need to consult with members of the accounting department and possibly other people as well to determine whether there will be requirements to access the old application after the upgrade is complete (e.g., some users might need to be able to access legacy data that is not going to be migrated to SQL Server 2005.)

You must also determine how to install the assembly that contains business rules. Because the same version must be used by two applications, the best solution is to install it as a shared assembly in the GAC. To do so, you need to digitally sign the assembly to make it a strong-named assembly.

SELF-CHECK

- What are the main benefits of a shared assembly?
- What is the primary difference between a strong-named assembly and an assembly that does not have a strong name?
- What must be installed in the GAC?

11.2 Planning a Deployment

When planning a deployment, you need to consider the environment in which the application needs to run, the existing environment in which it will be installed, and the type of deployment you will perform. Depending on the resources you used when building the application, the purpose of the application, and the application's end user, you might also need to consider licensing and other legal requirements, marketing, user training, and support. However, these considerations are beyond the scope of this text.

In this section, you'll learn about the deployment planning decisions that are most often the responsibility of the programmer. These include deciding what type of installation best meets your needs and identifying the changes you must make to the production computer.

11.2.1 Deployment Methods

Windows Forms–based applications support three types of deployment: XCopy deployment, ClickOnce deployment, and Windows Installer deployment. The type of deployment you choose depends on the complexity of the application, the types of changes that need to be made to the environment, and whether the application needs to be installed only within the corporate network or to the general public or other external users.

This section provides an overview of each deployment type and gives some guidelines for determining which type of deployment best meets your needs.

XCopy Deployment

XCopy deployment is as simple as copying the executable files from the development machine to the production workstations. This deployment method can be used only with simple applications, and it's a seriously limited deployment method because it doesn't allow you to perform custom actions, such as installing a shortcut on the user's desktop or a new font on the target computer. It also does not provide a way to install the .NET Framework.

This type of deployment is called XCopy deployment because you install the application on the target machine by simply copying the files in the application's Bin\Release folder (and any subfolders with custom files that might exist in this folder) to the target computer. No components are registered, and no other changes are made to the target computer. To remove the application, you simply delete the folder, and no trace of the application remains on the computer—except perhaps for a shortcut the user might have created on the desktop. You can also install multiple versions of the same application to different folders, which can run side by side. Each application folder contains its own EXE, DLLs, and dependencies, so they shouldn't interfere with one another. DLLs are treated as application files and need not be registered at the client computer, which is why you can remove them by deleting them.

XCopy deployment can also be used to update an existing application. To deploy a newer version on the client machine, you just copy the new files over the existing ones. The next time the user runs the application, he or she runs the new version of the application.

The XCopy deployment method should be used with applications that will be installed on a few clients only. You can create **BAT files** (i.e., files that use operating system commands to automate a process, also known as *batch files*) to automate the process of copying the application files to a client, but the XCopy technique is not a substitute for a real setup program or a ClickOnce deployment.

ClickOnce Deployment

ClickOnce deployment is ideal for **corporate intranets** (i.e., web servers and file servers deployed for use within a company's network). The application's files are copied to a virtual directory of the web server, a shared folder on a server, or a CD or DVD. With ClickOnce, you can either deploy the application to a web server (and have users execute the application as they would connect to a web application) or deploy a setup program, which installs the application to the client computer. It is a useful deployment option for small- to medium-sized applications.

There are three major benefits to ClickOnce deployment. First, using this deployment option allows for **self-updating** Windows applications. You can post the latest version of the application at the original location, and the next time the user runs the application, it will install and run the latest version. Second, any user can install most ClickOnce applications with only basic user security. With other technologies, administrator permissions are required. Finally, when this type of application is run from the server, the installation has little impact on the user's computer. The application is run from a secure per-user cache and adds entries only to the Start menu and the Add or Remove Programs list. For programs that do not need to access the GAC, this is a terrific deployment solution for distribution.

If you distribute a ClickOnce application through external media, the application is run with **full trust** (i.e., a code access level that allows it access to the Registry, file system, and external resources). **Code access security** provides the ability for administrators to limit which components or applications can run and what resources they can access, based on where they are located, the publisher (developer), and whether they are digitally signed. A detailed discussion of code access security is beyond the scope of this text.

Windows Installer Deployment

In this last deployment method discussed in this chapter, you create a Windows Installer package, distribute it to the target machines, and ask users to run the setup program, which installs the application and integrates it with the user's environment. A Windows Installer deployment can create shortcuts, add entries to the **Registry** (i.e., a file that contains configuration information for hardware and software components installed on a computer), manage user registration, and so on. Programs installed through Windows Installer can later be removed through the Add or Remove Programs utility (see Figure 11-1). A Windows Installer deployment is the most professional method of deploying an application, and it's the only option for distributing an application to the general public.

Windows Installer is a technology for distributing and installing applications through an executable file (usually named Setup.exe) and a Microsoft Installer (MSI) file. An **MSI file** is a database with all the data needed to install an application. The setup program is a **bootstrap application** (i.e., a small application that loads another program) that opens an MSI package and installs the application and its components on the client computer. Creating a simple Windows Installer package with Visual Studio is a straightforward process because the setup project can be part of the application. Creating a flexible installation program for a large application might become quite a task, but at the very least, you can design and test the setup project in the

Figure 11-1

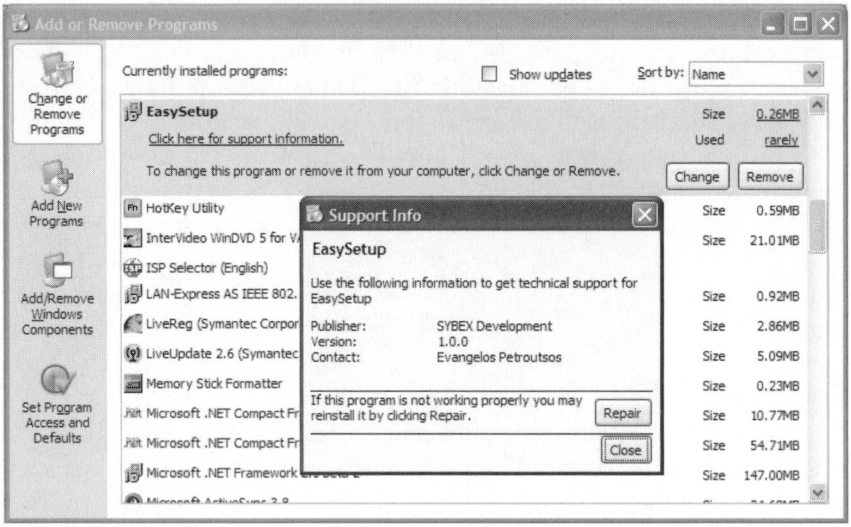

The Add or Remove Programs utility.

integrated development environment (IDE) of Visual Studio. You can even debug the installer in the IDE: You can install the application on the development computer and monitor the installation process. Third-party products are available to help you to build a Windows Installer package and setup program.

When you use Windows Installer to deploy an application, the information stored in the database remains at the client, so you can run the setup program again to either repair or uninstall the application.

11.2.2 Identifying Required Changes

As you create an application, you make changes to the development environment. You might install a font, use icons from the folder in which they exist on the development machine, install class library assemblies in the development machine's GAC, and so on. When the application is deployed to a production computer, it might not find a drive or folder that existed on the development computer or a class library that's not installed in the production computer's GAC. You should always keep in mind that your application will be distributed to other people's workstations. If you're using icons, you should copy them into a folder within the project and use them from that folder.

In addition, you should decide on your deployment method early in the process and deploy the application to a production machine from time to time. Production machines are set up differently from development machines (a major difference is that Visual Studio is not installed), and you might be surprised at how often an application that works as expected in the development environment misbehaves when installed on a production machine. The problem is usually simple to resolve, but you shouldn't postpone deployment problems to the very end of the development cycle.

Installing the .NET Framework

The client computers to which you deploy your .NET applications must have the correct version of the .NET Framework runtime installed. If they don't, the application won't run. The deployment techniques supported by Visual Studio 2005 provide the means to distribute the .NET Framework along with the application.

Before you can perform an XCopy deployment, you must make sure the .NET Framework has been installed on the target computer. To install the .NET Framework on a machine, you must run the Dotnetfx.exe setup program, which you can find on your Visual Studio 2005 development computer at C:\Program Files\Microsoft VisualStudio8\SDK\v2.0\BootStrapper\Packages\dotnetfx. This path assumes that Visual Studio was installed in the default location and that the version of the .NET Framework is 2.0. If the Dotnetfx.exe file exists in a shared folder, you can easily install the .NET Framework on any computer on the local network. After that, you can copy the executable files produced by the Visual Studio 2005 compiler to the client and execute them.

Deployment techniques other than XCopy support the installation of the .NET Framework, along with any other prerequisite components, such as ADO 2.0. You can include the .NET Framework in the setup application, which then detects the presence (or absence) of the .NET Framework on the target computer and proceeds accordingly. If the .NET Framework isn't installed on the client computer, the setup application installs it first and then continues with the installation of the application.

To install the .NET Framework on a client computer, the user must log on with administrator privileges. Installing the .NET Framework takes a few moments, but it's an unattended process, and it either installs the .NET Framework successfully or fails, in which case the original computer configuration is restored. You can install the .NET Framework on Windows 98 (and later) computers, and your applications also work under this pre-.NET operating system.

Class Libraries and Custom Controls

An important part of planning deployment is to ensure that all class library and custom control DLLs are installed on the production computer. This includes any classes you add references to and custom controls that you add to the toolbox, and subsequently to your application, that are not part of the .NET Framework.

You need to decide whether to install these assemblies as private assemblies or as shared assemblies. You might also need to ensure that you are legally allowed to distribute third-party components.

Other Dependencies

You need to make a list of non-executable files your application depends on. These might include help files and other documentation, data files, icons, graphics, and fonts. You need to make sure that these files are included with the project so that they can be deployed along with the application.

Regardless of how you plan to deploy the application, it is a good idea to store most dependent files in a subdirectory of the project directory (such as in a Resources folder). Doing so enables the application to consistently reference the files on the development computer and, after deployment, on the production computer.

Database Connections and Other Configuration Settings

Some configuration settings might be different in a production environment than in the development environment. For example, an application might access a database on a server when it is installed in a production environment but access a local copy of that database during development. You might also have user-specific configuration settings. For example, you might allow users to modify the font used on controls and menus or configure a path to where their documents are stored.

Along with the application, you can include a configuration file to store values. Application settings are stored in a file named app.config, which is created at design time. The app.config file can be modified after deploying the application without the need to recompile.

The configuration file is an **Extensible Markup Language (XML)** file. XML is an industry-standard specification for describing data, using a hierarchical structure. Although a detailed explanation of XML and configuration files is beyond the scope of this book, we will take a brief look at how the application configuration file is formatted and used in a Windows application. The format of an XML file is known as its **schema.** A sample app.config file is shown here to illustrate its format:

```
<?xml version="1.0" encoding="utf-8" ?>
<configuration>
  <configSections>
    <sectionGroup name="applicationSettings"

      type="System.Configuration.ApplicationSettingsGroup,
      System, Version=2.0.0.0, Culture=neutral,
```

```
      PublicKeyToken=b77a5c561934e089" >
          <section name="fileiotest.My.MySettings"


          type="System.Configuration.ClientSettingsSection,
          System, Version=2.0.0.0, Culture=neutral,
          PublicKeyToken=b77a5c561934e089"
          requirePermission="false" />
      </sectionGroup>
      <sectionGroup name="userSettings"


      type="System.Configuration.UserSettingsGroup,
      System, Version=2.0.0.0, Culture=neutral,
      PublicKeyToken=b77a5c561934e089" >
          <section name="fileiotest.My.MySettings"


          type="System.Configuration.ClientSettingsSection,
          System, Version=2.0.0.0, Culture=neutral,
          PublicKeyToken=b77a5c561934e089"
          allowExeDefinition="MachineToLocalUser"
          requirePermission="false" />
      </sectionGroup>
    </configSections>
    <connectionStrings>
      <add


          name=
"fileiotest.My.MySettings.ProductServiceConnectionString"
          connectionString=
"Data Source=.\SQLEXPRESS;AttachDbFilename=C:\Ch9DB\
Product Service.mdf;Integrated Security=True;Connect
Timeout=30;User Instance=True"
providerName="System.Data.SqlClient" />
    </connectionStrings>
    <system.diagnostics>
      <sources>
      <!-- This section defines the logging configuration
      for My.Application.Log -->
        <source name="DefaultSource"
         switchName="DefaultSwitch">
          <listeners>
              <add name="FileLog"/>
           <!-- Uncomment the below section
            to write to the Application Event Log -->
              <!--<add name="EventLog"/>-->
          </listeners>
        </source>
      </sources>
      <switches>
```

```
                <add name="DefaultSwitch"
                 value="Information" />
            </switches>
            <sharedListeners>
                <add name="FileLog"
type="Microsoft.VisualBasic.Logging.FileLogTraceListener,
Microsoft.VisualBasic, Version=8.0.0.0, Culture=neutral,
PublicKeyToken=b03f5f7f11d50a3a,
processorArchitecture=MSIL"
initializeData="FileLogWriter"/>
<!-- Uncomment the below section and
replace APPLICATION_NAME with the name of your application
to write to the Application Event Log -->
                <!--<add name="EventLog"
                    type="System.Diagnostics.
                    EventLogTraceListener" initializeData=
                    "APPLICATION_NAME"/> -->
            </sharedListeners>
        </system.diagnostics>
        <applicationSettings>
            <fileiotest.My.MySettings>
                <setting name="Datapath"
                 serializeAs="String">
                    <value>c:\appdata</value>
                </setting>
            </fileiotest.My.MySettings>
        </applicationSettings>
        <userSettings>
            <fileiotest.My.MySettings>
                <setting name="color"
                 serializeAs="String">
                 <value>255, 128, 128</value>
                </setting>
            </fileiotest.My.MySettings>
        </userSettings>
    </configuration>
```

Notice that the file is structured hierarchically and that each element has matched opening and closing tags. For example, the applicationSettings element opens with this tag:

```
<applicationSettings>
```

and closes with this tag:

```
</applicationSettings>
```

Some elements, such as the following, are self-closing:

```
<add name="FileLog"/>
```

Figure 11-2

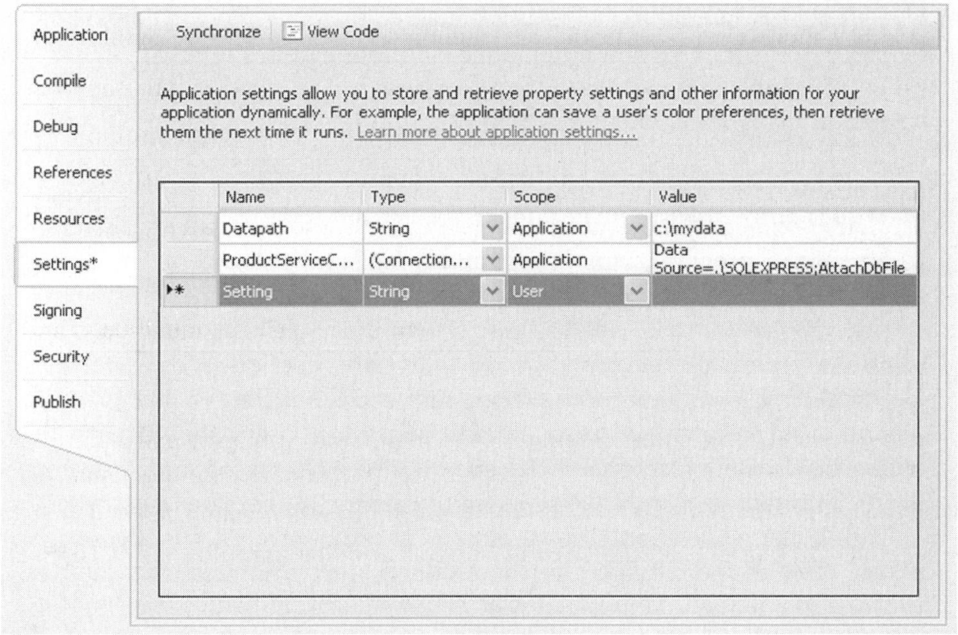

The Settings page.

XML is a case-sensitive language that ignores whitespace. This means that line breaks are not meaningful. To add a comment to an XML file, you use this syntax:

```
<!-- Comment goes here -->
```

The app.config file is added to the project automatically when you configure a database connection or when you define an application setting. User-specific settings are stored in a file named user.config, which is created at runtime.

You define application and user settings through the Settings page of a project's properties (see Figure 11-2). For each setting, you must provide a unique name, a data type, whether it is an application setting or a user setting, and a value. The data type can be any type that can be serialized to a string for storage in the XML file.

Database connections are defined under the <connectionSettings> element. Application settings you add are defined under the <applicationSettings> element. User-specific settings are identified and assigned default values under the <userSettings> element.

You can access the settings in code by using the My object's Settings property. All settings defined in the configuration file are accessible there. For example, the color setting can be accessed by using this code:

```
My.Settings.color
```

FOR EXAMPLE

Planning Deployment

Suppose you are a programmer on a development team responsible for updating your company's accounting program. The current program was written in Visual Basic 6.0 and stored accounting data in a Microsoft Access database. The new program is written using Visual Basic 2005, and it stores data in a SQL Server 2005 database.

The program will use an assembly that will also be used by the company's payroll program, which is currently under development by another team. The assembly should be installed as a shared assembly.

The application will also use the System.Data.SqlClient namespace and a custom control you purchased from a third-party developer. The company's logo will appear on the About screen, and a custom font is used to print reports. The program will also include help files. Users should have the option of installing a tutorial. They should also have the option of upgrading their current version of the program or running the versions side-by-side.

While the application is in development, each developer is accessing a private copy of the database. In the production environment, the database will be installed on a separate server. Users need to be able to set the font for all user interface elements.

You identify the following dependencies:

▲ .NET Framework 2.0 (which includes System.Data.SqlClient)
▲ A shared assembly
▲ A custom control
▲ The logo file
▲ The font used to print reports

You identify the following additional files that need to be installed:

▲ A tutorial
▲ Help files

You decide to use the Settings page of the project properties to modify the database connection string before deployment. You also create a UserFont property and set the user interface elements to use the font defined by the user. You add code to the Options dialog to allow users to change the font, and you use the My.Settings object to set the font to the one chosen by the user.

You decide to use Windows Installer as the deployment method to allow users to be able to select whether to upgrade or run side by side, to be able to select whether to install the tutorial, and to be able to install the shared assembly in the GAC.

- What type of deployment allows you to install a shared assembly in the GAC?
- When is an XCopy deployment most suitable?
- What type of deployment is self-updating?
- What is a dependency for all Visual Studio 2005 applications?
- How can you define application-wide settings that can be modified without recompiling the application?

11.3 Preparing for Deployment

Before you can actually deploy an application, you need to take some steps to ensure that your application is ready for deployment in a production environment. In this section we'll discuss some concepts related to testing an application, doing conditional compilation, and setting project options.

11.3.1 Test, Test, Test

Before you deploy an application, you need to make sure it will work correctly in the production environment. Testing a simple application with only one programmer might be fairly straightforward. However, testing more complicated applications (especially those with multiple programmers) is a time-consuming and complicated task.

Entire books are written on testing procedures and methodologies. The goal of this chapter is not to make you an expert in application testing but to introduce some of the terms you'll encounter on the job. First, it's important to understand that testing is a process that occurs throughout the lifetime of a project. During the design phase, you desk check your algorithms to make sure they work on paper. You validate the user interface design against the requirements. You create a **test plan** (i.e., a list of procedures for testing the features of the program) for testing the application during the development phase. The test plan might include **automated tests,** which are programs that exercise portions of the code, and **manual tests,** which are conducted interactively by the programmer or a dedicated software tester. The design plan might also require a **code review,** which is a process in which another programmer (typically a more experienced one) looks at your code to make sure it seems to do what it needs to and meets any standards that have been defined.

As you code each procedure, you test to ensure that it works the way it should and you fix any bugs you find. If you create a Class module, you create a test project as well and test the Class module to make sure it works correctly. Testing each module as you go along is called **module testing** and is a critical part of any project that includes any custom classes, especially if those classes were developed by different programmers.

After the individual parts of the program have been tested, it is time to perform **integration testing,** which focuses on finding problems that are caused by the way classes and consumers interact. Perhaps a class doesn't behave quite the way a consumer expects it to. This problem would (hopefully) be uncovered during integration testing.

At all phases of testing, it is important to thoroughly document the problems you find and, if possible, the steps necessary to reproduce them. **Reproducing** a problem (i.e., making it happen predictably) is important to finding the cause and to **regressing** (i.e., verifying the problem has been solved) the bug. The final phase of testing is **regression testing,** during which all bugs that were reported during integration testing are tested again to make sure the problem has been resolved and that no unexpected side effects have been caused by the fix.

After regression testing is complete, the application is ready to be deployed. However, testing doesn't usually stop there. Even the best-tested application fails occasionally. Therefore, it is important to keep track of problems discovered after deployment so that they can be fixed in the next version. In many cases, this will be the job of technical support or help desk personnel.

FOR EXAMPLE

Integration and Regression Testing

Suppose you are a programmer on a development team responsible for updating your company's accounting program. The current program was written in Visual Basic 6.0 and stored accounting data in a Microsoft Access database. The new program is written using Visual Basic 2005, and it stores data in a SQL Server 2005 database.

The program will use an assembly named BusinessRules that will also be used by the company's payroll program, which is currently under development by another team. The assembly should be installed as a shared assembly. You have been developing the reporting functionality of the application by using a stub of the assembly. You submit your code for integration testing, and testers report that errors occur when calling methods on some of the classes in the BusinessRules assembly.

The developer of the BusinessRules assembly says the assembly worked fine during module testing and that the other application is not having a problem with it.

You ask the testers to tell you the exact steps necessary to reproduce the problem. You install the version of the BusinessRules component being used for integration testing and reproduce the problem in the debugger. You find that the problem occurs only when negative numbers are passed to the methods. You report your findings to the developer, who makes the changes and provides you with a new version of the BusinessRules component. You regress the bug with the new version by attempting to call the methods using negative numbers. It works fine. You also try some numbers in other ranges to verify that the fix did not introduce any side effects. During the next integration test, the software testers should also regress the bug.

11.3.2 Conditional Compilation

There might be some code you want to run when debugging a project but that you do not want run in a production environment (and vice versa). For example, you might need to disable error handling during testing and enable it only when you compile a production version. To do so, you can use **conditional compilation,** which uses a special conditional statement to determine which code to compile. To use conditional compilation, you define a conditional compilation constant by using this syntax:

```
#Const constantName = value
```

Next, you use #If, #Else, and #End If statements to test the value and execute code accordingly. For example, suppose you want to display the actual error while testing but display a custom error when the application is deployed to a production environment. To accomplish this, you declare a conditional compilation constant as follows:

```
#Const testing = True
```

Then, in the exception handler, you use this code:

```
Catch ex As Exception
#If testing Then
    MessageBox.Show(ex.Message)
#Else
    MessageBox.Show _
        ("An error occurred calculating the total.")
#End If
```

11.3.3 Setting Project Properties

You have already seen how to configure the settings properties to enable application and user settings that can be managed through configuration files. Now we'll look at a few more properties you should set before deploying a project. To set properties for a project, you right-click the project and choose Properties.

The Application page of the project's properties is shown in Figure 11-3. Some settings on the Application page, such as the application type and the startup form, should be set appropriately already. However, you need to ensure that the assembly name property is set to the name of the executable (without the .exe extension). If you are creating a class library, you also need to verify the name of the root namespace. You usually want to associate the application with an icon other than the default icon. To do so, you choose Browse from the drop-down list and locate the icon file you would like to use. (An icon file is a special type of graphic that has the .ico extension.) Programs are available for creating custom icons, but their use is beyond the scope of this chapter.

You click Assembly Information to enter detailed information about the assembly (see Figure 11-4). This information is included in the **assembly manifest,** which stores **assembly metadata** (i.e., data about the assembly's identity,

Figure 11-3

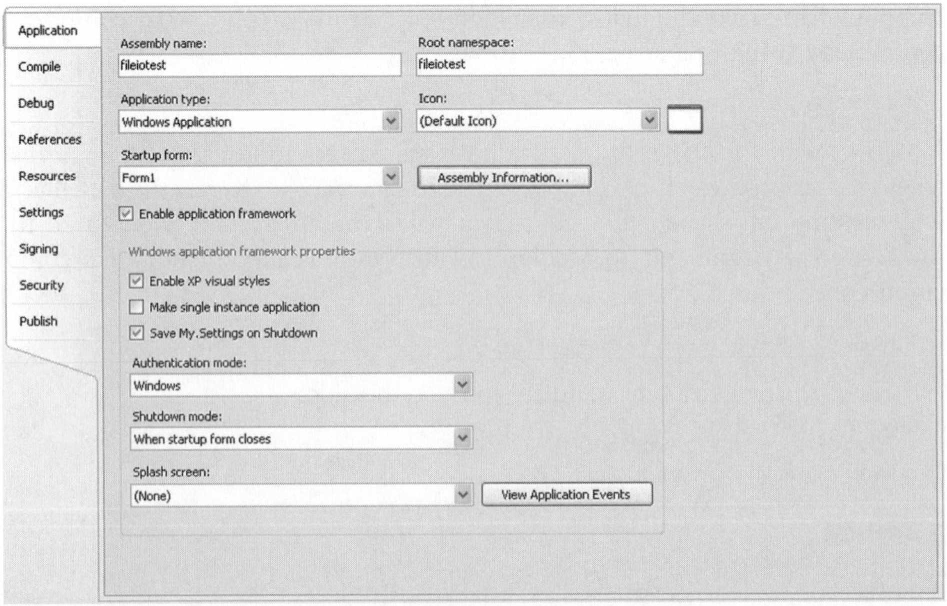

The Application page.

Figure 11-4

The Assembly Information dialog box.

the classes it references, and the files it includes). Notice that you can set informational properties, such as a description of the assembly, the company name, and copyright and trademark information. You can also specify properties that identify the assembly. These are the assembly's name, version, GUID, and neutral language.

The compile properties allow you to specify the output path for the compiled project. You can also configure other properties, but you should modify most of them before final testing, not right before deployment, because they can affect the way the program operates. The Advanced Compiler Settings dialog box (see Figure 11-5) allows you to set optimization features and compile for a specific platform. (These options are beyond the scope of this text.) You can also manage conditional compilation constants here (instead of declaring them with #Const in the code) and enable or disable the TRACE and DEBUG conditional compilation constants.

The References page of the project's properties allows you to view and manage the references currently set for the project, as shown in Figure 11-6. You click Unused References to generate a list of classes that are referenced but not used in the code. You can select to have those references removed so that they will not be treated as dependencies when you build the setup program.

Figure 11-5

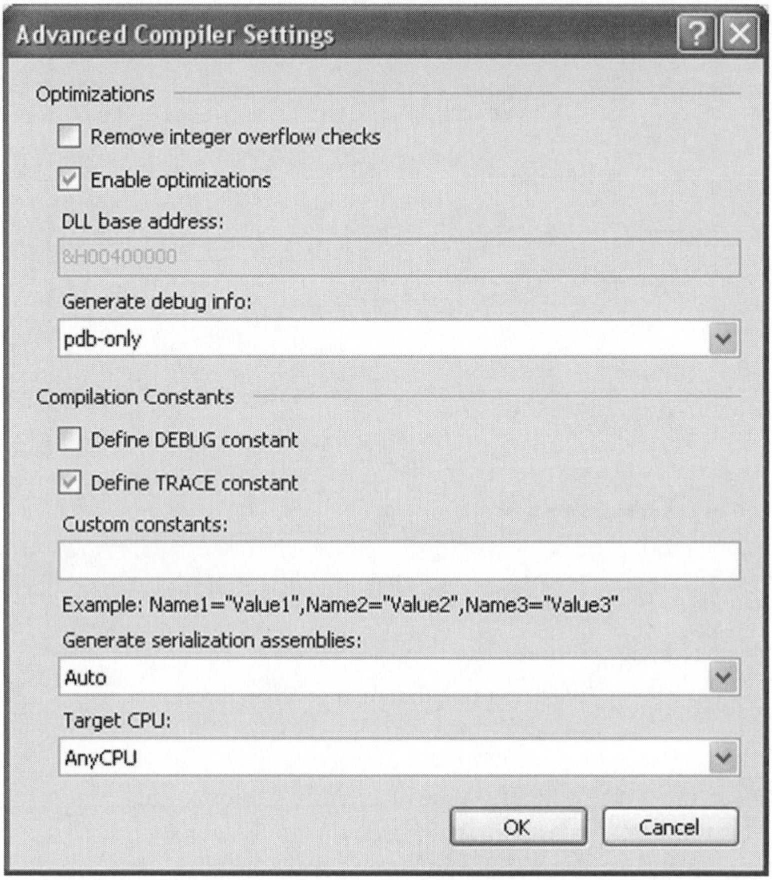

Advanced Compiler Settings dialog box.

The Signing page of the project's properties (see Figure 11-7) allows you to sign the assembly with a key pair, thus creating a strong-named assembly. You can select a key file that was issued by a certificate provider, create a key file (which is not as secure as obtaining one from a third-party certificate provider), or select to delay sign the assembly. When you **delay sign** the assembly, you associate only the public key with the assembly. The assembly is signed with the private key at a later time by an individual who is authorized to access the private key. This option is often used in companies that have dedicated personnel who have access to private keys. You cannot run a delay-signed assembly until it has been signed with the private key.

The other properties on the Signing page and the properties on the Security and Publish pages are used to configure ClickOnce deployment and are not discussed here.

Figure 11-6

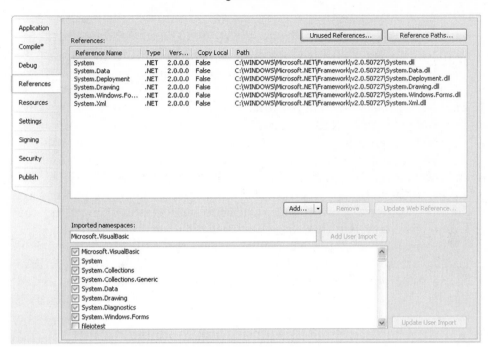

References page.

Figure 11-7

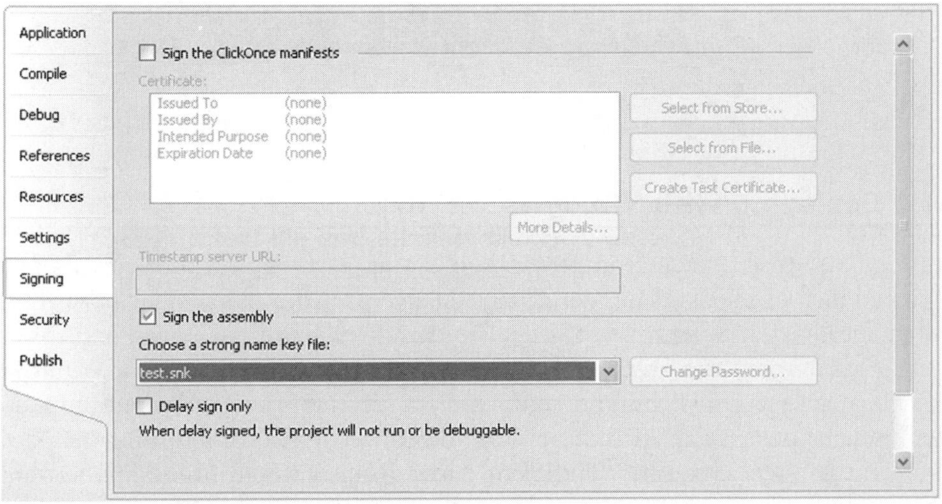

Signing page.

FOR EXAMPLE

Setting Project Properties

Suppose you are a programmer on a development team responsible for updating your company's accounting program. The current program was written in Visual Basic 6.0 and stored accounting data in a Microsoft Access database. The new program is written using Visual Basic 2005, and it stores data in a SQL Server 2005 database.

The program will use an assembly named BusinessRules that will also be used by the company's payroll program, which is currently under development by another team. The assembly should be installed as a shared assembly.

Before building the setup program for the application, you should set the icon to a custom icon and set assembly information properties. You should also verify that there are no unused references.

Before building the BusinessRules component, the developer should identify the key file to sign the assembly. If the developer does not have access to the private key, then the assembly should be signed using delayed signing.

SELF-CHECK

- What type of testing is primarily concerned with making sure reported problems have been fixed?
- What statement is used to prevent a block of code from being compiled when the Debug constant is set to True?
- Where do you configure an assembly's version number?

11.4 Deploying with Windows Installer

It's very easy to create a setup program for an application and then distribute it to a number of clients. The Windows Installer provides a lot of help, such as automatically adding entries to the Registry, installing additional fonts, and so on.

To learn about the process of deploying an application through a Windows Installer package, you'll build a setup project for the EasyDeployment application, which uses ADO.NET to access the database and expects to find the database on the target computer. The connection string is stored to the application's configuration file so that administrators can change it after installing the application to the client computers.

Figure 11-8

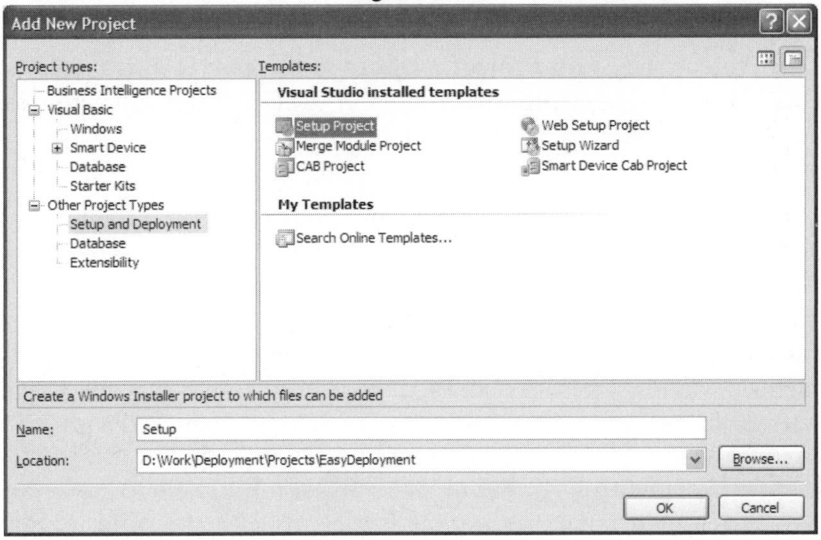

Selecting a setup project type.

11.4.1 Creating a Windows Installer Package

Visual Studio includes a special project type for creating a Windows Installer package: Setup Project. To add a setup project to a solution, you open the File menu and select Add and then New Project. The New Project dialog box appears. When you click the Setup and Deployment item in the Project Types box, you see the supported setup and deployment projects available with Visual Studio, as shown in Figure 11-8.

The following setup project types are supported:

▲ **Setup Project:** The **Setup Project** project type creates a Windows Installer package (i.e., an MSI package) and a bootstrap application that installs the application. Applications installed through setup projects are installed by default in the target computer's Program Files folder and can later be removed through the Add or Remove Programs snap-in. This is the type of setup project explores in this section.

▲ **Web Setup Project:** Similarly to the Setup Project type, the **Web Setup Project** project type creates a Windows Installer package, but it installs a web application to the web server's virtual directory.

▲ **Merge Module Project:** The **Merge Module Project** project type creates Merge modules, which contain the files that make up a specific component. Merge modules are usually later included in a setup project. The Microsoft Data Access (MDAC) component, for example, is usually packaged as a Merge module so that it can be included in the setup project of any application that depends on MDAC.

▲ **Cab Project:** The **Cab Project** project types create CAB (cabinet) files. **CAB files** might contain any number of files, and they're compressed to reduce the amount of data to be downloaded to the client. CAB files are often used to package components, and users can select to install individual components on the target machine.

▲ **Setup Wizard:** This wizard takes you through the steps of creating a setup project of the preceding four types.

▲ **Smart Device Cab Project: Smart Device Cab Project** is a wizard that takes you through the steps of creating a setup program for smart devices such as Windows mobile phones. This option is only available if you selected to install smart device support when you installed Visual Studio.

You select the Setup Project template and type the name of the project. In this case, you should name the project EasySetup. Visual Studio examines the application's project and detects any dependent components. It then adds the Detected Dependencies folder to the project, as shown in Figure 11-9.

On the designer's surface of the setup project, you see a simplified view of the target computer's file system. Basically, a setup program modifies the target computer's file system by installing files and other items (shortcuts). When

Figure 11-9

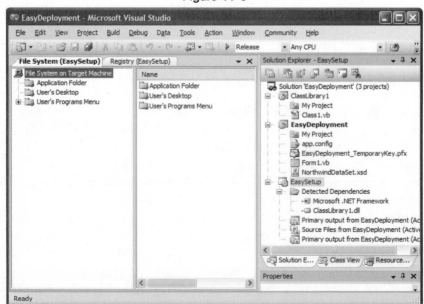

The Detected Dependencies folder.

you design the setup program, you specify how it will affect the target computer's file system, which is what you do on the design surface with visual tools: You specify which files will be copied where, which components will be registered, how to create shortcuts on the desktop, and so on. To view all the items of the target computer that you can affect from within your setup project, you right-click the setup project's name in the Solution Explorer and select View from the context menu. You then see a submenu with the following items:

▲ **File System:** This is your view of the target computer's file system. You can add items under most folders of the target computer's file system.

▲ **Registry:** This is a simple tool that allows you to add keys to the target computer's Registry during the installation. The same keys can then be read later by the application's code.

▲ **File Types:** This is a simple tool that allows you to establish associations between your application and files with a specific extension. You should not take over common associations, and certainly not without prompting the user first.

▲ **User Interface:** This tool allows you to specify the interface of the setup program by adding custom dialog boxes to perform actions that are specific to your application's setup program. To customize the setup program's interface, you can add one or more of a number of predefined dialog boxes.

▲ **Custom Actions:** This tool is intended for advanced setup projects, and it allows you to perform custom actions, depending on whether one of the following events is fired: Install, Commit, Rollback, and Uninstall. The custom actions are usually performed by separate executable files, which are invoked automatically if the corresponding event is fired. A server application's setup program, for example, might automatically start an executable to create a new database upon successful completion of the application setup.

▲ **Launch Conditions:** This tool allows you to define the **launch conditions** (i.e., the conditions that must be met at the target machine before the application is installed). For example, you can specify that the application be installed only if the target machine runs under Windows 2000 or require a specific component. You can provide a URL for installing the component if it is not already installed. One use of the launch condition is to ensure that the .NET Framework is installed. You can also search the target machine for a file or Registry key. This is useful, for example, if you need to determine whether a previous version is installed or whether the hardware can support the application.

11.4.2 Using the File System Editor

The most important editor is the File System Editor, which allows you to specify what will be installed on the target machine and where each item will be installed. At the very least, you must specify the project items that will be copied to the target computer. Certainly, you must copy the application's executable files (EXEs and DLLs). These files constitute the project's output. You right-click the setup project and from the context menu select Add. You see another menu with the following items, which represent the items you can add to the setup project:

▲ **Project Output:** This option is for the **project output:** the EXE and DLL generated by the compiler.

▲ **File:** This option leads to the Open dialog box, in which you can access any file to add to the setup program.

▲ **Merge Module:** You use this option to select a Merge module on the local machine and include it in the setup program.

▲ **Assembly:** You use this option to select one of the assemblies installed on the development machine and include it to the setup project.

At a very minimum, you need to add the project's output. To do so, you right-click the Application Folder item under the File System on Target Machine branch, and from the shortcut menu, you select Add and then Project Output. A new dialog box appears, as shown in Figure 11-10, in which you can select the project whose output you want to include in the setup program. The ComboBox control at the top of the Add Project Output Group dialog box contains the names of all projects in the solution (except for the setup project, of course). You select the desired project on the ComboBox control. The outputs of the selected project are displayed on a ListBox control, and you can select the desired output (which is Primary Output). The Configuration

Figure 11-10

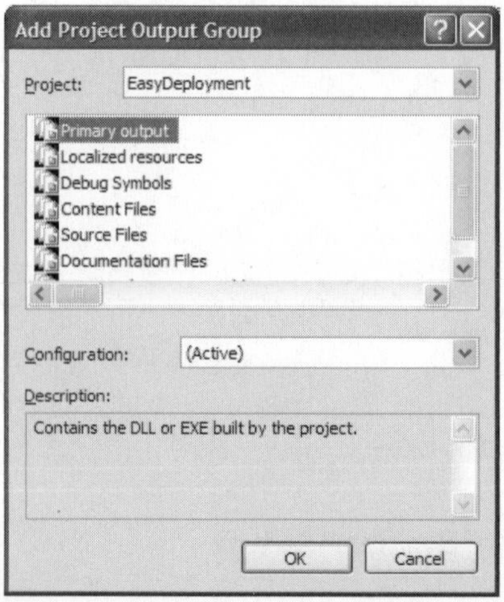

The Add Project Output Group dialog box.

ComboBox control at the bottom lets you select the project's configuration, whether it's the Debug or Release configuration of the project. The default selection is (Active), which is the configuration of the project when you built it for the last time.

The item Primary Output from EasySetup (Active) is added under the setup project in the Solution Explorer's window. Two dependencies are also picked up: the Framework redistributable and ClassLibrary1.dll.

The project's dependencies are detected automatically for you. These files are added to the project's Detected Dependencies list. If you can be sure that certain dependencies already exist at the target computer, you can omit them by selecting the Exclude command from the appropriate item's context menu. If an application is deployed and a dependency is missing, the application might not run. More often than not, developers don't exclude any of the dependencies. This means that the MSI file will be larger than it needs to be, but the deployed application is more likely to always work.

The following are the other types of output you can select from a given project:

▲ **Primary Output:** This is the EXE and DLL files generated by the compiler for the selected project.

▲ **Localized Resources:** This is the DLL that contains resources specific to a locale. **Localized resources** are the resources required to support a different language.

▲ **Debug Symbols:** When a project is compiled in Debug mode, a file with debugging information is created (it's a file with the extension.pdb). This file is used when the application is executed in the context of a debugger.

▲ **Content Files:** This includes any content files for the project.

▲ **Source Files:** This is the project's source files (you usually don't distribute the application's source code).

▲ **Documentation Files:** This is the project's documentation files.

▲ **XML Serialization Assemblies:** These are the XML serialization assemblies for the current project. **XML serialization** is the conversion of an object to XML so that it can be transported to a different application and reconstructed from the XML. A discussion of XML serialization is beyond the scope of this text. You should not add them unless you have custom objects you want to serialize in XML format.

When you add Primary Output from EasyDeployment to the setup project, the DLL that implements the class library is added under the Detected Dependencies item of the Solution Explorer. If you don't want to include one of the selected dependencies (because you know that a component has already been installed on the destination computer), you can right-click its name in the Solution Explorer window and select Exclude from the shortcut menu. You can also select Refresh from the Detected Dependencies item's context menu to force the IDE to reevaluate the dependencies.

When you're ready to build the setup project and deploy your application to another computer, you can test the setup application right in the IDE by selecting the Install and Uninstall commands of the setup project's context menu. Actually, you should run the installation project at this point and print the various dialog boxes that appear during the installation project. Then you can use those printouts as you explore the properties of the setup project and understand better how to customize the appearance of the dialog boxes that appear during the setup.

If you build the entire solution, the process takes a while because the setup project must be built as well. However, you can build each of the projects separately. To see the compiler's output, you switch to the setup project's Bin folder, where you see three items:

▲ **Setup.exe:** This is the bootstrap program that installs the application.
▲ **EasySetup.msi:** This is the MSI file (a Windows Installer file) that contains all the data needed to install, fix, and remove the application from the target computer.
▲ **Setup.ini:** This is the application's INI file.

These three files must be distributed to every computer on which the application will be installed.

Users can install the application by running the Setup.exe program. The dialogs displayed during the installation process provide simple instructions. The first window welcomes the user to the application setup and waits for the user to click the Next button. The next window suggests the path of the folder in which the application will be installed. Users can accept the default location (which is a new folder under the user's Program Files folder) or click the Browse button to select another folder. The Next button in this window takes the user to the Confirm Installation window, in which the user must click Next to start the installation. The process of installation takes a variable amount of time, depending on the number of files that must be copied, the speed of the computer, and whether the installation is being performed from media on the local computer or across the network. When the application's installation completes, the user is informed about the completion of the installation and is prompted to close the wizard's last window. You will see later in this chapter how to customize the dialog boxes that appear during the application's setup.

If you start the Add or Remove Programs utility in the Control Panel, you see that your application has been installed on the target machine. Users can use this snap-in to repair the application or uninstall it. If you locate the application's entry in the Add or Remove Programs utility, you see two buttons: Change and Remove. The Change button enables users to repair the installation by writing the original files on top of the existing ones, and the Remove button removes the application from that target computer.

11.4.3 Setup Project Properties

Each setup project has a few basic properties, which you can set in the Property Browser if you select the name of the setup project in the Solution Explorer window. These properties identify the manufacturer of the application and determine some basic characteristics, such as whether the setup project should detect and remove an earlier version of the same application. Some key properties of the setup project are the following:

▲ **Author:** You set this property to the name of the company (or individual) that developed the application. Its default value is the same as the Manufacturer property's value.

▲ **Description:** You set this property to any helpful text that describes the application.

▲ **Manufacturer:** This is a string with the application's manufacturer name. MSI uses this setting to create the name of the default folder during installation, so you must set it to a value that users can easily associate with your application (not necessarily the application's name).

▲ **ManufacturerURL:** This is your company's URL, which is displayed as a hyperlink on the product's support page.

▲ **ProductName:** This is a name that identifies the application.

▲ **Support Phone:** This is the phone number of a telephone support department for the application.

▲ **SupportUrl:** This is the URL of the application's support web site.

▲ **Version:** This is the version number of the Windows Installer package.

These settings are also used to compose the Support Info dialog box. To see this window after installation, you start the Add or Remove Programs tool from the Control Panel, select the EasyDeployment entry, and click the Click Here for Support Information hyperlink.

There are two additional properties of the setup project area that are interesting and determine the behavior of the setup program to some extent:

▲ **DetectNewerInstalledVersion:** This property, which is True by default, tells the Windows Installer to detect any newer version of the same application that has already been installed and, if there is a newer version, to prevent the installation of the application.

▲ **RemovePreviousVersion:** You set this property to True if you want the setup program to remove an older version of the application (if one exists) and then install the newer version.

Figure 11-11

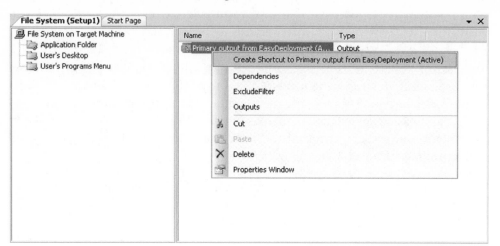

Creating a shortcut.

11.4.4 Creating Shortcuts

Most setup programs create a shortcut to the application on the user's desktop. You click the Application Folder item in the File System Editor and right-click the target file in the pane with this folder's contents (in this case, Primary Output from EasyDeployment). One of the commands of the context menu is the Create Shortcut to Primary Output from EasyDeployment. When you select this command (see Figure 11-11), a new shortcut is created. You should change the shortcut's name to Shortcut to EasyDeployment and then drag the shortcut and drop it on the User's Desktop item in the File System pane. The installation program creates a shortcut to the application's EXE file and places it on the user's desktop.

To associate an icon with a shortcut, as opposed to using the generic shortcut icon used by the operating system, you must add the icon file (i.e., a file with extension .ico) to the Application Folder item in the File System Editor and then set the Icon property of the shortcut to that file. The WorkingFolder property is the path to the application's **working folder** (i.e., the folder where the application is installed).

The User's Programs Menu item represents the user's Start | Programs menu, and you can add a new menu item for your application. You can place your application directly on the user's menu or create a subfolder with a descriptive name that contains the application. To do this, you right-click the User's Programs Menu item in the File System Editor and select Add Folder from the shortcut menu. A new folder is created under the selected item; you should rename it VB Tools. Then you right-click the new item, select Add from the context menu, and then select Project Output. In the Add Project Output Group dialog box that appears, you select Primary Output from EasyDeployment. When the application is installed, a new item is added under the User's Programs Menu item, and the application's EXE is added under this item. If you're installing multiple applications with the same setup program, you should place their EXE files in the same item of the User's Programs Menu item. This folder is usually named after the manufacturer of the applications.

You can manipulate the special folders on the user's file system from within your setup application. To do so, you right-click the item File System on Target Machine, and you see a list of special folders you can select from:

▲ Common Files Folder
▲ Fonts Folder
▲ Program Files Folder
▲ System Folder
▲ User's Application Data Folder
▲ User's Desktop
▲ User's Favorites Folder
▲ User's Personal Data Folder
▲ User's Programs Menu
▲ User's Send To Menu
▲ User's Start Menu
▲ User's Startup Folder
▲ User's Template Folder
▲ Windows Folder
▲ Global Assembly Cache Folder
▲ Custom Folder

You can add items to any of these locations. To install a font at the target computer, for example, you place the font in Fonts Folder on the target computer. Upon installation, the operating system on the client computer detects the presence of a new item in the Fonts folder, and it installs it automatically. If you have an application for encrypting files, for example, you can add it to the user's Send To menu. Every time the user opens a file's context menu by right-clicking its name, your application's name appears as a destination of the Send To command. An application that should be executed at startup must be placed in the user's Startup folder. Finally, you can create a folder specific to your application, by using Custom Folder, and place files in it.

11.4.5 File Types and Custom Commands

To associate an application with a specific file type, you switch to the File Types tab (by selecting View and then File Types from the setup project's context menu). On this tab, you see a single item: the File Types on Target Machine. You right-click this item and select Add File Type, and a new file type is added to the existing item.

After a file type has been created, you can modify its properties. To do so, you select it with the mouse and switch to the Properties window, in which you can set the name of the file type (e.g., the name Custom Data File Format) and one or more extensions, separated with commas (e.g., the .cff extension). The newly added file type is renamed Custom Data File Format (CFF). After the application is installed on a client computer, files with the .cff extension are opened with your application. When the user double-clicks such a file, for example, the EasyDeployment application starts. However, it doesn't perform any action because you haven't programmed any actions yet. Each file type has a few commands (i.e., verbs) associated with it.

When you right-click a text file, the first three commands in the context menu are Open, Print, and Edit. All three actions are performed on the specific file with the application associated with the text files on your computer. In most systems, the file is opened, printed, or edited with Notepad. To add actions to the new file type, you right-click the file type in the designer and select Add Action from the context menu. A new default action is added, and you can rename it, using a meaningful verb for the specific action. The first action is the default one—the action that is performed when the file is double-clicked. You can change the default action by right-clicking the action you want to be default and choosing Set As Default.

All other actions appear along with the default one in the file's context menu. To complete our example, you should add the following actions: &Open, &Print, and &Process. They are then listed as shown in Figure 11-12.

For each action, you must set three properties in the Properties window: the action's name, the action's verb, and the action's arguments. The action's name is what appears on the context menu, and the action's verb is a string that is passed to your application. The action's arguments are the values you want to pass to the application, and this property's setting is usually "%1" (including the quotation marks), which refers to the name of the selected file (i.e., the file on which the act will be performed).

Figure 11-12

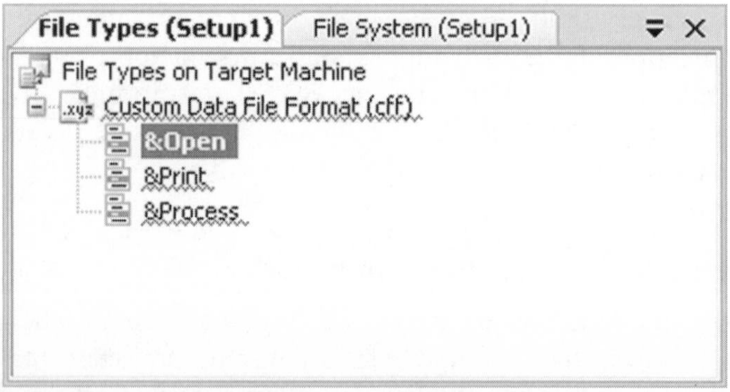

A file type with three actions.

You also pass to the application a switch value to indicate the desired operation. The Print command, for example, should pass to the application the following arguments (the first argument is the name of the command, followed by the file on which the application will act):

```
print "%1"
```

To use this feature, you must also add some code in the application's Load event handler, such as the statements shown in the following code segment:

```
If My.Application.CommandLineArgs.Count > 0 Then
    Dim switch As String = _
        My.Application.CommandLineArgs(0).ToString
    Dim file As String = _
        My.Application.CommandLineArgs(1).ToString
    Select Case switch
        Case "/open": MsgBox("Opening file " & file)
        Case "/print": MsgBox( _
            "Printing file " & file)
        Case "/process": MsgBox( _
            "Processing file " & file)
    End Select
    Application.Exit
End If
```

When the application starts and the main form is loaded, the code examines the number of arguments passed to the application. If the number of command-line arguments is zero, the program was invoked by the user, and it continues normally. If the application was called with command-line arguments, it means that it was invoked by Windows either because the user selected a command from a file's context menu or because the user dropped a file onto the application's shortcut. In either case, the code extracts the switch (i.e., a string prefixed by the/character that specifies the desired action) and the name of the file that initiated the application. Then it uses a Select Case statement to carry out the desired action and exits.

Another good place to insert any statements you want to execute before any other code in the application (even before the main form is loaded) is the application's Startup event handler. To view the Startup event handler, as well as all other application events, you open the project's Properties page and select the Application tab. Then you click View Application Events to see the Code window, in which you can select any of the MyApplication object's events.

11.4.6 Using the Registry Editor

A common operation for many installation programs is to add a few keys to the end user's Registry. You use the Registry Editor to add keys and values to the target computer's Registry. When you open the Registry Editor in the designer surface (by right-clicking the setup project's name in the Solution Explorer and selecting View and then Registry), you see the organization of the Registry, but you can only access the HKEY_CURRENT_USER and HKEY_LOCAL_MACHINE branches of the Registry. The HKEY_LOCAL_MACHINE\Software\[Manufacturer] key is created by default, but it hasn't been assigned a value yet. The [Manufacturer] key is replaced by the value of the Manufacturer property of the setup project when the setup application is executed at the target machine.

Adding new keys is straightforward: You right-click the desired branch in the left pane of the Registry window and select New Key from the context menu. The new key is named New Key #1, and you can change this name to anything. To set the key's value, you right-click the key's name and select the value type as String value, Environment String value, Binary value, or DWORD value.

11.4.7 Using the User Interface Editor

A setup program has a simple user interface, which consists of a number of dialog boxes that guide the user through the installation process. However, it's possible to add custom dialog boxes to the interface through the User Interface Editor.

To view the User Interface Editor, you switch to the Solution Explorer window and select View and then User Interface from the setup project's context menu. The designer's surface is like the one shown in Figure 11-11. Figure 11-13 shows the icons that represent the dialog boxes that make up the interface of the default setup program, in the order in which they appear. Each dialog box has a few

Figure 11-13

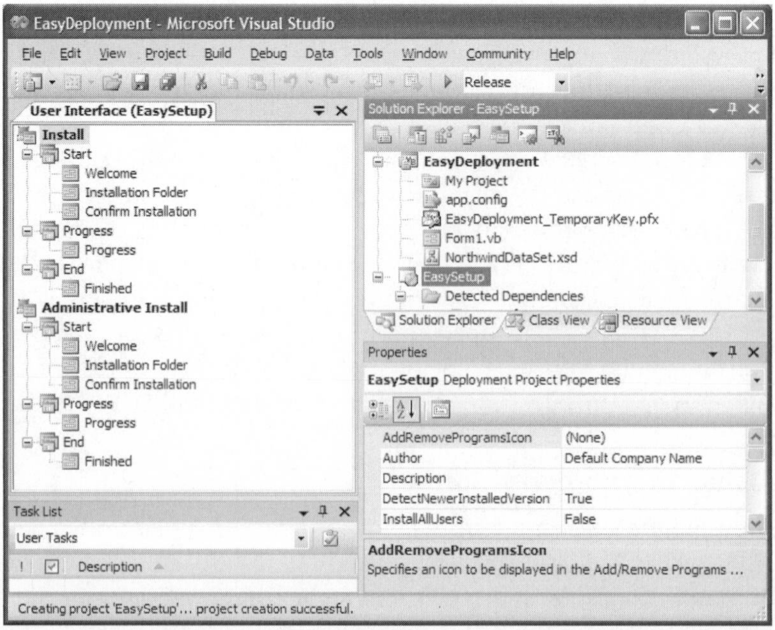

Dialog boxes.

properties, which you can use to customize the dialog box's appearance. To set the properties of a dialog box, select its icon in the right-hand pane.

To customize the setup program's interface, you set the properties of the dialog boxes. You select each dialog box in the left pane and look up its properties. Most dialog boxes have very few properties, such as a bitmap that will be displayed and a copyright warning.

To add a custom dialog box to the user interface, you right-click one of the steps in the installation process (i.e., Start, Progress, End) and select Add Dialog from the context menu. The Add Dialog dialog box contains the additional dialog boxes available for you to add. Most of them are made up of a small number of radio buttons, check boxes, and text boxes. Unfortunately, you can't edit these dialog boxes visually; you can't even view them at design time. You can set their properties and view them only while the application is being actually installed.

Some of the custom dialog boxes are quite simple. The License Agreement dialog box, for example, displays the application's license agreement (which is a text file) and the usual I Agree and I Don't Agree radio buttons. If the user doesn't select the Agree radio button, the installation process is aborted.

To see how custom dialog boxes work, you can add one to your sample setup application. You should add a dialog box that has two radio buttons and prompts the user to specify whether the project's source files should be installed. To do so, you right-click a step and select Add Dialog. Next you select the dialog box with two radio buttons and then set the new dialog box's properties as shown in Table 11-1.

The names of the properties are self-descriptive. The ButtonProperty property is basically a variable name that is set to the value of the selected radio button. This value can be used by another part of the setup program to control an action. In this case, you should use the input provided on the custom dialog box to determine whether the source files are installed. Figure 11-14

Table 11-1: Property Settings

Property	Setting
BannerText	Installation Options
BodyText	Install Source Files?
Button1Label	Include Source Files?
Button1Value	1
Button2Label	Skip Source Files
Button2Value	2
ButtonProperty	SOURCEFILES
DefaultValue	1

Figure 11-14

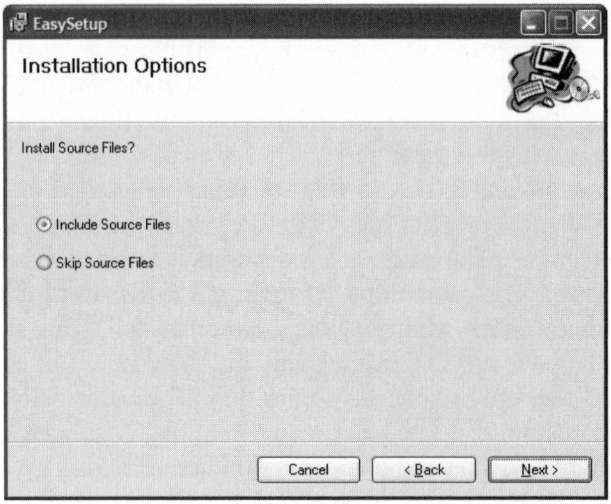

Creating a custom dialog box.

shows what the custom dialog box looks like during the application's installation.

You can switch to the File System Editor and add the application's source files to the setup project's output. From the Application Folder item's context menu, you select Add and then Project Output, and when the Add Project Output Group dialog box appears, you select the Source Files item for the EasyDeployment application. This action causes the source files to be included in the package and a new item to be added to the Application folder of the target machine.

To install the source files conditionally, based on the user's selection on the custom dialog box, you open the Property Browser of the item that represents the source files and locate the Condition property. This property determines the condition that must be met for the selected component to be installed. You set the Condition property of the source files as follows:

```
SOURCEFILES = 1
```

If the user checks the Include Source Files radio button on the custom form, the application's source files are copied by the installation program to the target computer's application folder. If the custom dialog box contains check boxes, you must take into consideration that users might check multiple check boxes. Each check box has a CheckBoxValue property, whose value is either Checked or Unchecked. The Condition property in this case should be set to a logical expression, like this:

```
CheckBox1Value = Checked And CheckBox2Value = _
    Unchecked
```

You should experiment a little with the custom dialog boxes to get exactly what you want. You can look up the default appearance of each custom dialog box in the documentation and then adjust the dialog boxes by using their properties. The custom actions you can take based on the user's choice(s) on these custom dialog boxes are quite limited. Some of the dialog boxes allow you to start a custom application. The Register User dialog box, for example, has an Executable property that you can set to the name of an EXE file. When the user agrees to register the application, the executable is invoked automatically. The Register User dialog box also exposes a property named Arguments, which you can set to a string with arguments to be passed to the executable that handles the user registration.

FOR EXAMPLE

Building a Windows Installer Setup Program

Suppose you are a programmer on a development team responsible for updating your company's accounting program. The current program was written in Visual Basic 6.0 and stored accounting data in a Microsoft Access database. The new program is written using Visual Basic 2005, and it stores data in a SQL Server 2005 database.

The program will use an assembly named BusinessRules that will also be used by the company's payroll program, which is currently under development by another team. The assembly should be installed as a shared assembly. You have been developing the reporting functionality of the application by using a stub of the assembly. You submit your code for integration testing, and testers report that errors occur when calling methods on some of the classes in the BusinessRules assembly.

You identify the following dependencies:

▲ .NET Framework 2.0 (which includes System.Data.SqlClient)
▲ A shared assembly
▲ A custom control
▲ The logo file
▲ The font used to print reports

You identify the following additional files that need to be installed:

▲ A tutorial
▲ Help files

(Continued)

The BusinessRules assembly and the custom control have already been packaged as Merge modules.

You add a setup project to the solution. You add Project Output and both Merge modules. You also configure the custom font to be added to the Fonts folder on the user's computer and the logo file and help files to be added to the application directory.

You verify that the .NET Framework is a launch condition. You also add a Search Target machine condition to check the Registry to determine whether the existing version is installed.

You configure setup to create a shortcut in the user's Programs menu and on the desktop. You add a custom dialog box to allow users to select whether to install the tutorial and create a shortcut to it in the user's Programs menu. You set the Condition property of the tutorial file.

SELF-CHECK

- When creating a Windows Installer project, which menu option allows you to add help files to a subdirectory of your application directory?
- When you add Primary Output for a Windows Application to a folder, what are you adding?
- You configure the SupportUrl property. Where will this URL appear?
- When creating a Windows Installer project, what menu option allows you to add menu items to the Start menu?
- You associate files that have the .abc extension with your application and add the actions &Open, &Edit, and &Print. What action will occur when the user double-clicks a file with the .abc extension?
- What property of a file do you set to cause it to be installed only if the user selects to install it?

SUMMARY

In this chapter, you've learned about deployment. You've learned how to plan a deployment, including identifying dependencies and choosing a type of deployment. You've also learned how to prepare an application for deployment and how to create a Windows Installer setup program.

KEY TERMS

Assembly

Assembly manifest

Assembly metadata

Automated test

BAT files

Bootstrap application

Build

CAB file

Cab Project

ClickOnce deployment

Code access security

Code review

Conditional compilation

Corporate intranet

Delay sign

Deployment

Deployment mechanism

Development environment

Digital signature

Extensible Markup Language (XML)

Full trust

Global Assembly Cache (GAC)

Globally unique identifier (GUID)

Hash value

Installation

Integration testing

Launch condition

Localized resources

Manual test

Merge Module Project

Module testing

MSI file

Private assembly

Private key

Production environment

Project output

Public key

Public Key Infrastructure (PKI)
  certificate

Registry

Regressing

Regression testing

Reproducing

Schema

Setup

Setup Project

Self-updating

Shared assembly

Smart Device Cab Project

Spoofing an assembly

Strong-named assembly

Test plan

Version number

Versioning

Web Setup Project

Windows Installer (WI)

Working folder

XCopy deployment

XML serialization

ASSESS YOUR UNDERSTANDING

Go to www.wiley.com/college/petroutsos to evaluate your knowledge of deployment concepts and techniques.

Measure your learning by comparing pre-test and post-test results.

Summary Questions

1. You are creating an update for an application. At minimum, what change should you make to the project properties?

    (a) Increment the version number.

    (b) Change the name of the assembly.

    (c) Sign the assembly with a different key file.

    (d) Remove unused references.

2. Your company has purchased a code-signing certificate from a third-party certificate authority. Only members of the information security department have access to the certificate's private key. You are building a component that will be installed in the GAC. What should you do?

    (a) Sign the assembly with a new key.

    (b) Deploy the assembly unsigned.

    (c) Delay sign the assembly.

    (d) Install the assembly as a private assembly.

3. What must you do before you can install an application via XCopy deployment?

    (a) Install the .NET Framework.

    (b) Sign the assembly.

    (c) Add a folder to the GAC.

    (d) Grant the application full trust.

4. A ClickOnce deployment can add shortcuts to the Start menu. True or False?

5. A Windows Installer deployment uses a bootstrap application and an MSI file. True or False?

6. You define a user-specific setting by using the Settings page of a project's properties. What information is added to the app.config file?

    (a) name

    (b) name and data type

    (c) name, data type, and default value

    (d) name and default value

7. How can you ensure that unnecessary dependencies are not added to a Windows setup project?

   (a) On the References page of project properties for the application, click Unused References.

   (b) Right-click the Detected Dependencies node of the setup project and choose Remove Unused.

   (c) Display Class View for the project, right-click References, and choose Remove Unused.

   (d) On the References page of the project's properties for the setup project, click Unused References.

8. Which phase of testing is most likely to reveal incompatibilities between a class and a consumer?

   (a) code review

   (b) integration testing

   (c) module testing

   (d) regression testing

9. You have defined a user setting named UserName and set it to default to Anonymous. You want to use the setting to personalize the user interface. You can set and retrieve the value through My.Settings.UserName. True or false?

10. You are using the BetaBuild conditional compilation constant to cause different error handling code to be executed. How can you define the setting value for the BetaBuild constant?

    (a) Change the value in the applicationSettings section of the app.config file.

    (b) Change the value in the userSettings section of the app.config file.

    (c) On the Compile page of project's properties, click Advanced Compile Options.

    (d) Define it as an application setting on the Settings page of the project's properties.

11. You are preparing to deploy a class library that will be used by a number of different applications. Those applications will need to be able to install the class library. What should you use to package the class library assembly for deployment?

    (a) CAB file

    (b) Merge module

    (c) MSI package

    (d) Smart Device Cab Project file

12. You are building a Windows Installer setup program for an application. You need to ensure that a specific version of the .NET Framework is

installed on each target computer before installing the application. How should you configure this requirement?

(a) Define a custom action.

(b) Add a dialog box to prompt the user to choose whether to install the .NET Framework

(c) Add a launch condition.

(d) Add the .NET Framework to the file system as a private assembly.

13. You need to allow a user to choose between three installation configurations. Each configuration installs different support files. What should you do?

(a) Add a setup project to the solution. Use the User Interface Editor to create a dialog box. Set the Condition property of each file to a value that corresponds to the configuration that installs it.

(b) Configure the project's properties to support a ClickOnce installation. List the files as dependent files and associate each with a hyperlink.

(c) Add three different Merge modules: one for each configuration. Use the User Interface Editor to create a dialog box. Set the Condition property of each Merge module to a value that corresponds to the configuration that installs it.

(d) Create three different CAB files. Use the Setup Wizard to build a dialog that allows users to choose a CAB file.

Applying This Chapter

1. You are writing a small application that uses two class library assemblies. The application is built specifically for that version of the assemblies, and you want to ensure that other applications do not replace that version with a newer version. The application will be deployed to a kiosk at the company. Users will log on at the computer and should be able to set background and foreground color preferences for the user interface. The assembly should have a custom icon, and a shortcut to the application should be created on the desktop.

(a) Discuss why XCopy deployment is best suited to the application.

(b) What task (if any) will need to be performed manually before deployment?

(c) What task (if any) will need to be performed manually after deployment?

(d) Where should you install the class library assemblies?

(e) How will you implement the requirement for user preferences?

(f) How will you implement the requirement for the custom icon?

2. You are designing the testing and deployment for an application that will be deployed to 100 users on your company's network. The application

includes business rules that are likely to change quarterly. The business rules are implemented in a Class module that is developed by another programmer. The business rules class contains company-critical formulas. Upper management is worried that a malicious person might try to replace the assembly with one that uses different calculations. The application also uses three custom components that are used to generate and print various report formats. Those components are being developed by other programmers.

(a) What type of deployment is most appropriate? Explain why.

(b) Describe how the three testing phases—module testing, integration testing, and regression testing—should be performed.

(c) What steps can you take to alleviate upper management's concerns about the business rules component?

(d) The company has decided that all assemblies should be strong named. Compare creating a new key to sign assemblies with delay signing of assemblies. Which is more secure and why?

3. You are planning the deployment for a game that will be sold in stores and distributed on DVD. You are also planning to send out trial versions that will be feature limited: Players will be able to use only one of three default characters. They will also not be able to progress beyond a certain level. In the full version, users can create characters. A user's characters should be available only when that user is logged on. The full version of the game will include expansion tile sets and sound effects. Users must be able to select whether to install the expansions. They must also be able to install or uninstall them at a later time.

(a) Choose the type of deployment best suited to the requirements of this application and explain why it is the best option.

(b) How should you implement the feature-restricted trial version?

(c) Describe how you can allow users to select to install expansion tiles and sound effects.

(d) How can you limit character availability to only the user who creates the character?

(e) What should you do to ensure that the .NET Framework is installed and that the video adapter is configured for at least the minimum resolution?

(f) You want to add a shortcut with a custom icon to the desktop. Describe the two properties you must set and identify any additional steps you must take.

(g) How can you provide users a link to your web site for technical support problems and bug fixes?

YOU TRY IT

Planning Deployment to the General Public

You are creating a Visual Basic 2005 application that will be used to design a garden layout. The application will be sold in home improvement stores, nurseries, and over the Internet. The application includes templates for flower gardens, vegetable gardens, and herb gardens. Users can select which templates to install during installation. They must also be able to add and remove them later.

The application includes a class library that gives planting information and another that provides companion planting suggestions for insect control. These class libraries access up-to-date information from a SQL Server database at the company. These class libraries will be updated annually and updates will be made available through the web site. The planting information library includes calculations that must be reviewed by a horticulturist before the application can be distributed.

The company is concerned about potential liability or an attack on the database if someone spoofed the planting information or insect control assemblies.

Users need to be able to launch the application from the Start menu or by double-clicking a garden plan file.

A user needs to enter his or her zip code after launching the application for the first time. The user's planting zone will be calculated and must be stored for later reference by any user who launches the application on that computer.

A trial version of the program will be available as a promotion for nurseries to carry the full version. The trial version, which expires after 30 days, does not provide planting and care instructions. You need to ensure that users cannot reinstall the trial version to reset the clock.

1. Plan how the application should be tested to meet requirements.
2. Plan how the application should be distributed. Your plan should include the deployment method and a discussion of why other methods will not work, any dependencies and how they will be deployed, and details about how your plan meets each requirement.
3. How should you prepare the application for distribution? Support your preparations by identifying how they are necessary to meet the requirements.

12

BUILDING WEB APPLICATIONS

Starting Point

Go to www.wiley.com/college/reese to assess your knowledge of web application development using HTML and ASP.NET.
Determine where you need to concentrate your effort.

What You'll Learn in This Chapter

▲ How web applications work
▲ HTML document structure
▲ Text-formatting tags
▲ Images and hyperlinks
▲ Tables
▲ HTML forms
▲ ASP.NET fundamentals
▲ State management

After Studying This Chapter, You'll Be Able To

▲ Create a webpage, using HTML
▲ Create a simple web application, using ASP.NET

INTRODUCTION

If there is one technology that caught on overnight and has affected more computer users than any other, it is the World Wide Web. The Web is the set of all public **web sites** (i.e., locations on the Internet that supply documents or applications you can access using a browser) and the documents they provide to their clients. The computers that host web site are called **web servers;** their service is to provide the documents to the clients who request them. **Clients** are the millions of personal computers connected to the Internet. To exploit the Web, all you need is a **browser,** such as Internet Explorer, that can request documents and render them on your computer.

This chapter is a compendium of information on how to apply your knowledge of programming to the Web—or, to use a popular phrase, how to leverage your knowledge of Visual Basic by applying it to the Web. To do so, you need a basic understanding of **Hypertext Markup Language (HTML),** the language used to build web documents, and a good understanding of how clients interact with the servers on the Internet. We'll start by looking at how a web application works. Next, we'll move on to discuss HTML fundamentals. The chapter concludes with a look at how to build a simple ASP.NET application.

12.1 Web Application Fundamentals

Understanding how a web application operates is key to successfully learning how to program one. There are fundamental differences between a web application and a Windows application. Having some knowledge of the underlying technology that makes a web application work can help you understand what you need to do to make a web application work correctly and to locate and correct bugs when they arise.

12.1.1 Understanding Internet Communication

The **Internet** is a global, distributed network of computers that use a common **protocol** (i.e., software that manages communication between two computers or two applications) to communicate: **Transmission Control Protocol/Internet Protocol (TCP/IP).** TCP/IP is based on standards because it has to be implemented consistently on all computers and operating systems. Indeed, TCP/IP is a truly universal protocol, but you needn't know much about it. It's there when you need it and allows your computer to connect to any other computer on the Internet.

TCP/IP is really a suite of protocols. TCP and IP allow computers to communicate at the network level. However, other protocols work on top of TCP and IP, including protocols that allow applications to communicate. One of these is **Hypertext Transfer Protocol (HTTP),** the protocol used by web applications. HTTP is optimized for requesting and supplying HTML documents.

12.1.2 Web Sites and Webpages

HTML is the language you use to prepare documents for online publication. **HTML documents** are also called **webpages;** a page is what you see in your browser at any time. Each web site, whether on the Internet or on an intranet, is composed of multiple related pages on a particular server, and you can switch among pages by following hyperlinks. A **hyperlink** is text that is associated with the address of a document or file on a web server. It is often displayed as blue, underlined text or distinguished from standard text in some other manner.

A webpage is basically a text file that contains the text to be displayed, some special commands that determine how the text will be rendered at the client, and references to other elements, such as images, sounds, and, of course, other documents. You can create HTML pages with a text editor such as Notepad, with a **"what you see is what you get" (WYSIWYG)** application such as Visual Studio, or with any number of web design tools. The result is always a plain-text file that computers can easily exchange. The browser displays this text file on the client computer by interpreting the rendering instructions and presenting the rest as content.

Webpages are stored on computers that act as servers: They provide pages to any computer that requests them. Each server computer has an address, or **uniform resource locator (URL),** that looks something like the following:

```
http://www.example.com
```

The first portion of the URL (in this example, http) is the protocol used in accessing the server, and the next part (in this case, www.example.com) is the name of the server on the Internet. All computers that use TCP/IP have a unique, four-octet numeric address, such as 193.22.103.18, known as the **Internet Protocol (IP) address.** You can navigate to a web server by using its IP address, but numeric IP addresses are difficult for humans to remember than names. Therefore, computers known as **Domain Name System (DNS)** servers look up the names in tables and translate them into IP addresses.

When a browser requests a specific document, it uses a URL that includes the filename of the document. It might also include the path to the document along with a set of parameters known as a **query string.** The following URL shows the request for the webpage named showMe.htm on www.example.com:

```
http://www.example.com/showMe.htm
```

If a document is not included, the web server responds by sending the web site's default document. On some web servers, the default document is named index.htm. On **Internet Information Server (IIS),** the document is named either default.htm or default.aspx. To pass a query string, you use a ? and one or more attribute/value pairs, as in the following example:

```
http://www.example.com/showMe.htm?country=USA
```

The computer that handles requests for a webpage must run a web server that acknowledges requests made by other computers—the client computers— and supplies the requested documents to the client's browser. IIS is the web server that comes with Windows.

12.1.3 About HTML

HTML is made up of text-formatting **tags** that are placed in a pair of angle brackets. The first, or opening, tag turns on a formatting feature, and the matching closing tag turns it off. To format a few words in bold, for example, you enclose them with the <b> and </b> tags, as shown here:

```
Some <b>words</b> in the sentence are formatted in
<b>bold</b>.
```

Of course, not all tags are as simple as this. The <table> tag, for example, which is used to format tables, requires additional tags, such as the <tr> tag, which delimits a new row in the table, and the <td> tag, which delimits a new cell in a row.

Tags often contain attributes, which are keywords with special meaning within a specific tag. The **anchor tag** (<a>), which is used to insert a hyperlink in the document, recognizes the href attribute, which provides the URL of the document. A hyperlink to the Microsoft home page on the Web would look something like this:

```
This <a href="http://www.microsoft.com">link</a>
leads to Microsoft's home page.
```

The text between the <a> and </a> tags is marked as a hyperlink (displayed in a different color and underlined). The href attribute in the <a> tag tells the browser which URL, or address, to jump to when a user clicks this hyperlink.

In addition to the formatting commands, HTML can handle a few controls, known as **HTML controls.** These controls include text boxes, radio buttons, check boxes, buttons (specifically, Submit and Reset buttons), and a few more simple controls. These are the controls you see on the various pages that prompt you for data such as names, addresses, credit card numbers, and so on. The user can enter data or make selections on these controls and submit them to the server by clicking the Submit button. The Submit button can have any caption, but its function is to submit to the server the data on the various controls on the page by appending them to the server's URL. Sometimes you see long URLs that consist of the site's URL followed by a question mark and a bunch of data (the query string mentioned earlier). What follows the question mark is the data that the client is submitting to the server. The server reads these values, processes them, and prepares a new page, which is downloaded to the client.

HTML is a standard specification. The latest version, HTML 4.01, is defined at http://www.w3.org/TR/1999/REC-html401-19991224/.

HTML and XHTML

HTML 4.01, the most recent version of the language, was released in 1999. In January 2000, the **World Wide Web Consortium (W3C;** a vendor-neutral organization responsible for web standards) released **XHTML** (Extensible HTML) version 1. This new standard is a reformulation of HTML to comply with XML syntax rules. XHTML uses almost the same set of tags as HTML, but with several restrictions:

▲ HTML 4 code is not case-sensitive; for example, you can enter the opening table tag as <table> or <TABLE>. Lowercase items work with old or new browsers, but uppercase ones don't work with future versions because XHTML doesn't read them. XML is case-sensitive, so a tag that includes uppercase letters is read differently than one that is all in lowercase.

▲ In HTML 4, attribute values need to be quoted only in certain circumstances. In XHTML, all attribute values must be in quotation marks.

▲ In HTML 4, some tags don't need to be closed. You can enter a <p> paragraph tag, type some text, and start the next paragraph with another <p>, without ever using a closing </p> tag. Browsers just figure it out; a new paragraph tag means the end of the previous paragraph:

```
<p>This is a paragraph.
<p>This is a new paragraph.
```

In XHTML, every element must be closed. This means that any element that includes content must have paired opening and closing tags, like this:

```
<p>This is a paragraph.</p>
<p>This is a new paragraph.</p>
```

To learn more about XHTML, you can view the XHTML specification at http://www.w3.org/TR/xhtml1/.

12.1.4 Server/Client Interaction

A web site that consists of HTML pages is interactive only in the sense that it allows the user to jump from page to page through hyperlinks. The client requests documents from the server, and the server supplies them. In this simple interaction model, webpages reside on the disks of the servers waiting to be requested by a client. Obviously, updating the information entails editing the HTML documents.

The disadvantage of this static model is that the client can't engage in a conversation with the server so that information can flow in both directions. The development of programs that execute on the server to build a dynamic response has enabled web authors to add dynamic content to the Web. The client can send specific requests to the server (e.g., "Show me the invoices issued last month," "Show me the customers in North America"). The server doesn't return a static page. Instead, it executes a script, or an application, that extracts "live" data from a database, formats the data as an HTML document, and sends the document to the client. The client sees up-to-date, accurate information.

The earliest technology for implementing server-side processing was **Common Gateway Interface (CGI).** CGI was difficult to program and maintain, and it did not perform well under a heavy load. Microsoft introduced **Active Server Pages (ASP)** as another server-side option. Both CGI and ASP read the query string from the request and make processing decisions based on the query string.

The latest version of ASP, **ASP.NET** 2.0, is a greatly improved version of ASP that allows you to program HTML pages in Visual Basic 2005. The first versions

FOR EXAMPLE

Deciding on Web Site Technologies

You have been hired by Excellence High School to provide a web presence. The initial web site will be informational only. The school wants to include an event calendar, allow teachers to post assignments, and provide other general information about the school. The students in the Visual Basic class will help you develop the web site.

Within two years, the school wants to be able to allow students to sign up for classes and check their grades and class progress online. Grades and class enrollment are stored in a database on a server.

You recommend HTML for the initial version of the web site because the site does not require a server-side solution. Also, using HTML will make it easy for teachers to post assignments online because even if they don't know HTML, they can save a Word document as HTML.

You recommend ASP.NET for the enrollment and grade reporting system. You explain that ASP.NET will allow you to perform tasks on the server, such as writing to and retrieving data from the database. You also explain that it is a better option than CGI or ASP because it performs better, offers more features, and is easier to maintain. You point out that another key advantage is that the students who are going to help are learning Visual Basic, and ASP.NET applications can be built using any .NET Framework language, including Visual Basic.

of ASP were limited to the HTML controls. ASP.NET, which was introduced with Visual Studio .NET, uses a new family of controls that exist on the server; you can program against these controls, just as you program Windows controls. Your code resides on the server and manipulates web controls. When it's time to send a response to the client, ASP translates the web controls into HTML controls and HTML code (and sometimes it generates JavaScript code to be executed at the client) and sends the client a page that can be rendered by a browser.

SELF-CHECK

- What protocol is used to access a web site?
- What tag is used to add a hyperlink to a webpage?
- Does the XHTML standard require closing tags for all elements?
- What tools are used for server-side processing?

12.2 HTML Fundamentals

Because HTML is the primary language for building webpages, it is important that you understand the structure of an HTML document and how to format a webpage using HTML. Remember that even if you build an application using a server-side tool, such as ASP.NET, the client's browser still receives HTML. In this section, you'll learn how to use several important HTML tags. You'll also learn about HTML controls and forms.

12.2.1 HTML Document Structure

If you store the following lines in a text file with the extension .htm (or. html) and then open it with Internet Explorer, you see the greeting "Hello, World!":

```
<html>
    <head>
        <title>Your Title Goes Here</title>
    </head>
    <body>
        Hello, World!
    </body>
</html>
```

To create the most fundamental HTML document, you must start with the <html> tag and end with the </html> tag. Within these tags should be a head section and a body section. The **body** of the document is the portion that is presented within the browser window. The document's **head**, marked with the <head> and </head> tags, is where you normally place the following elements:

▲ The document's title

▲ Information about the document, such as the meta and base tags

▲ Scripts

The title is the text that appears in the title bar of the browser's window and is specified with the <title> and </title> tags. **Meta tags** don't display anywhere on the screen, but they contain useful information regarding the content of the document, such as a description and keywords used by search engines. Here's an example of a page that uses meta tags:

```
<html>
    <head>
        <title>Your Title Goes Here</title>
        <meta name="Keywords"
            content="health, nutrition, weight
            control, chronic illness">
    </head>
    <body>
        Hello, World!
    </body>
</html>
```

Attributes

Many HTML tags understand special keywords, called **attributes**. The <body> tag, which marks the beginning of the document's body, for instance, recognizes the background attribute, which lets you specify an image to appear in the document's background. You can also specify the document's text color and its background color (if there's no background image) with the text and bgcolor attributes, respectively:

```
<html>
    <head>
        <title>Your Title Goes Here</title>
    </head>
    <body background="paper.jpg" bgcolor="yellow"
text="black">
        <h1>Tiled Background</h1>
        <p>The background of this page was created with a
small image, which is tiled vertically and horizontally by
the browser. If the image can't be displayed, the page will
have a solid yellow background. Either way, the text will
be black.</p>
    </body>
</html>
```

Background images are tiled, starting at the top-left corner and working their way across and then down the screen. Many HTML tags accept attribute parameters that position the element the tag represents precisely on the page. The good news is that you don't have to learn all these tags; if you're working with the Visual Studio integrated development environment (IDE), the designer inserts them for you.

12.2.2 Basic HTML Tags

HTML is easy for a Visual Basic programmer to learn and use. The small part of HTML presented here is all you need to start building functional webpages. Although you can use the visual tools of the Visual Studio IDE, it's often actually simpler to open an HTML file and edit it. At the very least, you should be able to locate basic structures in a page's HTML code, such as tables and controls. In this section, we'll discuss the most necessary tags for creating no-frills HTML documents, grouped by category. As you work with Visual Studio, you'll be switching between the design and HTML view of the same page, and you'll pick up more HTML as you go along.

Headers

Like documents prepared with a word processor, HTML documents can have headers, which separate sections of a document. You use the <hn> tag to insert a header. There are six levels of headers, starting with <h1> (the largest) and ending with <h6> (the smallest). To place a level 1 header in a document, you use the tag <h1>, like this:

```
<h1>Welcome to Our Fabulous Site</h1>
```

A related tag is the <hr> tag, which displays a horizontal rule and is frequently used to separate sections of a document. The document in Figure 12-1, which demonstrates the HTML tags discussed so far, was produced with the following HTML file:

```
<html>
    <head>
        <title>
            Document title
        </title>
    </head>
    <body>
        <h1>Sample HTML Document</h1>
        <hr>
        <h3>The document's body may contain:</h3>
        <h4>Text, images, sounds and HTML commands</h4>
    </body>
</html>
```

Figure 12-1

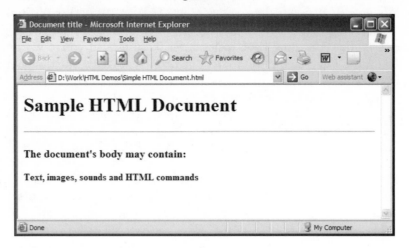

Header tags.

Paragraph Formatting

The formatting of paragraphs is determined by the font(s) used in the document and the size of the browser's window. HTML doesn't break lines into paragraphs whenever you insert a carriage return in the text file. To force a new paragraph, you must explicitly tell the browser to insert a carriage return by using the <p> tag. The <p> tag also causes the browser to insert additional vertical space. To insert a line break without the additional vertical space, you use the <br> tag.

Character Formatting

HTML provides a number of tags for formatting words and characters. Table 12-1 shows the basic character-formatting tags. The tags listed in pairs can be used

Table 12-1: Character-Formatting Tags

Tag	Effect
<b> or <strong>	Specifies bold text.
<font>	Specifies text characteristics, such as typeface, size, and color.
<i> or <em>	Specifies italic text (for emphasis).
<tt> or <code>	Turns on the "typewriter" attribute, so text is displayed in a monospace font; used frequently to display computer listings.

alternately for the same effect; for example, the <b></b> pair produces the same look as the <strong></strong> pair in most browsers.

The <font> tag specifies the name, size, and color of the font to be used, and it recognizes the following attributes:

▲ *size:* Specifies the size of the text in a relative manner. The value of the size attribute is not expressed in points, pixels, or any other absolute unit. Instead, it's a number in the range 1 (the smallest) through 7 (the largest). The following tag displays text in the smallest possible size:

```
<font size="1">tiny type</font>
```

The following tag displays text in the largest possible size:

```
<font size="7">HUGE TYPE</font>
```

▲ *face:* Specifies the font family. If the specified font does not exist on the client computer, the browser substitutes a similar font. The following tag displays the text in the Comic Sans MS typeface:

```
<font face="Comic Sans MS">Some text</font>
```

▲ *color:* Specifies the color of the text. Color values are specified as hexadecimal numeric values, like the following:

```
<font style="color: #ccffff">
```

Creating Lists

You may sometimes want to display data in either an **ordered** (numbered) **list** or an **unordered** (bulleted) **list.** You can create an ordered list by using the <ol></ol> tag pair. You can create an unordered list by using the <ul></ul> tag pair. In either case, you identify each item in the list by using the <li></li> tag pair. For example, the following code displays two lists: an unordered list of the ingredients and an ordered list of the steps to take.

```
<b>Ingredients:</b>
<ul>
    <li>Five limes</li>
    <li>2T Grenadine</li>
    <li>Sugar to taste</li>
    <li>2 quarts water</li>
    <li>Lots of ice</li>
    <li>Lime slices and maraschino cherries for garnish</li>
</ul>
<b>Instructions:</b>
<ol>
    <li>Squeeze limes into water.</li>
    <li>Add grenadine and sugar to taste.</li>
```

```
      <li>Stir.</li>
      <li>Add ice and garnish.</li>
</ol>
```

Figure 12-2 shows this HTML rendered in a browser.

Figure 12-2

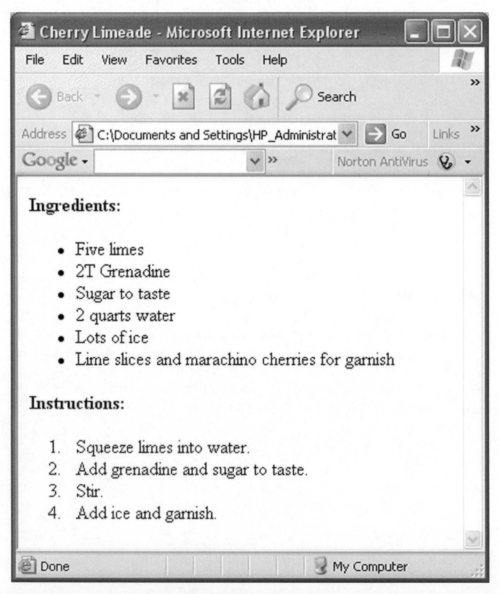

Ordered and unordered lists.

12.2.3 Inserting Graphics

Graphics play an important role in webpage design. Almost every page on the Web uses graphics, and some pages contain hardly any text. Graphics are not inserted in an HTML document directly. The document itself contains special tags that reference the image to be inserted by the browser when the page is opened. Because of this, the browser downloads the graphics files separately and places them on the page.

On the Web, where every byte counts and downloads must be fast, images must contain as much information as possible in as few bytes as possible. Despite the large number of graphics formats available today, two formats dominate the Web:

▲ JPEG (Joint Photographic Experts Group)
▲ GIF (Graphics Interchange Format)

These formats are used because they compress graphics files to a more manageable size. **JPEG** files can be compressed a good deal (albeit with some loss of detail), but they maintain a good image quality overall. The problems with a JPEG becomes evident when a compressed image is enlarged, but the graphics on webpages are meant to be viewed in the context of the webpage to which they belong, so this is usually not much of a problem. The **GIF** file format is an old one that supports only 256-color images, but it has a few really handy features. It's the only format that supports transparency, and its compression ratio is even better than JPEG's, without any loss of detail.

To insert an image at the current location in a document, you use the <img> tag with the src attribute, which specifies the image to be displayed. The width and height attributes determine the size of the image on the browser, regardless of the actual image size. If you specify only one of the two attributes, the image is resized proportionally in both dimensions. The following HTML code produces a page with a graphic centered across the page:

```
<html>
    <head>
        <title>Graphics on Web pages</title>
</head>
    <body>
        <center>
        <h1>Placing an Image on a Web page</h1>
        <img width=240 src="radiance.jpg" /><br />
        The moon, centered on the page
        </center>
    </body>
</html>
```

The <img> tag has the following syntax:

```
<img src="picture.jpg" />
```

The <img> tag is an **empty** (or **self-closing**) **element**—that is, it does not have content between the opening and closing tags. Therefore, you can close the tag by adding a space and a slash (/) character. The <img> tag recognizes additional attributes, but you must include the src attribute, which is the location of an image file on the server or any URL on the Web. When you use the following attributes with the <img> tag, the browser can manipulate the image in several ways:

▲ *align:* Aligns the image to the left, right, center, top, bottom, or middle of the screen.

▲ *width and height:* Specify the width and height of the image.

▲ *border:* Adds a border to the image, which is visible only if the image is a hyperlink.

▲ *vspace and hspace:* Clear space around the image vertically and horizontally. The empty space is specified in pixels.

▲ *alt:* Includes a text message to be displayed if the user has turned off graphics.

If you want to change the size of an image, you can specify the size with the width and height attributes, and the browser sizes the image to the new values. For instance, to create a straight vertical line 2 pixels wide, you simply use a square image 2 pixels on each side and set the <img> tag's width and height attributes as follows:

```
<img width="2" height="200" src="picture.jpg">
```

Your image stretches 200 pixels high. You can also use the width and height attributes to distort bitmaps. The border attribute specifies the width of the border to appear around an image. Borders 2 pixels wide automatically surround any image used as a hyperlink. You can eliminate this automatic border by setting the border="none" attribute.

One aspect that affects the appearance of images, especially when they are surrounded by text, is the amount of space between the image and surrounding text. You can clear space horizontally and vertically with the hspace and vspace attributes, respectively. You simply specify the amount of space, in pixels (e.g., hspace="10" or vspace="20").

The alt attribute displays alternative text for users whose browsers don't display images to speed up the loading of the page or perhaps to use screen reading software, such as Microsoft Narrator, to accommodate a visually impaired users. The attribute alt="Company Logo" tells the user that an image is not displayed in the browser. In addition, if the image takes a long time to download, the message "Company Logo" is displayed in the image's space on the page. If for some reason your images are not transmitted or don't show up, the user can still navigate your web site and get the picture, so to speak.

12.2.4 Using Tables

Tables are invaluable tools for organizing and presenting data in a grid or matrix. Tables are used in an HTML document for the same reasons they are used in any other document. There is, however, one additional reason for using tables with an HTML document: to align the elements on a page. A table's cell may contain text, hyperlinks, or images, and you can use tables to align these elements on the page in ways that are simply impossible with straight HTML. By using tables without borders, your audience won't see how you accomplished your feats of graphic design.

Basic Table Tags

Every table begins with the <table> tag and ends with the </table> tag. The attributes of the <table> tag allow you to specify whether the table has borders, the width of borders, the distance between cells, and the proximity of cell contents to the edge of the cell. You can specify the width and height of the table either in pixels or as a percentage of total screen size.

Within the <table> tags, each table row is marked by the <tr> tag. Each row's cells are marked by the <td> tag. Here's the structure of a simple table:

```
<html>
    <table>
        <tr>
            <td> Row 1, Column 1 </TD>
            <td> Row 1, Column 2 </TD>
            <td> Row 1, Column 3 </TD>
        </tr>
        <tr>
            <td> Row 2, Column 1 </TD>
            <td> Row 2, Column 2 </TD>
            <td> Row 2, Column 3 </TD>
        </tr>
        <tr>
            <td> Row 3, Column 1 </TD>
            <td> Row 3, Column 2 </TD>
            <td> Row 3, Column 3 </TD>
        </tr>
    </table>
</html>
```

If you create an HTML file with these lines and open it with your browser, you see the items arranged as a table, without any lines around them.

Aligning Cell Contents

The align and valign attributes specify the alignment of a cell's contents. The align attribute is used for horizontal alignment and can have the value left, center, or right. The valign attribute specifies the vertical alignment of the text, and it can have the value top, middle, or bottom. The default alignment is left (horizontal alignment) and middle (vertical alignment).

The <table> tag can also take the align attribute, but instead of aligning the table contents, it aligns the table itself. If you don't include an align attribute, the table is left-aligned in the browser's window. Most elements, including paragraphs (<p>) and images (<img>), can also use the align attribute, and if it's not present, they default to aligning left.

Table Width

All the examples you have looked at so far use the default table width, which is determined by the entries of the individual cells. If a column contains a very long entry, the browser wraps its contents to make sure that all columns are visible. However, it is possible to specify the width of the entire table by using the width attribute of the <table> tag. The width attribute can be a value that specifies the table's width in pixels or as a percentage of the window's width. For example, the following HTML defines a table that occupies one-half the window's width:

```
<table width="50%">
```

The following HTML defines a table that is 200 pixels wide, regardless of its contents and/or the window's size:

```
<table width="200">
```

If the window is less than 200 pixels wide, part of the table is invisible. To view the part of the table that's outside the window, you have to use the horizontal scrollbar.

Multiple-Row and Multiple-Column Cells

Quite often, tables don't contain identically sized rows and columns. Some rows might contain fewer and wider cells than the others, and some columns might span multiple rows. Figure 12-3 shows a table that has cells that span multiple columns and rows. These cells use the rowspan and colspan attributes, which let you create really elaborate tables. Either or both can appear in a <td> tag, and they merge the current cell with one or more of its adjacent cells on the same row (in the case of the colspan attribute) or column (in the case of the rowspan attribute). The number of adjacent cells to be merged is the value of the colspan and rowspan attributes; colspan="2" means that the current cell covers two columns.

The table in Figure 12-3 was created with the HTML code shown here.

```
<html>
    <head>
        <title>ROWSPAN - COLSPAN Examples</title>
```

```html
    </head>
    <body>
        <table border align="CENTER">
        <caption><b>ROWSPAN & COLSPAN
        Demo</b></caption>
        <tr>
            <td colspan="2"
            ROWSPAN="2">Source:<br>1991
        Census</td>
            <th colspan="2">Average</th>
        </tr>
        <tr>
            <th>Height</th>
            <th>Weight</th>
        </tr>
        <tr>
            <th ROWSPAN="2">Gender</th>
            <th>Males</th>
            <td>5.83</td>
            <td>195.5</td>
        </tr>
        <tr>
            <th>Females</th>
            <td>5.22</td>
            <td>167.8</td>
        </tr>
        </table>
    </body>
</html>
```

Figure 12-3

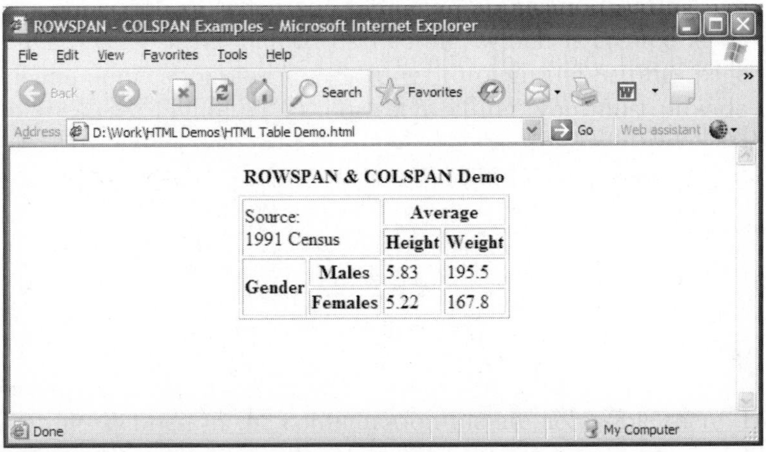

Table cells that span multiple rows and columns.

This example uses the colspan attribute in the appropriate <td> tags to force some cells of the first row to span two columns, and it uses the rowspan attribute to force some cells in the first column to span multiple rows. The <th> tag is a special table cell that indicates a table heading. Other than that, the new table is as simple as those in the previous examples.

FOR EXAMPLE

Creating an HTML Webpage

You have been asked to create an event calendar for Excellence High School. The event calendar page should include a list of hyperlinks to the pages for the principal and the staff members responsible for organizing various events. It should also include a table of events that lists the date, a graphic showing the type of event (i.e., football game, basketball game, drama production, band concert), and a description of the event. If multiple events occur on the same date, the date should be listed only once.

You create a webpage using the following HTML:

```
<html>
    <head>
        <title>Excellence High School Event
        Calendar</title>
    </head>
    <body>
        <h1>Excellence High School</h1>
            Excellence High School understands that stu-
dents need more than just academics. We pride ourselves
on the wide range of extracurricular activities we offer
to students.
            <p><b>Meet Our Staff</b></p>
            <ul>
            <li><a href="principal.htm">Ms. White,
            Principal</a>
            <li><a href="football.htm">Coach Reynolds,
            Football</a>
            <li><a href="basketball.htm">Coach
                    Phillips, Basketball</a>
                <li><a href="drama.htm">Mr. Carlson,
                Drama</a>
                <li><a href="band.htm">Mrs. Sampson, Band
                Director</a>
                <h2>Event Calendar</h2>
                <table border="1">
                <tr>
```

(Continued)

```
                        <th>Date</th>
                        <td></td>
                        <th>Event Description</th>
            </tr>
            <tr>
                    <td>October 5th</td>
                    <td><img src="football.gif"
                        alt="Football" width="75"/></td>
                    <td>Game vs. Reliable Academy</td>
            </tr>
            <tr>
                    <td rowspan= "3">October 12th</td>
                    <td> <img src="football.gif"
alt="Football" width="75"/></td>
                            <td> Game vs. Success High School</td>
                    </tr>
                    <tr>
                    <td><img src="basketball.gif"
                        alt="Basketball" width="75"/></td>
                    <td> Tryouts Practice 1</td>
            </tr>
            <tr>
                    <td><img src="drama.gif"
                        alt="Drama" width="75"/></td>
                    <td><u>As You Like It</u> by
                        William Shakespeare</td>
            </tr>
            <tr>
                    <td rowspan="2">October 13th</td>
                    <td><img src="band.gif" alt="Band"
                    width="75" /> </td>
                    <td> Spirit Rally </td>
            </tr>
            <tr>
                    <td><img src="drama.gif"
                        alt="Drama" width="75"/></td>
                    <td><u>As You Like It</u> by
                        William Shakespeare</td>
            </tr>
        </table>
        </body>
</html>
```

The resulting webpage is shown in Figure 12-4.

(Continued)

Figure 12-4

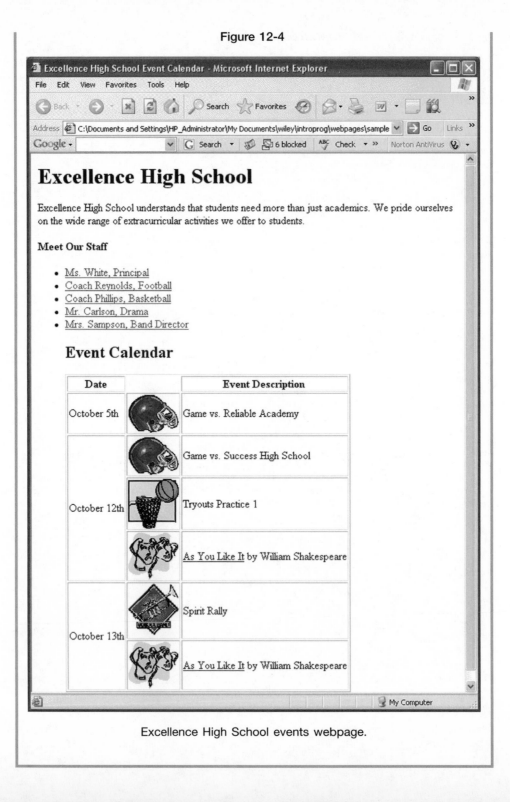

Excellence High School events webpage.

12.2.5 Using Forms and Controls

As you know, HTML pages contain controls that let the user enter information, similar to the usual Windows controls: text boxes, radio buttons, check boxes, and so on. These controls are rendered by the browser at the client, and they make the difference between HTML pages and web applications. Whereas HTML pages are for viewing only, **web applications** enable user interaction. The areas on the HTML page where these controls appear are called **forms,** and the controls themselves are called **intrinsic controls,** or HTML controls. HTML provides special tags for placing intrinsic controls on a form.

Before placing a control on a page, you must create a form that uses the <form> tag, whose syntax is as follows:

```
<form name="name" action="action" method="method">
</form>
```

All the controls must appear between the <form> and </form> tags. The optional name attribute is the name of the form and is used when a page contains multiple forms. The action attribute is the name of an application on the server that will be called to process the information. The method must be set to either "get" or "post". When it is set to "get", the values of the controls on the form are added to the query string. When it is set to "post", the values are included in the form sent to the application.

When the user clicks a submit button (which you'll learn to create a little later in this chapter), the browser creates a new URL and requests it as if it were a new page. This URL contains the name of the application specified with the form's action attribute, followed by the values of the controls on the forms. The method attribute specifies how the controls' values will be transmitted to the server. All the information the browser needs to contact an application on the server is contained in the <form> tag.

HTML provides support for the intrinsic controls described here. Figure 12-5 shows a webpage with a form that contains most of HTML's intrinsic controls. (You will see the HTML code that produced the page in this figure later in this section.)

The Text Control

The Text control is a box in which users can enter a single line of text (e.g., name, address). To insert a Text control on a form, you use the <input> tag with the type value set to "text", as in the following example:

```
<input type="text" name="firstName"
value="Enter first name here">
```

The value attribute specifies the initial value. After the user changes this entry, value holds the new string. The text in the Text control can be edited with the common editing keys (e.g., Home, Delete, Insert), but the text can't be formatted.

Figure 12-5

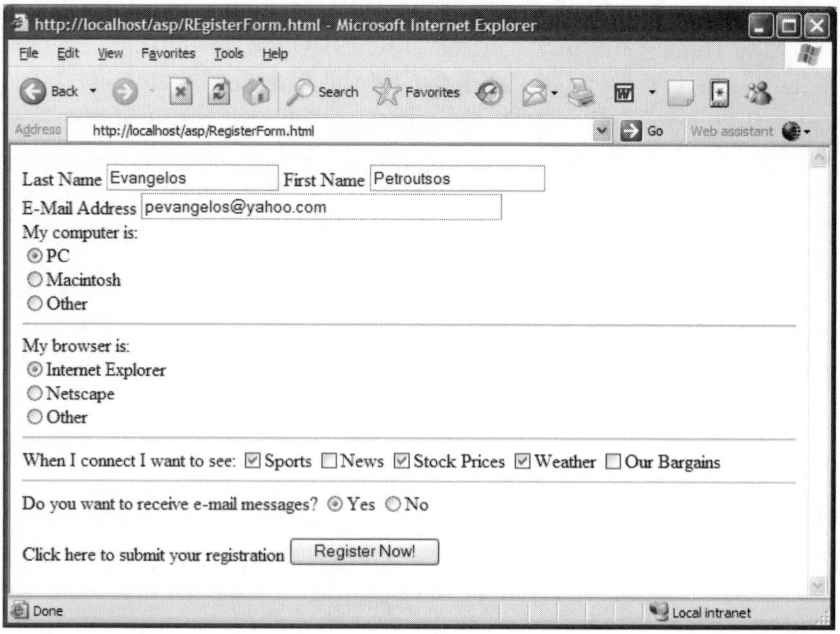

Intrinsic controls.

To control the size and contents of the control, you use the size and maxlength attributes. The size attribute specifies the size of the control on the form, in number of characters, and the maxlength attribute specifies the maximum number of characters the user can type in the control. A variation of the Text control is the Password control, which looks identical but displays an asterisk instead of the actual characters as they are typed.

The TextArea Control

The TextArea control is similar to the Text control, but it allows the entry of multiple lines of text. All the usual navigation and editing keys work with the TextArea control. For example, to place a TextArea control on a form, you use the <textarea> tag:

```
<textarea name="Comments" rows="10" cols="30">
The best editor I've ever used!</textarea>
```

Because the TextArea control allows you to specify multiple lines of initial text, it's not inserted with the usual <input> tag but with opening and closing <textarea> tags, with the control's text between them. You use the rows and cols attributes to specify the dimensions of the control on the page, in number of characters. Unlike the rest of an HTML document, the content between the two <textarea> tags is preserved when the text is displayed on the control; line breaks you insert, for instance, appear in the browser. Even if you include HTML tags in the initial text, they appear as text on the control. For example, this code:

```
<textarea name="Comments" rows="10" cols="30">
The <b>best</b> editor I've ever used!</textarea>
```

displays the following text inside the textarea element:

```
The <b>best</b> editor I've ever used!
```

The CheckBox Control

The CheckBox control is a little square with an optional check mark that acts as a toggle; every time the visitor clicks it, it changes state. You use a CheckBox control to present a list of options, from which the user can select one or more. To insert a CheckBox control on a form, you use the <input> tag, as in this example:

```
<input type="checkbox" name="Check1">
```

To initially check a CheckBox control, you specify the checked attribute in the corresponding <input> tag. The control's value can be ON or OFF (or 0 or 1), indicating whether it's checked (1) or cleared (0). The value attribute is examined by the script on the server and is never used at the client.

The RadioButton Control

The RadioButton control is round and contains a dot in the center. RadioButton controls are used to present lists of options, similar to the CheckBox control, but only one of a set can be selected at a time. Each time a visitor selects a new option, the previously selected one is cleared. To insert a RadioButton control on a form, you use a statement similar to the following:

```
<input type="radio" name="Radio1">
```

Although each CheckBox control has a different name, all the RadioButton controls in a group have the same name. This is how the browser knows which RadioButton controls belong to the same group and that only one control in the group can be selected at a time. To specify the control that will be initially checked in the group, you use the checked attribute. The following lines insert a group of four RadioButton controls on a form:

```
<input type="radio" name="Level"/>Beginner <br/>
<input type="radio" name ="Level"/>Intermediate <br/>
<input type="radio" name ="Level"
checked="checked"/>Advanced<br/>
<input type="radio" name ="Level">Expert <br/>
```

The Multiple Selection Control

The Multiple Selection control is basically a list of options similar to the Windows ListBox control. The visitor can select none, one, or multiple items in the list. The list is delimited with opening and closing <select> tags, and each item in the list is inserted with a separate <option> tag. To place a Multiple Selection List control on a form, you add the following lines:

```
<select  name="MemoryOptions"  size="3"
multiple="multiple">
     <option  value  ="16">16  MB</option>
     <option  value  ="32">32  MB</option>
     <option  value  ="64">64  MB</option>
     <option  value  ="128">128  MB</option>
     <option  value="256">256  MB</option>
</select>
```

The size attribute specifies how many lines to make visible. If you omit it, the list is reduced to a single line, and the user must use the up and down arrow keys to scroll through the available options. If the list contains more lines, a vertical scrollbar is automatically attached to help the user locate the desired item. The multiple attribute specifies that the visitor can select multiple items in the list by clicking their names while holding down the Shift or Ctrl key. If you omit the multiple attribute, each time an item is selected, the previously selected item is cleared.

The <option> tag has a value attribute that represents the value of the selected item. If the user selects the 64 MB option in the earlier list, the value 64 is transmitted to the server. Finally, to initially select one or more options, you specify the selected attribute:

```
<option  selected="selected"  value="128">  128
MB</option>
```

The Command Button Control

Clicking a command button triggers one of the following actions:

▲ Submits the data entered on the controls to the server.
▲ Resets all control values on the form to their original values.

The most important command button is the submit button. It transmits the contents of all the controls on the form to the server; the values are processed by an application whose URL is specified in the action attribute of the <form> tag. The reset button resets the values of the other controls on the form to their initial values. The reset button doesn't submit any values to the server. Most forms contain submit and reset buttons, which are inserted like this:

```
<input  type="submit"  value="Send  Data"  />
<input  type="reset"  value="Reset  Values"  />
```

The value attribute specifies the string that will appear on the button—its caption. The submit button reads the name of the application that must be contacted on the server (the <form> tag's action attribute), appends the values of the controls to this URL, and transmits it to the server.

Processing Requests on the Server

The RegisterForm.htm page, previously shown in Figure 12-4, contains several of the controls you can place on a webpage to request information from the user. The form section of the page is defined with the following tag:

```
<form action="ASP/Register.asp" method="GET">
```

The data collected on this page is transmitted to the application Register.asp on the same server when the user clicks the Register Now! button, and it is processed there. For now you must keep in mind that the browser automatically submits the controls' values to the server. All you have to do is specify in the <form> tag the URL of the program to intercept them on the server. The URL used in this example begins with the ASP folder. With no protocol, domain, or other parent folder specified, the ASP folder has to be in the same location as the current document, and the browser remembers where that is. The URL of this example is equivalent to http://www.myserver.com/ASP/Register.asp (where the first part of the address is the location of the HTML page with the form).

The rest of the code is trivial. It uses the <input> tag to display the various controls, and most of the controls are grouped into tables for alignment purposes. The following example lists the tags for the intrinsic controls only, omitting the table- and text-formatting tags in the interest of conserving space:

```
<form action="ASP/Register.asp" method="GET">
    Last Name
    <input type="text" size="20" maxlength="20"
    name="LName" />
    First Name
    <input type="text" size="20" maxlength="20"
    name="FName" />
    <br>
    E-Mail Address
    <input type="text" size="46" maxlength="256"
    name="EMail" />
    <br/>
    My computer is:<br />
    <input type="radio" checked="checked"
        name="Hardware" value="PC">PC<br />
    <input type="radio" name="Hardware"
    value="Mac" />Macintosh
    <br />
    <input type="radio"
        name="Hardware" value="OtherHardware"
        />Other<br />
    <hr/>My browser is:<br />
    <input type="radio" checked="checked"
        name="Browser" value="IE" />
```

```
Internet Explorer<br />
<input type="radio"
    name="Browser" value="Netscape"
    />Netscape<br/>
<input type="radio" name="Browser"
value="OtherBrowser" />Other
<br />
<hr/>
When I connect I want to see:
<input type="checkbox" name="Sports" value="ON"
/>Sports
<input type="checkbox" name="News" value="ON"
/>News
<input type="checkbox" name="Stock" value="ON"
/>Stock Prices
<input type="checkbox" name="Weather" value="ON"
/>Weather
<input type="checkbox" name="Bargains" value="ON"
/>
Our Bargains
<hr />
Do you want to receive e-mail messages?
<input type="radio" checked="checked"
    name="Mail" value="YES" />Yes
<input type="radio" name="Mail" value="NO" />No
<br /><br />
Click here to submit your registration
<input type="submit" name="Register"
value="Register Now!" />
</FORM>
```

If you click the Register Now! button, the browser displays a warning, indicating that it can't find the Register.asp application. This page can't be tested without a web server and the specified application. You can view its contents as you would any other page, but the page can't contact the server unless it is opened on a web server.

FOR EXAMPLE

Building a Form

Excellence High School wants to conduct an online survey to rate its current extracurricular offerings and determine whether students would be interested in other activities. You need to allow students to rank the current activities on a four-point scale, where 1 = Poor and 4 = Excellent.

(Continued)

You also want to list other proposed activities and have students select which activities interest them.

One of the students in the Visual Basic class taught herself how to build an ASP script that will be used to store survey results to a database.

You create a webpage using the following code:

```html
<html>
    <head>
    <title>Excellence High School Activity
    Survey</title>
    </head>
    <body>
    <form name="survey" action="post"
    method="survey.aspx">
        Please rate our current activities.
        <br />
        <table>
        <tr>
        <td>Football</td>
        <td><select name="FootballRank" size="1">
            <option value ="4">
            Excellent</option>
            <option value ="3"> A Very
            Good</option >
            <option value ="2">Good</option>
            <option value ="1">Poor</option>
        </select>
        </td>
    </tr>
    <tr>
        <td>Basketball</td>
        <td><select name="BasketballRank" size="1">
            <option value ="4">
            Excellent</option>
            <option value ="3">
            Very Good</option >
            <option value ="2">Good</option >
            <option value ="1">Poor</option >
        </select>
        </td>
    </tr>
    <tr>
        <td>Drama</td>
        <td><select name="DramaRank" size="1">
            <option value ="4">
```

(Continued)

```
                Excellent</option>
                <option value ="3">
                Very Good</option >
                <option value ="2">Good</option>
                <option value ="1">Poor</option>
        </select>
        </td>
    </tr>
    <tr>
        <td>Band</td>
        <td><select name="BandRank" size="1">
            <option value ="4">
            Excellent</option>
            <option value ="3">
            Very Good</option>
            <option value ="2">Good</option>
            <option value ="1">Poor</option>
            </select>
        </td>
        </tr>
    </table>
        <br />
        What other activities would you like to see?
        <table>
        <tr>
            <td><input type="checkbox"
            name="ChessClub">
                Chess Club</input></td>
            <td><input type="checkbox"
                name="Debate Team">
                Debate Team</input></td>
            <td><input
                type="checkbox" name="Gymnastics">
                Gymnastics</input></td>
        </tr>
        <tr>
            <td><input type="checkbox"
            name="Golf">Golf</input></td>
            <td><input type="checkbox"
            name="Tennis">Tennis</input></td>
            <td><input
                type="checkbox"
name="Rugby">Rugby</input>
            </td>
        </tr>
```

(Continued)

```
      </table>
      <input type="submit" value="Submit Survey" />
  </form>
  </body>
  </html>
```

The resulting webpage is shown in Figure 12-6.

Figure 12-6

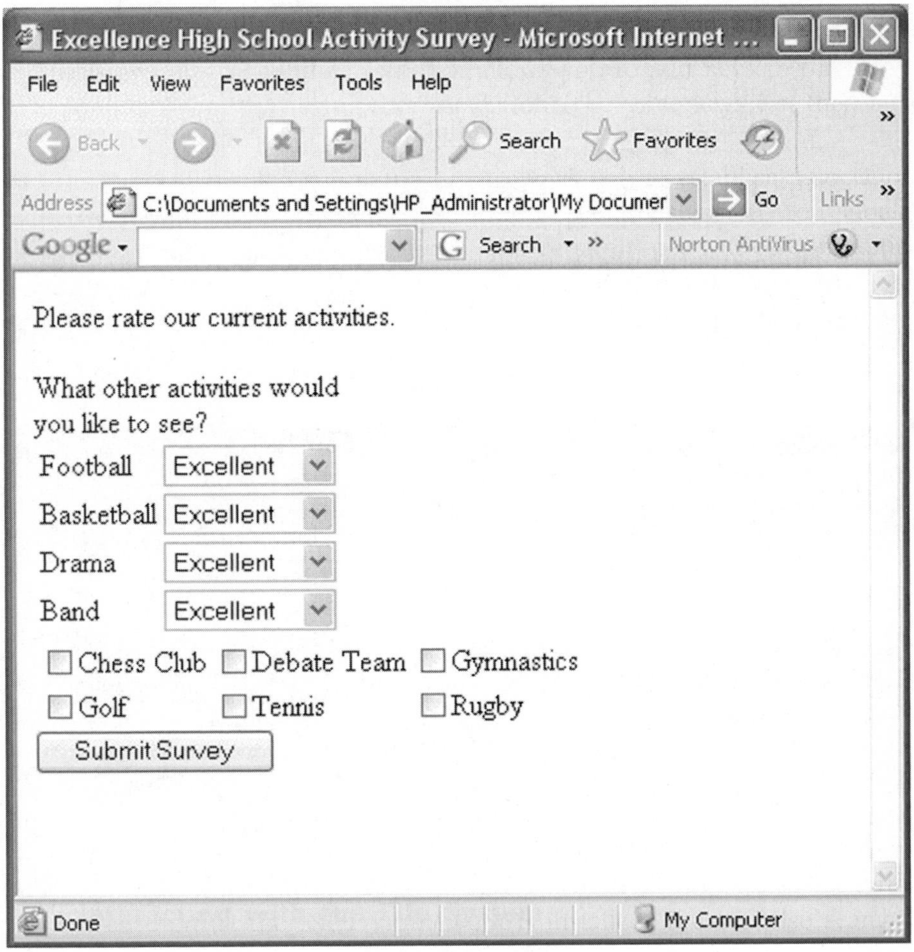

An event survey.

SELF-CHECK

- Where must a <title> tag be placed?
- Of <h1>, <h2>, <em>, and <strong>, which displays the largest text?
- Is font size for HTML text a relative size?
- What tag do you use to identify each element in a numbered list?
- Can a JPEG have transparent areas?
- What tag identifies a cell in a table?
- You are creating a form. What element will add a CheckBox control to the form?

12.3 Building a Web Application

In this section, you'll see how to build a web application similar to the application of the preceding section that uses an HTML form and HTML controls. The new application is called Register, and its form is shown in Figure 12-7.

Figure 12-7

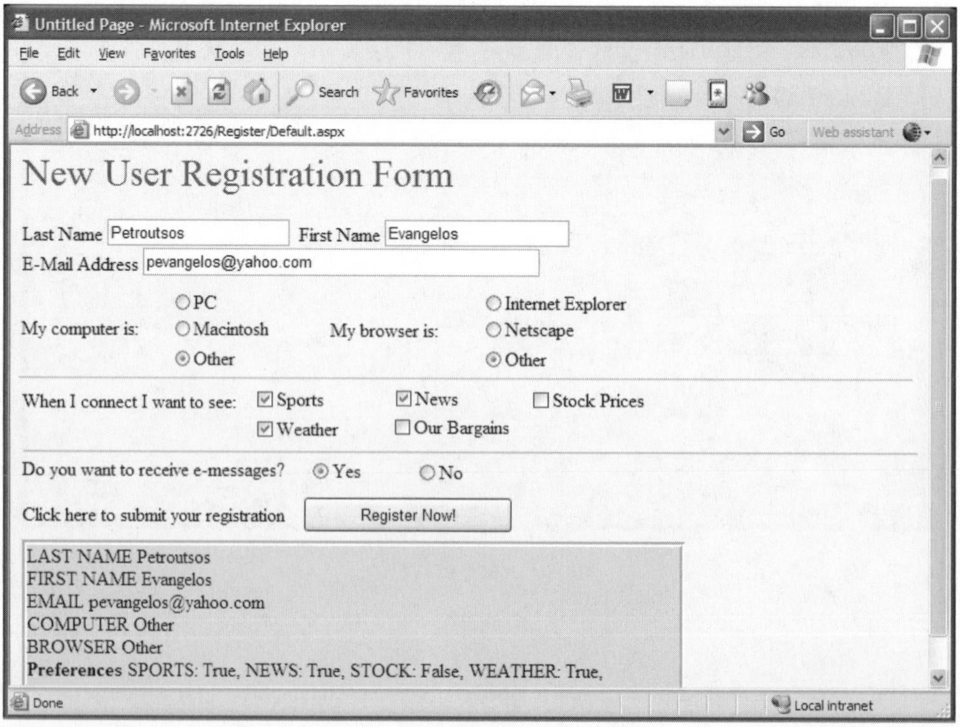

An ASP.NET application.

The first difference you will note between the two applications is that the new one displays the results on the same page. Typical web applications don't let you display new information on the same page that submitted the data to the server because it's easier to create a new page than to reconstruct the page that submitted the request. However, ASP.NET makes it very easy to display the results of the processing on the same page that invoked the script. The control on which the results are displayed is a Label control, which is initially empty. The most important difference, however, is that with the web application, you don't have to extract the control values from the query string to process the form. Instead, you can write simple Visual Basic code that reads the values of the controls directly, as if it were a Windows application.

12.3.1 Creating an ASP.NET Application

To create an ASP.NET application, you launch Visual Studio 2005. If you open the File menu and select New web site, you see the New web site dialog box, shown in Figure 12-8. When you select the ASP.NET web site item, the Location combo box lets you specify where to create the web site. Normally, a web site resides in a virtual folder of a web server and requires IIS. Visual Studio allows you to create a web site on the local or a remote web server, the local file system, or an FTP site. You can create the new site by using the local file system because the project model is directory based: The entire site is contained in a single folder. The web site can be moved to a production web server after it has been thoroughly tested. You should start all new web projects on the local

Figure 12-8

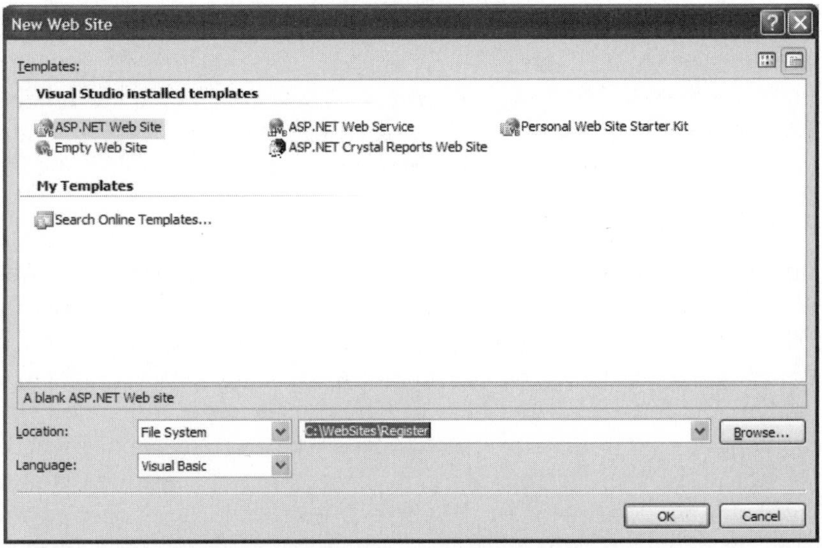

Creating a new web site.

file system so that you do not need to install IIS on your development computer. Although IIS is included with Windows, it presents a possible security risk, so many environments prohibit the use of IIS on desktop computers. The option Remote Sites option allows you to create a web site on a remote web server; you might use this option, for example, if you have to rent space on a web server for your site or if you want to work with your company's web server from home.

You click the Browse button on the New web site dialog box to open the Choose Location dialog box, where you can specify the location of the site. If you click the File System button on the left, you see the hierarchy of drives and folders on your system. By default, all new web sites are created under the C:\Documents and Settings*Username*\My Documents\Visual Studio 2005\web sites\ folder. You just enter the name of the new site's path and close the two dialog boxes.

The advantage of building a web site on the local file system is that you don't have to have IIS installed on your system; you can develop and test your new site with the ASP.NET Development Server, which is installed along with Visual Studio. This web server can't be accessed from the outside (it services requests from the local machine only), and you don't have to take any of the security measures necessary with IIS.

Finally, on the lower section of the New web site dialog box, you can select the site's language in the Language box. As you add pages to the site, you can specify different languages for different pages.

A single new item is added to the Solution Explorer automatically: Default.aspx. For the sake of this example, you should rename it RegisterForm. aspx. This is the equivalent of a Windows form, and it's the page users will see in their browsers. The main pane of the IDE shows the RegisterForm.aspx form in Design view. To place the various controls on the page, you select them in the toolbox and drop them on the form using the mouse. The toolbox contains a large number of controls (many of them new to ASP.NET 2.0), grouped in various categories according to their function. A few of them are used here.

12.3.2 Designing a Web Form

Designing a web form is no different from designing a Windows form: You place controls on the form, size them, set their properties, and you have built the web application's user interface. The web controls don't have as many properties as their Windows counterparts, but they have many more properties than HTML controls. One property that's common to all web controls is the EnableViewState property, which is set to True by default. This property determines whether the control's **state** (i.e., the current value and other property settings) is automatically saved during round-trips to the server. You should leave this property set to True so that each time the page is returned to the client, the controls retain their values. For example, if the user forgets to supply a value to a required field, you don't want to make the person retype everything. The controls maintain their values, and the user can edit the one in error.

By default, only Button controls cause postbacks to occur. A **postback** causes a round-trip to the server in order for server-side processing to occur. However, other controls have an AutoPostBack property, which you can set to True to cause the page to be posted back to itself every time the control's main event takes place. This event could be the TextChanged event of the TextBox control, the SelectedIndexChanged event of the ListBox control, and so on. The idea is to provide more direct interaction with the user, but the trip to the server introduces a noticeable (if not substantial) delay, even on the local network. If you set the AutoPostBack property of a TextBox control to True, the page is posted back every time the TextBox control loses the focus and its contents have been edited since it got the focus. The TextChanged event, which is fired at the server, can format the text on the control (i.e., convert the characters typed into upper-case or format a numeric value) and re-send the same page back to the client. The TextChanged event can't be fired with every keystroke, as is the case with a Windows application, because causing a postback for each keystroke would be very inefficient.

As you place controls on a page in Design view, they're laid out in flow mode, which is the default layout mode for a webpage. The IDE attempts to fit each element on the page to the right of the last element on the page. If there's not enough space, the element is placed on the following line, flush to the left side of the page. You can change the default behavior by changing each

Figure 12-9

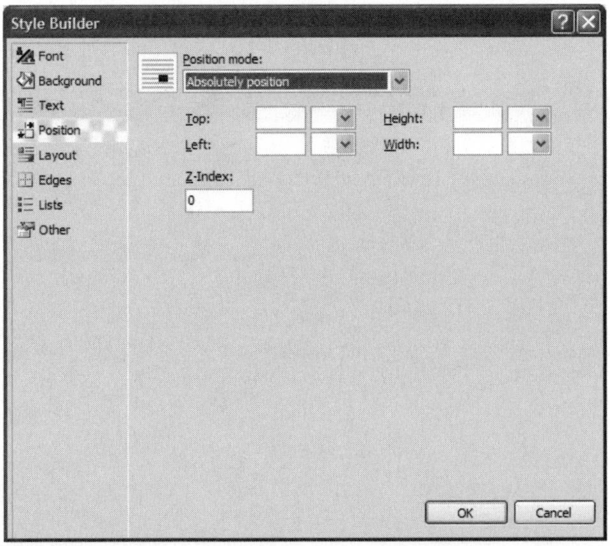

The Style Builder dialog box.

control's position mode. To do so, you right-click the control and from the context menu select Style to open the Style Builder dialog box, which is shown in Figure 12-9. Here you can set the control's style (e.g., its font, foreground and background colors, the style of lists and tables). You select the Position tab, and in the Position Mode combo box, you select Absolutely Position; then you click OK to close the dialog box. You can grab the selected control with the mouse and move it around. Not only can you move the control around, you can also select multiple controls and align them by using the commands on the Format | Align menu, as long as all controls have Position Mode set to Absolutely Position. In flow mode, you can't align controls as you wish. However, you can create elaborate tables and place the controls in their cells to make a perfectly aligned page.

If you want to freely position all controls on a page, you must change the default settings from the Options dialog box, which is shown in Figure 12-10. You select the Layout command and then select Position and Auto Position Options to open the Options dialog box with the CSS Positioning tab selected. You check the top option, as shown in Figure 12-10, to specify that all controls dropped on the page should be positioned in absolute mode.

12.3.3 Viewing the HTML for a Form

Although designing a web form is similar to designing a Windows form, there is one key difference: When you design a web form, you are actually creating HTML. You view the HTML by opening the .aspx file in Design view and clicking Source. However, the HTML you create has some important differences from standard client-side HTML. To demonstrate, the following is an example of the

Figure 12-10

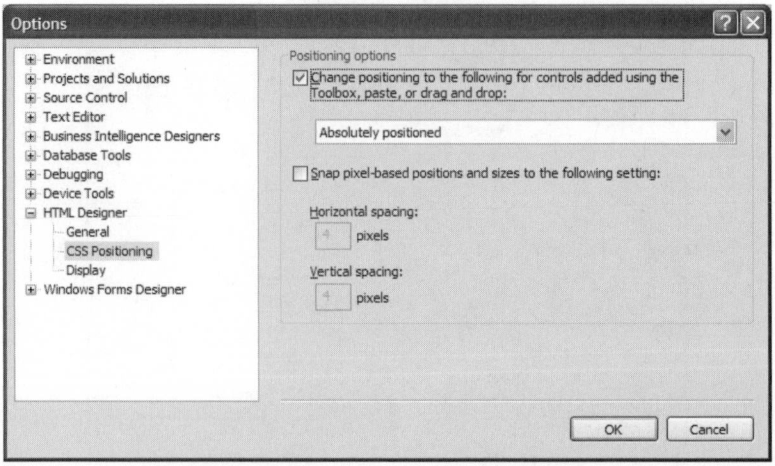

Positioning controls in absolute mode.

HTML that is generated when you create a web site and add a Label control and a TextBox control to the form:

```
<%@ Page Language="VB" AutoEventWireup="false"
    CodeFile="Default.aspx.vb" Inherits="_Default" %>
    <!DOCTYPE html PUBLIC "-//W3C//DTD XHTML 1.0
Transitional//EN" "http://www.w3.org/TR/xhtml1/DTD/xhtml1-tran-
sitional.dtd">
    <html xmlns="http://www.w3.org/1999/xhtml" >
    <head runat="server">
        <title>Untitled Page</title>
    </head>
    <body>
        <form id="form1" runat="server">
        <div>
        <asp:Label ID="Label1" runat="server"
        Text="Label"></asp:Label>
        <asp:TextBox ID="TextBox1"
        runat="server"></asp:TextBox></div>
        </form>
    </body>
    </html>
```

The first difference you should notice between this example and earlier examples is this line:

```
<%@ Page Language="VB" AutoEventWireup="false"
CodeFile="Default.aspx.vb" Inherits="_Default" %>
```

This is known as the **page directive,** and it gives ASP.NET the information it needs to perform server-side processing. In this example, it tells ASP.NET to use execute code in Default.aspx.vb. This file is known as the **code-behind file.** It also tells ASP.NET that the server-side code is written in Visual Basic. The Auto-EventWireup attribute lets ASP.NET know whether it should automatically wire all control events or whether the programmer will do it. It is set to False by default, and you should leave it set to False to improve performance. Finally, the Inherits attribute allows you to identify a page that serves as the base class. In this case, the page is the base class.

The next two lines let the browser know that Transitional XHTML is being used and provide the URL to the XML namespace that should be used for reference, if necessary. These are XHTML-specific elements and are not related to ASP.NET.

A critical point is that many elements include the runat="server" attribute. This attribute is required for an element to be accessed in the server-side code. For some elements, such as <form> and the web server control elements, runat="server" is required.

The final difference is the syntax for using web server controls:

```
<asp:Label ID="Label1" runat="server"
Text="Label"></asp:Label>
```

```
<asp:TextBox ID="TextBox1"
runat="server"></asp:TextBox>
```

Notice that web server controls always begin with the prefix asp:. This identifies a control as a web server control that is included with Visual Studio.

It's essential to understand that the HTML that includes the <asp:*control*> tags is *not* the HTML that is passed to the browser. The browser receives HTML generated by ASP.NET. In this particular case, the browser receives the following HTML:

```
<!DOCTYPE html PUBLIC "-//W3C//DTD XHTML 1.0
Transitional//EN"
"http://www.w3.org/TR/xhtml1/DTD/xhtml1-transitional.dtd">
    <html xmlns="http://www.w3.org/1999/xhtml" >
    <head>
        <title>
            Untitled Page
        </title></head>
    <body>
        <form name="form1" method="post"
        action="Default.aspx"
        id="form1">
        <div>
        <input type="hidden" name="VIEWSTATE"
        id="VIEWSTATE"

value="/wEPDwUKMTk0NjM3NDE0OWRkyoohU3ZzC8ucGNh84AnIBoUNG
TE=" />
        </div>

        <div>
        <span id="Label1">Label</span>
        <input name="TextBox1" type="text" id="TextBox1"
        /></div>

        <div>
        <input type="hidden" name="__EVENTVALIDATION"
            id="__EVENTVALIDATION"
value="/wEWAgLtpdLhDgLs0bLrBmu1g+TF+Iwv/7apRqK4eISBakzK" />
        </div></form>
    </body>
    </html>
```

Notice that when the <form> element in this HTML is rendered by the browser, its method attribute is set to "post", and its action is set to "D" "efault.aspx". This means that when the form is submitted, it posts the results to Default.aspx. Also notice that there the Label control is rendered as a <span> element, which is really just an area of static text. The TextBox control is rendered as an input element that has its type attribute set to "text". There are also two hidden fields that ASP.NET uses internally.

12.3.4 Coding an Application

Now you must add some code behind the Register Now! button. When this button is clicked, the values the user entered on the form are submitted to the server. All you have to do is read these values and display them on the Label control at the bottom of the form (the Values control). The application doesn't process the values, but after you know how to read them, you can store them in a database, prepare a new page with the specified settings, and so on. If you double-click the Register Now! button on the form, you will see the declaration of the Click event:

```
Private Sub Button1_Click(ByVal sender As _
    System.Object, ByVal e As System.EventArgs) _
    Handles Button1.Click
End Sub
```

This is clearly Visual Basic code. With ASP.NET, the code running on the server is no longer VBScript; you can write Visual Basic code, which is compiled and executed as needed. Note also that the code is inserted in its own file, the RegisterForm.aspx.vb file, which contains just code. This is the **code-behind approach,** which allows you to separate the HTML code (the design of the page) from the Visual Basic code.

ASP.NET simply lets you program the Click event of the Button web control as if it were a Windows Button control. When the user performs an action that results in a postback, the Page_Load event occurs. Next, the Button_Click event and all the other events that have occurred since the form was last displayed occurs when the page is posted back to the server. You cannot predict the order in which the control events will occur. Another important point is that the Page_Load event occurs each time the page is displayed. You can use the IsPostBack property of the Page object to execute different code in response to a postback than when the page is first requested.

To populate the Label control of this example, you insert the following statements in the Click event handler of the Button control:

```
Private Sub Button1_Click(ByVal sender As _
System.Object, _ByVal e As System.EventArgs) _
Handles Button1.Click
    Values.Text = "LAST NAME " & txtLName.Text
    Values.Text = Values.Text & "<br>" & _
        "FIRST NAME " & txtFName.Text
    Values.Text = Values.Text & "<br>" & _
        "EMAIL " & txtEMail.Text
    Values.Text = Values.Text & "<br>" & _
        "COMPUTER "
    If rdPC.Checked Then
        Values.Text = Values.Text & rdPC.Text
    End If
```

```
      If rdMacintosh.Checked Then
          Values.Text = Values.Text & rdMacintosh.Text
      End If
      If rdOther.Checked Then
          Values.Text = Values.Text & rdOtherPC.Text
      End If
      Values.Text = Values.Text & "<br>" & "BROWSER "
      If rdIE.Checked Then
          Values.Text = Values.Text & rdIE.Text & _
              "<br>"
      End If
      If rdNetscape.Checked Then
          Values.Text = Values.Text & _
              rdNetscape.Text & "<br>"
      End If
      If rdOther.Checked Then
          Values.Text = Values.Text & _
              rdOther.Text & "<br>"
      End If
      Values.Text = Values.Text & " <b>Preferences</b>"
      Values.Text = Values.Text & " SPORTS: " _
          & chkSports.Checked & _
          ","
      Values.Text = Values.Text & " NEWS: " _
          & chkNews.Checked & ","
      Values.Text = Values.Text & " STOCK: " _
          & chkStock.Checked & ","
      Values.Text = Values.Text & " WEATHER: " _
          & chkWeather.Checked _
          & ","
      Values.Text = Values.Text & " BARGAINS: " _
          & chkBargains.Checked
End Sub
```

To see what's sent to the client, you can right-click the form and choose View in Browser. Internet Explorer pops up, showing the page you designed. Before filling out the form, you should open the View menu and select Source to see the HTML that is being sent to the browser. We don't show all the code here, but it is plain HTML code that describes the contents of the page. The first TextBox control is inserted on the page with the following tag:

```
<input name="txtFName" type="text" id="txtFName"
    style="position: absolute" />
```

You should enter values on the controls and click the Register Now! button. The form is submitted to the server, where the application's code prepares the new page. The new page isn't created from scratch. The code sends out the same page, but this time, the Label control at the bottom of the form contains the values submitted to the server.

If you view the new page's source code, you see that the tag of the first TextBox control has become the following:

```
<input name="txtFName" type="text" _
value="Evangelos" id="txtFName"
   style="position: absolute" />
```

The value attribute was added to all controls on the form. This is what the EnableViewState property does: It causes the various controls to retain their values when a page is updated.

12.3.5 Maintaining State

You should keep in mind that a web application's code runs on a server and "sees" the values of the controls only when the client submits them (i.e., when the user clicks a button that submits the form to the server). While the form is open on the client's browser, the application doesn't even execute on the server. This is probably the most important difference between web applications and Windows applications: A web application isn't running at all times on the server. It starts every time the client submits a request to the server. It runs for a few milliseconds (or perhaps many seconds), generates a new page, and then terminates. It doesn't remain inactive; it simply dies when it's done. But what if you want to maintain the values of some variables between consecutive invocations of the server application?

The technique you use to maintain the values of some variables depends on whether you need to maintain the state information between successive requests to the same page (i.e., postbacks) or between multiple pages in the application. Let's look at handling state between postbacks first.

You have seen that controls can save their state during postback. This is known as maintaining **view state.** The view state is stored in a hidden control with the ID VIEWSTATE. You can store other values in view state by creating hidden controls on the form, or you can place values directly in view state by using the Page object's ViewState property, which is a collection of key/value pairs. The value can be any type of object, but you should keep in mind that storing large objects, such as a DataSet, in view state is not recommended because these objects must travel back and forth between the client and server during each round-trip. To add an object to the ViewState object, you call the Add method of the ViewState object. For example, to add the SalesTotal value of $35.50 to ViewState, you execute the following:

```
ViewState.Add("SalesTotal", 35.50)
```

To retrieve the SalesTotal value from the ViewState object, you execute the following:

```
Dim decTotal As Decimal
decTotal = ViewState("SalesTotal")
```

When a user connects to a web application, a **session** begins. That session remains in effect until the user closes the browser. The ability to store values throughout the user's session is known as maintaining **session state.** There are several ways to maintain state across the pages of a web application. The simplest method is to create a few variables through the Session object. The Session object represents a specific session; it's created when a new user connects to the server and released when the user leaves the site. The Session object is discussed later in this chapter, but here's how you can add two variables named Items and UID to the Session object and set their value to a number and a string, respectively:

```
Session("Items") = 3
Session("UID") = "anonymous"
```

If a variable of the same name exists already, its value is overwritten. Session variables should be used to store relatively small pieces of information that apply to all the pages of the application, such as the user's name, ID, or preferences.

Another method of maintaining state is to use an ID that uniquely identifies a session. This ID is generated by the SessionID property of the Session object. After you obtain an ID for the current session, you can store it in a Session variable and use it in code to identify the session. This ID is passed back and forth between the client and the server, and it maintains its value for the duration of the session. You can use this value as a key to a table in a database that contains information such as the items ordered by a user—or any other data you want to access from within multiple pages or multiple invocations of the same page.

Web developers sometimes need to pass cookies and store them on the client computer. A **cookie** is downloaded to the client and stored as a small file. It can store one or more values. Many users disable cookies on their computers due to privacy and security concerns, so you can't rely on this technique for all clients. If the client computer doesn't accept cookies, your application should be prepared to maintain its state using a different method. If the client accepts cookies, you can use them to store information you want to maintain between sessions, such as the basket's contents. A client that accepts cookies can place items in its basket and terminate the application without placing an order. The next time the client connects to your site, the items will still be in the basket.

You send cookies to the client computer by attaching them to the Cookies property of the Response object. The Cookies property is a collection of HttpCookie objects. An HttpCookie object has a name and, optionally, a value of type String. The following code attaches a cookie to the response:

```
Dim cBasket As New HttpCookie("basket", _
    "itm123, itm456")
Response.Cookies.Add(cBasket)
```

Cookies are passed in a request and can be accessed using the Cookies property of the Request object, as in the following example:

```
Dim cBasket As HttpCookie
Dim sItems As String
cBasket = Request.Cookies("basket")
If Not cBasket Is Nothing Then
    sItems = cBasket.Value
End If
```

You can retrieve a cookie by passing its name or its index in a collection. You should always test whether a cookie exists by using the Nothing keyword. If you try to retrieve the value of a cookie that does not exist, an error occurs.

FOR EXAMPLE

Designing an ASP.NET Application

Suppose you are designing a web application to allow students to sign up for classes online.

The first form the students should see will prompt them for their first name and last name. The principal wants students to be able to choose classes on a single form.

When a student submits the form, the classes should be checked to verify that the student meets the course prerequisites. If the student does meet the course prerequisites, the student's schedule should be written to the database, and another form displaying a printable class schedule should be displayed. If a student chooses classes he or she is not eligible to take, the same form should be displayed, with the classes the student cannot take highlighted in a different color and the missing prerequisites listed.

You are building the application as an ASP.NET application, using Visual Basic. You must determine how to manage state. Some students will be using browsers that have cookies disabled. You decide to use session state to store the user name and the classes selected between pages. You use view state to store the classes selected before the prerequisites are checked. You do not need to manually write the classes to view state because the EnableViewState property is set to True by default. You decide to use ListBox controls for the course selection and check for prerequisites in the SelectedIndexChanged event so that prerequisites are checked only for modified classes. However, after you present your design to the principal, he informs you that students can take a prerequisite course

(Continued)

concurrently with a course for which it is a prerequisite. Therefore, prerequisites need to be checked for all courses selected each time the form is submitted. You modify your design to do all processing inside the Page_Load event and use the IsPostBack property to check whether the request is a postback.

SELF-CHECK

- When does the Page_Load event occur?
- What identifies the name of a code-behind file?
- Can view state be accessed from any page in an application?

SUMMARY

In this chapter, you've learned how to create a webpage that includes lists, tables, and forms by using HTML. You've also learned the fundamentals of creating a web application by using ASP.NET.

KEY TERMS

Active Server Pages (ASP)	Empty element
Anchor tag	Extensible HTML (XHTML)
ASP.NET	Form
Attribute	Graphics Interchange Format (GIF)
Body	Head
Browser	HTML control
Client	HTML document
Cookie	Hyperlink
Common Gateway Interface (CGI)	Hypertext Markup Language (HTML)
Code-behind approach	
Code-behind file	Hypertext Transfer Protocol (HTTP)
Cookie	Internet
Domain Name System (DNS)	Internet Information Server (IIS)

Internet Protocol (IP) address

Intrinsic control

Joint Photographic Experts Group
    (JPEG)

Meta tag

Ordered list

Page directive

Postback

Protocol

Query string

Self-closing element

Session

Session state

State

Tag

Transmission Control Protocol/
    Internet Protocol (TCP/IP)

Uniform Resource Locator (URL)

Unordered list

View state

Web application

Webpage

Web server

Web site

What you see is what you get
    (WYSIWYG)

World Wide Web Consortium
    (W3C)

ASSESS YOUR UNDERSTANDING

Go to www.wiley.com/college/reese to evaluate your knowledge of web application development using HTML and ASP.NET.

Measure your learning by comparing pre-test and post-test results.

Summary Questions

1. A browser is the software responsible for rendering HTML. True or False?

2. A webpage uses a form to obtain shipping information for an order. The form sends the data to an ASP script. How does the ASP script retrieve the data?
   (a) from a query string
   (b) from view state
   (c) from session state
   (d) from control attributes in the webpage

3. Which of the following shows the correct structure for an HTML document?
   (a) `<html></html><head></head><body></body>`
   (b) `<head></head><html><body></body></html>`
   (c) `<html><head></head><body></body></html>`
   (d) `<html><head><body></body>></head><</html>`

4. You are creating a webpage that must adhere to the XHTML standard. Which of the following shows the correct way to create a table cell?
   (a) `<td>`This is a table cell
   (b) `<td>`This is a table cell`</td>`
   (c) `<TD>`This is a table cell
   (d) `<TD>`This is a table cell`</TD>`

5. The `<hn>` tag within the `<head>` section provides information to search engines. True or False?

6. You are creating a webpage using HTML. You want to display the city and state on a different line from the address. You do not want to add an additional vertical space. You also want to display the entire address in italic type. What HTML should you use?
   (a) `<i>`111 West Main St. `<p>` St. Louis, MO `</i>` `</p>`
   (b) `<strong>`111 West Main St. `<br>` St. Louis, MO `</strong>` `</br>`
   (c) `<i>`111 West Main St. `<br>` St. Louis, MO `</i>`
   (d) `<strong>`111 West Main St. `<p>` St. Louis, MO `</p></strong>`

7. To add a graphic to a webpage, you use the <img> tag and set its src attribute to the graphic's URL and its alt attribute to text that describes the graphic. True or False?

8. You are creating an HTML page that will display product information for a T-shirt company. For each T-shirt, the page should show a graphic, a price, and check boxes that allow the user to select a size. The XXL and XXXL T-shirts have a different price than the other shirts. You are using a table. Each T-shirt design is a separate row. What attribute will you use to align the cells so the price is listed only once for S, M, L, and XL T-shirts?

   (a) colspan attribute of the <tr> tag

   (b) colspan attribute of the <td> tag

   (c) rowspan attribute of the <tr> tag

   (d) rowspan attribute of the <td> tag

9. You are creating a web form that will be processed by a CGI script. You want to allow users to select a color from a list. Four colors are available, and only one color can be selected. Which HTML code will you use?

   (a)
```
<select name="Color" size="4">
<option value="red" />
<option value ="blue" />
<option value="green" />
<option value="yellow" />
</select>
```

   (b)
```
<select name="Color" size="1">
<option value="red" />
<option value ="blue" />
<option value="green" />
<option value="yellow" />
</select>
```

   (c)
```
<select name="Color" size="1">
<option value="red">Red</option>
<option value ="blue">Blue</option>
<option value="green">Green</option>
<option value="yellow">Yellow</option>
</select>
```

   (d)
```
<select name="Color" size="4">
<option value="red">Red</option>
<option value ="blue">Blue</option>
<option value="green">Green</option>
<option value="yellow">Yellow</option>
</select>
```

10. You are creating an ASP.NET application. You want to dynamically add controls to the form immediately after a user selects an option from a drop-down list. What should you do?

    (a) Set the AutoPostBack property of the drop-down list control to True.

    (b) Set the EnableViewState property of the drop-down list control to True.

    (c) Set the AutoPostBack property of the drop-down list control to False.

    (d) Set the EnableViewState property of the drop-down list control to False.

11. You are creating an ASP.NET application. You are converting an HTML form to an ASP.NET page named order.aspx. How should you modify the <form> tag?

    (a) Make it `<form id="order" action="post" method="order.aspx.vb">`.

    (b) Make it `<form id="order" runat="server">`.

    (c) Make it `<form id="order" action="post" method="order.aspx>`.

    (d) Remove it.

12. You need to preserve a value when navigating between two different webpages. Your application needs to work with all browsers, regardless of their security settings. To handle this, where should you store the value?

    (a) ViewState

    (b) a hidden control

    (c) a cookie

    (d) the Session object

Applying This Chapter

1. You are writing an order management application for a store that sells handmade quilts. The company currently sells all quilts for the same price. It wants to be able to charge different prices for twin, full, queen, and king-size quilts. Not all quilts are available in all sizes. The store also wants the application to recommend accessories based on the quilts chosen when the user clicks the button to check out. The company wants to store customer and order information in a database. The customer information will be used to make recommendations when the user visits the web site in the future.

    (a) What advantages will you realize by using ASP.NET to build the application?

    (b) You plan to build the application in ASP.NET. How will you handle changing the sizes available based on the quilt chosen?

(c) How will you handle displaying a different price for each size of quilt?

(d) How will the application remember which quilts have been selected when the user checks out?

2. You are updating a web application for a donation pledge site for a non-profit organization. The organization would like to allow donors to allocate percentages of their donations to specific areas. The web site must list five areas, with a list of projects in each area. Users must be able to click a project name to view detailed information on each project. Users must be able to select the percentage of their donations to be allocated to each area, but per-project allocation will be managed internally. Allocation must be done in 20% increments. The current version of the application uses an ASP page to receive data from the client. The ASP page will be updated to reflect the new functionality.

(a) You want to align the list of projects within each area by using a table. The columns should be labeled Area, Project, and Percentage. Assuming that Area1 has 3 projects associated with it and Area2 has 2 projects associated with it, what HTML code will you use?

(b) The detailed information about each project needs to include the key people working on the project and a summary of the project. The summary should include dates, goals, and a description of why it is important. Keywords should be displayed in italics. What tags will you use to format the data?

(c) The web site needs to be listed in search engines when potential donors search on keywords. How can you implement this functionality?

YOU TRY IT

Examining Commercial Web sites

In learning how to build a web application, it's a good idea to visit commercial applications and examine what they've done. Visit msn.com, amazon.com, and aol.com. Describe the technologies used to implement each of these sites. Answer these questions for each site.

1. Does the site perform server-side processing? Can you tell which technology it uses?
2. Locate the <form> tag, if any. How is data being sent to the server?
3. How does the site use images?
4. Does the site maintain state across multiple pages? across the same page?
5. Does the site use lists?
6. Does the site use tables? Why?
7. View the source code for the site. What tags are included in the <head> section?

Creating a Webpage

The best way to learn how to use HTML is to use it. Create a webpage for yourself, your company, or a friend. Include the following elements:

- At least one table
- At least one list
- Character- and text-formatting tags
- At least one image
- At least one hyperlink

Use Notepad to create the webpage. Remember to save it as an .htm document. Test the page by double-clicking the document to view it in a browser. Why don't you need a web server to test the page?

If you want to test the page in a live environment, see if your ISP offers free web site hosting. If it does not, find one of the free server hosts on the Internet. Search on "free web site host" or a similar string. Of course, exercise caution if the site requests personal information. If you feel at all uncomfortable, use a different host.

APPENDIX – ASCII CODES

Table X-1: Shows the ASCII codes for standard alphanumeric and symbolic characters.

Code	Char	Code	Char	Code	Char
033	!	065	A	097	a
034	"	066	B	098	b
035	#	067	C	099	c
036	$	068	D	100	d
037	%	068	E	101	e
038	&	070	F	102	f
039	'	071	G	103	g
040	(	072	H	104	h
041	)	073	I	105	i
042	*	074	J	106	j
043	+	075	K	107	k
044	,	076	L	108	l
045	-	077	M	109	m
046	.	078	N	110	n
047	/	079	O	111	o
048	0	080	P	112	p
049	1	081	Q	113	q

Table X-1: (continued)

Code	Char	Code	Char	Code	Char
050	2	082	R	114	r
051	3	083	S	115	s
052	4	084	T	116	t
053	5	085	U	117	u
054	6	086	V	118	v
055	7	087	W	119	w
056	8	088	X	120	x
057	9	089	Y	121	y
058	:	090	Z	122	z
059	;	091	[	123	{
060	<	092	\	124	|
061	=	093	]	125	}
062	>	094	^	126	~
063	?	095	_		
064	@	096	`		

The codes for non-printing and white space characters are shown in Table X-2.

Code	Character
000	Null character
001	Start of header
002	Start of text
003	End of text
004	End of transmission
005	Enquiry
006	Acknowledgement
007	Bell
008	Backspace

Table X-2: (*continued*)

Code	Character
009	Horizontal tab
010	Line feed
011	Vertical tab
012	Form feed
013	Carriage return
014	Shift Out
015	Shift In
016	Data Link Escape
017	XON Device Control 1
018	Device control 2
019	Device control 3
020	Device control 4
021	Negative Acknowledgement
022	Synchronous idle
023	End of transmission block
024	Cancel
026	End of medium
027	Substitute
028	Escape
029	Group separator
030	Request to send
031	Unit separator
032	Space
127	Delete

GLOSSARY

.NET Framework A set of libraries that provide applications with access to operating system features and other functionality.

.NET Framework Class Library (FCL) An object-oriented collection of reusable types that is included with the. NET Framework and can be accessed by any .NET language.

Abstract base class A class that provides only an interface, not an implementation. An abstract base class can be inherited, but not consumed.

Abstract class See Abstract base class.

Access key A keystroke combination that opens a menu or causes an event to occur. Access keys are defined by ALT+ a letter and identified by an underline.

Accessibility A characteristic that determines what code within a different module can access a variable.

Action objects The objects for which code is needed to respond to events.

Action query A query that alters the data in a database table.

Active Server Pages (ASP) A server-side scripting solution introduced by Microsoft.

AddHandler statement A statement that associates the name of an event with the event handler.

ADO.NET An architecture for accessing multiple relational databases. ADO stands for Active Data Objects.

Aggregate function A function that acts on selected fields of all rows returned by a query. For example, COUNT is an aggregate function that counts the number of rows with values.

Algorithm The step-by-step process—the logic—that will solve the problem. Also refers to a step-by-step description of a procedure written in pseudocode.

Anchor To cause a control to preserve its distance from the edge of a form when the form is resized.

Anchor tag The HTML tag used to define a hyperlink.

Application objects Objects that the programmer can create and use to improve the efficiency of the project.

Argument A data value passed from the calling procedure to the called procedure.

Arithmetic operator An operator that performs a mathematical computation.

Array A data structure for storing and processing a list of data values.

ArrayList class A member of the Collections namespace. It allows you to create a smart array.

As The reserved word that tells Visual Basic you are declaring a variable as a particular data type.

Asc() function A function used to convert a character to its numeric ASCII code value.

ASCII encoding An encoding format that supports only the ASCII character set. Generally used by legacy applications.

ASP.NET An enhancement to ASP. Server-side code is compiled to run more optimally. It can also be written in any. NET programming language.

Assembly A .NET Framework application or class library that has been compiled to run outside the development environment.

Assembly manifest An area of an assembly or a separate file within an assembly that contains assembly metadata, including information about the assembly's identity, files within the assembly, and assembly dependencies.

Assembly metadata Data that describes an assembly, including information about the assembly's identity, files within the assembly, and assembly dependencies.

Assignment operator The equal sign (=). Used to assign a value to a variable.

Attributes A keyword that appear within an HTML tag and is set to a value. Similar to control properties.

Automated tests Programs that are written to exercise portions of an application's code.

Base class   The class from which a derived class inherits functionality.

Base Ten   The standard mathematical notation in which each digit of a number is a power of 10.

Base Two   The mathematical notation in which each digit of a number is a power of 2. Computers store data in bytes using base two.

Batch (BAT) files   Files that use operating system commands to automate a process.

Binary   A base-two representation in which all data is represented as a pattern of ones and zeros.

Binary file   A file that is read and written as bytes.

Binary number system   A number system in which all values are either 1s or 0s.

Bit   A binary slot. Also known as a binary digit. The smallest unit of measurement for data storage.

Bit Shift Operator   An operator that moves the bit values of a variable to a different slot.

Bitwise Operator   An operate that modifies the bits in a value.

Black-box view   A methodology that allows a programmer to work with an object, knowing only the external interface (properties and methods) of that object, not the inner workings of the object. Encapsulation provides a black-box view of an object.

Blank form   Where you create the screens that allow a user to interact with your application.

Block variable   A variable declared within a block, such as within an If . . . Then or loop structure block. A block-level variable has a scope limited to the block in which it is declared. That means it cannot be accessed outside of the block.

Body   The portion of an HTML document enclosed between the <body> and </body> tags. It is where you place the text, graphics, and controls that should be displayed in the browser window.

Boolean   A property or variable that can be either True or False.

Bootstrap application   A small application that loads another program.

Break mode   A program state that allows you to access debugging tools, such as stepping through code, setting watches, and using the Locals window.

Breakpoint   An identified line of code that will cause the debugger to pause execution before the line of code is executed.

Browser   Software that can request send a request to a Web server and render the HTML response.

Bubble sort   An algorithm for sorting an array. When using a bubble sort, the high values sink to the bottom and the low values bubble to the top.

Bug   A program error.

Build   Compile source code into an executable file.

Button control   Simulates a push button on a form and is used to start, confirm, or cancel an operation.

Byte   A unit of measurement that equals 8 bits.

Bytecode   The intermediate language used by Java.

Cab Project   A Visual Studio project type that creates CAB files.

Cabinet (CAB) files   A file that might contain a number of other files that are compressed. Typically used when downloading an application over a slow link.

Call   See Invoke.

Cascading menu   A menu that includes submenu items that display when the mouse rests of the menu item.

Child class   A class that inherits properties and methods from a parent class. See also Derived class.

Child node   A node in a tree that has a parent. All nodes with the exception of the root node are child nodes.

Chr() function   A function used to convert an integer value to the character associated with it.

Class   A program that combines code and data. A class cannot run on its own, but must be used (consumed) by another application. A class is sometimes thought of as a blueprint for an object.

Class Designer   A Visual Studio feature that allows you to view the classes in your project.

ClickOnce deployment   A deployment method in which the application's files are copied to a deployment mechanism, such as a Web server, shared folder, CD, or DVD and users browse to the URL and launch (or install) the application.

Client   A computer that initiates a request for a Web page.

Clipboard   Windows feature that allows you to copy and paste data within an application and between applications.

Code   Programming instructions.

Code access security   An operating system feature that allows administrators to limit which components or applications can run and what resources they can access based on where they are located, the publisher (developer), and whether they are digitally signed.

Code module   A section of pure code that is known to all forms in a project.

Code review   A process in which another programmer looks at your code to make sure it seems to do what it needs to and meets any standards that have been defined.

Code View   The Visual Studio view that allows you to write source code.

Code-behind approach   The ASP.NET architecture that allows you to separate the Web page design from its functionality by placing the design elements in one file and the server-side code in a different (code-behind) file.

Code-behind file   An ASP.NET source code file that stores the server-side processing code for a page.

Collating sequence   The sort order for characters.

Comment   Documentation that is not compiled into executable code.

Common Gateway Interface (CGI)   An older server-side processing technology that uses a script, usually written in Perl, to receive and process a query string.

Common Language Runtime (CLR)   A program that compiles Microsoft Intermediate Language (MSIL) code to native processor code. It also provides the runtime environment for a .NET application.

Common user interface   A software concept in which multiple applications share similar user interface features, such as menu commands and dialog boxes.

Comparison Operator   An operator that compares two values and returns a Boolean result.

Compiler   A program that translates source code to machine code.

Compiler Option   A setting that determines what things are checked during compilation and what types of operations can be compiled without error. Option Explicit and Option Strict are two examples of compiler options.

Concatenate   To add a String variable or constant to the end of another String variable.

Concatenation   Appending one string onto the end of another.

Conditional compilation   A technique that uses a constant defined at compile time to determine which blocks of code to include in the compiled application.

Connection object   An ADO.NET object that defines and manages the connection to a database.

Constant   An object that stores a literal value. A constant is declared, can be assigned a type, and must be assigned a value. A constant's value cannnot change during program execution.

Constructor   A special routine that runs when an object is instantiated. It initializes variables and performs other preparation tasks to allow class members to be accessed.

Consumer   An application that declares and instantiates a class.

Container control   A control that can host other controls, such as the Panel or GroupBox control.

Context menu   A menu that is displayed by right-clicking on a form or control. It is context-specific and contains commands that relate to the item being clicked.

Control   A class that can be used as a user interface element. A control has properties, methods, and events. Controls used in Windows applications derive from the System.Windows.Forms.Control class.

Control structure   A structure that defines a type of logic.

Controls collection   A collection that contains all the controls on a form or container control.

Conversion function   Function that can be used to convert one data type to another data type.

Cookie   One or more values that are downloaded to a client and (optionally) stored in a file on the client's computer.

Coordinate system   A positional system that uses a pair of integer values to identify every point on a surface.

Corporate intranet   Web servers and file servers deployed for use within a company's network.

CurrencyManager   An ADO.NET object that manages the navigation through records for bound controls.

Data definition language (DDL)   SQL statements used to define the structure of a database, for example creating and modifying tables.

Data manipulation language (DML)   SQL statements used to select and modify data.

Data Type   A characteristic that determines the kind of data stored in a variable or constant and the memory it consumes.

Data Type Character   A short-hand character that can be used in a variable declaration instead of using As and the full name of the data type.

DataAdapter object   An ADO.NET object that maps data retrieved from the database to a DataSet. It is used to determine what data is selected and how database columns map to DataSet columns.

Database   A method of storing different types of data in such a way that the data can be easily manipulated and retrieved by a user.

Database management system (DBMS)   An application that manages the storage of relational data on disk.

DataColumn   An ADO.NET object that represents a single column in a table.

DataRow   An ADO.NET object that represents a single row in a table.

DataSet   An ADO.NET object that stores data within the application. It can include one or more tables.

DataTable   An ADO.NET object that represents a database table.

DataView   An ADO.NET object that provides a customizable view of a table.

Debugging   The process of finding and correcting any errors found.

Decision control structure   A logic structure that compares one value to another to decide on the direction the program should take.

Default constraint   A value that is used when one is not included in the INSERT statement.

Default constructor   A constructor which is created automatically for each class and accepts no arguments.

Delay sign   Associate a public key with an assembly so that it can be signed later by the private key. A technique typically used when programmers are not allowed to access the code signing private key.

Delimited file   A sequential file that uses a special character to separate fields and records.

Delimiter   A character that separates items in a list. For example, a period delimits on sentence from another in a document.

Deployment   The activity of delivering copies of an application to other machines so that the application runs in the new environment.

Deployment mechanism   The medium used to distribute the application. For example, CD, DVD, Internet, or shared folder.

Derived class   A class that inherits base functionality from another class.

Design View   The Visual Studio view that allows you to drag and drop controls onto forms, move controls around, and set their properties.

Designer window   The surface of the form in Design View.

Design-time error   An error that the Integrated Development Environment (IDE) can detect when the application is being designed. Normally caused by a typographical error or forgetting to declare a variable.

Desk checking   The process of checking the logic in an algorithm by walking through it using pencil and paper.

Development environment   The computer on which you write an application.

Digital signature   A Public Key Infrastructure (PKI) certificate that guarantees the executable has not been modified and that it originated from the party who signed the assembly.

Dim   The reserved word that tells Visual Basic you are declaring a variable.

Direct-access files   Files that can be input in any order.

Do...Loop   Executes a block of statements for as long as a condition is True; if the expression is False, the program continues and the statement following the loop is executed.

Dock   To attach a control to one or more edges of a form. A docked control grows and shrinks as the form is resized.

Domain Name System (DNS)   A protocol that translates names into IP addresses.

Dynamic array   An array that has no upper limit on the array size.

Dynamic link library (DLL)   A file that contains support classes and cannot be executed on its own.

Dynamic menus   Menus that change at runtime to display more or fewer commands.

Empty element   An element that does not have content between the opening and closing tags. Therefore, you can close the tag by adding a space and a slash (/) character.

Encapsulation   The requirement that it should never be possible to work with variables in an object directly; they must be addressed through the object's properties and methods.

Encoding   A standard for determining how bits are translated to characters.

End Of File (EOF) marker   An invisible binary marker that indicates that the last record in the file has been read.

Endless loop   See Infinite loop.

Enumerated Type   See Enumeration.

Enumeration   A custom data type that contains a set of legal constants that limit the possible values for a variable. The constants are mapped to descriptive words.

Error handler   A section of code that allows you to detect exceptions and take the necessary steps to recover from them.

Event   An action to which an object can respond.

Event handler   A procedure that is associated with one or more events.

Event procedure   The procedure where you add the code that should execute when the event occurs.

Event-driven programming   A programming methodology in which program actions are driven by events.

Exception handler   See Error handler.

Executable   A file that executes an application. It has the file extension .exe.

Exit statement   Allows you to exit prematurely from a block of statements in a control structure from a loop, or a procedure.

Exponentiation   An operation in which one operand is raised to the power of the other operand. For example 10^2 raises 10 to the power of 2, for a result of 100.

Extensible HTML (XHTML)   A reformulated HTML standard that complies with XML syntax rules.

Extensible Markup Language (XML)   An industry-standard specification for describing data using a hierarchical structure.

FCL   See .NET Framework Class Library.

Field   A single fact or data item; it is the smallest unit of named data that has meaning in a database.

Finally block   The structured exception handling block that executes at the end of normal execution or after executing a Catch block. A Finally block is used to perform clean-up, such as closing resources.

Flow   The steps a program must take to perform a task.

Flowchart   A graphical depiction of a program's flow.

Fly-out menu   See Cascading menu.

For Each loop   A loop construct that allows you to process an array without knowing the maximum number of elements in the array.

For . . . Next loop   Uses an a variable to increase or decrease in value during each repetition during the loop.

Foreign key   A field that identifies a record in another table or a different record in the same table.

Form   The class used to create a graphical window in a Windows application. An HTML page that includes input controls and a submit button. A form can be posted to a server-side script or application for processing.

Form event   An event that occurs when something happens to an instance of the Form class.

Format expression   A string value that identifies the format that should be used to display a numeric or date value.

Full join   A join that returns all the rows of both tables.

Full trust   A code access security level that allows an application or component to access the registry, file system, and external resources.

Fully-qualified name   When discussing classes, a fully-qualified name includes the class name and the namespace. It uses the format *namespace.classname*. You use a fully-qualified name to prevent conflicts when declaring and instantiating an object and multiple namespaces include the same class name.

Function definition statement   The name of the function, a list of parameters with type specifiers, and the return value data type.

Function   See Function procedure.

Function procedure   A procedure that returns a value.

GDI+   A library that includes classes for creating vector graphics, drawing text, and manipulating images.

General procedure   A procedure that is not associated with a specific event or control.

Gigabyte (GB)   A unit of measurement. Each gigabyte is equal to 1,024 megabytes.

Global Assembly Cache (GAC)   A file system directory used to store shared assemblies.

Global procedure   A procedure declared as Public in a Code module. Its scope is the entire project. This means that it can be called by any form in the project.

Global variable   A variable declared as Public in a Code module. Its scope is the entire project. This means that it can be accessed by any form in the project.

Globally unique identifier (GUID)   A hexadecimal value that will be unique on any computer where the assembly is installed.

Graphics Interchange Format (GIF)   A graphic format that supports only 256 colors. It also supports transparency. It offers a better compression ration than JPEG. Files are identified by the extension .gif.

Handled exception   An error that is handled within an application's code instead of the operating system.

Handles keyword   A keyword used when defining an event procedure. It precedes the name of the class and event.

Hash value   An integer value that uniquely identifies the object variable in the context of the current application. A value computed from the assembly's bits.

Hashtable class   A member of the Collections namespace that allows you to identify each element with a unique name.

Head   The section of an HTML document located between the <head> and </head> tags. It includes the document's title, information about the document, including META tags and BASE tags, and any client-side scripts.

High-level language   See Programming language.

HTML control   An element used on an HTML form that can pass a value to a script or application.

HTML documents   The HTML code that makes up the Web page displayed in the browser.

Hyperlink   Text that is associated with the address of a document or file on a Web server. A hyperlink is usually displayed in a different color (typically blue) and underlined.

Hypertext Markup Language (HTML)   The language used to create and format Web documents.

Hypertext Transfer Protocol (HTTP)   The protocol used by Web browsers and Web servers to manage HTML request and response.

Identity column   A column with a unique value generated by the database management system.

If . . . Then statement   A decision control structure that accepts an expression that evaluates to either True or False. Tests a condition. If the condition is True, the program executes the statements(s) that follow; if the condition is False, the application continues with the statement following the If statement.

If . . . Then . . . Else statement   Executes one block of statements if the condition is True and another block of statements if the condition is False.

Implementation inheritance   A type of inheritance in which a derived class inherits the functionality of an existing class, but can also add new members or revise inherited members through overriding them.

Imports keyword   The keyword used to identify a namespace that will be used in the project.

Index   A number that identifies an element's position in an array.

Inheritance   The capability to create child classes that descend from a parent class and inherit functionality from the parent class.

Initialize   To set an initial value.

Inner join   A join that includes only the rows that match the join condition.

Input/Output/Processing (IPO) Table   A design tool that shows the inputs to an object, the required outputs for that object, and the processing that is necessary to convert the inputs into the desired outputs.

Installation   The process of loading, configuring, and installing software.

Instance   An object based on a class and loaded into memory.

Instance method   A method that can only be called on an instance of a class, not on the class itself.

Instance variable   A variable that has a scope and lifetime limited to an instance of an object.

Instantiation   The process by which you create an instance of an object in memory. In Visual Basic, you instantiate an object using the New keyword.

Integrated Development Environment (IDE)   An application use to write and compile source code. It contains tools that facilitate writing and debugging programs.

Integration testing   The process of testing all classes and consumers to ensure that they interact as expected.

Intellisense A Visual Studio feature that displays the list of properties and methods for an object when the object name is typed in the code window and followed by a period.

Interactive development The ability to create an object, write code for it, and test it without need to write the entire program.

Interface The methods, properties, and events of a class.

Internet A global, distributed network of computers that use TCP/IP to communicate.

Internet Information Server (IIS) The Web server software included with Windows operating systems.

Internet Protocol (IP) address The unique four octet address of a computer on the Internet.

Intrinsic control See HTML control.

Invoke To cause a sub or function to execute.

Join A process that connects multiple tables in a query.

Joint Photographic Experts Group (JPEG) A file format that can be compressed, while maintaining good image quality. Identified by a .jpg extension.

Just-in-time (JIT)compiler A compiler that converts machine-independent intermediate language code to machine language.

Kilobyte (KB) A unit of measurement. Each kilobyte is equal to 1,024 bytes.

Label control Used to display text on a form that identifies controls, provides instructions for using your application, and generally communicates to the user.

Landscape A page orientation that is longer horizontally than vertically.

Launch condition A condition that must be met by the target computer in order for the application to be installed.

Leaf nodes Nodes in a tree that do not lead to any other nodes.

Left join A join that displays all records in the left table and only those records from the right table that match the join condition.

Lifetime The period of execution over which a variable retains its value.

List Data structure with items all on the same level that can be traversed one after the other.

Literal A value typed directly into code.

Local variable   See Procedure-level variable.

Localized resources   Resources (typically text strings) used to support a specific language.

Logic error   An error caused by a problem in the program logic. A logic error is difficult to diagnose and usually manifests itself as an unexpected behavior or result, not as an exception.

Logical Operator   An operator used to combine two Boolean values and return either True or False. See also Bitwise Operator.

Loop structure   A structure used to perform a repetitive task. A loop executes over and over until the exit condition is met.

Machine language   The language used to compile instructions that can be understood by the processor.

Manual tests   Tests that are conducted interactively by a programmer or software tester.

Me keyword   A keyword that returns a reference to the current form.

Megabyte (MB)   A unit of measurement. Each megabyte is equal to 1,024 kilobytes.

Memory   The dynamic, nonpersistent storage area where operating system code and program code is loaded.

Menu hierarchy   The organization of menu titles and subgroups.

MenuStrip control   Variation of the Strip control; implements menus.

Merge Module Project   A Visual Studio project type that creates a merge module. A merge module is used to install components (class libraries or customer controls).

META tag   A tag that does not display on the screen, but that contains information about the contents of the document. Search engines use meta tags to generate keywords.

Method   An action that can be taken on an object.

Microsoft Intermediate Language (MSIL)   The intermediate language used by .NET Framework languages, such as Visual Basic and C#.

Module testing   The process of testing each class module as it is developed.

Modulo   An operation that returns the remainder from a division as an Integer value. For example 5 Mod 3 = 2.

MSI file   A file that contains all the data needed to install an application. It has the extension.msi.

Multiple Document Interface (MDI) application   An application that allows you to work with multiple documents, each in a separate window.

MustInherit   A class declaration modifier that is used to create an abstract class.

MustOverride   A function or property modifier that tells the compiler that derived classes must provide an implementation for the member.

Mutually exclusive   A type of option that allows a user to select only one of the set.

My keyword   A Visual Basic keyword that allows you to access the Computer object and other system- and application-specific properties.

MyBase   A keyword that references the base class from which a class inherits.

MyClass   A keyword that references the derived class.

Name   The identifier for an object.

Namespace   A logical naming scheme that is used by the .NET framework to group related types, classes, and objects under a distinct umbrella. Its purpose is to ensure that two classes with the same name can be uniquely qualified.

Narrowing conversion   A data conversion in which the target data type cannot hold all the legal values of the original data type. For example, converting a Long to an Integer is a narrowing conversion because an Integer can hold only a subset of those values supported by the Long data type.

Nested If-Then-Else statement   A programming logic construct that includes multiple if conditions, all but the first nested inside else clauses.

New keyword   The keyword used to create an instance of an object in memory.

Node   An item in a tree.

Normalization   The process of breaking data into related tables that eliminate all possible forms of information duplication.

NotInheritable   A modifier that identifies a class as one that can be consumed, but not inherited by a derived class.

NotOverridable   A modifier that identifies a method or property that cannot be overridden.

Null value   A special value SQL Server assigns when a column does not contain a value.

Object   A running instance of a class.

Object-oriented language   A programming language that that encapsulates functionality into classes.

Operand   A value used to perform an operation.

Operator   A character or keyword that defines the operation to be performed.

Optional keyword   The keyword used to identify a parameter that does not need to be passed when the procedure is called.

Order of Precedence   The order in which the operations in a complex expression are performed.

Ordered list   The HTML term for a list of items with each item preceded by a sequential number.

Overloaded   A method or property that has multiple versions that accept different arguments.

Overloaded constructors   Constructors that accept arguments.

Overloaded method   A method that has multiple signatures, each of which accepts an argument list with a different number of arguments, arguments with different data types, or both.

Overridable   A keyword used to identify a method or property that can be overridden by a derived class.

Overrides   Provides a new implementation for a property or method implemented by the base class.

Page directive   An element at the top of an ASP .NET page that gives ASP .NET the information it needs to perform server-side processing.

Pairwise comparison   The comparison of two values in an array. Commonly used when sorting an array or finding the minimum or maximum value in an array.

Parameter   Name and type specifiers of data being passed to (and sometimes from) a procedure.

Parameterized constructor   See Overloaded constructors.

Parameterless constructor   See Default constructor.

Parent class   A higher-level class from which a child class inherits properties and methods. See also Base class.

Parent-child relations   Relations that can be described as "belongs to" or "owns".

Passing by reference   A method of passing arguments in which changes made to an argument within a procedure affects the variable passed as the argument by the calling procedure.

Passing by value   A method of passing arguments in which arguments are passed into a procedure, but not out of the procedure.

Petabyte (PB)   A unit of measurement. Each petabyte is equal to 1,024 terabytes.

Pinned   A docked window that does not slide in and out.

Polymorphism   The ability of a child class to add or modify functionality to make it different than the parent class, yet accessible using the same client-side code.

Pop-up menu   See Context menu.

Portrait   A page orientation that is longer vertically than horizontally.

Postback   A round-trip to the server that results in the same form being displayed.

Precision   The number of digits to the right of the decimal point.

Primary key   A unique identifier that is used to establish a relationship between the table in which it is unique and another table.

Priming   The process of initializing a variable used in a loop's exit condition before executing the loop.

Private assembly   An assembly installed in an application's bin directory and is private to the application.

Private key   The key that is used to encrypt or sign a document, message, assembly, or other data when using asymmetric encryption. A private key must be kept protected from unauthorized access.

Procedural programming   A programming methodology in which execution of the program starts with the first instruction and continues through the remaining instructions, making decisions as to which instructions will be executed depending on the data that are input.

Procedure-level variable   A variable declared within a procedure. A procedure-level variable has a scope limited to the procedure in which it is declared. That means it cannot be accessed outside of the procedure.

Production environment   The computer on which the deployed application is run.

Programming language   A language that can be compiled either to machine language or to an intermediate language.

Project A folder that organizes the files related to an application.

Project output The EXE or DLL generated by the compiler when an assembly is built.

Property A characteristic of an object.

Property procedure A special type of procedure that contains a Get and a Set section to allow you to implement code when a consumer requests or sets a property.

Protected friend A property or function scope modifier that identifies a member that is available to any derived class and other classes in the same project.

Protected A property or function scope modifier that identifies a member that can be accessed in the derived class, but cannot be accessed by a consumer.

Protocol Software that manages communication between two computers or two applications.

Pseudocode A way to describe program flow using natural language instead of the programming language syntax. Pseudocode is meant for human readers, not computers.

Public key The key used to decrypt an item encrypted using asymmetric encryption or verify the integrity of a digital signature hash.

Public Key Infrastructure (PKI) certificate A digital certification that proves an individual or company's identity and is used for asymmetric (public key/private key) encryption.

Query string The portion of a URL after the question mark. A query string is used to pass data to a script or application.

Random access files See Direct-access files.

Record A collection of one or more data items that are treated as a unit.

ReDim statement A statement used to change the upper boundary of an array.

Reference Pointer to a location in memory that stores an instance of an object.

Reference equality A condition that is true if both variables point to the same instance of a class.

Registry A file that contains configuration information for hardware and software components installed on a computer.

Regressing Attempting to reproduce a bug to verify that it has been fixed.

Regression testing   The phase of testing during which all reported bugs are retested to verify that they have been fixed and that there are no unexpected side effects from the fix.

Relational database   A database that has multiple tables that are related to each other by foreign keys.

Repetition control structure   A logic structure that is used to repeat one or more operations.

Reproducing   Making a problem (or bug) happen predictably.

Reserved Word   A keyword or function name used by Visual Basic. You cannot give a variable or constant the same name as any reserved words.

Return statement   The statement used within a function to set the value the function returns.

Return value   The data returned by a function.

Reusable code   Code that can be invoked repeatedly throughout the project or saved and added to other projects.

Rich Text Format (RTF)   Standard for storing formatting information along with the text.

Right join   A join that displays all records in the right table and only those records from the left table that match the join condition.

Root   The top node in a tree structure.

Root namespace   The namespace associated with a specific project.

Run time   The state an application is in when it is executing.

Runtime Error   An error that causes an exception or a hang when an application executes. A runtime error is caused because the computer is in an unexpected state or input values are unexpected.

Schema   The format of an XML file.

Scope   A characteristic that determines what code within a module can access a variable.

Select Case structure   Compares the same expression to different values.

Selection query   A query that selects and returns data, usually from a relational database. A selection query is performed using a SELECT statement.

Self-closing element   See Empty element.

Self-updating   The ability to post an application update on a server and have it automatically be used the next time the user runs the application.

Separator bar   A line that you add to a menu or toolbar to create a logical grouping.

Sequence control structure   A logic structure in which one program instruction follows another in order.

Sequential access files   Files from which data records must be input in the same order that they were output to the file.

Service Pack   An operating system or application update.

Session   The ASP.NET Web application object that persists from the time a user first connects to the application to when they close the browser.

Session state   The ability to store values across multiple pages within a user session.

Setup   See Installation.

Setup Project   A Visual Studio project type that creates a Windows Installer package for an application.

Shared assembly   An assembly that can be accessed by multiple applications on the computer. It is installed in the Global Assembly Cache and must be strong-named.

Shared class   A class that exposes methods and properties that can be accessed directly through the class name, instead of through an instance of the object.

Shared keyword   A keyword used to identify a shared method or shared property.

Shared method   A method that is shared by all instances of a class. A shared method can also be called on the class itself instead of on an instance of a class.

Shared variable   A variable that is shared by all instances of a class.

Short-circuit evaluation   Enables Visual Basic to stop evaluating operands if it can deduce the final result without them.

Shortcut key   A character that activates a control's event when pressed in conjunction with the Alt key. A keystroke that causes a menu item's event to occur, even if the menu that contains the item is not open.

Shortcut menu   See Context menu.

Side effect   An action that a function or procedure performs that is not the main purpose of the function or procedure. For example, opening a file or creating a database connection.

Signature A method's contract with the consumer. The signature includes the name of the method and the number and data types of arguments.

Smart Device Cab Project A Visual Studio project type that creates a Setup program for a smart device, such as a Windows mobile cell phone.

Solution A folder that organizes multiple projects.

Solution Explorer The window in the Visual Studio IDE that lists the projects in a solution and the files in a project.

Source code The human-readable instructions the program will execute.

Spoofing an assembly The process of creating an assembly that looks identical to a real assembly, but that does something different (usually malicious).

Startup Form The first form that displays when the application launches.

State The current value of control properties or variables.

Static variable A procedure-level variable that retains its value between executes of the procedure in which it is declared.

Status bar Displays dynamic status information about the application.

StatusStrip control Control that enables an application to display status information.

StreamReader class A class that includes methods that can be used to read data from a file.

String Textual data.

Strong-named assembly An assembly that is uniquely identified by a version number, globally unique identifier, and digital signature.

Structured exception handling A method of exception handling in which you execute statements inside a Try block and handle errors within a Catch block.

Structured Query Language (SQL) A nonprocedural programming language used for accessing relational data.

Subprocedure A module of code that does not return a value.

Subscript See Index.

Syntax The general grammar for using a subprocedure, function, or method.

Syntax error See Design-Time Error.

Tab Group A Visual Studio feature that allows you to display views of forms side-by-side.

Tab order   The order in which controls receive focus when the Tab key is pressed.

Table   A related collection of records, all having the same columns (fields).

Table alias   A shortened version of the table name defined in the FROM clause of a join and use in the SELECT, ON, and WHERE clauses to reduce typing when accessing columns with the same name in multiple tables.

Tags   HTML elements that control document formatting and represent controls. A tag is enclosed in angle brackets.

Template   A form that has the standard elements found on a form used for a specific purpose.

Terabyte (TB)   A unit of measurement. Each terabyte is equal to 1,024 gigabytes.

Test plan   Procedures for testing the features of a program.

Text file   A file that contains only text and is read and written as character or string data.

Textbox control   Enables a user to enter text into a field.

Tick   100 nanoseconds. A tick is usually used when high precision timing is essential.

Toolbar   A set of buttons that can be shown and hidden as a group.

Toolbox   A window that organizes controls and other objects that can be added to an application.

ToolStrip control   Similar to MenuStrip control, but supports a wider variety of items.

ToolStripContainer control   Control that has four containers that can contain ToolStrip, MenuStrip and StatusStrip controls.

Tooltip   A short textual description of an item. A tooltip appears when a mouse rests over a control or toolbar item.

Transmission Control Protocol/Internet Protocol (TCP/IP)   The universal suite of protocols common to all computers on the Internet.

Tree   A data structure that is most appropriate for representing hierarchical data.

Try . . . Catch . . . End Try block   A programming construct for implementing structured exception handling.

Two-dimensional array   An array that represents a table of data. A two-dimensional array has two index values: the first identifies the row position and the second identifies the column position.

Type specifier   The keyword that defines the parameter's data type. A type specifier has the format As *datatype*.

Undeclared variable   A variable that is used in code without explicitly declaring it.

Unhandled exception   An error that is not handled by the application, and therefore, must be handled by the Common Language Runtime (CLR). The CLR handles exceptions by displaying an unhandled exception dialog and usually terminating the program.

Unicode   A character encoding scheme that supports international character sets.

Unicode encoding   An encoding format that supports international character sets. Used by most modern applications.

Uniform Resource Locator (URL)   The address of a resource accessed using a browser or other Internet application.

Unordered list   An HTML term for a list of items, with each item preceded by a bullet character.

User interface   The parts of the program the user views and interacts with to perform a task.

User-defined type (UDT)   A structure that includes multiple variables.

Validation   The act of ensuring that data can be converted to the necessary data type and is within an expected range.

Variable   A memory location that stores a piece of data that can be changed during execution.

Vector   A set of mathematical properties that define a graphic's size, properties, and positing.

Vector graphic   A graphic represented by a set of mathematical properties (vectors) instead of as a grid of pixels. Typically used for line drawings.

Version number   A number that is incremented each time the application is updated.

Versioning   The process of incrementing the version number of a class to allow applications to use a version of a class library with which it is known to be compatible.

View state   The state of controls and variables during postback to the same page in an ASP.NET application.

Virtual class   See Abstract base class.

Visual Basic   A programming language.

Web application   A set of Web pages that provide more interactivity. Typically implemented using server-side processing.

W3C   See worldwide web consortium.

Webpage   The HTML code that is displayed by the browser.

Web server   A computer that runs special software that allows it to host Web sites.

Web Setup Project   A Visual Studio project type that creates a Windows Installer package for a Web application.

Web site   Location on the Internet that supplies documents or applications you can access using a browser.

What you see is what you get (WYSIWG)   Pronounced wizzy-wig. A method of creating a graphical user interface that allows you to position elements interactively. The tool displays the interface the way the user will see it.

While . . . End While loop   Executes a block of statements as long as a condition is True; when the End While statement is reach, control is returned to the While statement, which evaluates the condition again. If the condition is still True, the process is repeated. If the condition is False, the program resumes with the statement following End While.

Widening Conversion   A conversion in which the target data type is large enough to hold all possible values of the original data type. Converting an Integer to a Long is a widening conversion.

Window   A rectangular region on the screen with its own boundaries.

Windows Application project   The project template you use to build an executable that will run on a desktop computer running Windows and the .NET Framework.

Windows Explorer   A utility for examining and navigating your hard disk's structure.

Windows Installer (WI)   A technology for distributing and installing applications through an executable file (Setup.exe) and an MSI file.

Working folder   The folder where an application is installed.

World Wide Web Consortium (W3C)   A vendor-neutral organization responsible for Web standards.

X-coordinate   A value that represents the horizontal distance of a point from the origin.

XCOPY deployment   A deployment mechanism in which you just copy the application's directory and paste it onto the target computer.

XML serialization   The conversion of an object to XML so that it can be transported to a different application and reconstructed from the XML.

Y-coordinate   A value that represents the vertical distance of a point from the origin.

Zero-based array   An array that uses zero as the index for the first element.

SYMBOLS